THE MEDIEVAL WORLD VIEW

Bernard of Chartres used to compare us to dwarfs perched on the shoulders of giants. He pointed out that we see more and farther than our predecessors, not because we have keener vision or greater height, but because we are lifted up and borne aloft on their gigantic stature.

JOHN OF SALISBURY *(c. 1115–80)*
Metalogicon

THE MEDIEVAL WORLD VIEW

AN INTRODUCTION

Second Edition

WILLIAM R. COOK
RONALD B. HERZMAN

State University of New York, Geneseo

New York   Oxford
OXFORD UNIVERSITY PRESS
2004

Oxford University Press

Oxford   New York
Auckland   Bangkok   Buenos Aires   Cape Town   Chennai
Dar es Salaam   Delhi   Hong Kong   Istanbul   Karachi   Kolkata
Kuala Lumpur   Madrid   Melbourne   Mexico City   Mumbai
Nairobi   São Paulo   Shanghai   Taipei   Tokyo   Toronto

Published by Oxford University Press, Inc.
198 Madison Avenue, New York, New York, 10016
http://www.oup-usa.org

Library of Congress Cataloging-in-Publication Data

Cook, William R. (William Robert), 1943–
    The medieval world view / William R. Cook and Ronald B. Herzman.—2nd ed.
        p. cm.
    Includes bibliographical references (p.) and index.
    ISBN 0-19-513934-8 (acid-free paper) — ISBN 0-19-513935-6 (pbk. : acid-free paper)
        1. Civilization, Medieval. I. Herzman, Ronald B. II. Title.
    CB351 .C58 2003
    940.1—dc21   2002030316

Printing number: 9 8 7 6 5 4 3 2 1

Printed in the United States of America
on acid-free paper

For Ellen,
Veronica, and Anna

and

Our Children

CONTENTS

ACKNOWLEDGMENTS

We knew twenty years ago and we know even better today that books are not merely the work of those whose names are on the title page. It is a pleasure in this second edition to thank both those who have been our guides throughout our careers and those who have helped shape our careers and our ideas since the first edition of *The Medieval World View* was published in 1983. We are humbled when we reflect on the number of people who have been an important part of our work. Those whose books have helped shape ours, many of whom are not known to us personally, are named in the bibliography. In acknowledging our debts here, we have limited ourselves to those who have added something more than their research and insights to the making of this book.

All the various iterations of *The Medieval World View* have been subject to the scrutiny of our own students. We have been fortunate that so many of them at SUNY Geneseo, as well as some in the early 1980s at Attica Correctional Facility, have taught their teachers. A few of our Geneseo students must stand for many, literally thousands taught on our campus near Rochester, NY, and hundreds that we have brought to Europe. We have taught long enough that many of them now have distinguished careers. We thank first Mike Benton (a high school teacher in Ohio), Gerry Twomey (a priest on Long Island), and Wes Kennison (our Geneseo colleague and an elected public official). Their names appeared in the first edition, and their friendship has continued through the second. To these we add Glenn McClure, Greg Ahlquist, Lisa Lucenti Ahn, Laura Sythes, Tom Lombardi, Jim Hunt, Brian Carniello, Elissa Quinn, and Kim Ednie.

We have been likewise fortunate in our teachers and our mentors, both formal and informal. We thank especially Brian Tierney, the late David Herlihy, David Bevington, Giles Constable, John Fleming, Bruce Cole, Edward Peters, James Powell, Robert Hollander, Russell Peck, and Ewert Cousins. Among colleagues of our own and a later generation of scholars, we are grateful to the late Karen Pelz, William Stephany, Richard Emmerson, Thomas Heffernan, Thomas Burns, David Burr, Wayne Hellmann, Ann Derbes, Penn Szittya, our Geneseo colleagues Gary Towsley and Graham Drake, and our former students, Anne Clark Bartlett and Eve Salisbury.

Faculty and administrative colleagues at SUNY Geneseo have provided us both a stimulating intellectual environment and friendship. Two former chairs, Eugene Stelzig in English and the late Randy Bailey in History, can stand for the many faculty colleagues here at home who deserve our gratitude. Former president Carol Harter and president Christopher Dahl have celebrated our achievements even while helping to make them possible. It has been our pleasure to be their guides through the streets of medieval Siena.

Beginning in 1983 and continuing through the present, we have each been fortunate to direct ten seminars for the National Endowment for the Humanities in their Summer Seminars for School Teachers Program. We thank Kathe Hartnett and Lynn Kennison, our administrative assistants, without whose help these seminars would not have been nearly as efficient or nearly as enjoyable. On behalf of the three hundred gifted teachers with whom we have worked in this unique program of faculty enrichment, we mention by name the five who have been participants in both of our seminars: Chris Lorenc, Elida Giles, Anita Pilling, Frank Malley, and Gerry Kapolka. These folks are part of a large body of educators too often thought of simply as transmitters rather than creators of knowledge. From the enormous amount that they have taught us about the Middle Ages, we know better. These teachers are important contributors to intellectual dialogue on many levels. Many of the ideas in this book were refined in these seminars.

We have also presented many of the ideas in this book in earlier versions at monasteries and later in several Franciscan institutions throughout the United States. Men and women who have vowed the religious life have taught us in their questions and in their critiques, as well as in the way they live out their lives in ways relevant to the twenty-first century but rooted in medieval ideals. Our college is located a mere four miles from the Abbey of the Genesee; for three decades the monks their have befriended us and allowed us to draw from their wisdom and experience. For virtually all of that time, their superior, John Eudes Bamberger, has been the embodiment of the ideal abbot described in the Rule of Saint Benedict. Our debt to the monastic tradition would not be paid unless we also mentioned the late Dom Jean Leclercq, who gave us encouragement and wisdom when both were needed.

While we privilege individuals here, it would be remiss to ignore the fact that many institutions have over the years funded our research, given us opportunities to teach in Europe, organized conferences, invited us to give lectures, and in numerous other ways made our work easier, more pleasurable, and deeper. We mention two here, to stand once again for many. The International Congress on Medieval Studies at Western Michigan University is a conference like no other in its welcoming of young scholars, and as a clearing house of ideas for the almost 3000 medievalists who make their annual pilgrimage to Kalamazoo. The Teaching Company has enabled us to reach a wide audience of non-specialists with its video and audiotapes, and has helped us think through questions of audience useful for the second edition of *The Medieval World View*. We thank Tom Greenfield, who got us the gig, and Tom Rollins, who runs the company.

We wrote the first edition of the book when "cut and paste" was typically done with a pair of scissors and a pot of glue. In preparing the second edition, we were at the mercy of a younger and more skilled technogeneration for the more intricate scanning and formatting operations that went into the preparation of this manuscript. We thank in particular Brian di Paolo, Emily Spallina, and Katie Infantino for their assistance. The Geneseo Foundation provided some money to help get this work done. Michele Feeley and Marie Henry also provided valuable secretarial assistance. Four very thorough readers for Oxford University Press provided detailed and perceptive suggestions for the second edition. We made use of them whenever possible. In this and in many other ways Oxford University Press showed the same commitment that it showed for the first edition, and we are happy to thank our editor Linda Harris and senior editor Peter Coveney for their encouragement and expertise.

Our personal debts, like our professional ones, are legion. We have received continuous support from our families and friends, who have contributed more to this book than they know. Since the first edition, the truth of that statement has deepened. Both of our mothers, Veronica Herzman and Anna F. Cook, moved to Geneseo thirteen years ago, became close friends, and individually and together have provided guidance and wisdom for their sons. Herzman's children, Suzanne and Edward, have become teachers and can now officially offer professional as well as personal advice to both authors. Herzman also thanks the non-Geneseo branch of the family: Nancy and Chris Doran and Paul Herzman. Cook has adopted three sons, Paul Cook, and, since the first edition, Gualberto Fernandez and Angel Quintero; and he has been guardian for several other young men—Felix Bui, Jason Hayes, Obn Taylor, Hieu Huynh, Hanh Huynh, Hung Huynh, and Cuong Huynh. Our children, like our mothers, have become friends with each another. We look forward to a fourth generation of Cook-Herzman friendships.

Ellen Ferens Herzman has spent many years dealing with the fanaticism and eccentricities generated by this book and other Cook-Herzman extravaganzas, even though she had bargained only for Herzman in 1970. Gratefully, we dedicate the book to her. The other part of the dedication, to our mothers and children, also suggests something of the way in which this book is not only a collaboration between friends and colleagues, but between families as well. In this, we recognize our blessings.

INTRODUCTION

This book began as our response to the difficulties encountered by under-graduate students trying to understand the Middle Ages. As any teacher who must deal with a time and place remote from our own knows, the Middle Ages presents special problems to students, who for the most part are unaware of its quite different intellectual, aesthetic, institutional, and spiritual presuppo-sitions. The twelfth-century epic *Song of Roland* is a literary work of a very high order; it is also an extremely useful document with which to teach the ideals of feudal society and the spirit of the Crusades. Readers opening the *Song of Roland* for the first time, however, discover early on the disconcert-ing fact that Charlemagne is more than two hundred years old. Even if their immediate response is not to close the book, so long as their only standards of judgment are modern ones, they probably will not take the work seriously, refusing to believe that a culture that has no respect for "reality" has much to say to them. To understand and appreciate the work, they first need to un-derstand how exaggeration is a technique used to give prominence to what is most important in medieval documents, whether they be works of literature or art.

Any teacher of the Middle Ages could provide a hundred similar exam-ples, and it is for this reason that we have attempted to present the presup-positions of medieval society in a systematic fashion, by integrating primary texts and photographs into a narrative of the medieval world and its founda-tions. Thus, the book can be used to help understand and appreciate the Mid-dle Ages from the inside, that is, as the people of the Middle Ages saw them-selves. Perhaps more important, after reading the book one will have a better sense of how to approach any medieval literary text, artistic monument, his-torical document, or musical work in a more meaningful way. Although this is a relatively modest undertaking insofar as we are not offering a compre-hensive interpretation of the Middle Ages—though we do cover a lot of ter-ritory—it is at least in one sense original: we are not aware of any other book that attempts the same thing. In this introduction, therefore, it is appropriate to spell out the implications of our approach.

The most fundamental of these is that we are attempting to reconstruct important elements of the Middle Ages, in the phrase we have already used, "from the inside." To do this we emphasize the differences between that age and our own. The document most important for understanding the period is the Bible, a work necessary not only for understanding specifically religious subjects but for law, art, literature, and music as well. We approach the Bible from the standpoint of medieval exegesis rather than modern criticism. The chapter on the Bible, therefore, not only explains what the Bible is, but emphasizes those sections that were most frequently used in the Middle Ages, and gives clues, developed in subsequent chapters such as the one on Augustine, that explain how the Bible was read. It is likewise necessary to understand the contribution of Greece and Rome to the literature, art, or institutional history of the Middle Ages. However, the list of classical writers known and highly valued then was not necessarily the list most often studied today. And so on, down a rather extensive list of differences between medieval and modern culture.

A second implication of our approach follows from the first. To present the major developments of the Middle Ages in a somewhat systematic way, we deal with a highly complex period as a unity. There are dangers in this approach, which we think it would be wise to anticipate, especially given the current well-founded suspicion against totalizing systems. We ourselves of course do not think that the danger lies in faulty interpretations—though here we are obviously open to judgment—so much as it lies in being incomplete. In summarizing a phenomenon as complex as, say, feudal society, or a figure as monumental as Augustine, we understand very well that this trap is all but unavoidable. The risk we run of oversimplification, however, must be weighed against the primary goal of the book: to present that sense of the Middle Ages necessary to make any work of medieval culture more intelligible to a modern reader. We think that understanding the nature of feudal society or the place of Augustine can be aided by their placement within the larger context that the book develops. Equally significant, this context provides the most appropriate starting point for a more detailed study of the particular figures and movements presented in the book. Genuinely valuable scholarly contributions to all aspects of the Middle Ages abound; we have listed many of the more important and more accessible of these in our bibliography. The problem with them from a beginner's point of view is that the best are rarely written as introductions. Because these works are usually written not only by experts but for experts as well, much of their value will be lost to those who do not have some sense of the period.

The difference between what one sees as an expert and what one needs to see as a beginning student also allows us to say more about the problematic question of what kind of unity really does exist in the thousand-year period we call the Middle Ages. Can this unity, which we seem to presuppose, really be said to exist at all? Clearly, the differences between Augustine and Aquinas, Beowulf and Dante (or even Chaucer and Dante), or a Merovingian tribal king and Louis IX are enormous; and to ignore or to underestimate them is to ignore the actual texture of medieval religion, poetry, and monarchy. Those who argue against imposing a superficial unity on the Middle Ages perceive rightly the ever-present danger of reducing them to a Platonic model existing only in the mind of the scholar.

But it is also true that however great the differences between Augustine and Aquinas, they have many of the same concerns; for example, both deal with the relationship between human reason and divine revelation. Whatever different conclusions they come to, they still have more in common with each other than they have with, for example, a modern linguistic philosopher, for whom this relationship is not a concern. Literature provides similar examples of kinship. A Chaucer scholar easily recognizes enormous differences between Chaucer and Dante, differences in tone, temperament, and technique. But a modern student coming to either author for the first time will be greatly helped by knowing that each work is structured according to the ideal of a medieval pilgrimage, a literal journey that is a sign of a spiritual transformation; that similarity alone shows that Chaucer has more in common with Dante than either author has with Kafka or Don DeLillo. The changes that occurred in the thousand-year period between antiquity and the Renaissance can hardly be ignored. But they can be better understood by also recognizing that they all take place in a culture given a degree of homogeneity by the intellectual revolutions of subsequent times. To anyone familiar with the period, let alone to a scholar familiar with its political institutions, a Merovingian warrior-king seems to have almost nothing in common with a thirteenth-century king who presides over a complex legal and bureaucratic structure and who has a firm theoretical conception of the state. But even these differences will be grossly misinterpreted by the modern student to whom the very idea of kingship is utterly foreign, something our own presumed more sophisticated age need not take seriously. The Germanic warrior-king Clovis, for example, appears to be radically different from King Louis IX of France (1228–1270). However, both perceived themselves as Christian kings modeled on biblical exemplars and both quite consciously, albeit differently, recognized their debt to the model of the emperors of Rome. In other words, when looked at from a distance, from the vantage point provided by the twenty-first century, the people of the Middle Ages do indeed share a great deal. But the more scholars immerse themselves in the period, the more likely they are to take these differences between medieval and modern for granted, moving on to those discriminations within the period that are their real interest. This book takes the long view, the view that emphasizes the differences between medieval and modern, and hence a unity within the Middle Ages.

Moreover, this approach is aided by an affinity between the various medieval disciplines stronger than any that connects them in our own time. One example may suggest what the text itself embodies at greater length. A significant difference between the medieval and modern world is that our tendency is to look at truth as something to be created or discovered in the present, while truth in medieval society was perceived as having been discovered in the past. Because of this orientation there is throughout the period a visual and verbal iconography—a symbolic code by which figures and events can be identified—that remains relatively constant over the centuries. Saint Peter, to use an obvious and well-known example, is almost always pictured holding keys, a kind of shorthand referring to the text of Matthew's Gospel (Matt. 16: 18) in which Christ gives Peter the keys of His Kingdom. Some knowledge of this iconography is necessary not only to understand theological writings and saints' lives but also art, politics, and literature.

There has been a long-standing and almost continuous debate over the precise dates for the beginning and the end of the Middle Ages, testimony to the problem inherent in any attempt to classify the past with exactness. Figures such as Jerome and Augustine, however influential they were to become for the entire Middle Ages, belong nonetheless to the world of late antiquity. Figures such as Boethius and Gregory the Great, however much they draw from the ancient world, are usually classified as founders of the Middle Ages. Though this classification is somewhat arbitrary, it is nevertheless useful, and it is the one that we have adopted. We see the Middle Ages beginning with these so-called founders, the intellectual lights of that period that used to be dismissively referred to as the Dark Ages and now is more often called the early Middle Ages, the period stretching from the sixth century to the middle of the eleventh century. Therefore, the division of the book is threefold. Part 1 treats the antecedents of the Middle Ages, the classical and Christian backgrounds of medieval culture, ending in Late Antiquity with the monumental figure of Augustine. Part 2 deals with the early Middle Ages, beginning with the disintegration of the Roman Empire, including the Germanic invasions, the sixth and seventh-century founders, the renaissance associated with the figure of Charlemagne, and ending about the middle of the eleventh century. Part 3, "The High Middle Ages and Beyond," includes material from this point until about 1400.

There is a story we have heard that is probably only partly apocryphal about a course in English history from the Norman Conquest in 1066 to the battle of Bosworth Field in 1485. As the story goes, the instructor intended to begin with a few days of background. Those few days of background somehow turned into a few weeks of background. Those few weeks somehow managed to engulf the whole course, so that by Thanksgiving the teacher was still trying frantically to reach 1066. It was undoubtedly an excellent course, but not the one that was originally planned. We don't quite fall into that trap, in that we give equal time, pretty much, to the three major divisions of the book. But presenting as much material as we do in "The Foundations of the Middle Ages" is likewise our attempt to help teachers and students to avoid that trap.

Saint Peter by Lippo Memmi. Sienese, early fourteenth century. Paris, Louvre. Peter had been depicted with short white hair and curly beard since early Christian times. In this painting, he holds a book, the gospels, which is the guide for his life, and his "keys to the kingdom of heaven" (Matt. 16:18). One can see continuity in the representation of Peter by examining an earlier sculpted figure of the saint from Autun (Burgundy) on p. 186.

We have spent as much time as we have on the origins of the Middle Ages in order to let readers get on with the business of studying the major accomplishments and failures, which can best be understood once they have the background necessary to move directly to primary sources.

By modern standards, if not medieval ones, this book began a long time ago. In preparation for a course called "The Age of Dante," which we team-taught in Italy in the summer of 1975, we put together what turned out to be a very rough first draft. Before flying to Italy with our students, we had a week in the classroom to prepare them for what they would be reading and seeing. We put together a collection of medieval documents along with our own commentary, so that students with little or no medieval background would be better prepared to understand Dante and his world. The success of this battlefield experiment—one of our colleagues named our classroom week the boot camp of the mind—convinced us to try for something more elaborate and more permanent.

The Medieval World View was first published in 1983 and has stayed in print until the present. In moving from those mimeographed pages to publication—it really was a long time ago!—we kept the basic format, by including sections from primary sources, both written and visual. However, our commentary on these texts expanded and became part of a more continuous narrative. The published version is in no sense a sourcebook for the Middle Ages, since the texts we quote rarely go over a page or so in length. But as is obvious from what we have just said, the kind of book that it is owes a good deal to its beginnings, in that it was the texts that provided us with a starting point for our thinking about the book we wished to write, a book helpful for students coming to the Middle Ages for the first time, and, as it turned out, a book that has over the course of time also been helpful as an introduction to the Middle Ages for the general reader.

Why a new edition? For all practical purposes, the bibliography in the first edition ends with works published in 1981. The book becomes less useful to readers if the bibliography ceases to be a useful start to their own more specialized reading and research. One important reason for a second edition of *The Medieval World View* is to update that bibliography, so that both students and general readers can more easily move into the Middle Ages by following our suggestions. In addition to the daunting number of scholarly studies that have been published since that time, there have been a great many new (and more accessible) translations of primary sources. We have introduced new scholarly material and have dropped some works that are now outdated. We update some of the translations we use in the text and include them in the bibliography as well. Equally important, there has been an information revolution since the publication of the first edition. Medievalists have not been slow to embrace the new technology: websites with information on every figure from Abelard to Zeno; chatrooms of every description; The Dartmouth Dante Project, which makes commentaries on Dante from the fourteenth to the twentieth century available at the touch of a few keystrokes; and a host of other electronic resources are now standard fare in the world of medieval scholarship. We try to take account of these resources as part of the bibliographical apparatus for the new edition.

There is a great deal to be said for keeping the basic format of the first edition. As we have said, we are not aware of any other work that attempts the same kind of introduction to the Middle Ages. And this we have tried to do, with a few notable exceptions. The most important of these is that the book has a different conclusion. We ended the first edition at the year 1300, and included in our introduction a justification for that decision. In retrospect, we were wrong. A new chapter, on the fourteenth century, represents the biggest substantive change in the book. Carefully examining the tumultuous times that follow in the wake of what is sometimes called the medieval synthesis of the thirteenth century provides a more logical and a more useful conclusion to the book. And though there have been no other structural changes of quite the same magnitude, there have been many other changes that are nonetheless worth noting. An enormous amount has happened in medieval studies as well as in our own thinking about the Middle Ages since the publication of the first edition, and we have tried to find ways of taking this into account.

We said little about perceptions of gender in the first edition. A major presupposition of almost all classical, biblical, and medieval authors is that women are intellectually, socially, and in virtually all other ways inferior to men. This is an unfortunate aspect of our history, and one that we would do well not to ignore when studying the Middle Ages. But despite this pervasive prejudice, women nevertheless played important roles and accomplished an enormous amount during the Middle Ages in many areas, from piety to politics. This would of course include ways in which they have always been actors and agents of history, but for which they often do not receive explicit credit because there is not enough documentary evidence, such as child rearing and the transmission of cultural values. Women also wrote important and influential texts that can stand next to the best work of their male counterparts. The recovery and evaluation of these texts has been one of the most important projects of the last several decades in medieval studies. We have tried to take advantage of that work. To give a few examples: The chapter on the Bible discusses the figure of Wisdom as the feminine side of God. The chapter on monasticism includes more material about women and their importance in the monastic world. The chapter on Francis of Assisi now does more than simply mention Clare. And several important women writers, such as Hildegard of Bingen and Christine de Pizan, now have their place in the narrative.

We said little about Byzantium (the Eastern Roman Empire) and little about Islam in the first edition. Once again, we have added some specific references, including several new references to the Byzantine Empire and selections from a Crusade chronicle written from an Islamic point of view. These references are not meant to change the fact that we are writing from a primarily Western European point of view. But they help alert the reader to the fact that in the Middle Ages, those in the West were more aware of and had more interaction with the Byzantine world and with Islam than we often assume. These references can also serve the important function of reminding the reader that we *are* writing from a Western point of view, and that there are other perspectives from which to think about these events and issues and ideas. The bibliography likewise includes more material than the first edition relating directly to Byzantium and Islam. Beginning with primary texts as we have still seems to us to be the best way to open up the Middle Ages. But we also need to include a reminder that most people in the Middle Ages were not able to write, and so by definition we do not represent the views of those who could not write, or whose writings may have been suppressed. Although this book has little to say about those whose ideas have not been directly preserved, whether peasants or heretics, one of the interesting and important trends in recent medieval studies has been the attempt to find ways to listen to the marginalized. Readers should be aware of this trend.

The quotation from Bernard of Chartres that provides the epigraph for the book—that we are dwarfs on the shoulders of giants—is meant to be suggestive rather than programmatic, a useful entry into the text. We have tried to take into account its implications in the structure of our work by reminding the reader that the Middle Ages not only owed an enormous debt to the past—to its classical, Christian, and Germanic antecedents—but that it was in fact conscious of this debt as well. In the structure of the book, no less than for the thinkers of the Middle Ages, there is a constant backward glance to the achievements of the past.

Moreover, each phase of medieval culture was dependent on the achievements of the more immediate past as well as its premedieval foundations: it is impossible to understand the Renaissance of the Twelfth Century without an understanding of those elements of the classical past that they rediscovered and reinterpreted. But it is also impossible to understand the Twelfth-Century Renaissance without an appreciation of the Carolingian Renaissance of the early ninth century. In other words, classical and Carolingian writers can both be considered giants on whose shoulders the thinkers of the Twelfth-Century Renaissance rest. Our attempt to emphasize both the giants who existed before the Middle Ages and the giants who existed within the period itself is a thread that runs through each chapter, and which helps give coherence to our reading of the Middle Ages.

TIME LINE

CENTURIES PRECEDING THE MIDDLE AGES (ALL DATES C.E.)

14	Death of the Emperor Augustus
30	Crucifixion of Jesus Christ
c.64	Persecution of Christians by Nero
c.65	Deaths of St. Peter and St. Paul
98–117	Reign of Emperor Trajan
107	Martyrdom of St. Ignatius
155	Martyrdom of St. Polycarp
c.160–220	Life of Tertullian
161–180	Reign of Emperor Marcus Aurelius
c.185–254	Life of Origen
251–356	Life of St. Antony (becomes a monk c.269)
284–305	Reign of Emperor Diocletian

LATE ANTIQUITY AND THE MIDDLE AGES

312–337	Reign of Emperor Constantine
313	Edict of Milan
325	Council of Nicaea (1st ecumenical council)
330	Dedication of the City of Constantinople
c.340–397	Life of St. Ambrose
c.342–420	Life of St. Jerome
354–430	Life of St. Augustine
c.360–435	Life of John Cassian
378	Battle of Adrianople
379–395	Reign of Emperor Theodosius I (the Great)
381	Council of Constantinople (2nd ecumenical council)

THE MEDIEVAL WORLD VIEW

PART 1

The Foundations
of the Middle Ages

IRISH
SEA

York

BRITAIN

ATLANTIC
OCEAN

Trier

GAUL

Milan
Lyons

Marseille   Ravenna

ADRIATIC SEA

CORSICA
Rome

SPAIN

SARDINIA

SICILY
Agrigento

Hippo   Carthage

MEDITERRANE

THE ANCIENT WORLD

- - - - - Borders of Roman Empire at
           Its Greatest Expanse, c.120 C.E.

+++++ Approximate Division between Eastern
       and Western Roman Empire Beginning
       in the Reign of Diocletian (284–305)

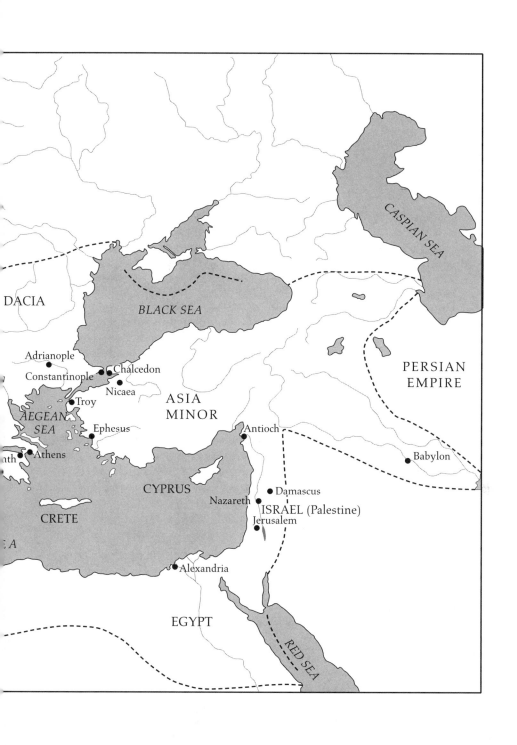

DACIA

BLACK SEA

CASPIAN SEA

PERSIAN
EMPIRE

Adrianople

Chalcedon
Constantinople
Nicaea
Troy

ASIA
MINOR

AEGEAN
SEA

Ephesus

Antioch

Babylon

ath Athens

CYPRUS

Damascus

Nazareth

CRETE

ISRAEL (Palestine)

Jerusalem

EA

Alexandria

EGYPT

RED SEA

CHAPTER 1

THE BIBLE

The Christian Bible was far and away the most influential text in the Middle Ages. For medieval (and modern) Christians, the Bible is divided into two parts: the Old Testament, which is a collection of books that tells the story of the Hebrew people, and the New Testament, a collection that provides the narrative and theological account of one particular Hebrew, Jesus Christ. Three-fourths of the Bible is made up of the Old Testament, the writings of the Hebrews. But when students and scholars set out to study the Middle Ages, they often pay far less attention to the New Testament than they do to the influence of classical antiquity and of early Christianity, let alone the Old Testament. Yet in the fourth century when Jerome translated the Bible into Latin in the version that became standard for the Middle Ages, he translated the Old Testament as well as the New, including what today are referred to as the Old Testament Apocrypha: books that did not remain part of the standard collection, or canon, of Scripture, but which are nevertheless also significant. And these Old Testament books were hardly ignored in the Middle Ages. They were read, studied, memorized, quoted, commented upon, embodied in the liturgy, and depicted in art, though usually in what was perceived as their relationship to the New Testament. Thus, a brief survey of the kinds of documents that make up the Old Testament is a necessary starting point for an understanding of the Bible and an understanding of the Middle Ages.[1]

The Old Testament was written over a much longer time than the New; perhaps a thousand years separate the composition of the earliest from the latest texts, and some of the stories existed either orally or in writing long before they reached the form in which they have been handed down. The Old Testament consists of legends, historical narrative, laws, poetry, allegory, prophecy, songs, and wise sayings. The first five books of the Old Testament (Genesis, Exodus, Leviticus, Numbers, Deuteronomy) are called the Law (English), the Torah (Hebrew), or the Pentateuch (Greek). These books present, often in symbolic terms, the story of creation, the fall of humanity, the choosing of the Hebrews by God, and their history until the death of Moses. Presumed in the Middle Ages to have been written by Moses, the Torah has always held a privileged place in Jewish and Christian understanding of the Bible. Many of the most familiar Bible stories are contained in these books: Adam and Eve, Cain and Abel, Noah, the Tower of Babel, Abraham, Isaac, Jacob, Joseph, the bondage in Egypt, the exodus into Palestine, the reception of the Ten Commandments. A significant portion of these books, however, is also taken up with legal material and ritual prescriptions. Although this ritual material is more or less ignored by Christians today, it captured the interest of medieval writers, and several long allegorical commentaries on the details of ritual and law were composed and widely known.

The next two books, Joshua and Judges, tell the story of the conquest of the Promised Land from the native inhabitants, the Canaanites. Perhaps the most famous stories in these books are Joshua at the battle of Jericho, and Samson and Delilah. In the Middle Ages, these books were seen as especially relevant to the Crusades, wars fought with the aim of reconquering the Promised Land, which had been captured by the Muslims in the seventh century. Imagery from Joshua and Judges pervades Crusade chronicles: the epitaph of the man who conquered Jerusalem in the First Crusade, for example, refers to him as another Joshua. More subtly, the theory of causation in Joshua and Judges—warriors will triumph in battle only if they act morally—is used to explain victories and losses in battle in the Crusades, and in warfare throughout the Middle Ages.

After the short book of Ruth come eight books, more or less historical in their orientation, that tell the story of the founding, flourishing, division, conquest, and restoration of the Hebrew monarchy. The stories of the anointing of Saul as first king of the Hebrews, the shepherd David's defeat of the Philistine giant Goliath, the civil war between David and Saul, and the victories and prosperity of David's reign after Saul had been killed are told in the First and Second Book of Kings, in modern translations called the First and Second Book of Samuel. (There are other differences between medieval and modern biblical terminology as well as differences in the numbering of some of the psalms.) The Third Book of Kings (First Book of Kings in modern translations) tells of the most wealthy and wise of all the Hebrew kings—Solomon—who, at the end of his life, turned away from the Hebrew God Yahweh (sometimes written Jehovah) to worship foreign idols. It then goes on to tell of the split between the north and south (respectively the kingdoms of Israel and Judah) after Solomon's death. The House of David ruled the south from Jerusalem while a succession of families attempted to rule in the north, eventually building a capital at Samaria. The Fourth Book of Kings continues to tell of the split and the falling away from the worship of Yahweh in both kingdoms, especially the northern one. The appearance of the prophets Elijah and Elisha in the Third and Fourth Book of Kings shows how moral authority among the Hebrews no longer rests with the monarchs, but has passed to their harshest critics. Fourth Kings also describes the destruction of the northern kingdom by the Assyrians in 722–721 B.C.E. and the destruction of the southern kingdom by the Babylonians in 587–586 B.C.E. It was with the fall of Jerusalem in 587–586 B.C.E. that the Hebrew monarchy came to an end and thousands of Hebrews were forced into exile in Babylonian territory. Whenever the theory and practice of monarchy are examined in the Middle Ages, the story of the rise and fall of the Hebrew monarchy is never far from the discussion.

There is no book in the Bible that gives a narrative of the actual events of the exile, but the books of Ezra and Nehemiah tell of the return from exile, the rebuilding of the Temple and the city walls, and the institution of religious reforms. After the restoration of the Temple in 516 B.C.E., the Hebrews were governed by foreign powers but generally were allowed to practice their religion undisturbed. There are no narrative accounts in the Old Testament extending from this time until the middle of the second century. However, when the Greek rulers of Palestine tried to enforce religious uniformity on the Hebrews around 160 B.C.E., a rebellion led by Judas Maccabaeus was successful in winning de facto freedom. The story of this revolt is narrated in the First and Second Books of Maccabees. After the revolt, there is no more historical narrative in the Old Testament.

In addition to these books, there are two other categories of books in the Old Testament. One category is the prophets. A prophet, as implied above with the mention of Elijah and Elisha, is a messenger whom God raises up to confront his people, especially the leaders, with their faults, and warn them of the consequences if they continue to sin. Prophets also carry their warnings into the near and even distant future by predicting what is to come. The prophets Elijah and Elisha are among the important figures who appear in the narrative books of Hebrew Scriptures. But prophets also speak in their own voice in a group of sixteen books that are named after individual prophets. This group consists of the four so-called major prophets (Isaiah, Jeremiah, Ezekiel, and Daniel) and the twelve minor prophets (Hosea, Joel, Amos, Obadiah, Jonah, Micah, Nahum, Habakkuk, Zephaniah, Haggai, Zechariah, and Malachi). This division into major and minor is not meant to indicate the quality or importance of the prophetic book but rather its length and its placement in Scripture.

Although the writings of the prophets stretch out over several hundred years, the most important prophetic literature was written at the time of the disintegration of the kingdoms of Israel and Judah and their destruction by the Assyrians and the Babylonians respectively. During this time the prophets continue to insist that these cataclysmic events have more to do with internal problems such as the Hebrews' own lack of social justice and their religious hypocrisy and idolatry than with external threats. Many texts from these prophets were either quoted directly or clearly alluded to in the New Testament, especially in Matthew's Gospel. Two examples will show how important some of these texts are to New Testament writers and to all subsequent Christian writers. The following text from Isaiah is quoted by all four evangelists as a prophecy of the ministry of John the Baptist:

A voice cries out:
"In the wilderness, prepare the way of the Lord,
make straight in the desert a highway for our God.
Every valley shall be lifted up, and every mountain and hill be made low,
the uneven ground shall become level, and the rough places a plain.
Then the glory of the Lord shall be revealed, and all people shall see it
    together,
for the mouth of the Lord has spoken." (Isa. 40:3–5)

The Gospels and Paul's Letters both emphasized that Christ was a direct descendent of King David. The expectation of a savior coming from the House of David is predicted by several prophets, including Jeremiah:

The days are surely coming, says the Lord, when I will raise up for David a righteous Branch, and he shall reign as king and deal wisely, and shall execute justice and righteousness in the land. In his days Judah will be saved and Israel will live in safety. And this is the name by which he will be called: "The Lord is our righteousness." (Jer. 23:5–6)

The final category of Hebrew Scripture is called the Writings, a collection of texts that provide models of conduct, advice, edifying stories, and magnificent poetry. Old Testament literary works were favorite sources of wisdom in the Middle Ages and were frequently commented upon by medieval writers. Included among these texts is the Book of Job, a long narrative poem about a good man who lost all his earthly possessions in a test of his faith. Job was frequently seen as an anticipation of Christ in the Middle Ages, thanks largely to the long Commentary on the Book of Job written by Pope Gregory I (d.604). He was also, like several other Old Testament figures, regarded as a saint in the Middle Ages, and churches were even dedicated to him. The Writings also include what was perhaps the best-loved and most pervasive book of the Old Testament in the Middle Ages, the Psalms, the Hebrew hymn book, a series of one hundred fifty songs which were believed to have been written by King David. These songs express the widest variety of moods and attitudes, ranging from laments to hymns of praise, from battle songs to wedding songs. Some sing of the love of the faithful for God while others cry out for the annihilation of their enemies. For example, one can contrast the two texts below:

Happy indeed is the man who follows not the counsel of the wicked; nor lingers in the way of sinners nor sits in the company of scorners, but whose delight is the law of the Lord and who ponders his law day and night. (Ps. 1:1–2)

O God, break the teeth in their mouths, tear out the fangs of these wild beasts, O Lord! Let them vanish like water that runs away: let them wither

like grass that is trodden underfoot: let them be like the snail that dissolves
into slime: like a woman's miscarriage that never sees the sun. (Ps. 57:7–9)

The Rule of Saint Benedict (c. 530) prescribed that the entire Psalter was to
be sung in monastic churches each week, and in cathedrals and parish churches
the Psalms were also sung regularly.

The books of Ecclesiastes, Wisdom of Solomon, and Proverbs were all
thought to have been written by King Solomon, and together with Ecclesiasticus (or the Wisdom of Jesus Son of Sirach), were seen to be thematically
connected to the idea of wisdom in its many manifestations, including wisdom
as the manifestation of the creative power of God, personified in both Proverbs
and Wisdom as a woman:

> She reaches mightily from one end of the earth to the other, and she orders
>   all things well.
> I loved her and sought her from my youth;
> I desired to take her for my bride,
> And became enamored of her beauty. (Wisdom 8:1–2)

The beginning of the Wisdom of Solomon—"Love justice you who rule
the earth"—is quoted in Dante's *Paradiso* and is emblazoned on a scroll in the
hands of Jesus in a fresco (1315) in the principal meeting chamber of Siena's
city hall. In Ecclesiasticus there is a brief summary, a highlights reel of the
heroes of Hebrew history, that was often used in the Middle Ages as a way
of teaching Christians the essentials of the Hebrew past. Wisdom literature
also included practical advice as well. A few examples from the Book of Proverbs
will illustrate the richness and variety of advice to be found there:

> Like a dog that returns to its own vomit, is a fool who reverts to his folly.
> (26:11)
>   Do not boast about tomorrow, for you do not know what a day may bring.
> (27:1)
>   The rod and reproof give wisdom, but a mother is disgraced by a neglected
> child. (29:15)

These and hundreds of other bits of wisdom provided both practical guides to
daily living and important philosophical principles in the Middle Ages. Within
this grouping of wisdom literature we should also mention the Song of Songs
because it, too, was considered to have been written by Solomon. A poem
charged with sexual imagery that celebrates the physical relationship between
a bride and a bridegroom, the Song of Songs was one of the most commented-
upon books of the Bible in the Middle Ages, most frequently treated allegorically, with Christ as the bridegroom and the Church as his bride.

It is important to say something about form as well as content in the Old
Testament since the vivid imagery of the Hebrew writers permeates the Middle Ages. They did not speak in abstractions but rather their language was al-

most invariably concrete and specific. They spoke in quite precise and detailed metaphor, as in the following Psalm:

> He who dwells in the shelter of the Most High and abides in the shade of the Almighty says to the Lord: "My refuge, my stronghold, my God in whom I trust."
>
> It is he who will free you from the snare of the fowler who seeks to destroy you; he will conceal you with his pinions and under his wings you will find refuge.
>
> You will not fear the terror of the night nor the arrow that flies by day, nor the plague that prowls in the darkness nor the scourge that lays waste at noon.
>
> A thousand may fall at your side, ten thousand fall at your right, you, it will never approach; his faithfulness is buckler and shield.
>
> Your eyes have only to look to see how the wicked are repaid, you who have said: "Lord, my refuge!" and have made the Most High your dwelling.
>
> Upon you no evil shall fall, no plague approach where you dwell. For you has he commanded his angels, to keep you in all your ways.
>
> They shall bear you upon their hands lest you strike your foot against a stone. On the lion and the viper you will tread and trample the young lion and the dragon.
>
> Since he clings to me in love, I will free him; protect him for he knows my name. When he calls I shall answer: "I am with you." I will save him in distress and give him glory.
>
> With length of life I will content him;
>
> I shall let him see my saving power. (Ps. 90 [91 in modern versions])

God is personal and concrete: "My stronghold," "his wings," and so on. Furthermore, the descriptions of God's power are specific. God will rescue a man from hurting his foot on a stone, which in ancient times could mean not being able to farm or harvest, and thus possibly starvation. This same passage is used by the devil in Matt. 4:6 and Luke 4:11 to tempt Christ. Texts like this were often used in medieval art, such as the statues of Christ standing on a lion and a viper, symbolizing enemies of the Church. This Psalm was one of the best known in the Middle Ages since the Rule of Saint Benedict prescribed its singing every day at the office of compline.

The second part of the Christian Bible, the New Testament, is much shorter than the Old Testament, much less varied in its literary forms, and written within a much shorter span of time, less than one hundred years. It consists of four Gospels; the Acts of the Apostles, an account of the early Church; thirteen letters attributed to Paul; the anonymous letter to the Hebrews, also believed in the Middle Ages to have been written by Paul; letters attributed to James, Peter, John, and Jude; and the Apocalypse or Book of Revelation.

Sculpture from the south porch of Chartres Cathedral. Thirteenth century. This statue puts into stone the image of Christ trampling the lion and dragon from Psalm 91.

The Gospels are the most familiar part of the New Testament because they contain the stories of the life and teachings of Jesus Christ. However, these accounts are not biographies in the modern sense. The Gospels present highly theologized pictures of Christ; their authors are more interested in presenting their audience with the "good news" of Jesus than a chronicle of his activities. The Gospels are conventionally divided into two groups: the synoptics (Matthew, Mark, and Luke) and John. In fact, there are crucial similarities among all four gospels. All four present as their central concern the crucifixion and resurrection of Jesus. And in all four the crucifixion and resurrection come at the end of the narrative, as its climax and focal point. Nonetheless, the division is useful. The synoptic Gospels, of which Mark is the earliest (c. 70 C.E.), share many stories that are not present in John. They have basically the same chronology of events; they describe the Last Supper and the institution of the Eucharist; in them Christ often speaks in parables. Nonetheless, there are also differences among them; for example, Mark has no nativity account. Matthew and Luke each describe Christ's birth, although with some significant differences between them. Each presents its own perspective on the meaning of Christ's life and teachings.

Matthew is the Gospel of fulfillment. Quoting the Old Testament nearly a hundred times, it constantly emphasizes how Christ fulfills and completes the revelation of God in the Old Testament. All the evangelists develop this theme somewhat, but Matthew far exceeds the others. Consider the following passages from the nativity narrative, which draw energetically from the figure of Joseph in Genesis, as well as from the prophets Isaiah and Jeremiah:

> Now the birth of Jesus the Messiah took place in this way. When his mother Mary had been engaged to Joseph, but before they lived together, she was found to be with child from the Holy Spirit. Her husband Joseph, being a righteous man and unwilling to expose her to public disgrace, planned to dismiss her quietly. But just when he had resolved to do this, an angel of the Lord appeared to him in a dream and said, "Joseph, son of David, do not be afraid to take Mary as your wife, for the child conceived in her is from the Holy Spirit. She will bear a son, and you are to name him Jesus, for he will save his people from their sins." All this took place to fulfill what had been spoken by the Lord through the prophet: "Look, the virgin shall conceive and bear a son, and they shall name him Emmanuel," which means, "God is with us." [quoting Isa. 7:14] (1:18–23)
>
> Then Joseph got up, took the child and his mother by night, and went to Egypt, and remained there until the death of Herod. This was to fulfill what had been spoken by the Lord through the prophet, "Out of Egypt I have called my son." [quoting Hos. 7:1] (2:14–15)
>
> When Herod saw that he had been tricked by the wise men, he was infuriated, and he sent and killed all the children in and around Bethlehem who were two years old or under, according to the time that he had learned from the wise men. Then was fulfilled what had been spoken through the prophet Jeremiah: "A voice was heard in Ramah, wailing and loud lamentation, Rachel weeping for her children; she refused to be consoled, because they are no more." [quoting Jer. 31:15] (2:16–18)

Perhaps this theme of fulfillment can best be summarized by a text from the Sermon on the Mount: "Do not think that I have come to set aside the law and the prophets; I have not come to set them aside, but to bring them to perfection" (5:17).

Luke, who was probably the best educated of the evangelists and best acquainted with the way the Greeks wrote history, gives a particularly beautiful literary work. Some principal themes are the universal message of Christ—Matthew by contrast was writing primarily for Jewish Christians—the exaltation of the lowly and poor, the importance of Mary, and the significance of Christ as a man of prayer and solitude. In his nativity narrative, Luke stresses the universal message of Christ in a song attributed to the prophet Simeon:

> "Master, now you are dismissing your servant in peace, according to your word; for my eyes have seen your salvation, which you have prepared in the

presence of all peoples, a light for revelation to the Gentiles and for glory to your people Israel." (2:29–32)

The exaltation of the poor and the importance of Mary are both present in the song of Mary:

> And Mary said: "My soul magnifies the Lord,
> and my spirit rejoices in God my Savior,
> for he has looked with favor on the lowliness of his servant.
> Surely, from now on all generations will call me blessed;
> for the Mighty One has done great things for me, and holy is his name.
> His mercy is for those who fear him from generation to generation.
> He has shown strength with his arm;
> he has scattered the proud in the thoughts of their hearts.
> He has brought down the powerful from their thrones, and lifted up the
>   lowly;
> he has filled the hungry with good things, and sent the rich away empty.
> He has helped his servant Israel in remembrance of his mercy,
> according to the promises he made to our ancestors,
> to Abraham and to his descendants forever." (1:46–55)

Luke also emphasizes repentance and forgiveness, illustrated by such stories as the Prodigal Son and the repentant thief who was crucified with Christ.

John's Gospel is different from the other three. It does not rely on parables as the other Gospels do. Rather, Christ speaks in a more sophisticated and philosophical way. Furthermore, the chronology differs from the synoptic Gospels. For example, Christ is crucified on the Passover in John and thus is identified with the sacrificial lamb of Exodus 12 while in the synoptics it is the Last Supper that takes place on the Passover and the crucifixion is the day afterward. There are several important themes in John, two of which appear in the opening verses. Christ is associated with light, and Christ is called the Word, who is shown to have been active in the works of creation. In fact, John's Prologue can be read as a commentary on and update of the creation stories in Genesis:

> In the beginning was the Word, and the Word was with God, and the Word was God. He was in the beginning with God. All things came into being through him, and without him not one thing came into being. What has come into being in him was life, and the life was the light of all people. The light shines in the darkness, and the darkness did not overcome it. (1:1–5)

Christ's identification with the paschal victim (the lamb sacrificed in commemoration of God's plague "passing over" the Hebrews when they were in Egypt) is clear in John:

> The next day he [John the Baptist] saw Jesus coming toward him and declared, "Here is the Lamb of God, who takes away the sin of the world!" (1:29)

According to John, Jesus' legs are not broken at the crucifixion, thus fulfilling a text in Leviticus that said that no bone of the paschal lamb was to be broken.

John's only parable is of Christ as the Good Shepherd, identifying Christ with the Messiah described by the prophets. This text, along with a different Good Shepherd parable in Matthew and Luke, is the source for early representations in art of Christ as the Good Shepherd as well as representations in later medieval literature.

> "I am the good shepherd. The good shepherd lays down his life for the sheep. The hired hand, who is not the shepherd and does not own the sheep, sees the wolf coming and leaves the sheep and runs away—and the wolf snatches them and scatters them. The hired hand runs away because a hired hand does not care for the sheep. I am the good shepherd. I know my own and my own know me, just as the Father knows me and I know the Father. And I lay down my life for the sheep." (10:11–15)

John carefully distinguishes between the letter and the spirit as the key to understanding Jesus. In fact, one of the literary devices John employs is to have the Pharisees and even sometimes Jesus' friends take his spiritual pronouncements literally. The famous "bread of life" passage illustrates the Johannine distinction between the letter, which is temporal, and the spirit, which is eternal. Christ has just fed the five thousand with five loaves and two fishes, and the crowds have followed him:

> So they said to him, "What sign are you going to give us then, so that we may see it and believe in you? What work are you performing? Our ancestors ate the manna in the wilderness; as it is written, 'He gave them bread from heaven to eat.'" Then Jesus said to them, "Very truly, I tell you, it was not Moses who gave you the bread from heaven, but it is my Father who gives you the true bread from heaven. For the bread of God is that which comes down from heaven and gives life to the world." They said to him, "Sir, give us this bread always." Jesus said to them, "I am the bread of life. Whoever comes to me will never be hungry, and whoever believes in me will never be thirsty. But I said to you that you have seen me and yet do not believe. Everything that the Father gives me will come to me, and anyone who comes to me I will never drive away; for I have come down from heaven, not to do my own will, but the will of him who sent me, that I should lose nothing of all that he has given me, but raise it up on the last day." (6:30–39)
>
> "Very truly, I tell you, whoever believes has eternal life. I am the bread of life. Your ancestors ate the manna in the wilderness, and they died. This is the bread that comes down from heaven, so that one may eat of it and not die. I am the living bread that came down from heaven. Whoever eats of this bread will live forever; and the bread that I will give for the life of the world is my flesh." (6:47–52)

All four Gospels have in common some special place among Jesus' followers for Peter. Three passages in particular became important to the Middle Ages since the popes were understood to be the successors of Peter and based their claims to power on Christ's words to Peter:

> Now when Jesus came into the district of Caesarea Philippi, he asked his disciples, "Who do people say that the Son of Man is?" And they said, "Some say John the Baptist, but others Elijah, and still others Jeremiah or one of the prophets." He said to them, "But who do you say that I am?" Simon Peter answered, "You are the Messiah, the Son of the living God." And Jesus answered him, "Blessed are you, Simon son of Jonah! For flesh and blood has not revealed this to you, but my Father in heaven. And I tell you, you are Peter, and on this rock I will build my church, and the gates of Hades will not prevail against it. I will give you the keys of the kingdom of heaven, and whatever you bind on earth will by bound in heaven, and whatever you loose on earth will be loosed in heaven." (Matt. 16:13–19)
>
> "Simon, Simon, listen! Satan has demanded to sift all of you like wheat, but I have prayed for you that your own faith may not fail; and you, when once you have turned back, strengthen your brothers." (Luke 22:31–32)
>
> When they had finished breakfast, Jesus said to Simon Peter, "Simon son of John, do you love me more than these [others do]?" He said to him, "Yes, Lord; you know that I love you." Jesus said to him, "Feed my lambs." A second time he said to him, "Simon son of John, do you love me?" He said to him, "Yes, Lord; you know that I love you." Jesus said to him, "Tend my sheep." He said to him the third time, "Simon son of John, do you love me?" Peter felt hurt because he said to him the third time, "Do you love me?" And he said to him, "Lord, you know everything; you know that I love you." Jesus said to him, "Feed my sheep." (John 21:15–18)

The Acts of the Apostles, attributed to Luke, is a continuation of his Gospel, beginning with the Ascension of Christ to heaven and then narrating important events in the first years of the Church. It tells of the Christian community in Jerusalem after Christ's earthly ministry; the stoning of the first Christian martyr, Stephen; the conversion of Paul; the missions of Paul to the Gentiles; and the establishment of gentile (non-Jewish) Christianity. One of the most important stories in Acts is Pentecost, the descent of the Holy Spirit:

> When the day of Pentecost had come, they were all together in one place. And suddenly from heaven there came a sound like the rush of a violent wind, and it filled the entire house where they were sitting. Divided tongues, as of fire, appeared among them, and a tongue rested on each of them. All of them were filled with the Holy Spirit and began to speak in other languages, as the Spirit gave them ability. (Acts 2:1–4)

It can be argued that as Luke's Gospel is the story of God the Son, Acts is the story of God the Holy Spirit, having come at Pentecost to guide the early Church.

In some ways the Letters of Paul are the most important part of the New Testament for the Middle Ages. The Greek word for letter is "epistle," which is how Paul's letters are often designated, especially in older translations. Although several letters traditionally ascribed to Paul are today regarded as works of his followers by many biblical scholars, medieval thinkers made no distinctions of authorship, nor did they doubt the complete consistency of the ideas expressed in the corpus of letters bearing his name. While the Gospels provided most of the stories and images for medieval art, Paul provided the basis for the development of Christian theology. Augustine, clearly the most influential theologian for the Middle Ages and beyond, was especially reliant on him. Paul had been a rigid, legalistic Jew—a Pharisee—who persecuted early Christians; he had looked on approvingly at the stoning of Stephen. However, according to Acts of the Apostles, he underwent a miraculous conversion to Christ on the road to Damascus, the model for later conversion stories, (e.g., Antony and Augustine):

> Meanwhile Saul [Paul], still breathing threats and murder against the disciples of the Lord, went to the high priest and asked him for letters to the synagogues at Damascus, so that if he found any who belonged to the Way, men or women, he might bring them bound to Jerusalem. Now as he was going along and approaching Damascus, suddenly a light from Heaven flashed around him. He fell to the ground and heard a voice saying to him, "Saul, Saul, why do you persecute me?" He asked, "Who are you, Lord?" The reply came, "I am Jesus, whom you are persecuting. But get up and enter the city, and you will be told what you are to do." (Acts 9:1–7)

Paul saw his mission as preaching the Gospel of Jesus Christ to non-Jews, and spent years traveling primarily in the eastern Mediterranean, establishing Christian communities and later writing them letters. He is believed to have died in the persecution of Nero in Rome, which began after the fire of 64 C.E.

Paul stresses the necessity of faith; this emphasis becomes a key to medieval theology. The following text from Paul's letter to the Romans makes the primacy of faith clear:

> For we hold that a person is justified by faith apart from works prescribed by the law. Or is God the God of Jews only? Is he not the God of Gentiles also? Yes, of Gentiles also, since God is one; and he will justify the circumcised on the ground of faith and the uncircumcised through that same faith. Do we then overthrow the law by this faith? By no means! On the contrary, we uphold the law. (Rom. 3:27–31)

Although Paul never suggests that human knowledge is of no value, the proper purpose of study and reflection is to lead a person to God:

> For what can be known about God is plain to them [the Gentiles], because God has shown it to them. Ever since the creation of the world his eternal

power and divine nature, invisible though they are, have been understood and seen through the things he has made. (Rom. 1:19–20)

For medieval theories of art, literature, music, science, and knowledge in general, there is no more important scriptural passage than this one. Augustine returns to it constantly, and virtually every other great medieval thinker uses it as well.

Paul's deep spirituality is sometimes misunderstood to mean that he rejected as evil worldly things or human flesh. One should consider Paul's own words about the material world and about humanity:

> I know and am persuaded in the Lord Jesus that nothing is unclean in itself; but it is unclean for anyone who thinks it unclean. (Rom. 14:14)

A great deal of medieval political theory derives either directly from Paul or indirectly from Paul through Augustine. Paul writes about the necessity for obedience to civil authority in the following influential passage:

> Let every person be subject to the governing authorities; for there is no authority except from God, and those authorities that exist have been instituted by God. Therefore whoever resists authority resists what God has appointed, and those who resist will incur judgment. For rulers are not a terror to good conduct, but to bad. Do you wish to have no fear of the authority? Then do what is good, and you will receive its approval; for it is God's servant for your good. But if you do what is wrong, you should be afraid, for the authority does not bear the sword in vain! It is the servant of God to execute wrath on the wrongdoer. Therefore one must be subject, not only because of wrath but also because of conscience. For the same reason you also pay taxes, for the authorities are God's servants, busy with this very thing. (Rom. 13:1–6)

Even medieval attitudes toward women derived to a great extent from Paul:

> But I want you to understand that Christ is the head of every man, and the husband is the head of his wife, and God is the head of Christ.
>
> For a man ought not to have his head veiled, since he is the image and reflection of God; but woman is the reflection of man. Indeed, man was not made from woman, but woman from man. Neither was man created for the sake of woman, but woman for the sake of man. For this reason a woman ought to have a symbol of authority on her head, because of the angels. Nevertheless, in the Lord woman is not independent of man or man independent of woman. For just as woman came from man, so man comes through woman; but all things come from God. (1 Cor. 11:7–12)

One should notice not only the subordinate place in which Paul put women, essentially accepting the conventions of his society, but also their new *importance* within Christianity. It is clear in Paul's letters as well as many other texts from the first Christian centuries that women played central roles in guiding and administering Christian communities. However, the continuing institutionalization of the Church eventually led to a male monopoly, at least in terms of the holding of *official* positions of authority.

As a Jew, Paul was thoroughly familiar with the Old Testament, and he often uses Old Testament stories in his letters. He sees Old Testament events as foreshadowings of things that occurred in the time of Christ: "That gospel, [i.e., good news] promised long ago by means of his prophets in the holy scriptures, tells us of his Son" (Rom. 1:2). This Pauline outlook is absolutely essential to understanding the way medieval people viewed the entire Old Testament (typology and figuralism are the words most often used to describe this foreshadowing of the New Testament in the Old). In the following text from 1 Corinthians, Paul reads events of the Jews' exodus from Egypt typologically:

> I do not want you to be unaware, brothers and sisters, that our ancestors were all under the cloud, and all passed through the sea, and all were baptized into Moses in the cloud and in the sea, and all ate the same spiritual food and all drank the same spiritual drink. For they drank from the spiritual rock that followed them, and the rock was Christ. Nevertheless, God was not pleased with most of them, and they were stuck down in the wilderness.
>
> Now these things occurred as examples for us, so that we might not desire evil as they did. Do not become idolaters as some of them did; as it is written, "The people sat down to eat and drink, and they rose up to play." We must not indulge in sexual immorality as some of them did, and twenty-three thousand fell in a single day. We must not put Christ to the test, as some of them did, and were destroyed by serpents. And do not complain as some of them did, and were destroyed by the destroyer. These things happened to them to serve as an example, and they were written down to instruct us, on whom the ends of the ages have come. So if you think you are standing, watch out that you do not fall. (1 Cor. 10:1–12)

This text shows the typological relationship between the passing through the Red Sea and Christian baptism, as well as between the feeding of the Hebrews in the desert and the Eucharist. Paul sees a primary significance of the Old Testament to be both symbolic and directly relevant to his own time, thus making it an integral part of Christian belief. He does not deny its historical truth but simply believes that this is not always the primary level of meaning. The following text from Paul's Epistle to the Galatians makes this point clearer:

> Tell me, you who desire to be subject to the law, will you not listen to the law? For it is written that Abraham had two sons, one by a slave woman and the other by a free woman. One, the child of the slave, was born according to the flesh; the other, the child of the free woman, was born through the promise. Now this is an allegory: these women are two covenants. One woman, in

fact, is Hagar, from Mount Sinai, bearing children for slavery. Now Hagar is Mount Sinai in Arabia and corresponds to the present Jerusalem, for she is in slavery with her children. But the other woman corresponds to the Jerusalem above; she is free, and she is our mother. (4:21–26)

Paul makes one of the most difficult but important connections between the Old and New Testament in Romans 5. Here he talks of Christ coming as a second Adam to undo the sin of the first:

Therefore, just as sin came into the world through one man, and death came through sin, and so death spread to all because all have sinned—sin was indeed in the world before the law, but sin is not reckoned when there is no law. Yet death exercised dominion from Adam to Moses, even over those whose sins were not like the transgression of Adam, who is a type of the one who was to come.

But the free gift is not like the trespass. For if the many died through the one man's trespass, much more surely have the grace of God and the free gift in the grace of one man, Jesus Christ, abounded for the many. And the free gift is not like the effect of the one man's sin. For the judgment following one trespass bought condemnation, but the free gift following many trespasses brings justification. (5:12–16)

This image of Christ as the new Adam is a medieval commonplace which can be seen in all facets of medieval culture. In many paintings of the Crucifixion, for example, the skull of Adam is at the foot of the Cross. The medieval legend of the true cross claims that the Cross of Christ was made from the tree in the Garden of Eden from which Adam has sinned; thus as one tree brought sin, so did that same tree bring life through the sacrifice of Christ. By the beginning of the Middle Ages, the idea of Mary as the new Eve also had developed. Thus, just as Eve (Eva in Latin) had sinned, so did the Angel Gabriel's greeting to Mary of "Ave" ("Hail," Eva spelled backward) begin the reversal of human destruction caused by sin.

Of the non-Pauline Epistles, only one will be discussed here—the anonymous Epistle to the Hebrews. It is important because it deals with the concept of Christ as priest, in particular as perpetual priest in the order of Melchizedek (a priest-king who meets Abraham in Genesis and is mentioned again in Ps. 109:4: "You are a priest forever, a priest like Melchizedek of old").

Every high priest chosen from among mortals is put in charge of things pertaining to God on their behalf, to offer gifts and sacrifices for sins. He is able to deal gently with the ignorant and wayward, since he himself is subject to weakness; and because of this he must offer sacrifice for his own sins as well as for those of the people. And one does not presume to take this honor, but takes it only when called by God, just as Aaron was.

So also Christ did not glorify himself in becoming a high priest, but was appointed by the one who said to him, "You are my Son; today I have begotten you;" as he says also in another place, "You are a priest forever, according to the order of Melchizedek." In the days of his flesh, Jesus offered up prayers and supplications, with loud cries and tears, to the one who was able to save him from death, and he was heard because of his reverent submission. Although he was a Son, he learned obedience through what he suffered; and having been made perfect, he became the source of eternal salvation for all who obey him, having been designated by God a high priest according to the order of Melchizedek. (Heb. 5:1–10)

This identification of Christ with Melchizedek, both priest and king, allows Melchizedek to become an important prefiguration of Christ in medieval art and the liturgy. Furthermore, Christ as priest and king becomes an important element in the development of theories of spiritual and royal authority.

The last book of the Bible, and to many the most puzzling and difficult, is the Book of Revelation, or the Apocalypse, as it was called in the Middle

Sculpture in the interior of Reims Cathedral. Thirteenth century. Melchizedek gives bread and wine to Abraham (Gen. 14:18). The physical food that Melchizedek gives to Abraham points toward Christ giving spiritual food to the Church. This representation of the event clearly interprets it as a prefiguration of holy communion given by a priest to a knight.

Ages. The word *Apocalypse* means a "Revelation" or an "unveiling," and refers
to a type of literature in which heavenly realities are mediated through a human sage. Part of the Old Testament Book of Daniel, considered to be one of
the four major prophetic books in the Middle Ages, is considered to be an apocalypse by modern scholars, and is the source of much of the imagery in the
Book of Revelation. Relating a series of visions in which the author, believed
in the Middle Ages to be the evangelist and apostle John (an attribution not
generally accepted today), Revelation describes in a dramatic and highly symbolic way the struggle between good and evil, especially as that struggle is to
be played out at the end of time. A sense of both the dramatic and the symbolic quality of Revelation can be seen from the following passage:

> After this I looked, and there in heaven a door stood open! And the first voice,
> which I heard speaking to me like a trumpet, said, "Come up here, and I will
> show you what must take place after this." At once I was in the spirit, and
> there in heaven stood a throne, with one seated on the throne! And the one
> seated there looks like jasper and carnelian, and around the throne is a rain-
> bow that looks like an emerald. Around the throne are twenty-four thrones,
> and seated on the thrones are twenty-four elders, dressed in white robes, with
> golden crowns on their heads. Coming from the throne are flashes of light-
> ening, and rumbling and peals of thunder, and in front of the throne burn
> seven flaming torches, which are the seven spirits of God; and in front of the
> throne there is something like a sea of glass, like crystal.
>
> Around the throne, and on each side of the throne, are four living crea-
> tures, full of eyes in front and behind: the first living creature like a lion, the
> second living creature like an ox, the third living creature with a face like a
> human face, and the fourth living creature like a flying eagle. And the four
> living creatures, each of them with six wings, are full of eyes all around and
> inside. (Rev. 4:1–8)

One thing to notice in this passage is the importance of numbers. Number symbolism is not unique to Revelation in Scripture, but it seems more abundant
and more complicated here than anywhere else. Seven is a number of completeness, echoing the days of creation; the twenty-four elders were taken to
represent the twelve of the Old (tribes of Israel) and the twelve of the New (the
apostles). The description of the four living creatures is a borrowing from Chapter 1 of Ezekiel. By the end of the second century, theologians had interpreted
them as symbols of the four evangelists, and so it was for the rest of the Middle Ages: Mark the lion, Luke the ox, Matthew the man, and John the eagle.

Another important text for dealing with number symbolism is the opening of the seven seals, one of several places in Revelation where the pattern
of seven is repeated (Rev. 6:1–8:2). Especially from the twelfth century on-
ward, scriptural exegetes interpreted the opening of these seals as the symbolic representation of successive events in the history of the church from the
coming of Christ to the consummation of the world at the Last Judgment. An

Portal sculpture. Church of Saint Trophîme, Arles, France. Twelfth Century. Christ is presented in glory, surrounded by the four beasts described in Revelation 4. From the second century on, they were understood to represent the four evangelists, clear here because each one holds a book.

apocalyptic mentality, that is, a sense of the imminence of the end of the world, frequently accompanied difficult times and cataclysmic events in the Middle Ages, and the influence of the Book of Revelation and its interpreters was especially pervasive during those times. As the last book of the Bible, and as a book that frequently borrows from the first book, the Book of Genesis, Revelation was also seen as a kind of summary or recapitulation of the entire Bible.

Near the end of Revelation, there is a description of heaven, the New Jerusalem:

> Then one of the seven angels who had the seven bowls full of the seven last plagues came and said to me, "Come, I will show you the bride, the wife of the Lamb." And in the spirit he carried me away to a great, high mountain and showed me the holy city of Jerusalem coming down out of heaven from God. It has the glory of God and a radiance like a very rare jewel, like jasper, clear as crystal. It has a great, high wall with twelve gates, and at the gates twelve angels, and on the gates are inscribed the names of the twelve tribes of the Israelites; on the east three gates, on the north three gates, on the south three gates, and on the west three gates. And the wall of the city has twelve foundations, and on them are the twelve names of the twelve apostles of the Lamb. (21:9–21)

This description of the heavenly Jerusalem, again illustrating the importance of numbers and the highly symbolic language of the book, is another text that is frequently depicted in medieval art. No book of the Bible is more frequently represented in art throughout the Middle Ages than the Book of Revelation.

The New Testament is not a collection of all early Christian literature but rather a collection of texts that was widely agreed upon only in the fourth century. Thus, there are many "gospels" and "apocalypses" that were written in the first Christian centuries but not included in Scripture; these make up the New Testament Apocrypha. In them are many stories not found in the canonical books of the New Testament that were immensely popular in the Middle Ages, and were important as sources of medieval literature and art. Among the most important works of this type are those that deal with the life of the Virgin Mary and the earliest stories of her Assumption into heaven.

Since the Bible begins at the beginning with the story of creation and ends at the end with the Last Judgment, people in the Middle Ages saw themselves to be actors on the stage of biblical history. They were part of its story. Not surprising, then, that the Bible was seen, as we note in our Introduction, as a guide not only to religious life in the Middle Ages, but to such diverse areas as law, art, literature, and music as well. How that synthesis came about is the subject of subsequent chapters. Our chapter on Jerome and Augustine, the great translator of the Bible into Latin and its most important expositor for the Middle Ages, will explicitly pick up once again the subject of biblical interpretation begun here in the first chapter. But biblical interpretation will also implicitly be a subject in the other chapters, shaping what we say there as well.

CHAPTER 2

THE CLASSICAL HERITAGE

When modern scholars divide European history into segments for convenience of study, the usual division is ancient, medieval, and modern, with ancient further subdivided into Greek and Roman. A further subdivision is now conventionally made which breaks the late Roman Empire into its own era, called Late Antiquity. Scholars living in the time of the Middle Ages would have seen no such divisions. They could not have seen themselves living between two ages, which is what the etymology of the word *medieval* means—a word used only since the eighteenth century. More important, in many crucial ways they did not see any distinct break between themselves and their classical forebears. In fact, elements from classical antiquity were taken over, modified, and used to such an extent that in some areas of thought the legacy of classical antiquity is as important to the Middle Ages as the Judaeo-Christian heritage.

The ancient Greeks were the "inventors" of more aspects of Western civilization than any other people. We credit them with creating drama, both tragedy and comedy; historical writing, especially associated with Herodotus and Thucydides; democracy as it evolved in Athens; many types of poetry, from the Homeric epics to Sapphic lyrics to the odes of Pindar; styles of monumental architecture—the Doric, Ionic, and Corinthian orders; and several branches of philosophy, including political philosophy, ethics, metaphysics, and much of what is now classified as natural science. This is a staggering list. But in some ways the single most important legacy of Ancient Greece to Western civilization generally and the Middle Ages in particular is the influence of its two greatest philosophers, Plato and Aristotle.

Plato (c.427–347 B.C.E.) and Aristotle (384–322 B.C.E.) lived in Athens within a generation of each other. Aristotle was Plato's student, although he wrote as much in reaction to his teacher as in continuity with Plato's thought. Much as he departed from the doctrine of his master, however, the two shared a number of important presuppositions about the nature of philosophical inquiry. Perhaps the most important of these is that both wrote in opposition

to a prevalent philosophical skepticism, that is, to a mode of philosophical inquiry that held that truth was ultimately relative and that human reason was
at best a faulty guide for answering questions about the nature of reality. For
both Plato and Aristotle the doctrine that truth is relative was philosophically
untenable, so much so that it is not inaccurate to view the thought of both
men as an extended critique of philosophical relativism. This alone made both
thinkers extremely congenial to the philosophers of the Middle Ages, who believed that truth existed and that, within certain limits, it was knowable. It is
hardly surprising then that the two most influential figures in the entire history of Western philosophy should likewise be the most influential to the portion of the Western tradition called the Middle Ages. The historian David
Knowles has described this influence in especially emphatic terms. Speaking
of the twelfth and thirteenth centuries in particular, he says that "it is possible to say that almost all the leading ideas of medieval philosophy, with the
partial exception of that branch of it later known as natural theology, were
identical with, or were directly derived from, ideas put into currency at Athens
between 450 and 300 B.C."[1]

The philosophy of Plato has become a model for all subsequent philosophies that find reality in a realm beyond the senses. By positing the doctrine
of "forms" or "ideas" Plato answered the question of what abiding reality
might exist beyond the seemingly endless flux of the world of things and suggests ways that humans might get a glimpse at it. This doctrine is often taken
to assert that any individual object existing in this world was only an appearance, an approximation to the real exemplar, or "form," which existed in a
world beyond the senses. Since true reality exists in a supra-sensible world,
everything that exists in the sensible realm is merely its reflection. Analogously, in the realm of ethics, he was concerned with the same problem—how
to account for stability in a world of seeming change. He asked what constant
reality might lie behind any individual action that could be considered good
or just. To cite an example Plato uses in the *Republic*: how can telling the truth
and lying in different situations both be understood as just acts? Behind these
individual actions he saw timeless ideas of "the good" and of "justice," of which
individual actions were the dim reflections. Thus, he is, both in his metaphysics
and his ethics, "the father of those who have held that Soul or Spirit or Mind
is the only reality, of those who regard all movements and activity as ultimately intellectual, of those who find the true life of the human spirit in an
upward striving toward the Divine."[2] Plato was not only concerned with the
unchangeable and unchanging reality that gives meaning to the flux of existence, but also with the relationship between the world of the senses and the
world of ideas, that is, with the process by which one might move from the
world of the senses to the world of intelligible reality. He was thus the father
of a tradition of mystical ascent to God subsequently developed by such pagan Neoplatonist thinkers as Proclus and Plotinus and Christian Neoplaton-

ists such as Pseudo-Dionysius. This tradition was later incorporated into the large body of mystical writing in the Middle Ages.

Ideas that can be traced back to Plato formed the fabric of philosophical thought in the Middle Ages, so much so that the entire period can be described philosophically as Platonic. What must be kept in mind, however, is that this influence, profound and all-pervasive as it unquestionably was, remained largely indirect, transmitted to the Middle Ages through some pagan Neoplatonists of late antiquity and through Christian Neoplatonic writers such as Augustine and Pseudo-Dionysius. Few of Plato's writings were directly known. In fact, of the twenty-six Platonic dialogues, only one, the *Timaeus*, was known to Western Europe during most of the Middle Ages; and that dialogue, dealing as it does with the creation of the universe and its mathematical form, was in some ways not typical, although it was of great importance, especially to the twelfth-century group of Neoplatonist philosophers connected with the school of Chartres. Much of medieval science is a reflection on the *Timaeus*. Later in the Middle Ages two more dialogues, the *Meno* and the *Phaedo*, came to be known. But Plato's influence was profound even where he was no more than a name, a wellspring from which philosophers, theologians, and mystical writers continued to draw.

Aristotle, like Plato, formulated a system that described the nature of reality and dealt with the problem of change, but his approach was significantly different. If Plato is the philosopher of the realm of the ideal, Aristotle is the philosopher of everyday experience. For Aristotle, philosophy begins in the realm of sense experience, and his analysis of the nature of being remains within the realm of experience. From the senses, he argued, the mind is able to apprehend the essence of a thing—that which makes a thing what it is— through a process of abstraction. He postulated that all being, which can be known first through the senses and then understood by the mind through the process of abstraction, can be understood as a combination of "matter" and "form." Matter is the element that gives a substance its individuality; form is the element that gives it universality. In other words, it is the form of a substance that determines what species, or general classification, a given substance belongs to. The form of a substance would determine, for example, that a certain object is a chair, the matter would determine that it is this particular chair. Aristotle used the relationship between matter and form to account for the multiplicity in the visible world—the same problem of things coming into existence and going out of existence that caused Plato to formulate the doctrine of ideas. If this relationship between matter and form is properly understood, then it can be seen that

> [i]f things are regarded not as being but as becoming or changing, then matter is the potential element, susceptible of a multiplicity of forms in succession, whereas form is the actuality; the relationship between matter and form,

potentiality and actuality, therefore, extends over the whole range of being from prime or pure matter, which cannot be perceived and which has no independent existence, to pure form which is the last and purest matter to come into being at the other end of the scale.[3]

These distinctions between matter and form, potentiality and actuality, became keystones of Thomas Aquinas's philosophy of being in the thirteenth century, especially in seeking to define God, to list God's qualities, and to delineate the distinctions between creator and created.

Other areas where Aristotle's thought has especial importance in the Middle Ages, chosen from the almost unthinkably large range of his accomplishments, are in the realms of ethics, political theory, logic, and science. In ethics and political theory, Aristotle begins with experience, with the actual observation of people in their relationships with each other in communities. In ethics, his analysis of virtue remained influential in the Middle Ages and well beyond. Virtue for Aristotle is located in the mean between two extremes, between an excess and a defect. The virtue of generosity, for example, would

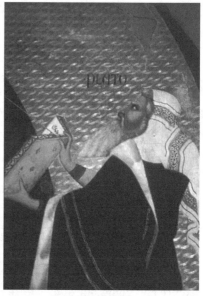

Two details of a painting, probably by Lippo Memmi, of the glorification of Saint Thomas Aquinas. Santa Caterina, Pisa. Fourteenth century. In these details, Aristotle (L) and Plato (R) show their books to Thomas Aquinas, thus indicating the saint's intellectual indebtedness to the greatest philosophers of classical antiquity. The writing in Plato's book is not visible to the viewers, perhaps suggesting that medieval thinkers got their knowledge of Plato indirectly rather than through reading his works.

consist in avoiding the excesses of prodigality and miserliness. The virtue of courage lies between foolhardiness and cowardice. One of the many medieval thinkers to make direct use of this definition of virtue was Dante, who uses it graphically in his punishment of the hoarders and the wasters in *Inferno* 7. Aristotle's political theory had a tremendous impact in medieval Europe beginning in the thirteenth century.

Aristotle's belief that humans are by nature political animals (i.e., who live in an organized society) and that the state is a positive force in bringing about the good life (rather than only being a necessary evil whose purpose is to keep order) had a great impact in both the theory and practice of statecraft. Aristotle's view of the state provided ammunition to secular rulers against claims of ecclesiastical interference and supremacy, and was a major element in the defeat of the idea of a universal Christian monarchy ruled by the pope. Thomas Aquinas's political writings were also derived directly from Aristotelian principles. Aristotle's system of formal logic was taken over by twelfth- and thirteenth-century writers seeking to order and synthesize centuries of tradition and a huge number of texts that often seemed to contradict one another. The great twelfth-century compilation of the Church's law, that is, canon law, which remained authoritative for centuries, was organized according to principles of Aristotelian logic; and works of theological synthesis such as the *Summa Theologiae* of Thomas Aquinas were only possible because of the reintroduction of Aristotelian logic.

Aristotle's scientific works were accepted as correct; and although some minor adjustments to and improvements on Aristotle's description of the natural world were made during the Middle Ages, his basic principles—such as that of a geocentric universe in which the heavenly bodies circled the earth embedded in crystalline spheres that were moved by the *primum mobile* (the outermost of these spheres)—remained authoritative in the Middle Ages and well into the seventeenth century. Aristotle's emphasis on discovering the final cause of events—that is, their ultimate purpose—remained the central concern of natural scientists in the medieval period, thus limiting the scope of scientific inquiry and subordinating science to theology because all discussion of the final cause of anything led toward God, the creator of all. Though not the only scientist revered in the Middle Ages (the astronomer Ptolemy and the physician Galen were both important), Aristotle was the preeminent authority in the fields of astronomy, physics, and biology.

For much of the Middle Ages, Aristotle, like Plato, was not known directly. Boethius translated some of his writings on logic c.500 C.E.; but for the most part, his works were not known in Western Europe from the eighth to the twelfth century. Compared to Plato, his influence was relatively minor until his works became known through Latin translations c.1200; from then on, Aristotle's influence was enormous. It is often argued in fact that the change from an essentially Platonic philosophic perspective to an essentially Aristotelian one is the crucial turning point in the history of medieval and indeed Western speculative thought. What must be kept in mind in describing this change, however, is that the Aristotelian system was more an addition to than a substitution for Platonism. Even in such an Aristotelian thinker as Thomas Aquinas, Platonic elements remain large and significant.

What was true of Plato and Aristotle in the Middle Ages was also true of most of the other achievements of the Greeks: they were not known firsthand. Medieval writers venerated Homer—Dante calls him the sovereign poet—but none of the writers who praised him had ever read more than the few lines of the *Iliad* or the *Odyssey* that Cicero and other Latin writers had quoted. They knew Homer by reputation, and they knew the story of Troy from the Latin prose versions of two writers known as Dares and Dictys (the version of Dares probably came from the sixth century C.E., that of Dictys from the fourth century C.E.). Furthermore, it was through Latin examples that so many of the other poetic forms that the Greeks developed were known to the Middle Ages. Catullus, Horace, and Ovid provided models for the lyric, rather than Pindar or Sappho. The tragedies of Aeschylus, Sophocles, and Euripides, and the comedies of Aristophanes and Menander were also unknown; for the Middle Ages the models of classical drama came principally from the tragedies of Seneca and the comedies of Terence. The models for the writing of history came not directly from Herodotus and Thucydides but from Sallust, Livy, and the biographer Suetonius. In architecture too, Greek styles were mediated through Rome. As the Romans had primarily borrowed and modified the Corinthian order of architecture from the Greeks, it was that decorative order that was most widely used in the Middle Ages. Since one can say that most of the Greek influence on the medieval period came from Roman adaptations of the Greek originals, a major legacy of Rome to the medieval world and beyond was the transmission and transformation of the achievements of the Greeks.

If one considers those Roman writers whose influence was significant, the list would vary depending on which part of the Middle Ages was examined. But it would be a long list, consisting of most of those authors who are now studied by students of Roman literature, but also consisting of writers such as Lucan and Statius—no longer studied widely in our own time but extremely influential to medieval writers. If one were forced to choose from among them, Cicero, Virgil, and Ovid would be most indicative of the types and range of the influence of the Latin classics on the Middle Ages. All three, figures of genius worth studying for their own sake as well as for their subsequent influence, were thorough students of Greek models.

Cicero was a statesman, writer, and political figure of the first century B.C.E. Both in form and content his writings were studied and imitated more than any other prose author. He was considered the master of Latin rhetoric, and thus his mode of expression was a model for students in monastic and cathedral schools, who learned Latin by a conscious imitation of classical models. Anyone who became a professed monk or a university student was exposed to Cicero; and even where the influence of his thought was not significant, educated clerics of the Middle Ages assimilated his sentence structure and his manner of expression. However, he was important for more than his prose style. Augustine, writing more than four hundred years later, credits Cicero with activating his own search for wisdom and thus ultimately for God in the *Confessions*. Cicero's stoic philosophy, adapted from the philosophical school that originated in Athens in the third century B.C.E., spoke of the need for humanity to conform to natural laws. This philosophy provided support for a Christian concept of natural law and for Christian ideas about the family of humanity. As one example of this aspect of Ciceronian influence, his writings on friendship served directly as models for twelfth-century writings on monastic friendship; Aelred of Rievaulx's work, *On Spiritual Friendship*, was modeled on Cicero's treatise *On Friendship*.

The following passage is from "The Dream of Scipio," a fragment of a longer work by Cicero entitled *On the Republic*. Although most of the text of *On the Republic* was lost to the Middle Ages, the fragment concerning Scipio's dream survived as an independent work, together with a commentary by the fourth-century writer Macrobius, and was among Cicero's most influential writings. In this passage, the Roman patriot and hero of the Punic Wars, Scipio Africanus, takes his grandson to "a certain place in heaven . . . assigned to all who have preserved, or assisted, or improved their country, where they are to enjoy an endless duration of happiness."[4] The grandfather uses this as an opportunity to inculcate a love of virtue in his grandson:

> "Consequently, should you renounce hope of returning to this place where eminent and excellent men find their reward, of what worth is that human glory which can scarcely extend to a small part of a single year? If, then, you shall determine to look on high and contemplate this mansion and eternal abode, you will neither give yourself to the gossip of the vulgar nor place your hope of well-being on rewards that man can bestow. Virtue herself, by her own charms, should draw you to true honor. . . . "
>
> When he had finished I said: "Truly, Africanus, if the path to heaven lies open to those who have deserved well of their country, though from my childhood I have ever trod in your and my father's footsteps without disgracing your glory, yet now, with so noble a prize set before me, I shall strive with much more diligence."
>
> "Do so strive," replied he, "and do not consider yourself, but your body, to be mortal. For you are not the being which this corporeal figure evinces; but the soul of every man is the man, and not the form which may be delineated with a finger. Know also that you are a god, if a god is that which lives, perceives, remembers, foresees, and which rules, governs, and moves the body over which it is set, just as the supreme God rules the universe. Just as the eternal God moves the universe, which is in part mortal, so does an everlasting soul move the corruptible body."[5]

A heavenly abode as the reward for virtue and the belief that the soul is immortal are two central concerns in this passage that were easily absorbed into the medieval Christian universe. In its original context, Cicero is referring specifically to political virtue—he is discussing the reward of the good statesman—but thinkers in the Middle Ages interpret the passage more broadly, that is, as applying to virtue in general. The dream vision, the dream as a mode of illumination, anticipates scores of dream-vision poems in the Middle Ages, with Macrobius's commentary on Cicero being one of the most important sources for the interpretation of various kinds of dreams, their natures, sources, and significance. The setting of Scipio's dream, the heavens, as a vantage point from which to view the earth and its strife and as a place to compare the harmony that exists above with the chaos below, also became a medieval commonplace. As one example of the continuing influence of this work, Chaucer, writing at the end of the fourteenth century, draws directly from the "Dream of Scipio" at the beginning of the *Parliament of Foules*.

The second writer is Virgil (70–19 B.C.E.), a poet who lived during the reign of Augustus. His epic poem, the *Aeneid*, itself modeled on the *Iliad* and the *Odyssey* of Homer, was both in form and content as much a model for poetry in the Middle Ages as the writings of Cicero were for prose. The poem describes the journey of Aeneas from the ruins of Troy to the shores of Italy, where he begins the foundation of Rome. His journey to Rome includes his stop at Carthage, where he recounts the fall of Troy (Book 2), including most memorably the Trojan horse and Sinon's betrayal. He has a tragic love affair with the Carthaginian queen Dido (Book 4), and takes a trip through the underworld to see his father (Book 6). All of these episodes exercised great influence on the imagination of the writers of the Middle Ages. Dido became an important character in medieval as well as later literary history. The trip to the underworld was a direct model for Dante, whose *Inferno* uses the geography, setting, and even some characters of Virgil's underworld. In Dante's political treatise, *On World Government*, the *Aeneid* is likewise his most frequently quoted classical authority and provides key arguments for his ideas of relationship between ecclesiastical and temporal authorities and his belief in world government. The following passage from the *Aeneid* (Book 6), the meeting of Aeneas and Dido in the underworld, illustrates the conflict between private desires and public duty that is at the heart of the poem:

> Among them was Phoenician Dido, who was roaming in the broad wood with her wound still fresh upon her. Troy's hero found himself near to her and as soon as he recognized her dimly through the shadows, like one who early in the month sees or thinks that he sees the moon rising through the clouds, his tears fell and he spoke to her in the sweet accents of love: "O Dido, unhappy Dido, was the news, then, true which was brought to me, that you had perished, had taken the sword, and trodden the path to its end? Ah, could I have been the cause of your death? By the stars, by the high Gods, I swear by any

truth there may be in the depths of the earth, that it was not by my own will, your Majesty, that I departed your shores; but rather was I imperiously forced by that same divine direction which compels me now to pass through the shadows in this world of crumbling decay under deepest night; and I could not have known that my leaving you would have caused you so terrible a grief. Stay your step and withdraw not from my sight. Whom do you seek to escape? My speaking to you now is the last indulgence which fate can give me." By such words Aeneas tried to soften her, and invited tears. But in her the anger blazed and grimly she glared, holding her gaze averted and fixed on the ground; she was no more moved by what Aeneas had begun to say than if she had been hard flint or a standing block of Parian marble. At length she flung herself away, and, in hatred still, fled back into the shadows offered her by the wood, where Sychaeus, her husband in former days, had sympathy for her distress and matched his love to hers. Aeneas was shocked by her unjust fate; and as she went long gazed after her with tearful eyes and pity for her in his heart.[6]

The journey of Aeneas to his true home had strong resonances with the medieval Christian concept of pilgrimage. Augustine's spiritual autobiography, the *Confessions*, moves from Carthage to Rome, no doubt in direct and conscious imitation of the journey of Aeneas. In the Middle Ages, continuing a tradition developed in late antiquity, commentaries were written on the *Aeneid* that allegorized the journey of Aeneas as the journey of the soul seeking wisdom. Among the most important of these medieval commentaries was that of Bernardus Silvestris, writing in the twelfth century. Such commentaries contributed to Virgil's enormous reputation as a sage in the Middle Ages. He was regarded as a prophet as well, a pagan who anticipated the truths of Christianity, in large part because of a Christian interpretation of the following passage from his fourth *Eclogue*.

> Now is come the last age of Cumaean prophecy: the great cycle of periods is born anew. Now returns the Maid, returns the reign of Saturn: now from high heaven a new generation comes down. Yet do thou at that boy's birth, in whom the iron race will begin to cease, and the golden to arise all over the world, holy Lucina, be gracious; now thine own Apollo reigns. And in thy consulate, in thine, O Pollio, shall this glorious age enter, and the great months begin their march: under thy rule what traces of our guilt yet remain, vanishing shall free earth ever from alarm?[7]

In the Middle Ages, people were sure they recognized a prophecy of Christ's incarnation in this passage. Furthermore, the fact that Virgil was writing at the time of Augustus, in whose reign Christ was born, supported this interpretation. It was regarded as no mere coincidence.

The third writer is Ovid (43 B.C.E.–17 C.E.), who also lived during the reign of Augustus, though a generation after Virgil. It was Ovid's version of the stories and legends of the gods and heroes of classical mythology that came down to the Middle Ages, allowing them to become part of the storehouse of imaginative energy for subsequent literature. His long narrative poem, the *Metamorphoses*, tells the stories of the classical gods and heroes from creation to his own time, linking them together through the theme of change. For example, in the story of the rape of Europa, Jove changes from his divine form to a bull in order to seduce the maiden Europa more easily. The story of Pygmalion, from Book 10 of the *Metamorphoses*, was as popular to the Middle Ages as it has continued to be in our own time:

> When Pygmalion saw these women, living such wicked lives, he was revolted by the many faults which nature implanted in the female sex, and long lived a bachelor existence, without any wife to share his home. But meanwhile, with marvelous artistry, he skillfully carved a snowy ivory statue. He made it lovelier than any woman born, and fell in love with his own creation. The statue had all the appearance of a real girl, so that it seemed to be alive, to want to move, did not modesty forbid. So cleverly did his art conceal its art. Pygmalion gazed in wonder, and in his heart there rose a passionate love for this image of a human form. . . .
>
> The festival of Venus, which is celebrated with the greatest pomp all through Cyprus, was now in progress, and heifers, their horns gilded for the occasion, had fallen at the altar as the axe struck their snowy necks. Smoke was rising from the incense, when Pygmalion, having made his offering, stood by the altar and timidly prayed, saying: "If you gods can give all things, may I have as my wife, I pray—" he did not dare to say: "the ivory maiden," but finished: "one like the ivory maiden." However, golden Venus, present at her festival in person, understood what his prayers meant, and as a sign that the gods were kindly disposed, the flames burned up three times, shooting a tongue of fire into the air. When Pygmalion returned home, he made straight for the statue of the girl he loved, leaned over the couch, and kissed her. She seemed warm: he laid his lips on hers again, and touched her breast with his hands—at his touch the ivory lost its hardness, and grew soft; his fingers made an imprint on the yielding surface, just as the wax of Hymettus melts in the sun and, worked by men's fingers, is fashioned into many different shapes, and made fit for use by being used. The lover stood, amazed, afraid of being mistaken, his joy tempered with doubt, and again and again stroked the object of his prayers. It was indeed a human body! The veins throbbed as he pressed them with his thumb. Then Pygmalion of Paphos was eloquent in his thanks to Venus. At long last he pressed his lips upon living lips, and the girl felt the kisses he gave her, and blushed. Timidly raising her eyes, she saw her lover and the light of day together.[8]

With Ovid, thinkers of the Middle Ages were forced to wrestle with the problem of whether stories that were obviously not literally true were dangerous or whether they were valuable. Could the story of Pygmalion, let alone the stories of Jove and his amorous adventures, hold anything of value for medieval Christians? Although Ovid and other writers of imaginative literature as well continued to be regarded in some quarters as highly suspect, they were defended by the concept of the "beautiful lie," the idea that a poet weaves an outer coat that, however fanciful, covers an inner truth. False stories could teach true doctrine. Though the debate continued throughout the Middle Ages, this defense allowed imaginative literature to be written and enjoyed in the Middle Ages, and to draw on the resources of the classical poets. When a story such as Pygmalion was retold in the Middle Ages—as it was at the end of the long allegorical poem called the *Romance of the Rose* (c.1285)—it was often utilized for purposes quite different from the original. Sometimes the stories were moralized and given explicitly Christian meanings; sometimes they were given contemporary applications by writers who saw in them meaning for their own time, just as Virgil and Ovid themselves took stories and legends that originally came from the Greeks and made them applicable to their age. Although writers felt free to make these stories their own, freely changing their purpose as well, poets in the Middle Ages (and beyond at least as late as the nineteenth century) simply assumed an awareness of classical mythology. Authors such as Jean de Meun (author of the second part of the *Romance of the Rose*), Dante, and Chaucer drew deeply from Ovid in their own poetry. Ovid's work, like Virgil's, also became the subject of allegorical commentaries.

In the Middle Ages, as in classical times, historical writing was considered a branch of literature; and like the other literary genres discussed above, the language and themes of Roman historical writing were taken over by the historical writers of the Middle Ages. While today many scholars consider Tacitus (c.55–c.120 C.E.) as the greatest historian of Rome, he was almost unknown in the Middle Ages. Livy (59 B.C.E.–17 C.E.), the great historian writing in the Age of Augustus, was highly respected in the Middle Ages although he became even more important to the republican writers of the Renaissance. However, two other Roman historians were also quite well known and imitated. The first is the imperial biographer Suetonius (c.69–c.140 C.E.). Despite his scandalous stories of the emperors, his twelve imperial biographies were important models for medieval secular biography, most noticeably Einhard's account of the life of Charlemagne. The other historian of great importance is Sallust (86–34 B.C.E.), a contemporary of Cicero whose two extant works have strong moral overtones. This is precisely the reason Sallust was so popular in the Middle Ages, for history was perceived as a branch of ethics whose purpose was to teach moral lessons by providing positive and negative exemplars. The tendency of modern historians to avoid moral judgments and not to assign praise or blame would have been totally foreign to medieval writers of history as well as to ancient writers such as Sallust. Moreover, history was considered to be a part of the study of rhetoric in ancient Rome and the Middle Ages. Thus, the literary conventions of history did not encourage simple narrative of literal truth but rather allowed and encouraged some rearrangement and embellishment of the facts in order to make the moral clear. These elements of ancient historiography combined with elements of biblical historical writing in the Middle Ages to allow for exaggeration and distortion of the facts (as contemporary historians would perceive them). Because of our modern, more "scientific" and "objective" view of history, many nineteenth- and twentieth-century writers have tended to disparage medieval historical writings. Only if we recognize the purposes and conventions of those texts, can we appreciate the greatness of historians such as the Venerable Bede or Geoffrey of Monmouth.

Sallust and Suetonius were contemporaries of many of the events they wrote about and even eyewitnesses to some of them. The belief that contemporary history was the most creative and the most useful form of historical writing existed in the ancient world and became the most important type of medieval historical writing. Writers such as the Venerable Bede and Gregory of Tours begin their work in the distant past, believing that an understanding of the past was crucially important, but they also carried these works through to the present to concentrate on the events of their own time.

A second important legacy from Rome to the medieval world was its law. Although the Greeks had theorized extensively about the nature of law, the science of jurisprudence was really invented during the growing complexity of the late Roman Republic. One of the products of this new science was a carefully defined concept of the state. Furthermore, philosophers of the same period, borrowing from the Greeks, developed a highly sophisticated theory of natural law. During the period of the Roman Empire, the largest and most complex state that had yet existed in the West, it was necessary that the numerous laws of the Empire be codified, that is, ordered and organized so that they could be a unifying factor in an empire that at one point in time during the second century C.E. stretched from the Irish Sea to the Persian Gulf. Ironically, the greatest law codes were compiled as the Empire was breaking up. In fact, the most important codification of Roman law occurred after the fall of the Empire in the West. Commissioned by the Byzantine Emperor Justinian (r. 527–565), his Code remained the basis of Byzantine law for almost a thousand years. This Code was not only a great compilation of laws but also contained commentaries on the law by the greatest Roman jurists. For several centuries the Justinian Code remained unknown in the West, although early medieval kings used the less complete fifth-century Theodosian Code extensively. In the twelfth century, however, the Code of Justinian was rediscovered in the West. From that time on, emperors quoted directly from it in objecting to ecclesiastical authority; kings used it as a model for constructing their own legal systems; Church lawyers were inspired to codify the Church's canon law. Much of the language of early parliamentary documents in England and elsewhere was drawn from Roman law; even the common law system in England owes much more to Roman law than has sometimes been acknowledged. The medieval dependence on Roman law is an important legacy of the Middle Ages to modern times; as late as the nineteenth century, the Justinian Code was used as a model both in Europe and America.

A third legacy from Rome to the Middle Ages was the idea of empire. Rome was neither the first power to have a large empire nor the first to consider the benefits of a world governed from one center. Alexander the Great had conquered much of the world and had talked of universal human brotherhood. However, it was the Romans who built on this notion and who passed it on. And most important, it was the Romans who institutionalized it. Alexander's empire was his personal conquest; when he died the empire was divided. The Romans ruled a vast empire from the late republican period (first century B.C.E.) until the disintegration of the Empire in the West (in the fifth century C.E.) and the fall of Constantinople in the East (1453 C.E.). Thus, an idea was combined with a process of institutionalization. The Romans in fact considered ruling as their chief skill and as their destiny. The ideal of Rome as ruler is nowhere better exemplified than in Book 6 of Virgil's *Aeneid*. Consider what Aeneas's father says to his son during the visit to the underworld, when Aeneas comes to learn his own destiny and hence the destiny of Rome:

> Others, for so I can well believe, shall hammer forth more delicately a breathing likeness out of bronze, coax living faces from the marble, plead causes with more skill, plot with their gauge the movement of the sky, and tell the rising of the constellations. But you, Roman, must remember that you have to guide the nations by your authority, for this is to be your skill, to graft tradition onto peace, to show mercy to the conquered, and to wage war until the haughty are brought low.[9]

This is of course more a statement of the ideal of Roman rule than its reality, but it was a passage known, quoted, and believed in the Middle Ages, an ideal that no one was ready to dismiss lightly.

The concept of empire far outlived the reality of a unified Mediterranean world. By the end of the fourth century there was a permanent split in the Roman Empire between the Latin West and the Greek East. In the East, the Byzantine emperors in Constantinople (who would have referred to themselves simply as Roman emperors) regarded themselves as the true heirs of the Empire, seeing their city as a new (and Christian) Rome. And indeed, in both splendor and in power the new Rome had outstripped the old by this time. However, with the rise of Charlemagne, the Empire was reconstituted in the West into what we have come to call the Holy Roman Empire. It appeared for a time that the emperors in the West who succeeded Charlemagne would continue to be rulers in fact as well as in theory, but this did not come to be. However, long after the Empire ceased to be the most important political power in Western Europe, there were those who still looked to the em-

Cross of the Holy Roman Emperor Lothar. Aachen, Germany. Ninth century. This imperial cross contains an ancient cameo of the Roman Emperor Augustus (d. 14 C.E.). Its position in a medieval cross suggests continuity between the Empire of ancient Rome and the reconstituted Empire begun by Lothar's grandfather, Charlemagne.

peror as the de jure head of the West. Dante placed his hopes in the reestablishment of the Empire's authority in the West in his treatise *On World Government,* written between 1315 and 1320. In the *Inferno,* he placed Brutus and Cassius on either side of Judas at the very bottom of hell because they had assassinated the first emperor, Julius Caesar, and thus had tried to subvert Rome's destiny to rule. In the middle of the fourteenth century, long after the emperors had ceased to be a major political factor, a famous fresco by the painter Andrea da Firenze depicted the emperor as the highest political authority in the West. The actual boundaries of the Holy Roman Empire changed often in the Middle Ages, but the claim can be made that the Empire lasted in some form until 1806. In the East, after the fall of Constantinople in 1453, the rulers in Moscow claimed to be heirs of the Roman imperial tradition and saw Moscow as the third Rome; they even took the title of the emperors—caesar, or in Russian, czar.

A fourth legacy from Rome is the Latin language; for as we have already implied in our discussion of Cicero, Virgil, Ovid, and the Roman historians, Latin remained a living language throughout the Middle Ages, a mark of continuity with the classical past. Indeed, Latin served as the international language of the European Middle Ages. It was the language of the Church and thus of virtually all religious writing, including the liturgy. It was the language of the universities and the schools, and thus of all philosophical writing. (In the later Middle Ages, students in the Oxford colleges were fined if they were caught speaking anything but Latin within their colleges' precincts.) It was the language of literature, at least until the late Middle Ages when there was a shift toward the vernacular languages—Jean de Meun wrote in French, Dante in Italian, Chaucer in English. Though learned by imitation from models of Roman prose and poetry, Latin continued to change throughout the Middle Ages. Vocabulary expanded as many Germanic words were incorporated into the language; and style, syntax, and grammar changed as well. The influence, moreover, was reciprocal; Latin style, syntax, and vocabulary also influenced the vernacular languages: modern English, for example, has a large number of Latin-based words although it is a Germanic language. Yet these very changes were a sign of the vitality of the language, allowing for the expression of what was unique and original in medieval culture, from early Christian hymns to the writings of Thomas Aquinas and beyond. As in so many other areas, medieval people borrowed language from classical antiquity but adapted it to their own needs. It can be argued that it was the revival of classical Latin as the ideal in the Renaissance that gradually turned Latin into an artificial language. In trying to eliminate all postclassical accretions and to imitate Cicero directly in their own writings, Renaissance humanists in fact contributed to its demise.

To a great extent, the achievements of biblical and classical thinkers took place independently of one another. The Greek historian Herodotus, for example, traveled throughout the Near East, writing extensively about the Egyptians and Persians while hardly mentioning the Jews. Yet by the time he made his journey, the Pentateuch was complete, and the prophecies of Isaiah and Jeremiah were already recorded. By the time of Augustus, there were Jewish settlements throughout the Mediterranean, and the Old Testament had been translated into Greek. Nevertheless, writers such as Virgil remained largely ignorant of Jewish history and literature. However, with the spread of Christianity beginning with Saint Paul, the two cultures began to interact with one another; Paul himself was a Jew, a Christian, and a Greek-educated Roman citizen. In philosophy, in the concept of empire, in literature, law, language, art, and architecture, the classical heritage is one of the wellsprings of medieval culture. The next two chapters will examine the spread and development of Christianity by emphasizing the beginnings of the interaction of biblical and classical cultures and values.

CHAPTER 3

EARLY CHRISTIANITY

By the middle of the fifth century, Christianity was the dominant religion of the Roman Empire, and essential doctrines had been well defined through the actions of synods and especially four great councils. The Church had attained great wealth, and its leaders were among the most important persons of the Empire. By this time there was also a rich Christian tradition preserved in liturgy, art, and stories of its holy men and women. To understand this extraordinary growth and development and its importance for the Middle Ages, we need to go back to the infancy of Christianity.

THE BEGINNINGS OF CHRISTIANITY

We saw in Chapter 1 that the four canonical Gospels tell the story of Jesus and his earliest followers, although there is great debate among scholars today about how historically accurate these accounts are. Our chief sources for the history of the earliest Christian communities are Acts of the Apostles and the letters of Paul. Together they present a picture of both teaching and practice in the years following Christ's earthly ministry. Immediately after Jesus' Passion and resurrection, there were few who accepted him as the long-awaited Messiah. Acts of the Apostles suggests that they may not have been more than 120 in all. Yet within just a few years, several thousand Jews in and around Jerusalem came to believe in Jesus as the Messiah. With the conversion and apostleship of Paul (c.33 C.E.) came the initiative to take the "Good News" about Jesus among the Gentiles (non-Jews) in the eastern Mediterranean. Paul began his Christian ministry preaching Christ to the Jews but found that most of them rejected his message:

> It was necessary that the word of God should be spoken first to you. Since you reject it and judge yourselves to be unworthy of eternal life, we are now turning to the Gentiles. For the Lord has commanded us [Paul and his companion Barnabas], saying,

"I have set you to be a light for the Gentiles,
So that you may bring salvation to the ends of the earth."
(Acts 13:46–47; last two lines are taken from Isaiah 49:6)

Paul taught these gentile Christian converts that they were not obligated to follow Jewish practices such as circumcision and dietary regulations. Although most of the earliest Christian communities contained both Gentiles and practicing Jews, within two or three generations the vast majority of Christians were Gentiles; and Jews who accepted Jesus as Messiah no longer were welcome in synagogues. Furthermore, by the end of the first century C.E., Christianity was no longer centered in Palestine, although this is in large part because of the Romans' destruction of Jerusalem in 70 C.E. after a Jewish revolt against Roman rule.

This predominantly gentile Church (the Greek word *ecclesia*, translated as Church, means "assembly") thus became a separate religion. This development is of the greatest significance in Christian history, for Christ was a Jew, and his earliest followers were Jews who adhered to the laws of the Old Testament. The period of separation of Judaism and Christianity saw the development of both anti-Christian and anti-Jewish attitudes. It is fair to say that in some Christian writings of that time and the following centuries we see the beginnings of Christian dislike and denunciation of the beliefs and practices of Judaism. Certain anti-Jewish beliefs became firmly implanted in Christianity and were one aspect of Christian thought throughout the Middle Ages and far beyond. One early passage that illustrates the beginnings of anti-Semitism is found in the letter of Saint Ignatius of Antioch (martyred 107) to the Magnesians:

> So lay aside the old good-for-nothing leaven [of the Old Testament], now grown stale and sour, and change to the new, which is Jesus Christ. . . . To profess Jesus Christ while continuing to follow Jewish customs is an absurdity. The Christian faith does not look to Judaism, but Judaism looks to Christianity, in which every other race and tongue that confesses a belief in God has now been comprehended.[1]

Despite the separation from Judaism, Christians continued to accept the Old Testament as the revealed word of God, although they followed Paul in giving a specifically Christian meaning to it, that is, they saw the events of the Old Testament in terms of their relationship to Christianity.

Perhaps even in Paul's lifetime, there were some converts to Christianity who attempted to combine their new religion with a philosophy that had developed in the eastern part of the Roman Empire called Gnosticism. Although not all Gnostics held identical beliefs, a basic tenet is the opposition between the material and spiritual realms. Gnostics saw all material things as intrinsically evil and all spiritual things as intrinsically good. Thus, a common Gnostic view of the story of creation in Genesis was that it is about an evil god or a rebellious spirit since it is the story of the making of evil things. Gnostics interpreted the New Testament to be about a pure spirit who only *appeared* to be human. Most Christians saw Gnostic interpretations of Scripture as both erroneous and dangerous. The general Christian rejection of Gnostic interpretations of Scripture, however, did not mean that the philosophy of Gnosticism ceased to impact the development of Christianity. In the fourth century, for example, the young Augustine, before his conversion to Christianity, was an adherent of a non-Christian Gnostic sect called the Manichees (after the Gnostic teacher Mani). Although Augustine unequivocally renounced his Manichean beliefs (see Chapter 4), some scholars have argued that certain views of Augustine and other Church Fathers, especially on forms of asceticism, can be traced to Gnostic views. As late as the twelfth and thirteenth centuries, there was a major revival of Christian Gnosticism in southern France and northern Italy called the Albigensian (after the French city of Albi) or Cathar movement (from a Greek word meaning "the pure ones"). The impact of this "alternate church" led to the calling of a crusade against other Christians and influenced Pope Innocent III's decision to establish a new religious order founded by Francis of Assisi (see Chapter 10). As late as the fourteenth century, there were remnants of Cathar beliefs and institutions found in villages in the Pyrenees.[2]

THE DEVELOPMENT OF CHURCH OFFICES

In the earliest Christian community in Jerusalem, according to Acts of the Apostles, the apostles handled all the work of the community, from preaching to presiding at liturgical ceremonies to caring for the goods held in common. As the community grew, a certain specialization soon became necessary. Furthermore, as Christian communities developed over time in cities around the Mediterranean, the problem of unity within a community became acute, especially when there were differences of opinion about who Jesus was and how to follow him faithfully. At first, it was possible to refer disputes to persons of great authority such as the apostles or Paul. But how were differences to be resolved and unity preserved when the apostles were no longer alive?

One solution to the problem of unity within a community was to designate a single person, someone who had received the authority to preside at rituals and was often called a priest, as the spokesman for and arbiter within a community, and this chief priest would also appoint (later ordain) new priests. This official came to be called the bishop (in Greek, *episcopos;* hence words such as "episcopal" and "episcopacy").

Since many regarded direct commission by Christ or personal inspiration from God as the only legitimate bases of authority in the Church, the question of the source of episcopal power was an important one in early Christian communities. The principle of apostolic succession, which was already being formulated by the end of the first century, was the generally accepted solution. Simply, apostolic succession means that the authority which Christ conferred upon the apostles is passed on to properly chosen successors—that is, Christ established offices rather than merely giving authority to individuals. The bishops' claim to obedience is explicit in Ignatius of Antioch's (d.107) letter to a Christian community in Asia Minor:

> Your obedience to your bishop, as though he were Jesus Christ, shows me plainly enough that yours is no worldly manner of life, but that of Jesus Christ Himself, who gave His life for us that faith in His death might save you from death. At the same time, however, essential as it is that you should never act independently of the bishop—as evidently you do not—you must also be no less submissive to your clergy [i.e., priests], and regard them as apostles of Jesus Christ our Hope, in whom we shall one day be found, if our lives are lived in Him.[3]

Some bishops came to be regarded as especially important because they were leaders of Christian communities first headed by apostles; thus their succession to the apostles was uniquely direct. In particular, the bishop of Rome (from the fifth century on usually called the pope, from a Latin word meaning father) was so regarded because it was believed that Peter, the so-called prince of the apostles, established and headed the Christian community there. Both Peter and Paul, the apostles respectively to the Jews and Gentiles and thus together to all people, were martyred and buried in Rome. It must also have seemed natural for Christians to look to Rome since it was the political center of the world. In addition, of all the apostolic sees (seats of bishops), Rome was the only one in the Latin-speaking West while there were three in the Greek East that were sometimes at odds with one another. Sometimes other bishops would ask advice from the bishop of Rome because of the prestige of his office as the leading bishop of the Empire, the first among equals. As early as the latter part of the second century, we find a description of the special importance of the see of Rome in a treatise by Irenaeus, bishop of Lyons (d.c.200):

> But since it would be very long in such a volume as this to enumerate the successions of all the churches, I can by pointing out the tradition which that very great, oldest, and well-known Church, founded and established at Rome by those two most glorious apostles Peter and Paul, received from the apostles, and its faith known among men, which comes down to us through the successions of bishops, put to shame all of those who in any way, either through wicked self-conceit, or through vainglory, or through blind and evil opinion, gather as they should not. For every church must be in harmony with this Church because of its outstanding pre-eminence, that is, the faithful from everywhere, since the apostolic tradition is preserved in it by those from everywhere.[4]

By the fifth century, a full-fledged theory of papal *jurisdictional* supremacy emerged. We must not equate the development of this idea with a claim that all Christians were required to use the same practices or that Rome would dictate to regional and local churches. Pope Leo I (the Great, r.440–461) is perhaps most responsible for the so-called Petrine (derived from the name Peter) theory, the ultimate foundation of claims of papal supremacy. Leo argued from Matt. 16:18–19 (see Chapter 1 for the text) that Peter received the power to govern the Church from Christ and that this power was inherited by Peter's successors. Peter was believed to have founded and led the Christian community in Rome; consequently, the bishops of Rome were his successors. Leo's claim was recognized by the Fourth Ecumenical Council (Council of Chalcedon) in 451: "Peter has spoken through Leo." Leo explained the meaning of Matt. 16:18–19 in a sermon preached in 443:

> The dispensation of Truth therefore abides, and the blessed Peter persevering in the strength of the Rock, which he has received, has not abandoned the helm of the Church, which he undertook. For he was ordained before the rest in such a way that from his being called the Rock, from his being pronounced the Foundation, from his being constituted the Doorkeeper of the kingdom of heaven, from his being set as the Umpire to bind and to loose, whose judgments shall retain their validity in heaven, from all these mystical titles we might know the nature of his association with Christ. And still today he more fully and effectually performs what is entrusted to him, and carries out every part of his duty and charge in Him and with Him, through Whom he has been glorified. And so if anything is rightly done and rightly decreed by us, if anything is won from the mercy of God by our daily supplications, it is of his works and merits whose power lives and whose authority prevails in his See. . . . For throughout the Church Peter daily says, "Thou art the Christ, the Son of the living God" (Matt. 16:16), and every tongue which confessed the Lord, accepts the instruction his voice conveys.[5]

In some sense, Leo's claim is a specific application of the principle of apostolic succession, that is, the authority that Christ specifically conferred upon Peter is specifically passed on to Peter's successors as leaders of the Roman Church. It is important to note that Leo was not claiming personal infallibility but rather universal jurisdiction in the Church. This means that he is the final voice in settling disputes among bishops, disputed elections to ecclesiastical offices, and similar sorts of controversies. Although the Petrine theory was well defined after the mid-fifth century, it was a theory that was not universally accepted, especially in the Eastern parts of the Roman Empire.

CHRISTIAN AND PAGAN

Christianity was born in the Greek-speaking Eastern part of the Roman Empire and appeared soon after in the Latin-speaking West. Since the entire New

Church of San Biagio, Agrigento, Sicily. Twelfth century. This church was built directly upon the remains of an ancient Greek temple of the fifth century B.C.E. dedicated to Demeter and Persephone, visually demonstrating that Christians consciously built upon the foundations of classical antiquity. The foundation is easy to see here because the temple was larger than the church.

Testament was written in Greek, Christianity from its beginnings co-existed and interacted with the thought and writings of the Greeks and Romans. The inevitable tensions between Christianity and the world of classical learning intensified in the third century. Most of the earliest Christian converts had come from the lower strata of society, including a significant number of slaves. The instability of the Empire after 180 and a changing and generally more pessimistic world view developing in the late second and third centuries provided a context for the conversion of significant numbers of educated, prominent people to Christianity. Such converts did not simply abandon all knowledge they had accumulated in pagan schools, and consequently they were often interested in defining the relationship between pagan learning and Christian revelation. Justin Martyr, toward the end of the second century, had argued that much of the wisdom of the great pagan thinkers was compatible with Christian teaching. He even believed that men such as Socrates had some limited revelation from God and, like the great Old Testament figures, were "Christians before Christ."[6] In Alexandria, the center of Greek learning, the study of pagan works and the use of classical tools of critical scholarship were first put to the service of Christianity. The foundation had been prepared in part by a group of Greek-speaking Jewish philosophers, the most important of whom was Philo (20 B.C.E.–50 C.E.), who were concerned with reconciling Jewish tradition and Greek thought.

The most important Christian scholar of this era was Origen (d.254). Some of his theological speculations, such as his belief that at the end all people would be saved, led to controversies over his writings for centuries after his death, including several formal condemnations of Origenism, partly because his followers often went beyond what he himself had said. Here, we shall be concerned with three facets of Origen's work that were influential in the development of Christian thought. First, he was a firm believer in the use of reason and hence the value for Christians of pagan learning. Here is Origen's reply to a letter of praise from one of his students:

> [Y]our natural aptitude is sufficient to make you a consummate Roman lawyer and a Greek philosopher too of the most famous schools. But my desire for you has been that you should direct the whole force of your intelligence to Christianity as your end. . . . And I would wish that you should take with you on the one hand those parts of the philosophy of the Greeks which are fit, as it were, to serve as general or preparatory studies for Christianity, and on the other hand so much of Geometry and Astronomy as may be helpful for the interpretation of Holy Scriptures. The children of the philosophers speak of geometry and music and grammar and rhetoric and astronomy as being ancillary to philosophy; and in the same way we might speak of philosophy itself being ancillary to Christianity.[7]

Second, Origen recognized the need for accurate texts and translations of Scripture. His use of the tools of textual criticism was of great influence generally and on Saint Jerome in particular. Third, Origen was himself a great interpreter of Scripture. He rejected simple literal readings, since as a scholar he recognized obvious historical discrepancies and impossibilities; rather, he emphasized the allegorical levels of interpretation as most important:

> There is something else that we must realize. The main aim of scripture is to reveal the coherent structure that exists at the spiritual level in terms both of events and injunctions. Wherever the Word [Christ] found that events on the historical plane corresponded with these mystical truths, he used them, concealing the deeper meaning from the multitude. But at those places in the account where the performance of particular actions as already recorded did not correspond with the pattern of things at the intellectual level, Scripture wove into the narrative, for the sake of the more mystical truths, things that never occurred—sometimes things which never could have occurred, sometimes things that could have but did not. . . . It was not only in the relation of events before the coming of Christ that the Spirit arranged things in this way. Because he is the same Spirit and comes from the one God, he has acted in the

same way with the gospels and the writings of the apostles. Even they contain a narrative that is not at all points straightforward; for woven into it are events which in the literal sense did not occur. Nor is the content of the law and commandments to be found in them entirely reasonable.[8]

The idea that Scripture, especially the Old Testament, contains allegory can be traced back to Paul. However, Origen created a rational, systematic approach to interpreting Scripture allegorically; and he goes farther than most Church Fathers—a general term used to designate all major orthodox Christian writers before c.600—in admitting the possibility that even the New Testament contains material that may be historically untrue. Later biblical commentators borrowed much from Origen in presenting their own theories of biblical exegesis. Both Jerome and Augustine used allegorical interpretations, often derived directly from Origen, but combined with a firmer belief in the historical truth of Scripture.

Not all Christians shared Justin's and Origen's enthusiasm for pagan learning. A North African Latin-speaking Christian named Tertullian (d.c.220) believed that the truth of Scripture so excelled that of the pagan writings as to render the latter useless. He also argued that Christians should separate themselves as much as possible from pagan society in order not to be corrupted by it:

> What has Athens to do with Jerusalem, the Academy [Plato's school in Athens] with the Church? . . . We have no need for curiosity since Jesus Christ, nor for inquiry since the Gospel. . . . Tell me what is the sense of this itch for idle speculation? What does it prove, this useless affectation of a fastidious curiosity, notwithstanding the strong confidence of its assertions? It was highly appropriate that Thales, while his eyes were roaming the heavens in astronomical observation, should have tumbled into a well. This mishap may well serve to illustrate the fate of all who occupy themselves with the stupidities of philosophy.[9]

Tertullian went farther than his rejection of classical culture and seemed to reject reason itself in his famous phrase, "I believe because it is absurd."[10] Even in the very language of his condemnations, however, Tertullian is using the satire and invective developed by pagan Latin writers. Even though he turned it against the pagans themselves, he was able to do so only because of his classical education. Although few Christian writers followed Tertullian's extreme negative view with regard to the value of pagan learning, he represents an uneasiness and fear of knowledge not drawn directly from Scripture that was an element in the thought of many more moderate Christians.

Tertullian and Origen represent the two extremes in their attitude toward the pagan world's achievements. Most of the writers influential for the Middle Ages, such as Jerome and Augustine, fall somewhere in between. In various forms, the debate about the value of pagan learning for Christians continued throughout the Middle Ages and also remains a part of contemporary discussions, for example, in debates about evolution and creationism. The issue, though in a more nuanced form, was central in disputes such as those between Bernard of Clairvaux and Peter Abelard in the twelfth century and between some Franciscan and Dominican theologians in the thirteenth.

PERSECUTION AND TRIUMPH

The early Church faced persecution. Christ himself was put to death by a Roman governor under pressure from Jewish leaders in Jerusalem. The apostles and their followers in Jerusalem faced the possibility of persecution once they became numerous enough to be a perceived threat to Judaism by the religious leaders. The first Christian martyr was Stephen, killed by the Jews c.35, and Luke recorded the story of his death in Acts of the Apostles:

> [At Stephen's preaching the Jews] covered their ears, and with a loud shout all rushed together against him. Then they dragged him out of the city and began to stone him; and the witnesses laid their coats at the feet of a young man named Saul [later Paul]. While they were stoning Stephen, he prayed, "Lord Jesus, receive my spirit." Then he knelt down and cried out in a loud voice, "Lord, do not hold this sin against them." When he had said this, he died. (Acts 7:57–60)

Stephen's last words are meant to remind the reader of Christ, who uttered similar words of forgiveness to his killers from the cross. Often images of Stephen in medieval art show him holding a rock or with a rock striking his head.

The most famous of the early persecutions of Christians, and the first launched by a Roman emperor, took place during the reign of Nero. He had been accused of having started a great fire in Rome in the year 64 in order to clear an area where he wished to build a grand new house—the origin of the old saying that Nero fiddled while Rome burned—and he needed a scapegoat. So he blamed the fire on the small, weak, and unpopular Christian community, which he understood to be a sect of Judaism. The persecution was confined to Rome and was not an attempt to wipe out the infant religion. However, both Peter and Paul were probably martyred during this persecution, Peter in the circus of Nero near a place called the Vatican, where four hundred years later a great basilica was built in his honor.

For almost two hundred years after Nero, there were scattered Christian persecutions, but all were short-lived and local. Most occurred in response to local problems (a bad crop, for example, where the populace may have believed that the Roman gods were punishing them for tolerating non-worshipers in their midst) or because the Christians were so different from other Roman cit-

izens. Christians generally did not attend the cruel entertainments so popular
with the masses or offer sacrifices to the Roman gods, considered as much a
patriotic as a religious act in imperial times. While many early Christians were
pacifists and refused to serve in the army, ironically Christianity was spread
in part by Christian soldiers stationed all over the Empire. Sometimes Christians were harassed by being "rounded up" for questioning. Probably the attitude of the Emperor Trajan (r.98–117) was typical of imperial policy toward
Christians in this period. In the following text, he is answering a provincial
governor who had expressed concern about the Christian "problem":

> You have acted quite properly, Pliny [called Pliny the Younger, the governor
> of the province of Bithynia in Asia], in examining the case of those Chris-
> tians brought before you. Nothing definite can be laid down as a general rule.
> They should not be hunted out. If accusations are made and they are found
> guilty, they must be punished. But remember that a man may expect pardon
> from repentance if he denies that he is a Christian, and proves this to your
> satisfaction, that is by worshipping our gods, however much you may have
> suspected him in the past. Anonymous lists should have no part in any charge
> made. That is a thoroughly bad practice, and not in accordance with the spirit
> of the age.[11]

Among the second-century martyrs was Ignatius of Antioch (d.107). In
surviving letters, he suggests his willingness to die for his faith, his conviction that martyrdom was the surest way to heaven, and his recognition that
to die for Christ was the closest possible imitation of Christ's own passion:

> All the ends of the earth, all the kingdoms of the world would be of no profit
> to me; so far as I am concerned, to die in Jesus Christ is better than to be
> monarch of the earth's widest bounds. He who died for us is all that I seek;
> He who rose again for us is my whole desire. The pangs of birth are upon me;
> have patience with me, my brothers, and do not shut me out from life, do not
> wish me to be stillborn. Here is one who only longs to be God's; do not make
> a present of him to the world again, or delude him with the things of earth.
> Suffer me to attain to light, light pure and undefiled; for only when I am come
> thither shall I be truly a man. Leave me to imitate the Passion of my God.[12]

Another second-century martyr was Polycarp (d.155). An excellent account of his martyrdom survives, but perhaps the most important aspect of
the text is the description of what the pious Christians did after his death:

> So, after all, we did gather up his bones—more precious to us than jewels,
> and finer than pure gold—and we laid them to rest on a spot suitable for that
> purpose. There we shall assemble, as occasion allows, with glad rejoicings; and
> with the Lord's permission we shall celebrate the birthday of his martyrdom.
> It will serve both as a commemoration of all who have triumphed before, and
> as a training and a preparation for any whose crown may be still to come.[13]

This text suggests that as early as the second century there was interest in preserving the relics (physical remains) of a holy person and that the day of his death—his birthday in heaven—was celebrated. In the Middle Ages, the celebration of the feast days of the saints, especially the martyrs, and the veneration of relics were two of the most important forms of popular piety. Relics were much sought after—bought, given as gifts, and even stolen. They were regarded as the means through which innumerable miracles were performed. A place with the relics of a saint was indeed a holy place, and people often traveled long distances to visit such a site. Since Christians believe in the resurrection of the body at the Last Judgment, there was a strong belief in the real presence of a saint where his or her relics were preserved. Thus, people journeyed extraordinary distances to visit tombs such as those of the apostle James in Spain, Peter and Paul in Rome, Mary Magdalen in France, Thomas à Becket in England, and countless others. Even the crusades to the Holy Land were often described in terms of a pilgrimage to the places where Jesus lived, died, and was raised from the dead. Though there are many reasons for the development of cults of saints, veneration of relics, and pilgrimage in the Middle Ages, we can trace the roots back as far as the middle of the second century.

A saint is one who is in heaven and thus eternally in God's favor. From the first century, Christians who died martyrs' deaths were presumed to be in heaven. There was at this time no formal process of canonization, the process by which one was declared a saint; the fact of martyrdom was sufficient evidence for veneration. With the end of large-scale persecutions in the fourth century, the definition of sainthood was enlarged to include those who professed Christianity and lived an exemplary Christian life. This class of saints is called confessors. Until the twelfth century, canonization varied from one area to another, and local cults sprang up in virtually all cathedrals and monasteries. Declaring someone a saint usually amounted to little more than placing the saint's relics in a place to be venerated and proclaiming that person's sanctity. From the end of the twelfth century until the present, canonization has been the prerogative of the pope, who collects evidence of sanctity and declares a person to be a saint. Pope John Paul II (r. 1978–) has formally canonized more saints than all of his predecessors combined.

In the year 250, a new type of persecution began under the Emperor Decius. He ordered all citizens of the Empire to sacrifice to the Roman deities under penalty of death. This decree was intended to wipe out Christianity. Fortunately for Christians, this persecution was short-lived because Decius died in 251. However, a similar persecution was ordered by the Emperor Valerian in 258, and it lasted until 261. Among the victims of these persecutions were the great theologian Cyprian of Carthage and the deacon Laurence (often spelled Lawrence). His story and those of other martyrs remained popular throughout the Middle Ages, as evidenced by their frequent appearances in sculpture, painting, and stained glass. His life continued to be rewritten and embellished. Here, for example, is a version taken from Jacobus de Voragine's *Golden Legend*, an enormously popular thirteenth-century collection of saints' lives:

> That same night the saint was haled before Decius. When Hippolytus [a Roman official] wept and cried out that he was a Christian, Laurence said to him: "Hide Christ in the inner man, listen, and when I call, come!" Decius said to Laurence: "Either you will sacrifice to the gods, or you will spend the night being tortured!" Laurence: "My night has no darkness, and all things gleam in the light!" Decius gave his orders: "Let an iron bed be brought, and let this stubborn Laurence rest on it!" The executioners stripped him, laid him out on the iron grill, piled burning coals under it, and pressed heated iron pitchforks upon his body. Laurence said to Valerian [another Roman official]: "Learn, wretched man, that your coals are refreshing to me but will be an

Martyrdom of Saint Eustace and his family. Fresco, fourteenth century. Monastery of Pomposa, Italy. Eustace, a Roman martyr, was put to death by being roasted inside a hollow bronze bull. Above the depiction of the martyrdom, the souls of Eustace and his family are taken to heaven by angels. Like many other stories of Roman martyrs, this one is interesting for its ingenuity. It is adapted from a form of torture used by Greeks in Sicily centuries earlier.

eternal punishment to you, because the Lord himself knows that being accused I have not denied him, being put to the question I have confessed Christ, and being roasted I give thanks!" And with a cheerful countenance he said to Decius: "Look, wretch, you have me well done on one side, turn me over and eat!" And giving thanks, he said: "I thank you, O Lord, because I have been worthy to pass through your portals!" And so he breathed his last.[14]

The genre of literature that recites the lives of saints is called hagiography (from the Greek *hagios*—"holy"—and *graphein*—"to write"). Hagiography was extraordinarily popular in the Middle Ages. The stories were colorfully written with much action and adventure. The heroes and villains were as easy to spot as they are in old white-hat/black-hat cowboy movies. These writings were not attempts to provide biographies of holy people but rather were attempts to edify, instruct in the virtues, and present idealized models for imitation.

The disregard for historical accuracy is obvious in the text above where the author has Decius as the emperor, then Valerian, then Decius again. Even the most casual tourist visiting the churches and museums of Europe cannot fail to see evidence of the enormous popularity of the stories of the saints in the Middle Ages. However, interest in the lives was more than merely entertainment and edification for the masses. The greatest writers of the Middle Ages, among them Bernard of Clairvaux and Bonaventure, also wrote or rewrote saints' lives. Of equal importance, these hagiographical conventions were often incorporated even into secular literary genres by writers such as Geoffrey Chaucer.

The growing Christian Church survived the persecutions of Decius and Valerian, and was generally left in peace during the next forty years. In fact, some buildings were constructed for Christian worship in the latter half of the third century. However, the Emperor Diocletian (r.284–305), as part of his program to stabilize the Roman Empire, was concerned that the primary loyalty of Christians was not to the state. He began the most serious and wide-ranging persecutions in 303; they continued—with some interruptions—until his successor Constantine's Edict of Milan in 313. Thousands of Christians died in Diocletian's attempt to rid the Empire of Christianity. Out of this persecution, too, came some of the Church's most famous martyrs, including Lucy, Margaret, Vincent, and Sebastian. A contemporary account of one bishop's encounter with the persecutors perhaps gives the best picture of what was involved:

The magistrate Magnilianus said to him: "Are you Felix the bishop?"

"I am," answered Bishop Felix.

"Hand over whatever books or parchments you possess," said the magistrate Magnilianus.

"I have them," answered Bishop Felix, "but I will not give them up."

The magistrate Magnilianus said: "Hand the books over to be burned."

"It would be better for me to be burned," answered Bishop Felix, "rather than the divine Scriptures. For it is better to obey God rather than men."

The magistrate Magnilianus said: "The emperors' orders come before anything you say."

Bishop Felix answered: "God's commands come before those of men."[15]

After Diocletian's retirement in 305, there was civil war among several claimants to the imperial title. Among them was Constantine, son of one of Diocletian's caesars (assistant emperors). He was proclaimed emperor by his army in York, England, in 306; but he became effective ruler of the Western half of the Empire only after defeating his rival Maxentius at the battle of Milvian Bridge on the outskirts of Rome in 312 and did not rule the entire Roman Empire until 323. According to tradition, on the eve of the battle, Constantine had a vision of the cross and heard a voice telling him he would conquer by that sign. He had Christ's monogram marked on his soldiers' shields the next morning. Whatever the historical accuracy of this popular story, Constantine and his coemperor issued the Edict of Milan in 313, which brought the Empire's persecution of Christians to an end and granted toleration to all religions. In the years following the edict, Constantine came more and more to favor Christianity, although he was not baptized until just before his death in 337. Among his favors to Christianity were the proclamation of Sunday as a holiday, the elimination of branding on the face as punishment because humans are made in the image of God, the grant of exemptions from government service to the clergy, and gifts of buildings and property to the Church.

Although some historians have argued that Constantine's conversion to Christianity was politically motivated and perhaps even a political ploy, there is no good reason to doubt the sincerity of his adherence to Christianity, even though he understood its basic tenets quite differently than many of his fellow Christians did. But if Constantine had hoped that Christianity would cement his empire together, he realized soon after the Edict of Milan that there were serious divisions within the Church. One issue arose directly from the persecution of Diocletian. Unlike Bishop Felix, some clergy submitted Christian books to the Roman authorities to be burned, and even sacrificed to pagan gods in order to escape execution. After the persecution, some of these priests and bishops wanted to take up their offices in the Church again. In North Africa, a dispute broke out because some Christians, later called Donatists, after Donatus, a bishop who replaced one of the "traitors," refused to recognize these "traitors" as priests and bishops. The bishop of Rome, a synod of bishops meeting in France, and Constantine himself (in 316, long before he was baptized) condemned Donatism; the emperor even used his power to attempt to put an end to it. This is the first instance of an emperor using political authority to try to settle an essentially theological controversy among Christians. Despite continued imperial support of the winning position—its supporters always described their views as orthodox, a word meaning right teaching—Donatism persisted in North Africa until the Muslim conquest in the seventh century. In the fifth century, the North African Bishop Augustine was a strong opponent of Donatism and wrote powerful treatises supporting the orthodox position.

The Donatist and orthodox views represent two competing beliefs concerning the nature of the Church. The former perceived the Church to be a community of saints, the holy ones of God, from which sinners were to be excluded. On the other hand, the orthodox position was based on a broader conception of the Church as a mixed body of saints and sinners, all benefiting from the community and the sacraments—the rites through which God's grace is channeled to the community of believers. Furthermore, the orthodox believed that properly ordained clergy administered the sacraments validly even if they themselves were not of good character because ultimately, they argued, it was Christ who administered the sacraments, and he could supply grace by means of the sacraments even through unworthy agents. The victory for the orthodox position was of great importance to the development of the Church, whose membership for much of the medieval period consisted of almost the entire population of Western Europe. However, on occasion, church reformers attacking clerical corruption in the Middle Ages came very close to the Donatist position. Among these are the eleventh-century reformer Cardinal Humbert and the fourteenth-century English theologian John Wyclif. Several popular heresies in the Middle Ages also included Donatist tenets.

The Donatist problem was not, however, the most charged theological problem Constantine had to face. More fundamental was defining the relationship between God the Father and Christ. A third-century theologian, Sabellius, had argued that God the Father and Christ were the same. This position provoked a response, and by the time of Constantine there was widespread agreement that important distinctions needed to be made between God the Father and God the Son. However, accepting that there were indeed distinctions did not mean that there was agreement on the nature of those distinctions. A priest from Alexandria named Arius (d.c.336) argued that Christ was not co-eternal with the Father but rather was the first fruit of creation: "There was a time when he [Christ] was not." In *Paradiso* 13, Dante mentions Sabellius and Arius as representatives of Christian heresy. He suggests that the problem with those who adhered to their views was their inability to see any merits in the other position. The idea that what heretics do is to take part of the truth (in the case of the Sabellians, the unity of God the Father and God the Son; in the case of the Arians, the distinctions between God the Father and God the Son) and confuse it for the whole truth is Dante's working definition of heresy in *Inferno* 10. Arius stressed the differences between

God and Father and God the Son and spoke of them as being of different "substances," a philosophical term best rendered in modern English as "essences" or "being." Encouraged by his ecclesiastical advisors, Constantine summoned a council of bishops, almost entirely from the Eastern part of the Empire, which met at Nicaea in Asia Minor in 325. Constantine himself presided over this gathering, now referred to as the First Ecumenical (from the Greek word meaning "the inhabited world") Council even though he was not a baptized Christian at the time. The Council condemned Arianism and approved a statement concerning the proper relationship of God the Father to his Son probably suggested by Constantine himself although undoubtedly based on the advice of trusted bishops. This formula was incorporated into a statement of belief called the Nicene Creed (from the Latin *credere* meaning "to believe"). This creed received significant additions at the Second Ecumenical Council, held at Constantinople in 381, incorporating a greater recognition of the Holy Spirit as part of the Godhead, and one additional change was later added in Latin-speaking Christendom. This final version is worth presenting here in its entirety. The creed is important not only for its condemnation of Arianism and strong proclamation of the Trinity, but also because in the Middle Ages it was incorporated into the Mass and thus was the principal declaration of belief made by the faithful in the West. The Creed is divided into four parts; the first three concern the parts of the Trinity and the fourth concerns the Church. The section that deals specifically with the challenge of Arianism is in italics:

> We believe in one God,
> the Father, the Almighty,
> maker of heaven and earth,
> of all that is, seen and unseen.
> We believe in one Lord, Jesus Christ,
> the only Son of God,
> *eternally begotten of the Father,*
> *God from God, Light from Light,*
> *true God from true God,*
> *begotten, not made, of one Being [substance] with the Father.*
> *Through him all things were made.*
> For us men and for our salvation
> he came down from heaven:
> by the power of the Holy Spirit
> he became incarnate from the Virgin Mary, and was made man.
> For our sake, he was crucified under Pontius Pilate;
> he suffered death and was buried.
> On the third day he rose again in accordance with the Scriptures;
> he ascended into heaven
> and is seated at the right hand of the Father.
> He will come again in glory to judge the living and the dead,

and his kingdom will have no end.
We believe in the Holy Spirit, the Lord, the giver of life,
who proceeds from the Father and the Son.
With the Father and the Son he is worshipped and glorified.
He has spoken through the Prophets.
We believe in one holy catholic and apostolic Church.
We acknowledge one baptism for the forgiveness of sins.
We look for the resurrection of the dead,
and the life of the world to come.
Amen.[16]

Not all of Arius's followers abandoned their beliefs after Nicaea, and a significant number of bishops who signed the Nicene formula later reverted to Arianism. Constantine himself leaned toward Arianism after Nicaea and was baptized on his deathbed by an Arian bishop in 337. His three sons, who ruled from 337 to 361, also leaned toward Arian beliefs. There were even brief periods when the Nicenes seemed to be in a minority and even faced persecution as heretics. Generally, Arianism was confined to the East; the Latin-speaking West was firmly Nicene. In the 360s and 370s the pendulum swung back toward the Nicene position; and the Second Ecumenical Council, meeting in Constantinople in 381, once again condemned Arianism. This was its death blow within the Roman Empire.

Despite the triumph of the Nicene position, Arianism would continue to have a great impact on the history of early medieval Europe. Between the two ecumenical councils that condemned Arianism, Christianity spread for the first time to the Germanic Goths living outside the empire through the missionary work of Ulfilas (c.311–383), who had learned his Christianity from and was consecrated a bishop by an Arian. Thus, Christianity was taken to the Germans in its Arian form. Later, the Goths entered the Roman Empire and eventually occupied and ruled significant portions of it. Other Germanic tribes—Vandals, Burgundians, and later the Lombards—also became Arian. Collectively, these tribes ruled most of the Western Roman Empire by 500: the Goths controlled most of Italy and Spain, the Vandals were in North Africa, and the Burgundians occupied part of Gaul (France). The Germanic invasions thus were not only a political and military threat but a religious one as well. Nicene bishops, including the bishop of Rome, found themselves surrounded by people whom they regarded as dangerous heretics. Some of the Germanic chieftains persecuted Nicene Christians. The sixth-century bishop Gregory of Tours recounts the story of a Nicene martyr in Arian Spain:

> About this time Trasamund began to persecute the Christians and by tortures and all sorts of executions forced the whole of Spain to accept the heresy of the Arian rite. It so happened that a young girl of strong religious convictions was dragged forward for this torment. She was extremely wealthy and according to the class-distinctions of this world she belonged to a noble senato-

rial family. What is nobler still than all this, she was strong in the Catholic faith and served Almighty God in a faultless way. . . .

As she was dragged off to be re-baptized against her will and compelled to suffer immersion in the filthy font, she shouted: "I believe the Father with the Son and the Holy Ghost to be of one substance." As she said this she stained all the water with her blood, for her menstrual period began. Then she was submitted to a legal interrogation, and tortured by the rack, the flames and the pincers. Finally she was consecrated to Christ our Lord by having her head cut off.[17]

Only in the seventh century did Arianism disappear as the Germanic tribes gradually accepted the orthodox (Nicene) position on the relationship of the Father to the Son.

After Constantine, Christians ruled the Roman Empire except for the two-year reign of the Emperor Julian the Apostate (r.361–363). The importance of Constantine's conversion and the beginning of imperial support for Christianity after three centuries of indifference or persecution is hard to overestimate. Among the most immediate changes were the number and kind of converts. Until Constantine, Christians were a small minority but highly dedicated to their faith, as evidenced by the willingness of many to be martyred; when people became Christians, they obviously did not do so for any material advantage. But with imperial sponsorship of Christianity, countless thousands converted because Christianity was the religion of the emperor and thus perhaps a good way to get ahead in the Empire. Within a century of Constantine's reign, emperors decreed Christianity to be the only legal religion of the Empire and restricted military and civil service to Christians. Those ready to die for the faith had to learn to deal with and accept many "lukewarm" Christians and consequently to redefine the very nature of the Church.

Since post-Constantinian Christianity was a safe and even favored religion, martyrdom with rare exceptions was no longer possible. How then could those deeply devoted Christians show their willingness to lose all for Christ, as the venerated martyrs of the past had done? One reaction was the growth of asceticism (from the Greek word meaning "athletic training"), a vigorous self-denial of worldly pleasures, which was sometimes viewed as a kind of "daily martyrdom" (see Chapter 6). The ascetic movement was not confined to men and women living as hermits or in monastic communities in the deserts of Egypt, Palestine, and Syria. Even before the victory of Christianity in the fourth century, widows and unmarried women in Rome and other places, often from noble families, made vows of celibacy and poverty, sometimes choosing to live in poor and even squalid conditions.

Another significant change after Constantine occurred in the role of bishops. They began to wear insignia once used only by imperial civil servants, and the emperors treated them as religious counterparts to imperial officials. Even the "'throne" or *cathedra* that came to be used by bishops in their churches was modeled on the seat of high-ranking imperial officials. (The word "cathedral," meaning a church that is the seat of a bishop, derives from this piece of imperial regalia adapted to Christian use.) The bishops of Rome were among those who adopted imperial regalia; in addition, the popes began to use the title and privileges once held by the chief pagan priest of Rome—the *pontifex maximus*. The popes also sponsored large building projects, including the construction of churches on the spots where famous Christians had been martyred. Among these was the Church of Saint Peter, built on the site of Nero's circus in the Vatican. The pope came to live in a palace called the Lateran, which Constantine bequeathed to the head of the Roman Church. It was next to this palace that the cathedral of Rome, Saint John in Lateran, was built. For most of the Middle Ages, the residence of the pope was the Lateran palace. Only in the fifteenth century did the popes permanently move to a papal palace across the Tiber in the Vatican.

Throughout the Empire, the Church began to acquire wealth from both imperial and private gifts. The fact that bishops were often the heads of wealthy corporate communities added to the importance of the episcopal office. The control of wealth by the Christian clergy meant that they were important to the economy and governance of the Empire. This is one reason the emperors were so interested in the disputes within Christendom. We have already seen how Constantine became directly involved in what were essentially theological disputes with the Donatist and Arian problems. On the other hand, bishops sometimes sought to exercise their spiritual authority over a Christian emperor to influence essentially political policy. The best example of this involves the Emperor Theodosius (d.395) and the bishop of Milan, Saint Ambrose (d.397). For political reasons Theodosius carried out a massacre in the Greek city of Thessalonica (modern Thessaloniki) in the year 390. When the emperor returned to Milan, which by this time was effectively the capital of the Western part of the Empire because of its proximity to the most important military operations, Ambrose chastised him and forbade him to enter the cathedral of Milan until he did public penance for his sin. Theodosius did public penance. On another occasion, a group of zealous Christian monks had burned a synagogue in the Eastern part of the Empire; Theodosius ordered the local bishop to restore the synagogue with Church funds. Ambrose's biographer Paulinus recounts what happened upon the emperor's return to Milan:

> Moreover, after he [Theodosius] had returned to Milan, he [Ambrose] preached on this very topic in the presence of the people, and the emperor was present in the church at the time. In this sermon he introduced the person of the Lord as speaking to the emperor: "I made you emperor from the lowest; I handed over to you the army of your enemy; I gave to you the supplies which he had prepared for his own army against you; I reduced your enemy into our power; I established one of your sons on the throne of the empire; I caused you to triumph without difficulty—and do you give triumphs

to me over my enemies? " And the emperor said to him as he was descending the pulpit: "You spoke against us today, Bishop." But the bishop replied that he had not spoken against him but for him. Then the emperor: "Indeed, I issued a stern order against the bishop concerning the rebuilding of the synagogue. Moreover, the monks must be punished."[18]

Ambrose forced Theodosius to recall the order to rebuild the synagogue by refusing to celebrate Mass until he received Theodosius's promise of obedience in this matter. This same Theodosius was the first emperor to persecute people who were not orthodox Christians, that is, both heretics such as the Arians and pagans. In 391, he issued a decree that was essentially designed to prohibit paganism:

> No person shall pollute himself with sacrificial animals; no person shall slaughter an innocent victim; no person shall approach the shrines, shall wander through the temples, or revere the images formed by mortal labour, lest he become guilty by divine and human laws. Judges shall also be bound by the general rule that if any of them should be devoted to profane rights and should enter a temple for the purpose of worship anywhere, either on a journey or in a city, he shall be immediately compelled to pay fifteen pounds of gold.[19]

Thus, in less than a century Christianity had gone from a persecuted minority religion to the official religion of the Roman Empire, the religion required of all public officials.

Throughout the Middle Ages, people were aware that the conversion of Constantine marked a (perhaps *the*) major change in the history of the Church. Reformers and critics of the Church often lamented that Constantine's gifts to the Church and all the consequences of imperial favor had ultimately led to a corruption of Christian values and Christian ecclesiastical offices. For example, Dante, meeting avaricious popes in hell, moans: "Ah, Constantine, of how much ill was mother, not your conversion, but that dowry the first rich father took from you"(*Inferno* 19.115–17).[20]

Similarly, here are the words of the important fifteenth-century Bohemian reformer John Hus:

> This [spiritual poison] was intimated when Emperor Constantine first enriched the Roman bishop, having given him estates; for a voice was heard from heaven saying: "Today poison has been poured into the Christian communion."[21]

A widely held belief in the Middle Ages was that Constantine actually conferred upon the pope the authority to govern the Western half of the Roman Empire; the legend was put in written form in the eighth century. This text, known as the Donation of Constantine, was from time to time a major point of dispute between the Holy Roman Emperors and the popes. Elaborate theories of church-state relations relied on the donation. Some writers such as Dante denied the legality and thus the validity of the transferal of imperial

Donation of Constantine. Fresco, c. 1250. Church of the Santi Quattro Coro-
nati, Rome. This painting represents the papal point of view of the relation-
ship between Church and Empire, for we see a humble and subordinate Con-
stantine conferring the symbols of temporal rule upon Pope Sylvester I.

power to the pope. However, it was not until the mid-fifteenth century that
the Italian humanist Lorenzo Valla demonstrated authoritatively that the Donation of Constantine was a forgery.

Another major dispute concerning the nature of Christ arose toward the
end of the fourth century, and led to the calling of the Third and Fourth Ecumenical Councils, the last councils to be concerned primarily with Christological questions. Although the precise theological positions are complex, the
crux of the dispute concerned the relationship of Christ's divinity to his humanity. One position, developed in Alexandria, argued that Christ was fully
divine but did not have all human traits; in particular, He did not have the
limitations of a human mind. More extreme adherents of this position, the
Monophysites (from the Greek word meaning "one nature"), believed that
Christ had only one complete nature, that is, a complete divine but only an
incomplete human nature. An opposing position came originally from Antioch but was eventually centered in Constantinople when its leading propo-
nent, Nestorius, became bishop of that city. The essence of this position is that

Christ had two completely separate natures, and its adherents emphasized the importance of his human nature. The Third Ecumenical Council in 431 at Ephesus condemned this Nestorian position by decreeing that Mary is the Mother of God—*Theotokos* in Greek (the Nestorians had argued that Mary was the mother of the human nature of Christ but not mother of his divinity). Although the adoption of the term *Theotokos* was for the purpose of clarifying a Christological position, it represents the key moment in the development of Mary's essential role in salvation history. The first church in Rome dedicated to the Virgin, known today as Santa Maria Maggiore, was constructed just after the Council of Ephesus and contains a decorative program that emphasizes the theology of Mary as Mother of God. The Nestorians faced persecution, and many fled to the Persian Empire. In later centuries, Nestorian missionaries traveled to China where, especially in the thirteenth century, they were remarkably successful, establishing churches in Beijing for example. When Marco Polo and some Franciscan missionaries arrived in China in the thirteenth century, they were surprised to find a rather flourishing albeit "heretical" Christian community there.

The Council of Ephesus failed to settle this Christological controversy since moderates and Monophysites continued to argue the rightness of their beliefs. A council at Ephesus in 449 upheld the Monophysite position over the objections of Pope Leo I. However, a new emperor summoned a council to Chalcedon in 451, now known as the Fourth Ecumenical Council. It denounced the Monophysite position as heretical and defined Christ as having two complete natures, human and divine, each retaining all its properties but indissolubly united at the Incarnation. As mentioned earlier, the Council of Chalcedon also appeared to recognize papal primacy by accepting a letter containing the claim that "Peter had spoken through Leo."

Like the other condemned groups before them, the Monophysites continued to exist, though almost exclusively in the Eastern part of the Roman Empire; they were particularly strong in Egypt. Monophysitism was a major divisive element in the Eastern Roman Empire until all the strongholds of the Monophysites were captured by the Muslims in the seventh century. These conquests occurred in part because there was little loyalty in those places to a persecuting emperor in Constantinople. Several Monophysite churches exist today, including the Coptic church, the Jacobite church in Syria, and the Armenian church.

The development of the doctrines and institutions of Christianity, the focus of this chapter, demonstrates the interaction between classical and biblical culture. Taking place as it did primarily in the eastern Mediterranean, this interaction occurred within a Greek cultural and linguistic framework. Though somewhat later, a parallel interaction took place in the Latin-speaking West, a development that we will trace in the next chapter by an examination of two of its greatest figures, Jerome and Augustine.

CHAPTER 4

THE LATIN FATHERS
Jerome and Augustine

With the exceptions of the writings of Tertullian and Cyprian (d.258), virtually all the surviving Christian writings before the fourth century were in Greek, even in the western Mediterranean. It was only in the fourth and fifth centuries, as the Roman Empire became permanently divided between East and West, that a largely independent theological tradition developed in the Latin-speaking West.

The first major figure was Saint Jerome (c.342–420), who grew up in Italy and studied in Rome where he was baptized and served as a secretary to Pope Damasus I. However, Jerome lived most of his adult life in the Holy Land, at a monastery in Bethlehem. He was an important writer on asceticism, an influential biblical scholar (often drawing heavily from Origen), an author of saints' lives, and a pastor. Indeed, one of Jerome's primary ministries (and one for which he has not received enough credit) was his pastoral care of women. Many noteworthy women supported him and benefited from his guidance, even though he remained skeptical about the spiritual capacities of their sex. However, it is as a translator of the Bible that he is best known.

Although there were Latin versions of Scripture before Jerome, it was he who retranslated most of both Testaments from their original languages into the version that eventually became standard in the West for more than a thousand years. This translation is usually referred to as the Vulgate (from the Latin *vulgus* meaning "common"), because it was the Bible common to medieval Europe. Jerome's introductions to and commentaries on many books of the Bible also became standard starting points for biblical commentary in the Middle Ages. Anyone who has ever studied a foreign language will appreciate how a translator has to use certain metaphors and approximations of meaning. Jerome's choices as a translator determined how readers understood and knew the Scriptures. Since his translations remained authoritative for so long, any errors he made became a part of the received biblical tradition in the West throughout the Middle Ages.

Jerome wrote several important works in addition to his biblical scholarship. Educated in the pagan classics like many other Christians, he was concerned with the proper relationship between them and Scripture. Though his viewpoint does not remain entirely consistent from one mood or period to another, the overall tone is clear: Christian writers can use classical works, though with caution and in a role subordinate to Scripture. Consider the following two passages from the writings of Jerome:

> While the old serpent was making me his plaything, about the middle of Lent, a deep-seated fever fell upon my weakened body, and while it destroyed my rest completely—the story seems hardly credible—it so wasted my unhappy frame that scarcely anything was left of me but skin and bone. Meantime preparations for my funeral went on; my body grew gradually colder, and the warmth of life lingered only in my throbbing breast. Suddenly I was caught up in the spirit and dragged before the judgment seat of the Judge; and here the light was so bright, and those who stood around were radiant, that I cast myself upon the ground and did not dare to look up. Asked who and what I was I replied: "I am a Christian." But He who presided said: "Thou liest, thou art a follower of Cicero and not of Christ. For where thy treasure is, there will thy heart be also." Instantly I became dumb, and amid the strokes of the lash—for He had ordered me to be scourged—I was tortured most severely still by the fire of conscience, considering with myself that verse, "In the grave, who shall give thee thanks?" Yet for all that I began to cry and to bewail myself, saying, "Have mercy upon me, O Lord; have mercy upon me."[1]

> He [Paul] had read in Deuteronomy the command given by the voice of the Lord that when a captive woman had had her head shaved, her eyebrows and all her hair cut off, and her nails pared, she might then be taken to wife. Is it surprising that I too, admiring the fairness of her form and the grace of her eloquence, desire to make that secular wisdom which is my captive and my handmaid, a matron of the true Israel? Or that shaving off and cutting away all in her that is dead whether this be idolatry, pleasure, error, or lust, I take her to myself clean and pure and beget by her servants for the Lord of Sabbaoth? My efforts promote the advantage of Christ's family, my so-called defilement with an alien increases the number of my fellow-servants. . . . Ezekiel shaves his head as a type of that Jerusalem which has been an harlot, in sign that whatever in her is devoid of sense and life must be removed.[2]

In other words, one should not ignore or reject the wisdom of the Greeks or Romans, but must select those elements from the classical heritage that are useful to achieve salvation only with great caution.

Saint Augustine lived during the waning days of the Roman Empire in the West. Born in what is now Algeria in North Africa in 354, he traveled to

Fresco of Saint Augustine teaching. Ottaviano Nelli, fourteenth century. Church of Sant'Agostino, Gubbio, Italy. This painting illustrates the fact that Augustine was a teacher in North Africa and Italy in the late fourth century. Perhaps more importantly it shows that Augustine is a teacher who needs to be heeded in the present.

Italy, and converted to Christianity in 386 under the influence of Ambrose, bishop of Milan and an influential Christian writer, who along with Jerome, Augustine, and Gregory, came to be known as the Latin Doctors. After Augustine's conversion, he became bishop of Hippo in North Africa; when he died in 430, Germanic invaders, the Vandals, were closing in on the city. An educator, a polemicist, a pastor, and a preacher, in addition to being a prolific writer of theology and philosophy, Augustine's importance to the Middle Ages and beyond cannot be overemphasized. He is one of the two or three most influential thinkers in all of Christian thought, and perhaps *the* seminal figure in determining the way Western Europe understood reality in the Middle Ages. He wrote on almost every topic, and even to survey what he has done in any complete fashion would be impossible; but by examining three of his important works, one can see something of both the breadth and depth of his influence. *On Christian Teaching* presents a theory of how to read Scripture.[3] The *Confessions* is his autobiography and thus contains the pattern of his conversion to Christianity. *The City of God* is an interpretation of all of history seen as the struggle between the heavenly and the earthly, the city of God and the human city.

To understand the influence of *On Christian Teaching*, one must first recall what has been said about the absolute centrality of the Bible to the Middle Ages. Those who judge by the influence the Bible has now, even for practicing Christians, will underestimate its importance to medieval culture. Perhaps at no time in Western history has a culture been so influenced by a single book. Modern scholars will read a great many more books in the course of their careers than their medieval counterparts, the explosion of material in all fields being one of the significant cultural changes that has taken place since the Middle Ages. But those books that medieval scholars knew, they knew exceedingly well. The book that they knew best was the Bible.

Not only was the Bible itself known in a way all but foreign to modern readers, but much of the scholarly writing in late antiquity and the Middle Ages consisted of commentary on its various parts. Many important works, such as Ambrose's commentary on the Gospel of Luke, Gregory the Great's *Moralia on* Job, and Bernard of Clairvaux's sermons on the Song of Songs, to take three well-known examples from among hundreds, are exegeses of the Bible. Augustine himself wrote many such works. The last part of his *Confessions* is a commentary on the book of Genesis, and one of his longest works is a series of commentaries and sermons on the Psalms. The Bible, then, was known, studied, and commented upon. Much of it was actually known by heart by the great scholars and thinkers, and those who could not read learned about it through sermons and the visual arts. Most of the sculpture, stained glass, and painting of the Middle Ages examined and interpreted biblical narrative.[4]

It follows from the importance of the Bible that Augustine's theory of biblical interpretation would have resonances with many areas of thought not specifically connected to theology. *On Christian Teaching* is an important text both to the history of ideas and the history of literary theory, defining an aesthetic influential to the entire Middle Ages. Augustine presents a distinction at the beginning of Book I that provides a basis not only for subsequent arguments in this work but to his thought as a whole. He distinguishes between the use and enjoyment of any object:

> To enjoy something is to hold fast to it in love for its own sake. To use something is to apply whatever it may be to the purpose of obtaining what you love—if indeed it is something that ought to be loved. (The improper use of something should be termed abuse.) Suppose we were travellers who could live happily in our homeland, and because our absence made us unhappy we wished to put an end to our misery and return there, we would need transport by land or sea which we could use to travel to our homeland, the object of our enjoyment. But if we were fascinated by the delights of the journey and the actual travelling, we would be perversely enjoying things that we

should be using; and we would be reluctant to finish our journey quickly. Being ensnared in the wrong kind of pleasure and estranged from the homeland whose pleasures could make us happy. So in this mortal life we are like travellers away from our Lord [2 Cor. 5:6]: if we wish to return to the homeland where we can be happy we must use this world [cf. 1 Cor. 7:31], not enjoy it, in order to discern "the invisible attributes of God, which are understood through what has been made" [Rom. 1:20] or, in other words, to derive eternal and spiritual value from corporeal and temporal things. The things that are to be enjoyed, then, are the Father and the Son and the Holy Spirit, and the Trinity that consists of them. . . . [5]

This passage obviously has far-reaching implications in that it helps to explain the proper attitude toward anything whatsoever, be it money, property, sex, or God. To see this as the beginning of a theory of aesthetics, however, is perhaps not so obvious. Augustine believed that this attitude must also govern one's approach to language. Words too are to be used rather than enjoyed, which means that one must not see them as things in themselves, but as signs pointing to something else. In one sense, of course, this is obvious, in that words are often referential. It would be self-defeating, when reading the word *horse*, to concentrate on the word itself, rather than on the four-legged animal to which the word refers. But when reading Scripture, Augustine tells us, one is to go beyond merely seeing the object that the word refers to; one must see words themselves as pointing toward a spiritual truth that exists behind the physical reality. He is elaborating a theory of symbolism. In Scripture, language is a means of leading the reader from the visible to the invisible. It is no accident that Augustine quotes Paul–"Invisible things are understood by the things that are made" (Rom. 1:20)—no fewer than six times throughout *On Christian Teaching*. He tells us about both ways of seeing words as signs:

> There are two reasons why written texts fail to be understood: their meaning may be veiled either by unknown signs or by ambiguous signs. Signs are either literal or metaphorical. They are called literal when used to signify the things for which they were invented: as, for example, when we say *bovem* [ox], meaning the animal which we and all speakers of Latin call by that name. They are metaphorical when the actual things which we signify by the particular words are used to signify something else: when, for example, we say *bovem* and not only interpret these two syllables to mean the animal normally referred to by that name but also understand, by that animal, "worker in the gospel," which is what scripture, as interpreted by the apostle Paul, means when he says, "You shall not muzzle the ox that treads out the grain" [1 Cor. 9:9 and 1 Tim. 5:18, quoting Deut. 25:4].[6]

Discovering the spiritual meaning that the words of Scripture point toward is the task of the serious student of Scripture, according to Augustine. Much of *On Christian Teaching is* devoted to ways in which this is to be done.

The qualities of mind that Augustine sees as necessary to this task are intertwined with the very quality of one's life; he is concerned with showing that understanding Scripture is always more than simply an academic study. To understand the spiritual meaning of Scripture, one must lead a life spiritually in accord with Scripture. Similarly, one should ask about an author's character as well as learning when considering a text's authority and reliability. In talking about how it is possible for one to misunderstand the spirit behind certain sections of the Old Testament, he tells us:

> Likewise we must take care not to regard something in the Old Testament that is by the standards of its own time not wickedness or wrongdoing, even when understood literally and not figuratively, as capable of being transferred to the present time and applied to our own lives. A person will not do this unless lust is in total control and actively seeking the complicity of the very scriptures by which it must be overthrown. Such a wretch does not realize that these things are written down for a useful purpose, to enable men of good conscience to see, for their own spiritual health, that a practice which they reject can have a good application, and that a practice which they embrace can be damnable, if the love shown by its followers (in the first case) or their greed (in the second) is taken into account.[7]

Augustine implies that one's own cupidity is the biggest obstacle to understanding Scripture. His theory helps to explain why certain parts of Scripture seem obscure; until one is able to pierce beneath the veil of the story itself to see the spiritual truth it contains one may indeed think that the surface story of Scripture is sometimes strange and unintelligible. Augustine wishes the reader to know both the difficulty of that enterprise and the importance of devoting one's life to it. A question that logically follows, however, is why Scripture should be written in such a seemingly obscure fashion. Why does God not offer spiritual truth simply, rather than in a roundabout fashion? His answer to this question is one of the most important sections of *On Christian Teaching*, and became one of the most influential statements on interpretation for the Middle Ages:

> But casual readers are misled by problems and ambiguities of many kinds, mistaking one thing for another. In some passages they find no meaning at all that they can grasp at, even falsely, so thick is the fog created by some obscure phrases. I have no doubt that this is all divinely predetermined, so that pride may be subdued by hard work and intellects which tend to despise things that are easily discovered may be rescued from boredom and reinvigorated. Suppose someone were to make the following statements: that there exist holy and perfect men by whose lives and conduct the church of Christ tears away those who come to it from their various superstitions, and somehow, by inspiring them to imitate their goodness, incorporates them into itself; and that there exist servants of the true God, good and faithful men who, putting aside

the burdens of this life, have come to the holy font of baptism, arise from it born again with the Holy Spirit, and then produce the fruit of a double love, that is love of God and love of their neighbour. Why is it, I wonder, that putting it like this gives less pleasure to an audience than by expounding in the same terms this passage from the Song of Songs [4:2], where the church is addressed and praised like a beautiful woman: "Your teeth are like a flock of shorn ewes ever ascending from the pool, all of which give birth to twins, and there is not a sterile animal among them"? Surely one learns the same lesson as when one hears it in plain words and without the support of the imagery? And yet somehow it gives me more pleasure to contemplate holy men when I see them as the teeth of the church tearing men away from their errors and transferring them into its body, breaking down their rawness by biting and chewing. And it is with the greatest of pleasure that I visualize the shorn ewes, their worldly burdens set aside like fleeces, ascending from the pool (baptism) and all giving birth to twins (the two commandments of love), with none of them failing to produce this holy fruit.[8]

This passage describes a movement from the visible to the invisible: Augustine makes it clear that the purpose of figurative language is not the pleasure to be gained in the language itself, but the truth to which the figurative language leads. The example he uses, by virtue of its jarring effect on a modern sensibility, reinforces this. The image takes the reader on a ride through the intestinal tract of a sheep and ends with a sheep bath, which only makes sense after one solves the intellectual puzzle it presents. Augustine thus claims that the reader gains intellectual satisfaction from the actual process of the discovery of truth, a satisfaction separate from the contemplation of this truth. The difficulty of the image increases the satisfaction. Augustine states explicitly that those things that are easily gained are not greatly valued. Conversely, one values the truth behind what he calls a "most dense mist" precisely because of the work that one must put into uncovering it. Since the example is rather extreme, it forcefully illustrates a significant difference between medieval and modern aesthetic theory: the function of imagery was not so much to arouse a spontaneous emotional attitude in observers, as to encourage them to "seek an abstract pattern of philosophical significance beneath the symbolic configuration."[9]

Augustine also treats the question of what sort of limits exist in the number of interpretations in a given scriptural passage:

So anyone who thinks that he has understood the divine scriptures or any part of them, but cannot by his understanding build up this double love of God and neighbor, has not yet succeeded in understanding them. Anyone who derives from them an idea which is useful for supporting this love but fails to say what the author demonstrably meant in the passage has not made a fatal error, and is certainly not a liar.[10]

Sculpture of the Mystic Mill. Monastery of Mary Magdalen, Vézelay, France. Twelfth century. Most of the sculpted capitals in this monastic church do not contain New Testament stories but rather are taken from the Old Testment or, as in this case, present allegories of the relationship between Old and New, thus exemplifying Augustine's idea that difficult images invite thought and meditation and thus lead to increased intellectual satisfaction. In this image, Moses places the rough grain of the Old Testament into a mystical mill, Christ. Paul fills his sack with the flour of the New Testament.

This statement does not give a carte blanche invitation to the reader. At the same time it is clearly open-ended, suggesting that even authorial intention is not so important as the promotion of the doctrine of charity.

In another section of *On Christian Teaching*, Augustine, like Jerome, writes about the possible uses of classical culture:

> Any statement by those who are called philosophers, especially the Platonists, which happen to be true and consistent with our faith should not cause alarm, but be claimed for our own use, as it were from owners who have no right to them. Like the treasures of the ancient Egyptians, who possessed not only idols and heavy burdens, which the people of Israel hated and shunned, but also vessels and ornaments of silver and gold, and clothes, on which leaving Egypt the people of Israel, in order to make better use of them, surreptitiously claimed for themselves (they did this not on their own authority but at God's command, and the Egyptians in their ignorance actually gave them the things of which they had made poor use) [Exod. 3:21–22, 12:35–36]—similarly all the branches of pagan learning contain not only false and supersti-

tious fantasies and burdensome studies that involve unnecessary effort, which each one of us must loathe and avoid as under Christ's guidance we abandon the company of pagans, but also studies for liberated minds which are more appropriate to the service of the truth, and some very useful moral instruction, as well as the various truths about monotheism to be found in their writers. These treasures—like the silver and gold, which they did not create but dug, as it were, from the mines of providence, which is everywhere—which were used wickedly and harmfully in the service of demons must be removed by Christians, as they separate themselves in spirit from the wretched company of pagans, and applied to their true function, that of preaching the gospel.[11]

Here, Augustine reads the quotation from Exodus, "that they are to claim gold and silver trinkets from their neighbor" (3:22), according to his own allegorical method. So understood, it becomes an explanation of the proper attitude toward pagan culture generally and, as such, becomes another important contribution to the much-debated question of what to do with the classical culture bequeathed to the Middle Ages. Augustine's answer, that one should take what is good, use it, and leave the rest behind, describes what actually happens to the culture of antiquity. One is justified in taking elements from the pagan past because they contain truth that can be converted to Christian uses. This principle helps to explain, for example, why in a medieval manuscript illumination containing a work of Cicero, the author is often pictured as a Christian monk. As modern readers with a different kind of time-consciousness, our instinctive reaction is to see such a transformation as simplistic or naive. But medieval people really show a sensible and sophisticated attitude, once one accepts their premise. They wished to show the relevance of the past and so they see people and events of the past as constantly present, whether in the portrayal of Cicero as a monk or of an Old Testament prophet using fifteenth-century English place names in a mystery play. In medieval painting or sculpture, figures who lived at different places and times are often depicted together on the same surface. This juxtaposition is also a way of bringing past and present together, showing that thematic connections are more important than temporal differences. Our reaction—to see only their distortion of the past—is perhaps another kind of naivete, the opposite side of the coin from the medieval view. In some ways we tend to neglect the continuity between our age and the past, and as a result tend to focus on the differences.

The *Confessions*, Augustine's autobiography, is perhaps the first and surely one of the greatest autobiographies in the history of the West, as well as one of its great spiritual treasures. But the form of the *Confessions* is not quite the same as more modern examples of the genre, which frequently include as many events as possible in constructing a person's life. Narrative completeness for Augustine is of less importance than following his principles of scriptural interpretation. He constructs the *Confessions* as a consciously ar-

Capital of Christ carrying his cross. Church of Saint Austremoine, Issoire, France. Twelfth century. In this representation of Christ carrying his cross, Roman soldiers are dressed as medieval knights in chain mail. Much Roman sculpture survived in the Middle Ages, so this way of representing the soldiers is not based on ignorance of what Roman soldiers looked like. Instead, it represents an attempt to bring the past into the present and so make it meaningful to its intended audience.

ticulated movement from the visible events in his life to the invisible reality of their meaning. Just as in reading Scripture one is led to an inner truth more important than the visible means by which this truth is presented, the events of Augustine's life are subordinated to a pattern of conversion toward which these events lead. His portrayal of the facts of his life is a means to an end

Sculpted panel of the Deposition of Christ from the Cross. Antelami, twelfth century. Church in Bardone, Italy. Not only are the main characters involved in the crucifixion present in this panel, but on the right are Adam and Eve, occupying the same space and thus appearing to be present at the crucifixion. The point of the sculpture is therefore theological rather than historical. Christ's death on the cross cancels the penalty for the sin of Adam and Eve.

rather than an end in itself; and the end of the *Confessions* is Augustine's conversion, his turning away from self and toward God. Thus, his conversion becomes the necessary condition for the proper understanding of Scripture. In fact, the last several books of the *Confessions* provide an explication of the beginning of the book of Genesis. As in *On Christian Teaching*, but far more personally, the *Confessions* affirms that how one reads a text and how one lives a life cannot be separated. As *On Christian Teaching* becomes a model for the understanding and interpretation of Scripture, so the *Confessions* becomes one of the most important models for the pattern of conversion, a pattern that exerted extraordinary influence on the thought of the Middle Ages.

The story of someone who turns away from self and toward God did not originate with Augustine. In fact, he relates in the *Confessions* how his own conversion was influenced by other famous conversion stories, that of Saint Antony of the Desert (251–356) as told by Saint Athanasius (c.296–373) and the most famous conversion in the New Testament—Paul on the road to Damascus—which is told in the Acts of the Apostles. But these stories are told by others. Augustine tells his own story. In the following excerpt, a friend sees an opened copy of Paul's letters in Augustine's house, and this leads him to talk about his own conversion, realizing that Augustine's interests are close to his own:

Then it occurred to him to mention how he and three of his colleagues (the date I do not know but it was at Trier [Germany]), when the emperor was detained by a circus spectacle in the forenoon, went out for a walk in the garden adjacent to the walls. There they strolled in couples, one as it turned out with Ponticianus [an acquaintance of Augustine], the other two separately wandering off on their own. In their wanderings they happened on a certain house where there lived some of your [God's] servants, poor in spirit: "of such is the kingdom of heaven" (Matt. 5:3). They found there a book in which was written the Life of Antony. One of them began to read it. He was amazed and set on fire, and during his reading began to think of taking up this way of life and of leaving his secular post in the civil service to be your servant. For they were agents in the special branch. Suddenly he was filled with holy love and sobering shame. Angry with himself, he turned his eyes on his friend and said to him: "Tell me, I beg of you, what do we hope to achieve with all our labours? What is our aim in life? What is the motive of our service to the state? Can we hope for any higher office in the palace than to be Friends of the Emperor? And in that position what is not fragile and full of dangers? How many hazards must one risk to attain to a position of ever greater danger? And when will we arrive there? Whereas, if I wish to become God's friend, in an instant I may become that now." So he spoke, and in pain at the coming to birth of a new life, he returned his eyes to the book's pages. He read on and experienced a conversion inwardly where you alone could see and, as was soon evident, his mind rid itself of the world. Indeed, as he read and turned over and over in the turbulent hesitations of his heart, there were some moments when he was angry with himself. But then he perceived the choice to be made and took a decision to follow the better course. He was already yours and said to his friend: "As for myself, I have broken away from our ambition, and have decided to serve God, and I propose to start doing that from this hour in this place. If it costs you too much to follow my example, do not turn against me." His friend replied that he would join him and be associated with him for such great reward and for so great a service.[12]

This interlocking pattern of conversions—Augustine's own is influenced by his friend's, and his friend's is influenced by that of Antony of the Desert—helps to explain why the *Confessions* is such an important document to the Middle Ages. As the life of Antony was a model for Augustine's friend, and indirectly for Augustine himself, so Augustine's life became a model for subsequent ages. His preeminence can be only partly explained on the grounds that the *Confessions* is a masterpiece of Latin prose. In titling the work *Confessions*, Augustine makes use of several senses of the word *confess*. Most obviously, he uses the word to mean "these are my deeds—I confess that I have committed them." He also uses the word to mean "to bear witness," a sense it developed in the early Church through the deeds of those who bore witness to Christ. "Confessor" is the Latin translation of the Greek word *martyr*. His conversion makes him a witness and model for the future that parallels the conversion of pagans to Christianity in the late Empire. In other words, Augustine symbolizes what happened to the culture of late antiquity as a whole. In a passage that suggests the sense of crisis and change in the whole culture, Augustine narrates the story of his friend Alypius, who undergoes a kind of conversion in reverse—away from God and toward self. Yet like Augustine's own conversion, we are presented here with a radical turning, one that overwhelms the whole being. His friend is taken to the gladiatorial shows and is overwhelmed with bloodlust:

> Alypius did not indeed abandon the earthly career of whose prizes his parents had sung to him. He had arrived in Rome before I did to study law. There he had been seized by an incredible obsession for gladiatorial spectacles and to an unbelievable degree. He held such spectacles in aversion and detestation; but some of his friends and fellow-pupils on their way back from a dinner happened to meet him in the street and, despite his energetic refusal and resistance, used friendly violence to take him into the amphitheatre during the day of the cruel and murderous games. He said: "If you drag my body to that place and sit me down there, do not imagine you can turn my mind and my eyes to those spectacles. I shall be as one not there, and so I shall overcome both you and the games." They heard him, but none the less took him with them, wanting perhaps to discover whether he could actually carry it off. When they arrived and had found seats where they could, the entire place seethed with the most monstrous delight in the cruelty. He kept his eyes shut and forbade his mind to think about such fearful evils. Would that he had blocked his ears as well! A man fell in combat. A great roar from the entire crowd struck him with such vehemence that he was overcome by curiosity. Supposing himself to be strong enough to despise whatever he saw and to conquer it, he opened his eyes. He was struck in the soul by a wound graver than the gladiator in his body, whose fall had caused the roar. The shouting entered by his ears and forced open his eyes. Thereby it was the means of wounding and striking to the ground a mind still more bold than strong, and the weaker for the reason that he presumed on himself when he ought to have relied on you [God]. As soon as he saw the blood, he at once drank in savagery and did not turn away. His eyes were riveted. He imbibed madness. Without any awareness of what was happening to him, he found delight in the murderous contest and was inebriated by bloodthirsty pleasure. He was not now the person who had come in, but just one of the crowd which he had joined, and a true member of the group that had brought him. What should I add? He looked, he yelled, he was on fire, he took the madness home with him so that it urged him to return not only with those by whom he had originally been drawn there, but even more than them, taking others with him. Nevertheless, from this you delivered him by your most strong and merciful hand, and you taught him to put his confidence not in himself but in you (Isa. 57:13). But that was much later.[13]

As the passage shows, Alypius does not concede to the temptation little by little; he gives into it completely, violently. The completeness of the "conversion" reminds the reader of other examples of the same type of turning such as Peter's abrupt denial of Christ or Judas's betrayal of Christ in the Gospels. The passage embodies a pattern that is the exact inverse of the *Confessions* as a whole. But more is implied than simply a contrast to Augustine's own life. The reader is told at the end of the passage that Alypius eventually returns to God, and his defeat was a paradoxically necessary first step toward his conversion. He learned not to rely on himself; the triumph of a true conversion can come only when one has learned to rely on God. Alypius is not merely a random example whose pride in his own self-sufficiency is being crushed; he is also a type of the entire rationalistic and individualistic culture of classical antiquity, a culture whose insufficiency is also embedded in the movement of the passage. In classical Roman literature, rational self-discipline and moderation is the ideal. A self-reliant individual should be able to keep from intemperance by nature. In this passage, individual self-reliance and the sufficiency of pagan culture are both overwhelmed. The pattern of Augustine's conversion suggests where sufficiency is to be found: "Our heart is restless until it rests in you."[14]

Augustine's friendship with Alypius reaches a climax when Augustine is a means for Alypius's own conversion to Christianity. While earlier friendships led Augustine to bad deeds or, after the death of one friend, to deep despair and self-pity, the friendship between Augustine and Alypius is one that aids both in their journeys to God. Thus, Augustine in the *Confessions* has clearly and deliberately given his readers a Christianization of the ideal friendship that Cicero had presented for the classical world more than four centuries earlier.

One can also see the *Confessions* as a particularly sophisticated example of the genre of hagiography. The story of how a holy man or woman lived was, as we have seen, one of the most popular genres in the Middle Ages, and the pattern of the saint's conversion from a life of sin to a life of virtue was very often its core. A popular example of such a conversion story can be seen in the life of Saint Pelagia, as it is told in the important thirteenth-century collection called *The Golden Legend*:

> Pelagia was the first among the women in the city of Antioch—first in possessions and wealth, and in beauty of form. She was also ostentatious and vain in her bearing, and licentious in mind and body. One day she was promenading through the city with a maximum of display: one could see nothing on her but gold and silver and precious stones, and, as she passed, the air was filled with the aroma of a variety of perfumes. Ahead of her and following her went a retinue of youths and maidens, likewise richly adorned. She was seen by a holy father, Veronus, bishop of Heliopolis (now called Damietta),

who began to weep bitterly because the woman put more care into pleasing the world than he did into pleasing God. He threw himself face down on the pavement, beating his brow on the ground, and bedewed the earth with his tears, saying: "Almighty God, pardon me, a sinner, because the attention a courtesan has given to her adornment for one day exceeds the effort of my whole life. Do not let the outward show of a harlot put me to shame in the sight of your awesome majesty! She adorns herself for earthy eyes with the utmost care, whereas I, having resolved to please you, my immortal Lord, fail to do so because of my negligence." To those who were with him he said: "I say to you in truth, God will bring this woman forward against us at the Judgment, because to please her earthly lovers she has painted herself so meticulously, and we give so little care to pleasing our heavenly Spouse!"

Having said these and similar things, Veronus suddenly fell asleep and dreamed that while he was celebrating mass, a black, malodorous dove flew around him, but when he dismissed the catechumens, the dove disappeared. After mass it came back, and the bishop plunged it into a tub of water. The dove came out clean and shining white, and flew away so high that it could no longer be seen, and the bishop woke up.

Then one day he went to the church and preached. Pelagia was present and was so stricken with remorse that she sent a letter to him, in which she said: "To the holy bishop, disciple of Christ, Pelagia, disciple of the devil. If you prove truly to be a disciple of Christ, who, I have heard, came down from heaven for sinners, you will receive me, a sinner but a repentant one."

On the third day thereafter, she prepared and assembled everything she owned and gave it all to the poor. A few days later, without letting anyone know, she left by night and went to Mount Olivet, where she donned the robe of a hermit, moved into a small cell, and served God in strict abstinence. She was held in high esteem and was called Brother Pelagius.[15]

As this example shows, the saint's life was a genre that could provide both popular entertainment and moral instruction, combining a vivid, entertaining (and often sensational) surface with a clear and explicit moral. This combination helps explain why the conversion of prostitutes—a theme that goes back to the Bible—was such a popular story in the twelfth and thirteenth centuries.

The actual conversion scene in the *Confessions*, though more sophisticated and less sensational, contains essentially the same movement as the story of Pelagia And like Pelagia's conversion, there is certainly a sensational element to Augustine's: the temptations against which he has been fighting a losing battle since adolescence are quite specifically sexual. In one of the most frequently quoted passages of the *Confessions*, Augustine reveals the power that illicit sex had over him by describing a prayer that he used to recite: ". . . I prayed to you for chastity and said 'Grant me chastity and continence, but not yet.' I was afraid that you might hear my prayer quickly, and that you might too rapidly heal me of the disease of lust which I preferred to satisfy rather than surpress."[16] In an equally famous passage, he describes the moment of his conversion, the moment when "not yet" becomes "now":

> Rivers streamed from my eyes, a sacrifice acceptable to you (Ps. 50:19), and (though not in these words, yet in this sense) I repeatedly said to you: "How long, O Lord? How long, Lord, will you be angry to the uttermost? Do not be mindful of our old iniquities" (Ps. 6:4). For I felt my past to have a grip on me. It uttered wretched cries: "How long, how long is it to be? Tomorrow, tomorrow." "Why not now? Why not an end to my impure life in this very hour?"
>
> As I was saying this and weeping in the bitter agony of my heart, suddenly I heard a voice from the nearby house chanting as if it might be a boy or a girl (I do not know which), saying and repeating over and over again: "Pick up and read, pick up and read." At once my countenance changed, and I began to think intently whether there might be some sort of children's game in which such a chant is used. But I could not remember having heard of one. I checked the flood of tears and stood up. I interpreted it solely as a divine command to me to open the book and read the first chapter I might find. For I had heard how Antony happened to be present at the gospel reading, and took it as an admonition addressed to himself when the words were read: "Go, sell all you have, give to the poor, and you shall have treasure in heaven; and come, follow me" (Matt. 19:23). By such an inspired utterance he was immediately "converted to you" (Ps. 50:15). So I hurried back to the place where Alypius was sitting. There I had put down the book of the apostle [Paul] when I got up. I seized it, opened it and in silence read the first passage on which my eyes lit: "Not in riots and drunken parties, not in eroticism and indecencies, not in strife and rivalry, but put on the Lord Jesus Christ and make no provision for the flesh in its lusts" (Rom. 13:13–14).
>
> I neither wished nor needed to read further. At once, with the last words of this sentence, it was as if a light of relief from all anxiety flooded into my heart. All the shadows of doubt were dispelled.[17]

Both to show Augustine's method and his subsequent influence, this passage is of exceptional importance. The meaning of the passage once again makes sense only when the reader moves beneath the surface to the substance: Augustine presenting his conversion in the strongest possible terms, showing how radical and complete was the turning away from himself and toward God. Once this is understood, the surface narrative makes more sense. It is a means toward that end. Is it likely that events happened exactly as Augustine describes them? Did he really hear the voice? Did he really open up to the right page of Scripture? All the details that are likely to strain the credulity of the modem reader are in part the wrong questions, questions of surface and not substance. These dramatic details are presented in such striking and memorable form in order to bring out the important substantial meaning.

The influence of the previous passage, and implicitly the influence of the *Confessions* as a whole, can be seen by the frequency with which it is referred to in subsequent works. It is used in later literature as an icon—a definitive emblem—of radical conversion. In the fourteenth century Dante brings the language of Augustine's conversion into Canto 5 of the *Inferno*, the canto of the lustful. When Francesca da Rimini describes how it came about that she subjected reason to desire by committing adultery with her lover Paolo, making a radical turn from God toward herself, the language she uses is the language of conversion, almost identical to the language of Augustine. She too learns from a book; as Augustine finds the right passage in Scripture, she finds the right passage in the story of Lancelot. And crucially, like Augustine, she reads no further:

> One day, for pastime, we read of Lancelot, how love constrained him; we were alone, suspecting nothing. Several times that reading urged our eyes to meet and took the color from our faces, but one moment alone it was that overcame us. When we read how the longed-for smile was kissed by so great a lover, this one, who never shall be parted from me, kissed my mouth all trembling. A Gallehault [pander] was the book and he who wrote it; that day we read no farther in it.[18]

Thus, Dante's poem is enriched for readers who understand the implications of a deeply imbedded literary allusion. This kind of literary influence is central to medieval literary art and culture. It is a language similar to the "language" of visual arts of the Middle Ages, where there is also a code, a standard iconography, that remains constant for hundreds of years. Anyone seeing a picture of a person with a halo in a medieval painting would know it was a saint—anyone that is, who knows the code, who understands the conventional language where "halo" stands for "saint." It is such works as the *Confessions* that provide the iconography for subsequent writers. To a much greater extent than is true in modern literature, medieval poetic language is a language that is already charged with meaning, a language, as in the example from Dante above, where stories that seem to have such immediate local references, and which are so "realistic," are very often also charged with the literary energies of previous stories. Unless one reads "intertextually," meaning will be lost in the reading of medieval literature.

The proper interpretation of Scripture is a major concern of the *Confessions* as well as of *On Christian Teaching*. In an important section Augustine treats the relationship between the Old and New Testaments. Augustine had been misled by the interpretations of the Manichees, one of whose tenets was the absurdity of much of the Old Testament. It was not until Augustine met his great teacher Ambrose that he learned another, "correct" interpretation of the Old Testament:

> That "man of God" (2 Kgs. 1:9) received me like a father and expressed pleasure at my coming with a kindness most fitting in a bishop. I began to like

Martyrdom of Saint Sebastian. Panel painting, fourteenth century. Museo dell'Opera del Duomo, Florence. Saint Sebastian was tortured by being pierced with arrows. Just as arrows become the way of identifying Sebastian, other instruments of torture and martyrdom (or parts of the body that were tortured) become the well-known symbols of many other saints. In the way that Sebastian is represented, the artist is also clearly identifying his suffering with Christ's crucifixion.

him, at first indeed not as a teacher of the truth, for I had absolutely no confidence in your Church, but as a human being who was kind to me. I used enthusiastically to listen to him preaching to the people, not with the intention which I ought to have had, but as if testing out his oratorical skill to see whether it merited the reputation it enjoyed or whether his fluency was better or inferior than it was reported to be. I hung on his diction in rapt attention, but remained bored and contemptuous of the subject-matter. My pleasure was in the charm of his language. It was more learned than that of Faustus [a leader of the Manichees], but was less witty and entertaining, as far as the manner of his speaking went. But in content there could be no comparison. Through Manichee deceits Faustus wandered astray. Ambrose taught the sound doctrine of salvation. From sinners such as I was at that time, salvation is far distant. Nevertheless, gradually, though I did not realize it, I was drawing closer.

I was not interested in learning what he was talking about. My ears were only for his rhetorical technique; this empty concern was all that remained with me after I had lost any hope that a way to you might lie open for man. Nevertheless together with the words which I was enjoying, the subject matter, in which I was unconcerned, came to make an entry into my mind. I could not separate them. While I opened my heart in noting the eloquence with which he spoke, there also entered no less the truth which he affirmed, though only gradually. First what he said began to seem defensible, and I did not now think it impudent to assert the Catholic faith, which I had thought defenseless against Manichee critics. Above all, I heard first one, then another, then many difficult passages in the Old Testament scriptures figuratively interpreted, where I, by taking them literally, had found them to kill (2 Cor. 3:6). So after several passages in the Old Testament had been expounded spiritually, I now found fault with that despair of mine, caused by my belief that the law and the prophets could not be defended at all against the mockery of hostile critics.[19]

Here Augustine learns that the Old Testament must be explained figuratively rather than only literally, a process beginning with the perception that it cannot be understood in isolation from the New, as the Manichees had claimed. Events in the Old Testament are to be understood as prefigurations of events in the New, completing their meaning by their relationship to events in the New. Augustine, unlike Origen, never denies that these events have historical importance in themselves; nor does he reduce them simply to allegories (he states this explicitly in Book 17 of the *City of God*). Nevertheless, they do point forward to events in the New Testament. Thus, the Fall of Man in the Garden of Eden anticipates the temptations of Christ in the desert; Cain's killing of Abel is an anticipation of the betrayal of Christ; Abraham's sacrifice of Isaac likewise anticipates the sacrifice of Christ; David, as king and prophet in the Old Testament, anticipates the fullness of kingship and prophecy of Christ in the New.

In each of these Old Testament prefigurations, there is a similarity to the event prefigured, but equally important, there are differences. In the story of Abraham and Isaac, for example, Abraham, the father of the Hebrew people, is analogous to God the Father, as Isaac is analogous to Christ the Son. Since Abraham is not God, this is only an analogy. Another significant difference in the story of Abraham and Isaac as a prefiguration of the sacrifice of Christ is that at the last moment God intervenes and Isaac is not sacrificed; yet Christ does sacrifice himself for the sins of humanity. Insofar as the events in the Old Testament are similar to the events they prefigure, the history of salvation can be seen as a timeless whole: what is to come is in some sense present in what has been. Insofar as these events are different from what they prefigure, however, they show that the events of salvation history are in linear progression from the Old Testament to the New, from the creation to the last judgment.

Much of medieval biblical commentary consists of explaining the relationship between the Old and New Testaments. These commentaries are often sophisticated and subtle. As a way of thinking, their influence can be found everywhere. The structure of the great medieval play cycles of the fourteenth and fifteenth centuries, for example, is based on this figural relationship; the plays begin with creation and move toward the last judgment. Each play can be seen both as part of a linear progression and as microcosm of the whole of salvation history. Countless examples in medieval art likewise embody the relationship between Old and New. In the great stained glass program at Chartres, for example, the lancet windows under the south rose show the four evangelists, each seated on the shoulders of one of the Old Testament prophets. A visual counterpart to Bernard of Chartres's image of "dwarfs seated on the shoulders of giants" quoted at the beginning of this book, the evangelists are smaller, but they are also able to see farther.

In scope and size, *City of God* is the most important of Augustine's writings, and along with the *Confessions* the work that exerts the largest influence on the thought of the Middle Ages. On the surface, the *City of God* is a work about politics and history. However, nothing better illustrates the inadequacy of applying modern categories to medieval patterns of thought than this classification. The *City of God* was written in response to an event that shook the foundations of the world of Augustine's time: the looting of Rome by the Goths in 410, an unprecedented event that meant that the most visible sign of continuity and permanence in civilization was in chaos. Everyone naturally sought explanations for this catastrophe. The one advanced by pagan intellectuals of the time was that Rome was sacked because of the influence of the Christians; this would never have happened, they argued, had its citizens adhered to the pagan virtues and the pagan gods. Augustine, responding to this charge, turns it around; Rome fell not because it was too Christian, but because it was not Christian enough. Augustine sees what our age would classify as a political issue in moral terms, a classification that re-

Manuscript illumination of David and Christ. Winchester Bible, Winchester Cathedral, England. Twelfth century. The Beatus initials—that is, the first letter of the first word of the first psalm, Beatus vir or Happy is the man— are painted to suggest the relationship between David, who in the Middle Ages was believed to be the sole author of the Psalms, and Christ. In the loops of the first "B" the shepherd boy David rescues a sheep from a bear and a lion. In the second "B" Christ, the Good Shepherd, expels an evil spirit from a boy possessed by a demon (Mark 9:17), and Christ delivers souls from hell. The events in the life of David (1 Sam. 17:34, 37) prefigure events in the life of Christ, and also suggest that the Psalms can be read as prefigurations of events in the New Testament. (The Dean and Chapter of Winchester Cathedral)

mains true throughout the Middle Ages. Such an attitude is expressed as late as the Hundred Years War, for example, a millennium after Augustine: when the tide of battle began to turn against the English, many blamed the inability of their nobles to live up to the ideals of Christian knighthood.

Augustine argues throughout the *City of God* that if one looks closely at Roman society as it really is, one will see that it is not a commonwealth—that is, it is not a community acting with the interest of its citizens at heart. Seeing the city for what it is, one will see that change, flux, and devastation are its very nature:

If, then, the home, every man's haven in the storms of life, affords no solid security, what shall one say of the civil community? The bigger a city is, the fuller it is of legal battles, civil and criminal, and the more frequent are wild and bloody seditions or civil wars. Even when the frays are over, there is never any freedom from fear.[20]

Cities such as Rome, by nature unable to endure permanently, are at best means to an end. Our life on earth is a pilgrimage to the only lasting city, the heavenly Jerusalem. The earthly city can provide only a temporary home for men and women as they go about the business of journeying toward their permanent home, although working to make that temporary home a just and peaceful one is important. This is the dichotomy that structures the entire work: the City of God, the heavenly Jerusalem of love; or the human city, the earthly city of pride. Augustine borrows the idea of citizenship from Roman political theory to describe the inhabitants of the two cities. If one is content to be a citizen of the earthly city, then one can do no more than accept the transient pleasures which that city offers. By contrast, those who desire citizenship in the City of God understand that they are pilgrims on earth, and that the earthly city can only be used, never enjoyed for itself. Augustine expands on classical ideas of friendship and combines them with the Christian concept of love, arguing that all virtuous societies must be rooted in both of them. A just society must be a community of friends with a common goal, united in love.

Augustine examines the dichotomy of the two cities from a number of interrelated perspectives. Perhaps the most important of these is the way in which this same dichotomy operates within each of us:

I have already stated in the foregoing books that God chose to make a single individual the starting-point of all mankind, and that his purpose in this was that the human race should not merely be united in a society by natural likeness, but should also be bound together by a kind of tie of kinship to form a harmonious unity, linked together by the "bond of peace." And this race would not have been destined for death, in respect of its individual members, had not the first two human beings (of whom one was created from no one, and the other from him) incurred death as the reward of disobedience: and so heinous was their sin that man's nature suffered a change for the worse; and bondage to sin and inevitable death was the legacy handed on to their posterity.

Now the reign of death has held mankind in such utter subjection that they would all be driven headlong into that second death, which has no ending, as their well-deserved punishment, if some were not rescued from it by the undeserved grace of God. The result is that although there are many great peoples throughout the world, living under different customs in religion and morality and distinguished by a complex variety of languages, arms, and dress, it is still true that there have come into being only two main divisions, as we may call them, in human society: and we are justified in following the lead of our Scriptures and calling them two cities. There is, in fact, one city of men who choose to live by the standard of the flesh, another of those who choose to live by the standard of the spirit. The citizens of each of these desire their own kind of peace, and when they achieve their aim, that is the kind of peace in which they live. We need to examine first what is meant by living "by the rule of the flesh" and "by the rule of the spirit."[21]

The macrocosm of the state is a reflection of the microcosm of the individual. Political truth is linked to more fundamental truths: historical truth, since the fall of Adam and Eve, is ultimately responsible for the struggle between flesh and spirit in each person, which Augustine describes by means of the dichotomy between the human city and the City of God; and moral truth, since Adam's fall can be seen in each one of us, sons and daughters of Adam within whom the battle between flesh and spirit is being fought. Augustine sees the same fundamental reality governing areas that today belong to widely different realms of experience: history, psychology, morality.

For an understanding of what the very words *flesh* and *spirit* mean, one must read in a spiritual, that is to say allegorical, way. Augustine goes on to define the meaning of the word *flesh* using direct textual criticism, by analyzing Paul's letter to the Galatians 5:19–21. A consideration of Paul's letter enables us to answer the question of what is meant by "living by the rule of the flesh." For among "the works of the flesh" that he said were obvious, and which he listed and condemned, we find not only those concerned with sensual pleasure, such as fornication, impurity, lust, drunkenness, and drunken orgies, but also those that show faults of the mind, which have nothing to do with sensual indulgence.

> For anyone can see that devotion to idols, sorcery, enmity, quarrelsomeness, jealousy, animosity, party intrigue, envy—all these are faults of the mind, not of the body. Indeed, it may happen that a man refrains from sensual indulgence because of devotion to an idol, or because of the erroneous teaching of some sect; and yet even then, though such a man seems to restrain and suppress his carnal desires, he is convicted, on the authority of the apostle, of living by the rule of the flesh; and it is the very fact of his abstention from fleshly indulgence that proves that he is engaged in "the works of the flesh."[22]

It is a matter of seeing correctly, which for Augustine means seeing that God is the end toward which all things should move:

> I have already said that two cities, different and mutually opposed, owe their existence to the fact that some men live by the standard of the flesh, others by the standard of the spirit. It can now be seen that we may also put it in this way: that some live by man's standard, others by God's. St. Paul puts it very plainly when he says to the Corinthians, "For since there is jealousy and

quarrelling among you, are you not of the flesh, following human standards in your behaviour?" Therefore, to behave according to human standards is the same as to be "of the flesh," because by "the flesh," a part of man, man himself is meant.[23]

There are also close connections in the *City of God* with Augustine's own pilgrimage from himself to God, which is the subject of the *Confessions*. Pilgrimage suggests the relationship that should exist between the City of God, which is above, and the life that we lead here below. Augustine talks of this relationship in describing the "historical" origins of the two cities, moving from Adam's fall to the story of Cain and Abel:

> Scripture tells us that Cain founded a city, whereas Abel, as a pilgrim, did not found one. For the City of the saints is up above, although it produces citizens here below, and in their persons the City is on pilgrimage until the time of its kingdom comes. At that time it will assemble all those citizens as they rise again in their bodies; and then they will be given the promised kingdom, where with their Prince, "the king of ages," they will reign, world without end.[24]

Throughout subsequent history, followers of Cain are all those who think the human city is permanent, all those who live according to the flesh. Followers of Abel are those pilgrims who recognize, in the words of the late-fourteenth-century English poet, Geoffrey Chaucer, that "Here is no home, here is but wildernesse."

Augustine's influence on political theory in the Middle Ages is enormous. Deeply influenced by Paul, he argues that the subjugation of humans to other humans, including the formation of government itself, is a result of sin:

> Now, as our Lord above says, "Everyone who commits sin is sin's slave," (John 8:34) and that is why, though many devout men are slaves to unrighteous masters, yet the masters they serve are not themselves free men; "for when a man is conquered by another he is also bound as a slave to his conqueror" (2 Pet. 2:19). And obviously it is a happier lot to be slave to a human being than to a lust; and, in fact, the most pitiless domination that devastates the hearts of men, is that exercised by this very lust for domination, to mention no others. However, in that order of peace in which men are subordinate to other men, humility is as salutary for the servants as pride is harmful to the masters. And yet by nature, in the condition in which God created man, no man is the slave either of man or of sin. But it remains true that slavery as a punishment is also ordained by that law which enjoins the preservation of the order of nature, and forbids its disturbance; in fact, if nothing had been done to contravene that law, there would have been nothing to require the discipline of slavery as a punishment.[25]

Humans would have no need for government had it not been for the Fall; government is thus a kind of punishment. This becomes more explicit when Au-

gustine talks of the rule of the wicked, as in the following passage on the in-
famous Emperor Nero:

> Yet even to men like this the power of domination is not given except by the
> providence of God, when he decides that man's condition deserves such mas-
> ters. God's statement on this point is clear, when the divine Wisdom says, "It
> is through me that kings rule, and through me that tyrants possess the land."[26]

This generally negative attitude toward the state became especially influential in the eleventh century when the papacy asserted itself against the major secular power of the time. Papal apologists argued for the inherent superiority of the Church over the state on the basis that the state is a result of
sin while the Church on earth is a representation of the heavenly city to which
all should aspire. Only with the revival of Aristotle in the thirteenth century
did this view face a serious philosophical challenge. But, however imperfect,
government is also necessary for Augustine. Civic institutions are what keep
people from being either too aggressive and public, or too passive and private.

Augustine's theory of history derives in large part from his interpretation of Scripture. Although he saw all human history as part of the universal
story of salvation, a continuum from creation to the last judgment, he saw divisions within this story, seven discrete ages of history:

> Now if the epochs of history are reckoned as "days," following the apparent
> temporal scheme of Scripture, this Sabbath period will emerge more clearly
> as the seventh of those epochs. The first "day" is the first period, from Adam
> to the Flood; the second from the Flood to Abraham. Those correspond not
> by equality in the passage of time, but in respect of the number of genera-
> tions, for there are found to be ten generations in each of those periods.
>
> From that time, in the scheme of the evangelist Matthew, there are three
> epochs, which take us down to the coming of Christ; one from Abraham to
> David, a second from David to the Exile in Babylon, and the third extending
> to the coming of Christ in the flesh. Thus we have a total of five periods. We
> are now in the sixth epoch, but that cannot be measured by the number of
> generations, because it is said, "It is not for you to know the dates: the Fa-
> ther has decided those by his own authority." After this present age God will
> rest, as it were, on the seventh day, and he will cause us, who are the seventh
> day, to find our rest in him.[27]

The implications of this way of looking at history are extremely far reaching.
Most obviously, it reinforces in yet another way the importance of the Bible
as a document central to medieval thought and Augustine as one of its definitive interpreters, providing as it does the pattern for all human history. Second, by linking the days of creation to the ages of history, Augustine shows
in this passage that God's direct action in history is present throughout time,
as well as in its beginnings at creation. The relationship between the seven
days of creation and the seven ages of history was in fact frequently and sys-

tematically elaborated by medieval thinkers, including as representative examples Isidore of Seville at the beginning of the seventh century, the Venerable Bede in the eighth, and Bonaventure in the thirteenth. It was further elaborated by an analogy between the seven ages of history and the seven ages (we would now call them stages) of an individual life that range from birth to death, thus showing that there is a relationship between microcosm and macrocosm and that individual human lives recapitulate the whole of human history. Third, according to this scheme, Christians live in an old world. Humans are now living in the sixth epoch, which began with the coming of Christ at the Incarnation. The second coming of Christ at the last judgment will usher in the seventh and last age, the age of rest. As the passage clearly indicates, Augustine himself denies that it is possible to know how long the present age will endure, believing that attempts to calculate the precise dates of the end are misdirected and sinful.

Nevertheless, the belief in a world that is old and about to pass away with the second coming of Christ is always implicit in medieval thought, emerging explicitly from time to time especially at moments of catastrophe, upheaval, and unrest. Reflection on the chaos of such times caused people to believe that the signs of the end of the world and the second coming, thought to be predicted in the book of Revelation, were being fulfilled in the present, including the all-out conflict between the forces of good and evil, the appearance of the Antichrist, and the appearance of various beasts such as the one described in Rev. 11:7. This sense of imminence, or Apocalypticism, as it is called, was not necessarily the province of radical and extreme thinkers. From the fifth century to the end of the Middle Ages and beyond, apocalyptic expectations were an important element in European religious and political life; in literature these expectations influenced such diverse but "orthodox" works as the *Song of Roland*, Dante's *Divine Comedy*, and *Piers Plowman*. More radical reformers at the end of the Middle Ages (and throughout the Reformation as well) tended by contrast to believe in millenarianism. Interpreting the text of Rev. 20:1–10, which refers to a period of a thousand years, they posited the establishment of a thousand-year kingdom of peace, plenty, and goodness on earth that would precede the end. Augustine had argued especially vigorously against millennial expectations, asserting that Rev. 20:1–10 did not refer to a literal thousand-year period, but rather symbolized the establishment of Christ's Church on earth from Pentecost to the second coming.

Medieval thought and institutions did not spring from the earth fully developed but emerged from the achievements and failures of classical civilization, the biblical world, and the first centuries of Christianity. In Part 1, we have laid the groundwork—giving readers the prerequisites for studying the Middle Ages seriously. Without this groundwork, texts, institutions, and events in the Middle Ages will often appear to be unintelligible. Now we are ready to examine those centuries that we call medieval.

PART 2

THE EARLY
MIDDLE AGES

EUROPE IN THE
EARLY MIDDLE AGES

- - - - Indicates Empire of Charlemagne c.800

Names of Germanic tribes indicate
area of permanent settlement.

CASPIAN SEA

BLACK SEA

BYZANTINE EMPIRE

Constantinople

CYPRUS

CRETE

SEA

•Damascus
•Nazareth

Jerusalem

•Alexandria

EGYPT

RED SEA

•Mecca

CHAPTER 5

THE TRANSITION FROM
ANCIENT TO MEDIEVAL

The first part of the book examined the Judaeo-Christian and Greco-Roman sources of medieval civilization and the beginnings of their contact and interaction, which took place within the context of the Roman Empire. However, only forty-six years after the death of Augustine, the Roman Empire no longer had an emperor in the West, and the emerging Latin-Christian culture was forced to develop without its strong institutional and psychological base. Furthermore, other cultural and social traditions began to interact with this Latin-Christian culture, especially those of the Germanic invaders but also those of the Celtic peoples, in particular the Irish. The transition from ancient Rome to the Middle Ages is one of the most important chapters in the development of Western civilization.

In his monumental work *The Decline and Fall of the Roman Empire* (1776), Edward Gibbon declared that the second century C.E. was the best time to have been alive in all of history. Gibbon may have exaggerated, but there surely is much to support his position. An empire relatively free of foreign attack or domestic crises stretched from the wall of Hadrian—roughly the border between England and Scotland—to the Persian Gulf, encompassing the entire Mediterranean and parts of three continents. To those alive at the time, it may well have seemed that this huge empire and its way of life would last forever. Yet, beginning in 180, the Empire suffered through a century of political instability; and although in the next century the powerful emperors Diocletian (r.284–305) and Constantine (r.312–337) carried out major reforms that probably prolonged its life, they failed to return the Empire to its unchallenged military position or its earlier quality of life. Following the death of Constantine, the story of the Empire in the West is one of almost constant defensive war and political disintegration, until in 476 its last emperor was deposed almost without notice or immediate impact.

The second century, Gibbon's age of prosperity and stability, was not without its unresolved problems. One of them was the method of imperial succession. In the first eighty years of that century, the emperors were all hand-picked successors of their sonless predecessors, all competent administrators and generals. However, Marcus Aurelius (d.180) chose to leave the Empire to his incompetent son Commodus, whose excesses led to his assassination and ushered in a century of political instability, highlighted by frequent military coups. Moreover, Marcus Aurelius was forced to fight Germanic invaders along the Danube frontier; and though he was essentially successful, the Germans continued to exert pressure along that hard-to-defend northwestern border of the Empire until their large-scale migrations in the fourth century. A plague during Marcus Aurelius's reign had a significant impact on agriculture, trade, and the army. The resulting shortage of soldiers offered a temptation to the Germanic tribes to raid the Empire across the Rhine-Danube frontier, which was almost irresistable when combined with the fact that the Roman generals and their armies frequently left border posts to march on Rome and claim the imperial title. In fact, Rome never solved the problems brought about by a decline in population; and the Empire's eventual collapse is to a significant degree a result of Rome no longer having a population adequate to make its various economic and political systems work.

A century after Marcus Aurelius the Empire appeared to enter a new period of stability under Diocletian, a peasant who rose to power through the army. In his twenty-one-year reign, he was able to renew and reorder the Roman state. Because of the shortage of soldiers and the threat of generals desiring the imperial title, the army was reorganized; non-Roman citizens, including many Germans in the West, soon became its main element. The Empire was divided into two administrative parts, with Diocletian and a "junior emperor" administering each of the two halves. To ensure stability and production of necessary products, the emperor forced people to remain fixed in their professions and to train their children to succeed them; many farmers were required to remain on the land even if they could not make enough money to live. The Empire entered a new period in other ways as well: court ceremonies became more elaborate, and the emperor became a more remote figure, surrounded by eunuchs from the East. When he appeared in public, he wore jewel-encrusted clothes and shoes. Toward the end of his reign, Diocletian became convinced that Christianity was a serious obstacle to the consolidation of the Empire, and he carried out the great persecution described in Chapter 3.

With the retirement of Diocletian in 305 came a struggle to determine his successor. In the West, Constantine became emperor after the Battle of Milvian Bridge in 312. Although best known for his conversion to Christianity, he is also an important figure in the political history of the Empire, retaining Diocletian's reforms and making further changes in the structure of the army. He also decided to build a splendid new city in the East in his own honor.

Choosing the site of the old Greek city of Byzantium, located on a narrow strait connecting the Mediterranean and the Black Seas, he erected Constantinople. By the end of the century, it had become the administrative capital of the Empire in the East, a new and a Christian Rome.

After the death of Constantine, there were no long periods of peace or stability in the Western part of the Empire. It was invaded almost continuously, especially by the Germans. One of the most significant events of the fourth century was the showdown between the Germanic Goths and the imperial forces at Adrianople in modern Bulgaria in 378. The Emperor Valens was killed, and after the battle the Goths and later other Germanic tribes were pretty much able to live and loot within the borders of the Empire at will.

From Adrianople until the extinction of the Western part of the Empire in 476, the German invasions and the brief but important invasion by the Huns under their brilliant leader Attila dominate imperial history. During this period, both the Goths and the Vandals sacked the city of Rome; Western emperors were often little more than puppets of German generals; violence and rapine were practiced by both German and Roman armies; and the Germans hired by Rome to fight other Germans often turned against their employers. It was a military, political, economic, and religious (the Germans were either Arian Christians or pagans) crisis that the Empire could not solve. By the end of the fifth century, the Roman Empire existed only as an idea and a memory in the West, although the political events of the fifth century had almost no direct effect on the culture of the Roman Empire. And although the sixth-century emperor in Constantinople, Justinian (r.527–565), tried to reconstitute the Roman Empire, gaining control of much of the western Mediterranean, his conquests were neither complete nor permanent. Byzantine power in the West eroded steadily after his death, and by 754 Byzantine territory in the West consisted only of parts of southern Italy and Sicily. Despite the fact that Byzantium retained a foothold in Italy until 1071, it played only a nominal role in the politics of the West after the mid-eighth century.

However, this does not mean that Byzantine civilization ceased to be important to the West culturally. In the tenth century, a Byzantine princess was regent for her son, the Holy Roman Emperor Otto III; and Byzantine craftsmen were major contributors to the cultural revival there known as the Ottonian Renaissance. Eleventh- and twelfth-century Byzantine artists executed magnificent mosaics in Sicily and Venice. Much thirteenth-century Italian painting is correctly described as Byzantine. Latin scholars working with Byzantine manuscripts in Constantinople in the mid-thirteenth century translated the complete works of Aristotle. These influences of East upon West are representative of an almost continuous interaction and cross-fertilization between Byzantine East and Latin West.

The Byzantine Empire and the West were neighbors. In the earliest medieval centuries, Constantinople exercised a great deal of political influence on the development of the West, especially in Italy. With the threat of Islam and the re-emergence of a Western Empire under Charlemagne, the two halves of the old Roman Empire were less political rivals than neighbors whose developments led them in different directions. However, the Western crusading movement, strongest from the end of the eleventh until the middle of the thirteenth century, created a new political dynamic between East and West because the Holy Land had been Byzantine territory until the Muslims conquered it in the seventh century. Of most direct concern here is the Fourth Crusade's attack on and conquest of Constantinople in 1204, which put a Latin-speaking emperor on the throne there until 1261.

Tensions between Greek- and Latin-speaking Christians were apparent at least as early as the fourth century. With the disintegration of the Roman Empire, Greek Christians in the Byzantine Empire and Latin Christians in the West developed increasingly different theologies and practices. For example, Augustine, writing in Latin, had virtually no influence on the development of Christianity in the East, while he was *the* most important shaper of Western Christian thought. Despite differences and even temporary schisms between East and West, the two main bodies of Christians remained in communion until 1054. Although there were important efforts to reconcile these two bodies of Christians, all of them failed to achieve permanent reunion.

From the previous discussion of the Byzantine Empire in its relationship with the West, one should not infer that the Empire centered in Constantinople is historically important primarily because of its influence on the West. Although Byzantine studies in Western Europe and America is a small and highly specialized field and relatively few works written in the Byzantine Empire are available in English translation, this civilization, which flourished for centuries and gave a continuous history to the concept of the Roman Empire until the Turks conquered Constantinople in 1453, is an important one in its own right. The popular view that it produced impressive but static works of art and a corrupt and highly bureaucratic government is both inaccurate and unfair. One of the tasks of medievalists of the next generation is to paint a broader picture of medieval Christian civilization that includes both its Greek- and Latin-speaking parts.

Before returning to our focus on Western Europe, it is necessary to remind ourselves that the Roman Empire was not a European empire but, rather, one situated around the Mediterranean. When most Westerners look at a map of that part of the world today, what they see is Western Europe, bounded on the east by the old Soviet Empire and on the south by the Mediterranean. The coast of North Africa is very different and "foreign" civilization. Although there was something of a linguistic split between the Greek East and the Latin West, the Mediterranean bound together people living on three continents into one empire and to a great extent one culture. It is only a bit of an oversimplification to suggest that how "Roman" a person was could best be determined by figuring the distance he or she lived from the Mediterranean. Hence, Saint Augustine, who was born in Africa just a few miles from the Mediterranean coast, was thoroughly Roman. Many more substantial remnants of Roman civilization survive today in Libya and Lebanon and Turkey than in northern France and England. Thus, one of the main story lines that emerges out of the collapse of Roman authority over the entire Mediterranean is how Europe, especially Western Europe, became a cultural and religious "unit" in which York and Antwerp and Marseille and Rome had more in common with each other than with Carthage and Constantinople. It is fair to say that one of the achievements of the Middle Ages was the creation of Europe.

GERMANIC CULTURE AND SOCIETY IN THE WEST

Many Germanic tribes appear and disappear in the records of their movement into the Roman Empire; the most important are those that were the successors of the Romans as the rulers in the West. In the fifth century, the Vandals, who were Arian Christians, occupied Latin-speaking North Africa and came in constant conflict with its Catholic population. One should recall that Augustine's city of Hippo was under Vandal attack at the time of his death in 430. The Byzantine Emperor Justinian defeated the Vandals, his first military campaign in the West. However, Byzantine rule lasted only about a century. By 700, the armies of Islam had dispossessed the Eastern Empire of North Africa; this conquest proved to be permanent, bringing it into a cultural and religious sphere quite different from its earlier Roman-Christian heritage.

Most of the Iberian Peninsula came under the control of the Visigoths, Arian Christians who became Catholic only in 587, probably for strategic rather than purely religious reasons. Despite a reasonably high level of prosperity and cultural development in the seventh century, the kingdom fell quite rapidly to Muslim invaders from across the Mediterranean in 711–13. For three hundred years, all but small, isolated parts of the peninsula were under Muslim rule. In the eleventh century, these surviving Christian regions took the offensive against Islam. This so-called *Reconquista* was successful in wresting most of the peninsula away from the Muslims within a century, although it was completed only with the conquest of Granada, the last Muslim stronghold, in 1492.

The Romans abandoned Britain, on the periphery of the Empire, in 410 when all available soldiers were needed closer to its heart. The island's Roman-Christian heritage was damaged and to a large extent driven underground by a series of invasions, which had already begun before Roman withdrawal. Angles, Saxons, and Jutes (pagan Germanic tribes from the southern shore of the North Sea) raided and began to settle in England, eventually conquering all but the western and northern extremities of Britain. The Anglo-Saxons did not subdue the romanized Celtic Christian population easily, however. About 500, a Celtic military victory slowed the Anglo-Saxon conquest of Britain by perhaps as much as fifty years. Centuries later, stories of one of the Celtic leaders traditionally called King Arthur, mixed with Celtic folklore, became a primary source for authors of the romance (see Chapter 9). The Anglo-Saxons did eventually defeat the Celtic Britons, and many of them fled to Cornwall and Wales, where Christianity and their Celtic heritage and language survived. Modern Welsh is a direct descendant of the language of these Britons.

Many Germans beginning in the third century entered the Roman Empire as employees—soldiers hired to defend imperial borders against other Germans. Thus, there were many Romanized Germans in the Empire in late antiquity. Other Germans entered as invaders; for example, many came in 406 when the Rhine River froze, making entry into Roman territory easy. The Franks originally entered the Empire in the pay of Rome, and came to control the northern part of Gaul before 500. By the middle of the sixth century, they had wrested control of southwestern Gaul from the Visigoths and southeastern Gaul from the Burgundians, thus ruling what is now roughly France plus Germany west of the Rhine. The Franks were pagan until the baptism of their able King Clovis (d.511) as a Catholic. Although the Frankish kingdom suffered from interminable civil wars, often splitting into virtually independent kingdoms upon the death of a king, the dynasty of Clovis, the Merovingian dynasty, ruled at least in name until 751. From the mid-seventh century on, however, Merovingian kings were almost without exception feeble in both mind and body, and the rule of the kingdom soon passed de facto to the family that had made itself the hereditary mayors of the palace, later called the Carolingians. It was the Carolingian mayor of the palace, Charles Martel, who defeated the Muslims at the important battle of Tours/Poitiers in 732–733; his son Pepin (whose son was Charlemagne), with papal approval, took the crown from the Merovingians in 751.

Odoacer, the German general who deposed the last Roman emperor in Italy in 476, belonged to a small tribe. In 493, he was defeated in battle by Theodoric the Ostrogoth (d.526), who, despite his Arian Christianity, had the support of the Catholic emperors in Constantinople. Theodoric's court was centered in Ravenna, the last imperial capital in the West, and contained men of great genius, including Boethius and Cassiodorus. However, Ostrogothic rule in Italy did not long survive Theodoric; Justinian, investing enormous resources in the enterprise, conquered Italy in a series of destructive wars that severely damaged its central economic and cultural position in the world. Despite Justinian's efforts, Byzantine rule lasted no longer than had the Ostrogothic; beginning in 568, three years after his death, the Arian Lombards invaded Italy from the North and quickly captured virtually all of northern and central Italy save Ravenna and Rome. These Lombards eventually became Catholic while remaining political enemies of both the pope and the Byzantine Empire; they ruled most of Italy until 774, when Charlemagne took their iron crown for himself.

Not all Germans moved into the Roman Empire. To the east of the Rhine were Germanic peoples such as the Saxons and the Bavarians. They remained pagan until the eighth century when missionary activity in the first half of the century and Charlemagne's armies in the second brought Christianity and the culture that accompanied it. To the north, in Scandinavia, were other Germanic peoples, who remained pagan until some of them, known to us as Vikings, invaded and settled in Britain and the Frankish kingdom, where they accepted Christianity in the ninth and tenth centuries. Shortly thereafter, missionaries brought Christianity to the inhabitants of Scandinavia itself.

The culture and society of the Germans and the ideas and institutions they brought with them into the Roman Empire are in some ways more difficult to describe with precision than the process of migration. Historians are hampered by the fact that Germanic cultures were not written cultures until they came into contact with the Roman world, and especially with Christianity. Thus, the earliest written records about the Germans come from Roman authors. In the second century C.E., the great Roman historian Tacitus described their customs. Although he was more interested in teaching his own society moral lessons than objectively describing German customs and although he perceived the Germans in Roman terms, Tacitus's descriptions are nonetheless useful. Here his comments describe the military character of Germanic society:

> To abandon your shield is the basest of crimes; nor may a man thus disgraced be present at the sacred rites, or enter their council; many, indeed, after escaping from battle, have ended their infamy with the halter.[1]

> They transact no public or private business without being armed. It is not, however, usual for anyone to wear arms till the state [a Roman concept that Tacitus here applies to a very different culture] has recognized his power to use them. Then in the presence of the council, one of the chiefs, or the young man's father, or some kinsman, equips him with a shield and a spear.[2]

Tacitus also explains the personal relationship between a chieftain and his warriors:

> When they go into battle, it is a disgrace for a chief to be surpassed in valor, a disgrace for his followers not to equal the valor of the chief. And it is an infamy and a reproach for life to have survived the chief, and returned from the field. To defend, to protect him, to ascribe one's own brave deeds to his renown is the height of loyalty. The chief fights for victory; his vassals fight for their chief.[3]

This martial quality and sense of personal loyalty between chief and vassal became important elements of medieval society, elements vital to a proper understanding of such important literary works as *Beowulf* and the *Song of Roland* and to the kinds of relationships usually described as feudal.

The military character of Germanic society posed the same difficult problem of cultural assimilation that the conversion of Constantine had earlier, for Christianity in its origins was essentially pacifist. As late as the fourth century the most popular saints included men who refused to fight in the army or who left the military in order to pursue lives of holiness, for example, Saint Sebastian and Saint Martin of Tours. Although Ambrose condoned violence and Augustine developed a theory of the just war, the Church hardly glorified violence, let alone to the extent that the Germans did. When Germans such as Clovis accepted Christianity, they saw Christ not as the Prince of Peace but as a warrior god; that is, they accepted him in terms they understood and interpreted his life and teachings in ways seemingly different from their original intent. Any time two different sets of values are brought together in a society, both are ultimately changed. During the time of the Germanic kingdoms, legends of warrior saints such as Saint George were created. We can thus speak of the "germanization" of Christianity as well as of the Christianization of the Germans. Though the Church came to tolerate and sometimes even encourage violence, as late as the tenth and eleventh centuries it also organized peace movements to try to diminish the violence within Europe. Only in the twelfth century, the heyday of the Crusades, did the acceptance and even glorification of violence become an integral part of the Catholic tradition.

Germanic law differed in many essentials from Roman law. In particular, Germanic law was personal while Roman law was territorial. A Lombard was judged by Lombard law no matter where he was—*who* a person was determined the law that governed him. Any person within the boundaries of the Roman Empire was subject to Roman law no matter what ethnic group he belonged to—*where* a person was determined what law governed him. The surviving law codes of the Germans—the codification and publication of law was itself a Roman borrowing, as was the Latin in which they were written—contain elements of both personality and territoriality, but ultimately the Roman principle won out.

The idea of the state was an integral part of Roman law and Roman political philosophy; the Germans however had no conception of the state. A Germanic king did not perceive himself as the ruler of all the people within a clearly defined territory but rather as the leader of a group of free warriors. The land a king controlled was treated as personal property and usually divided among his male heirs. It was centuries before the Roman idea of the state fully replaced the Germanic idea of kingship.

Germanic law allowed bloodfeuds: it permitted an injured family to seek revenge against the offender's family. Obviously, this was a custom that led to a great deal of violence, often escalating to become a serious problem of tribal unity and even survival. To mitigate this problem, the Germanic tribes, borrowing from the Roman system of fining the one guilty of a crime, developed the *wergild*, the money value of a person that was to be paid wholly or in part to the injured family, depending on the nature of the crime. The following selections from Rothair's Edict of 643, the earliest surviving laws of the Lombards, illustrate the use of the *wergild* in conjunction with the Roman system of fines:

> **49.** On cutting off noses. He who cuts off another man's nose shall pay half of that one's wergild as composition.
>
> **50.** On cutting off lips. He who cuts off another man's lip shall pay sixteen soldi as composition [compensation]. And if one, two or three teeth are thereby exposed, he shall pay twenty soldi as composition.[4]

Not every person's *wergild* was the same, as is clear from a list of penalties for murder in the early sixth-century Burgundian Code:

> Then the guilty party shall be compelled to pay to the relatives of the person killed half his wergild according to the status of the person: that is, if he shall have killed a noble of the highest class, we decree that the payment be set at one hundred fifty soldi, i.e., half his wergild; if a person of the middle class, one hundred soldi; if a person of the lowest class, seventy-five soldi.[5]

Germanic law was localized, putting much of the responsibility for justice on small groups—the family and the neighborhood in particular—to report crimes and to swear to a person's innocence. Out of this Germanic sense of local responsibility eventually come both the grand jury, a body to inquire and gather evidence, and the trial jury, a body to determine innocence and guilt. Both developed in medieval England.

On occasion, Germanic law called for trial by combat to determine guilt, or even trial by ordeal; for example, a suspect's guilt or innocence would be determined by requiring the suspect to hold a bar of red-hot iron until it burned the hand. If the burn healed, the person was innocent; if it did not, the person was guilty. These primitive methods of judgment, which were understood to be God's judgment, survived in some parts of Europe until the thirteenth century, a time when Roman law was once again being studied. In literature, one finds trial by combat in the twelfth-century *Song of Roland*.

When the Germans entered the Empire, they brought not only their political and social institutions but also their languages and cultures. In areas where Roman influence remained the greatest—modern Italy, France, and Spain, for example—vernacular languages developed from Latin, although they were not unaffected by Germanic tongues. But in England, Germany, and Scandinavia the vernacular languages were and indeed still are Germanic. Thus, the very medium of thought and expression in a large part of Europe in the Middle Ages came from the Germans. In art, Germanic elements of style, especially the tendency toward abstraction, exerted a strong influence throughout the Middle Ages, the abstract quality of early medieval art contrasting with the more realistic art of the Roman Empire. The Germanic style, which is evident in such striking interlace designs as the treasure from the Anglo-Saxon Sutton Hoo burial ship, later blended with elements from the Celtic and classical traditions to produce much of the great manuscript illumination and sculpture of the Middle Ages. Stories from the heroic Germanic past, its gods and heroes, are another important transmission. These stories too blended with other traditions, as in the fruitful synthesis of pagan and Christian in Old English poetry, seen in such poems as *Beowulf,* "The Dream of the Rood," "The Wanderer," and "The Seafarer." Stories from Germanic mythology also became incorporated into such Christian literary forms as saints' lives. Even the modern English names for the days of the week come from Germanic mythology.

The Germanic peoples looked to their past as preserved in oral tradition to find a model for the way things should be. They believed that law, for example, had been perfect in their past but was obscure and corrupt in the present. Thus, good law was to be discovered, not made. Although they sometimes allowed for new laws to be created by inventing a past for them, it was not until the revival of Roman law in the twelfth and thirteenth centuries that new laws could consciously be legislated. The idea that one had to find truth by looking to the past and stripping away modern accretions found resonances in both the Christian and classical traditions, in which people looked back to the Garden of Eden or the Golden Age. These three traditions thus reinforced one another in the Middle Ages. The decline of the world since the golden days is a concept of singular importance in medieval literature and historiography.

The collapse of the Roman Empire in the West ushered in a period of violence and chaos, a decline of culture and literacy, as well as other woes. The following text from a letter dated 473 of Sidonius Apollinaris, a Roman living in Gaul, suggests the experience of the Germanic invasions:

> There is a rumor that the Goths have moved their camp into Roman soil; we luckless Arvernians are always the gateway to such incursions, for we kindle our enemies' hatred in a special degree; the reason is, that their failure so far to make the channel of the Loire the boundary of their territories between the Atlantic and the Rhone is due, with Christ's help, solely to the barrier which we interpose. As for the surrounding country, its whole length and breadth has long since been swallowed up by the insatiate aggression of that threatening power. But we have little confidence that our reckless and dangerous courage will be supported by our hideously charred walls, our palisades of rotting stakes, our battlements worn by the breasts of many a sentinel; our only comfort is in the aid of the Rogations [prayers for deliverance said in procession] which we introduced on your advice.[6]

Sidonius's despair of victory without supernatural intervention is eloquent testimony to the effect of the invasions on the Roman population. However, we also need to remember that the Romans were hardly a gentle and peaceable folk, either in their military campaigns or in the punishment of their own citizens—martyrdom stories of Christians by Roman governors providing examples of the latter.

Perhaps the most famous statement of political and cultural decline following the destruction of the Roman Empire in the West comes from the late sixth-century historian Gregory of Tours, himself of Roman lineage:

> A great many things keep happening, some of them good, some of them bad. The inhabitants of different countries keep quarreling fiercely with each other and kings go on losing their temper in the most furious way. Our churches are attacked by heretics and then protected by the Catholics; the faith of Christ burns bright in many men, but it remains lukewarm in others; no sooner are the church-buildings endowed by the faithful than they are stripped bare again by those who have no faith. However, no writer has come to the fore who has been sufficiently skilled in setting things down in an orderly fashion to be able to describe these events in prose or verse. In fact in the towns of Gaul the writing of literature has declined to the point where it has virtually disappeared altogether. Many people have complained about this, not once but time and time again. "What a poor period this is!" they have been heard to say. "If among all our people there is not one man to be found who can write a book about what is happening today, the pursuit of letters is really dead in us!" I have often thought about these complaints and others like them. I have written this work to keep alive the memory of those dead and gone, and to bring them to the notice of future generations. My style is not very polished, and I have had to devote much of my space to the quarrels between the wicked and the righteous.[7]

Gregory vividly describes one example of the cruelty of the age, in this case inflicted upon the Franks by another Germanic tribe called the Thuringians:

> Hostages were exchanged and our Franks were ready to make peace with them. The Thuringians murdered the hostages in all sorts of different ways. They attacked our fellow-countrymen and stole their possessions. They hung our young men up to die in the trees by the muscles of their thighs. They put more than two hundred of our young women to death in the most barbarous way: they tied their arms round the necks of their horses, stampeded these animals in all directions by prodding them with goads, and so tore the girls to pieces; or else they stretched them out over the ruts of their roads, attached their arms and legs to the ground with stakes, and then drove heavily-laden carts over them again and again, until their bones were all broken and their bodies could be thrown out for the dogs and birds to feed on.[8]

As stark as the story of violence and destruction is, it is equally important to realize that the Germanic kings were not seeking to destroy Roman civilization so much as to make it their own. Of course their perception of the

Roman tradition was through Germanic eyes; nevertheless, much of the change that took place with the coming of the Germans was not intended to be destructive. For example, Clovis, the first Christian king of the Franks, sought to legitimize his authority by receiving Roman titles from the emperor in Constantinople and imitating imperial largesse:

> Letters reached Clovis from the Emperor Anastasius [of Constantinople] to confer the consulate on him. In St. Martin's church he stood clad in a purple tunic [the imperial color] and the military mantle, and he crowned himself with a diadem. He then rode out on his horse and with his own hand showered gold and silver coins among the people present all the way from the doorway of St. Martin's church to Tours cathedral. From that day on he was called Consul or Augustus.[9]

As early as the sixth century, the Merovingians created a myth that traced the origins of the Franks back to Troy, giving themselves a common and thus equal ancestry with the Romans. In the following text, the author makes clear Theodoric the Ostrogoth's attempt to continue the traditions of Rome:

> He so governed two races at the same time, Romans and Goths, that although he himself was of the Arian sect, he nevertheless made no assault on the Catholic religion; he gave games in the circus and the amphitheatre, so that even by the Romans he was called a Trajan or a Valentinian, whose times he took as a model; and by the Goths, because of his edict, in which he established justice, he was judged to be in all respects their best king. Military service for the Romans he kept on the same footing as under the emperors. He was generous with gifts and the distribution of grain, and although he had found the public treasury nothing but a haystack, by his efforts it was restored and made rich.[10]

One of the most important steps in the process of the integration of the Germans with those whom they conquered was their acceptance of orthodox Christianity. The change from Arianism to Catholicism was a turning point in the history of both the Visigoths and the Lombards, but even more important to the history of Europe was the conversion of the Franks and the Anglo-Saxons from paganism to Catholic Christianity. According to tradition, the conversion of the Franks was initiated by the conversion of their King Clovis, a story Gregory of Tours deliberately parallels to Constantine's conversion nearly two centuries earlier:

> Finally war broke out against the Alamanni and in this conflict he [Clovis] was forced by necessity to accept what he had refused of his own free will. It so turned out that when the two armies met on the battlefield there was great slaughter and the troops of Clovis were rapidly being annihilated. He raised his eyes to heaven when he saw this, felt compunction in his heart and was moved to tears. "Jesus Christ," he said, "you who Clotild [Clovis's wife] maintains to be the Son of the living God, you who deign to give help to those in

travail and victory to those who trust in you, in faith I beg the glory of your help. If you will give me victory over my enemies, and if I may have evidence of that miraculous power which the people dedicated to your name say that they have experienced, then I will believe in you and I will be baptized in your name. I have called upon my own gods, but, as I see only too clearly, they have no intention of helping me. I therefore cannot believe that they possess any power, for they do not come to the assistance of those who trust in them. I now call upon you. I want to believe in you, but I must first be saved from my enemies." Even as he said this the Alamanni turned their backs and began to run away. . . .

King Clovis asked that he might be baptized first by the Bishop [Remigius]. Like some new Constantine he stepped forward to the baptismal pool, ready to wash away the sores of his old leprosy and to be cleansed in flowing water from the sordid stains which he had borne so long. As he advanced for his baptism, the holy man of God addressed him in these pregnant words: "Bow your head in meekness, Sicamber. Worship what you have burnt, burn what you have been wont to worship."[11]

The mention of leprosy refers to a legend that Constantine was miraculously cured of the disease upon his baptism. Gregory's description of Clovis's baptism shows how ritual and splendor helped convert the Germans to Christianity:

The public squares were draped with coloured cloths, the churches were adorned with white hangings, the baptistry was prepared, sticks of incense gave off clouds of perfume, sweet-smelling candles gleamed bright and the holy place of baptism was filled with divine fragrance.[12]

The conversion of Clovis meant the conversion of the Franks: three thousand of Clovis's warriors were baptized the same day. The Roman population that the Franks governed was Christian, and thus the Franks had long been in contact with Christianity. But there was little or no instruction in the faith for most Franks; there were simply mass baptisms. Therefore, their formal conversion did not immediately make the Franks thoroughly Christian; nor did it make them forsake their old gods, their sacred places, or their magic.

Gregory of Tours, in his *Glory of the Confessors*, gives us a rare glimpse how the process that we see in the conversion of King Clovis took place less spectacularly and more gradually in the countryside. Gregory explains how a local bishop began the process of turning pagans (the Latin word *paganus* means someone who lives in the countryside) into Christians:

At a fixed time a crowd of rustics went [to a lake near the town of Javols] and, as if offering libations to the lake, threw [into it] linen cloths and garments that served men as clothing. Some [threw] pelts of wool. Many [threw] models of cheese and wax and bread as well as various [other objects]. . . . [T]hey brought food and drink, sacrificed animals, and feasted for three days. . . .

Much later a cleric from that city [of Javols] became bishop and went to the place. He preached to the crowds that they should cease this behavior lest they be consumed by the wrath of heaven. But their coarse rusticity rejected his preaching. Then, with the inspiration of the Divinity, this bishop of God built a church in honor of the blessed Hilary of Poitiers at a distance from the banks of the lake. He placed relics of Hilary in the church and said to the people: "Do not, my sons, do not sin before God! For there is [to be] no religious piety to a lake. Do not stain your hearts with these empty rituals, but rather acknowledge God and direct your devotion to his friends." . . . The men were stung in their hearts and converted. They left the lake and brought everything they usually threw into it to the holy church.[13]

In all likelihood, Gregory provides a "speeded up" account of the conversion of this particular group of peasants, and even after their conversion they continued to practice their rituals, albeit in a different place and to honor a different deity. Since the traditional religions recognized many gods, the use of saints and sometimes the invention of saints' stories eased the transition from polytheistic to monotheistic religious practices.

If this amalgamation of pagan and Christian occurred more or less haphazardly in the kingdom of the Franks, it was given a theoretical basis and papal approbation by Gregory I (the Great) in a letter of 601 that he addressed to the missionaries he had sent to convert the Anglo-Saxons:

[We] have come to the conclusion that the temples of the idols among that people should on no account be destroyed. The idols are to be destroyed, but the temples themselves are to be aspersed with holy water, altars set up in them, and relics deposited there. For if these temples are well-built, they must be purified from the worship of demons and dedicated to the service of the true God. In this way, we hope that the people, seeing that their temples are not destroyed, may abandon their error and, flocking more readily to their accustomed resorts, may come to know and adore the true God. And since they have a custom of sacrificing many oxen to demons, let some other solemnity be substituted in its place, such as a day of Dedication or the Festivals of the holy martyrs whose relics are enshrined there. On such occasions they might well construct shelters of boughs for themselves around the churches that were once temples, and celebrate the solemnity with devout feasting. They are no longer to sacrifice beasts to the Devil, but they may kill them for food to the praise of God, and give thanks to the Giver of all gifts for the plenty they enjoy. If the people are allowed some worldly pleasures in this way, they will more readily come to desire the joys of the spirit. For it is certainly impossible to eradicate all errors from obstinate minds at one stroke, and whoever wishes to climb to a mountain top climbs gradually step by step, and not in one leap. It was in this way that the Lord revealed Himself to the Israelite people in Egypt, permitting the sacrifices formerly offered to the Devil to be offered thenceforward to Himself instead. So He bade them sacrifice beasts to Him, so that, once they became enlightened, they might abandon one element of sacrifice and retain another. For, while they were to offer the same beasts as before, they were to offer them to God instead of to idols, so that they would no longer be offering the same sacrifices.[14]

It would be difficult to overestimate the importance of this statement. We have already observed that ideas from Greco-Roman culture were adapted to Christian use and shown how Jerome and Augustine justified this practice, but theirs was a rather different situation. Greco-Roman culture was the highly sophisticated culture of the Roman Empire within which Christianity originated and grew. Gregory here allows customs and practices from a foreign, nonliterate culture to be adapted to Christian use. This clearly aided further missionary activity to the Germans and later to non-Germanic peoples as well: even in the sixteenth century, some Catholic missionaries to America and India based their work on the theory of conversion that Gregory had enunciated almost a millennium earlier. Gregory's instructions also ensured the survival of elements of pagan culture that would have otherwise been neglected or destroyed. A poem such as *Beowulf* probably survived because a pagan story had been Christianized. The traditional yule log ceremony still practiced in some churches in England was originally a pagan Germanic custom.

Missionaries encountering Anglo-Saxon customs associated with purification after childbirth sent this question back to Pope Gregory shortly after their arrival: "How soon after childbirth may she [a mother] enter churches?"[15] The question itself is instructive, showing that the problems they encountered were as much concerned with daily activities and common practices as with matters of abstract theology. Gregory's answer is also instructive:

> As to the interval that must elapse after childbirth before a woman may enter church, you are familiar with the Old Testament rule: that is, for a male child thirty-three days and for a female, sixty-six. But this is to be understood as an allegory, for were a woman to enter church and return thanks in the very hour of her delivery, she would do nothing wrong.[16]

One discovers from this text how the allegorical method of scriptural exegesis which Augustine made popular in the West gives Gregory the opportunity to deal effectively and creatively with problems that arose in a world quite different from that of Palestine in biblical times and yet remain faithful to a belief in the inerrancy of Scripture.

The writings of the Venerable Bede (673–735), our main source for the conversion of England, show that the missionaries to England made use of art and ritual much as Remigius had done a hundred years earlier with Clovis and the Franks:

> But the monks were endowed with power from God, not from the Devil, and approached the king carrying a silver cross as their standard and the likeness

of our Lord and Saviour painted on a board. First of all they offered prayer to God, singing a litany for the eternal salvation both of themselves and of those to whom and for whose sake they had come.[17]

Only after this ceremony did the missionaries preach the word of God to King Ethelbert of Kent.

The missionaries also benefited from the fact that like Clovis, Ethelbert had a Christian wife who played a major role in his conversion. Women were also important to the development of Christianity in England generally. Some evangelized directly while others established nunneries that were centers of Christian learning. Marrying a Christian woman to a pagan remained an important means of conversion of powerful men and their families. Neither the dedication of missionaries nor the wisdom of Gregory the Great was sufficient to ensure immediate conversion. Ethelbert of Kent refused to force his subjects to become Christians. Traditional societies do not easily change their religion. Moreover, the Anglo-Saxon kingdoms often reverted to paganism after the death of a Christian king or in response to a disaster such as loss in battle or a bad crop. In fact, when Ethelbert of Kent died, he was succeeded by his pagan son. Gradually over the course of the seventh century, however, England became a Christian land. One reason for the ultimate success of Christianity was the continuing close link between the papacy and England. Until the Norman conquest in 1066, England's chief contact with the continent was not with the Frankish kingdom across the English Channel but directly with Rome. Up to the time of the Protestant Reformation in the sixteenth century, there continued to be a special relationship between England and the papacy.

The papacy sent more than men to England; it also sent the materials necessary to establish Christianity there:

> They [envoys from Rome] brought with them everything necessary for the worship and service of the Church, including sacred vessels, altar coverings, church ornaments, vestments for priests and clergy, relics of the holy Apostles and martyrs, and many books.[18]

It was important for the English church to learn not only the language of Christianity but also the form of its liturgy. Thus, a famous Roman cantor was sent to England:

> Benedict [Biscop, Abbot of Wearmouth] received Abbot John and conducted him to Britain, where he was to teach his monks the chant for the liturgical year as it was sung at Saint Peter's, Rome. In accordance with the Pope's instructions, Abbot John taught the cantors of the monastery the theory and practice of singing and reading aloud, and he put into writing all that was necessary for the proper observance of festivals throughout the year. This document is still preserved in this monastery, and many copies have been made for other places. John's instruction was not limited to the brethren of this monastery alone; for men who were proficient singers came from nearly all

the monasteries of the province to hear him, and he received many invitations to teach elsewhere.[19]

The papacy continued to provide learned leaders for the infant English church:

> Theodore of Tarsus [c.602–690] was the first archbishop whom the entire Church of the English obeyed, and since, as I have observed, both he and Hadrian were men of learning both in sacred and in secular literature, they attracted a large number of students, into whose minds they poured the waters of wholesome knowledge day by day. In addition to instructing them in the holy Scriptures, they also taught their pupils poetry, astronomy, and the calculation of the church calendar. In proof of this, some of their students still alive today are as proficient in Latin and Greek as in their native tongue.[20]

With the coming of Christianity to England came Latin and to some extent even Greek culture. The Church established schools and libraries, giving England a sophisticated written culture. By the eighth century, English schools were probably the best in Europe, producing the Venerable Bede, arguably the greatest historian of the Middle Ages and the most learned man in Europe at the time, and Alcuin, chief architect of educational reform on the continent under Charlemagne.

England developed a thriving Latin culture; however, unlike other Germanic people, the English also developed a written vernacular. The missionaries had brought not only a religion and a culture but also the vehicle for the transmission of the existing traditions of the Anglo-Saxons. The earliest surviving text in Anglo-Saxon is the laws of Ethelbert of Kent. Bede reproduces in his history a poem of Caedmon in Anglo-Saxon dating from 680. This written vernacular culture, flourishing throughout the Anglo-Saxon period, produced such poems as *Beowulf* and the "Dream of the Rood" and translations of such seminal Latin works as Boethius's *Consolation of Philosophy* and Gregory the Great's *Pastoral Care*.

Anglo-Saxon Christianity did not develop solely from the Roman tradition. Irish monks had arrived in the north of Britain in 565 with their own distinct form of Christianity, the product of a unique cultural synthesis. In the fifth century, Ireland, never a part of the Roman Empire, embraced Christianity, thanks to the efforts of Saint Patrick. But in some ways Christianity in Ireland developed quite differently from Christianity inside the territory of the Empire. First, Latin, never spoken in Ireland, had to be learned in order to understand Christian culture (the Bible, the liturgy, the writings of the Fathers). Since Latin was always a scholarly language in Ireland, it was not subject to as much change as it was in those areas under the control of the Germans. Latin thus remained most classical in a part of the world that had never been subject to Rome. Second, Ireland, organized by clans, had no cities, so there were no natural centers to establish bishops. Consequently, Ireland came to be organized monastically rather than episcopally, and bishops there were usually subordinate to their abbots. Third, the Irish monks practiced a zealous and somewhat extreme asceticism.

One peculiarity of this monastic Christianity was the peregrination: a monk would simply set off as a wanderer by land or sea, going where God took him. This literal exile from one's home, a symbol of life on earth as an exile from one's true home in heaven, is a partial explanation for Irish missionary activity in England and on the continent. The following text is from Jonas's life of Saint Columbanus (c.550–615), an important Irish missionary on the continent. It illustrates the close connection between exile and pilgrimage on the one hand and missionary activity on the other:

> After he had been many years in the cloister, he longed to go into strange lands, in obedience to the command which the Lord gave Abraham: "Get thee out of thy country, and from thy kindred, and from thy father's house, into a land that I will show thee." . . . Having collected a band of brethren, St. Columban[us] asked the prayers of all, that he might be assisted in his coming journey, and that he might have their pious aid. So he started out in the twentieth year of his life, and under the guidance of Christ went to the seashore with twelve companions. Here they waited to see if the mercy of the Almighty would allow their purpose to succeed, and learned that the spirit of the all-merciful Judge was with them. So they embarked, and began the dangerous journey across the channel and sailed quickly with a smooth sea and favorable wind to the coast of Brittany [in what is now northwestern France but not under Merovingian rule at the time]. Here they rested for a while to recover their strength and discussed their plans anxiously, until finally they decided to enter the land of [Merovingian] Gaul. They wanted zealously and shrewdly to inquire into the disposition of the inhabitants in order to remain longer if they found they could sow the seeds of salvation; or in case they found the hearts of the people in darkness, go on to the nearest nation.[21]

As Celtic missionaries arrived on the island of Britain, some serious conflicts developed between the two traditions—Roman and Irish—over such issues as the dating of Easter. In 663–664, the Synod of Whitby, held at a double monastery (one with separate parts for men and women) and presided over by the *abbess*, resolved all disputes in favor of the Roman practices, and gradually the Irish themselves began to adopt Roman practices and eventually the Rule of Saint Benedict for their monasteries. However, Celtic Christianity had a great impact upon the development of the Church in England. In addition to reinforcing the high level of scholarship brought from Rome, the Celtic style of manuscript illumination became the basis for the English style. In the seventh century, Irish monks on the continent sought to reform the Church there, and built a series of monasteries as far south as Bobbio in Italy. These monasteries gradually accepted the Rule of Saint Benedict, but their strict asceticism and high level of scholarship influenced continental monasticism.

The Irish monks developed a unique penitential system. In the early Church adult baptism was the norm, and thus the forgiveness of sins committed after baptism was not a central pastoral issue. Serious sinners were banned from the community until they performed public penance, and this ritual usually could not be repeated. However, with the triumph of Christianity and the growth of the practice of infant baptism, forgiveness for sins committed after baptism and reconciliation of the sinners with God and with their communities became tremendously important. A general confession and absolution became common on the continent. Irish monks, however, adopted a system of private confession to a priest who assigned a specific penalty to the sinner. Books called penitentials, containing the proper penalties for a great variety of sins, were compiled for use by confessors. Here is an example of an assigned penalty:

> A [priest] or a deacon who commits natural fornication, having previously taken the vow of a monk, shall do penance for seven years [usually by performing weekly fasts and other works during this time period]. He shall ask pardon every hour; he shall perform a special fast during every week except in the fifty days (between Easter and Pentecost). . . . He shall at all times deplore his guilt from his inmost heart, and above all things he shall adopt an attitude of the readiest obedience. After a year and a half he shall take the Eucharist and come for the kiss of peace and sing psalms with his brethren, lest his soul perish utterly through lacking so long a time the celestial medicine.[22]

The following articles concerning negligence toward the consecrated host provide an insight into the great number of contingencies these penitentials deal with:

1. He who fails to guard the host carefully, and a mouse eats it, shall do penance for forty days.
2. But he who loses it in the church, that is, so that a part falls and is not found, twenty days. . . .
7. One who vomits the host because his stomach is overloaded with food, if he casts it into the fire, twenty days, but if not, forty days.
8. If, however, dogs consume this vomit, one hundred. . . .
19. He who acts with negligence towards the host, so that it dries up and is consumed by worms until it comes to nothing, shall do penance for three forty-day periods on bread and water.
20. If it is entire but if a worm is found in it, it shall be burned and the ashes shall be concealed beneath the altar, and he who neglected it shall make good his negligence with forty days [of penance].
21. If the host loses its taste and is discoloured, he shall keep a fast for twenty days; if it is stuck together, for seven days.[23]

One can see from the following articles how the Church in Ireland dealt with the details of daily life in terms of sin and punishment. These rules show

how elements of the purity laws of the Pentateuch influenced the system and also illustrate ways in which the society was being thoroughly christianized. Even dealing with a mouse or an incontinent cat had religious overtones!

12. He who gives to anyone a liquor in which a mouse or a weasel is found dead shall do penance with three special fasts.

13. He who afterwards knows that he has tasted such a drink shall keep a special fast.

14. But if those little beasts are found in the flour or in any dry food or in porridge or in curdled milk, whatever is around their bodies shall be cast out, and all the rest shall be taken in good faith. . . .

18. Whoever eats or drinks what has been tainted by a household beast, namely, the cat, shall be healed with three special fasts.[24]

The Irish penitential system was adopted in England and on the continent in the eighth and ninth centuries. It remained an integral part of the Church's system of pastoral care for several centuries, although alternative ideas about penance developed in the twelfth and thirteenth centuries that focused more on intent than action, and are a direct ancestor of Catholic practice today. Great preachers of repentance in the Middle Ages, such as Francis of Assisi, operated largely within the context of this system. When the system was abused—and it often was—the abuse was pointed out by reformers and poets such as Dante and Chaucer. Penance in virtually the form created by the Irish monks was defined as one of the seven sacraments of the Church before the end of the Middle Ages.

The Irish missionary zeal, which had brought them to both Britain and the continent, became integrated into Anglo-Saxon Christianity and was largely responsible for a succession of English missionary monks to the continent from the end of the seventh to the middle of the eighth century. Of these the most significant is Saint Boniface (originally known as Wynfrith, 680–754), a man extremely important in the development of the medieval world for many reasons. First, he brought Christianity to the Germans east of the Rhine. Boniface had placed himself under the direct authority of the pope before embarking on his mission and thus brought the new church in Germany into the same kind of close relationship with Rome that England enjoyed. His approach to missionary work came out of the tradition Gregory the Great had established for missionaries to the Anglo-Saxons a century before. An English bishop sending advice to Boniface explains how to convert the Germans in a manner that was consistent with Gregory's admonition:

And so I have with affectionate good will taken pains to suggest to Your Prudence a few things that may show you how, according to my ideas, you may most readily overcome the resistance of those uncivilized people. Do not begin by arguing with them about the origin of their gods, false as those are, but let them affirm that some of them were begotten by others through the intercourse of male with female, so that you may at least prove that gods and goddesses born after the manner of men are men and not gods and, since they did not exist before, must have had a beginning. Then when they have been compelled to learn that their gods had a beginning since some were begotten by others, they must be asked in the same way whether they believe that the world had a beginning or was always in existence without beginning. If it had a beginning, who created it? Certainly they can find no place where begotten gods could dwell before the universe was made. I mean by "universe" not merely this visible earth and sky, but the whole vast extent of space, and this the heathen can imagine too in their thoughts. But if they argue that the world always existed without beginning, you should strive to refute this and to convince them by many documents and arguments. . . . Do they think the gods are to be worshiped for the sake of temporal and immediate good or for future and eternal blessedness? If for temporal things, let them tell in what respect the heathen are better off than Christians. What gain do the heathen suppose accrues to their gods from their sacrifices, since the gods already possess everything? Or why do the gods leave it in the power of their subjects to say what kind of tribute shall be paid? If they are lacking in such things, why do they not themselves choose more valuable ones? If they have plenty, then there is no need to suppose that the gods can be pleased with such offerings of victims.[25]

Thus, conversion began with already existing beliefs; the entire statement is based on the premise that the Germans should be reasoned with rather than marched into the river for mass baptisms like Clovis's warriors. Although Boniface constantly struggled with pagan survivals and revivals, and was martyred by pagans in Germany in 754, much of Germany was essentially Christian by the time of his death. What Boniface could not eradicate by word and example Charlemagne destroyed in a series of wars by the end of the century.

In 742, Boniface turned his attention to the Frankish kingdom. With papal support and the aid of a reform-minded Carolingian mayor of the palace, he set out to renew the Frankish church, placing it more firmly in the sphere of papal influence and Roman practice. He realized that there were dangers in a reform sponsored and enforced by a layman, but he also knew that without such support the Church had little power to enforce its decrees.

Without the support of the Frankish prince I can neither govern the members of the Church nor defend the priests, clerks, monks, and maids of God; nor can I, without orders from him and the fear inspired by him, prevent the pagan rites and the sacrilegious worship of idols in Germany.[26]

However, lay sponsorship and enforcement of ecclesiastical reform meant a greater degree of lay control over the Church and use of its property for secular ends.

The decrees of one Frankish synod which Boniface supervised suggest the range of problems in the Church; these are particularly interesting in light of the fact that the Franks had by this time been Christian at least in name for almost two and one-half centuries:

> We have decreed, according to the canons, that every bishop within his own diocese and with the help of the count, who is the defender of the Church, shall see to it that the people of God perform no pagan rites but reject and cast out all the foulness of the heathen, such as sacrifices to the dead, casting of lots, divinations, amulets and auguries, incantations, or offerings of animals, which foolish folk perform in the churches, according to the pagan custom, in the name of holy martyrs or confessors, thereby calling down the wrath of God and his saints, and also those sacrilegious fires which they call "Niedfeor," and whatever other pagan practices there may be.[27]

The close link forged between the papacy and the Franks largely through Boniface had enormous political consequences. In 751, Boniface anointed the Carolingian Pepin as king of the Franks on behalf of the pope. This special relationship between the new Frankish dynasty and the papacy led directly to the pope's coronation of Pepin's son Charlemagne as Roman Emperor in the year 800.

GREGORY THE GREAT AND THE PAPACY

Following the collapse of the Roman Empire in the West, the papacy found itself in a weak position because most of Western Europe was ruled either by Arian heretics or pagans. The popes were forced to look toward Constantinople for protection and support despite theological and cultural differences between East and West. While the Byzantine Emperor Justinian was bringing Italy under his rule, the bishops of Rome rejoiced. However, Justinian continued to support the bishop of Constantinople, in opposition to the papal claim of universal jurisdiction. Furthermore, Justinian's conquests were not permanent, for as we have seen, in 568 the Arian Lombards began to overrun most of Italy; and Byzantine preoccupation with its Balkan and eastern borders and later with Muslim incursions into its territory precluded further significant military involvement in Italy.

At the end of the sixth century, in a period of papal impotence in Western Europe and of an unstable relationship between the papacy and the Byzantine Empire, came the pontificate of Gregory the Great (r.590–604), often called the founder of the medieval papacy. Gregory, a monk with a well-deserved reputation for holiness at the time of his election, accepted and, in fact, furthered Leo the Great's claims of papal authority. In a letter to the Bishop of Alexandria, he brought the three most important Petrine texts together to put forth a claim of universal papal jurisdiction:

> For who can be ignorant that holy Church has been made firm in the solidity of the Prince of the apostles, who derived his name from the firmness of his mind, so as to be called *Petrus* from *petra*. And to him it is said by the voice

of the Truth, "To thee I will give the keys to the kingdom of heaven" (Matt. 16:19). And again it is said to him, "And when thou art converted, strengthen thy brethren" (Luke 22:32). And once more, "Simon [i.e., Peter], son of Jonas, lovest thou me? Feed My sheep" (John 21:17). Wherefore, though there are many apostles, yet with regard to the principality itself the See of the Prince of the apostles alone has grown strong in authority. . . . For he himself adorned the See to which he sent his disciple as evangelist. He himself established the See in which, though he was to leave it, he sat for seven years.[28]

Gregory had spent time in Constantinople as a papal ambassador before his election and had come to doubt that the papacy could count on imperial help. Thus, his policy was to make the papacy independent of Byzantium. For example, he made peace with the Lombards without informing the emperor. He also took charge of provisioning and defending the city of Rome so that it would not be dependent upon an imperial army.

We have already seen how Gregory's missionaries in England assured papal influence there and later helped to strengthen papal authority throughout northern Europe through the work of men such as Boniface. Related to his desire to spread Christianity was his concern for the education of people who were already at least nominally Christian. Concerned that his flock was worshiping paintings in church, the bishop of Marseille had ordered their destruction. Gregory's prohibition of this order presents the theory of the use of art in Christian instruction that became standard in the Middle Ages:

> For to adore a picture is one thing, but to learn through the story of a picture what is to be adored is another. For what writing presents to readers, this a picture presents to the unlearned who behold it, since in it even the ignorant see what they ought to follow; in it the illiterate read. Hence and chiefly to the nations, a picture is instead of reading. And this ought to have been attended to especially by thee who livest among the nations, lest, while enflamed inconsiderately by a right zeal, thou shouldst breed offense to savage minds. And, seeing that antiquity has not without reason admitted the histories of saints to be painted in venerable places, if thou hadst seasoned zeal with discretion, thou inightest undoubtedly have obtained what thou were aiming at, and not scattered the collected flock but rather gathered together a scattered one; so the deserved renown of a shepherd might have distinguished thee, instead of the blame of being a scatterer lying upon thee.[29]

This statement of Gregory's—echoing once again the theme of moving from visible to invisible—became the dominant attitude of the Church toward art in the Middle Ages. Christian art flourished in the West with little opposition before the Protestant Reformation of the sixteenth century, and richly decorated Romanesque and Gothic churches were in a real sense the books of the laity.

Gregory's writings were of enormous importance for the Middle Ages. He was regarded as one of the four Latin Doctors, along with Jerome, Ambrose, and Augustine. Perhaps his best-known work in the Middle Ages was the *Pastoral Care*, a standard manual of conduct for bishops and later more directly applicable to the work of parish priests. As the title suggests, Christ and his representatives, the bishops, are seen as shepherds. This image, which Gregory employs effectively in the letter quoted above, comes, of course, from the Gospels. The Good Shepherd was the most common depiction of Christ in the art of the catacombs and in churches built immediately following the conversion of Constantine. Bishops, as Christ's representatives on earth and as successors of the apostles, should be shepherds of their flocks in imitation of Christ the Good Shepherd. Gregory's achievement was to address the question of what it meant to be a good shepherd in a world quite different from that of the Bible. A passage from the *Pastoral Care* demonstrates Gregory's development of the pastoral image and its application to the episcopate.

> Further, there are some who investigate spiritual precepts with shrewd diligence, but in the life they live trample on what they have penetrated by their understanding. They hasten to teach what they have learned, not by practice,

Mosaic of Christ the Good Shepherd. Tomb of Galla Pacidia, Ravenna, Italy. Fifth century. The theme of Christ as the shepherd keeping watch over his flock becomes for Pope Gregory the Great the model for clergy to imitate. The photograph of the Beatus initial on p. 80 is another way that the image of Christ the Good Shepherd was understood in the Middle Ages.

but by study, and belie in their conduct what they teach by words. Hence it is that when the pastor walks through steep places, the flock following him comes to a precipice. Therefore, the Lord complains through the Prophet of the contemptible knowledge of pastors, saying "When you drank the clearest water, you troubled the rest with your feet. And my sheep were fed with that which you had trodden with your feet, and they drank what your feet had troubled" (Ezek. 34:8).[30]

The image of bishop and priest as shepherd remained central to theologians such as Saint Bernard of Clairvaux in the twelfth century and John Wyclif in the fourteenth. And later, when poets ridiculed wicked and greedy clergy of their own time, they turned to Gregory's *Pastoral Care.* Chaucer's description of his ideal priest, the Parson, in the *General Prologue to the Canterbury Tales,* uses Gregory's description of a good shepherd almost verbatim. Dante criticizes the popes in his own time with such phrases as "lawless shepherd."

Gregory was also known throughout the Middle Ages for his great work of biblical exegesis, the *Moralia* [i.e., an exposition of the moral level of biblical interpretation as defined by Augustine] on the Old Testament Book of Job. In it Augustine's approach to Scripture is made more accessible. The following passage illustrates the movement from visible to invisible, using the Old Testament figure Job as a prefiguration of Christ:

> For when the light of a candle is kindled in the dark, the candle, which causes other objects to be seen, is first seen itself. And so, if we are truly endeavoring to behold the objects which are enlightened, it is necessary for us to open the eyes of our mind to that Lightening which gives them light. But it is this which shines forth in these very discourses of blessed Job, where the shades of allegory too have been driven away, as though the gloom of midnight had been dispelled, a bright light as it were flaming across them. As when it is said, "I know that my redeemer liveth, and in my flesh I shall see God." Paul had doubtless discovered this light in the night of history, when he said, "All were baptized in Moses in the cloud and in the sea, and all ate the same spiritual meat, and all drank the same spiritual drink. But they drank of the spiritual Rock that followed them, but the Rock was Christ." If then the Rock represented the redeemer, why should not the blessed Job suggest the type of Him, since he signified in his suffering Him whom he spoke of in his voice? And hence he is not improperly called "Job," that is to say "grieving," because he sets forth in his own person the image of Him, of Whom it is announced long before by Isaiah, that He Himself "bore our griefs." It should be further known, that our Redeemer has represented himself as one person with Holy Church, whom He has assumed to Himself. For it is said of Him, "Which is the head, even Christ." And again it is written of His church, "And the body of Christ, which is the Church."[31]

In Gregory's *Dialogues,* a series of conversations about holy men and women, one book is devoted to the life of Saint Benedict. It helped to set a pattern for later works of hagiography, together with Athanasius's life of Saint Antony and Augustine's *Confessions,* and was in large part reponsible for spreading the fame of Benedict and his Rule (see Chapter 6). Another of Gregory's achievements was his codification of Church liturgy and music. Perceiving the need for some unity in the order of Church services, he established a basic pattern for the liturgy and compiled chants appropriate for the various services and seasons. Although he probably wrote none of these himself, they, and others written later in the same style, have come to bear his name: Gregorian chant.

Gregory's writings became widely known almost immediately, his place as one of the great saints of the Church assured. Nevertheless, during the seventh century, his goal of papal independence from Byzantium remained unrealized. In fact, it was more than a century before the papacy's influence north of the Alps encompassed much more than the Anglo-Saxon kingdoms. One reason for the revival of Gregory's policies was the election of Gregory II in 715. This second Gregory, who had also lived in Constantinople before his election, chose his papal name purposefully; and his accomplishments made him a worthy successor to his namesake. It was he who commissioned Boniface to convert the Saxons and other Germanic peoples.

By the middle of the eighth century, the Germans and Franks had close ties to Rome while Roman relations with Byzantium continued to deteriorate. In 751, Pope Zacharias supported Pepin's taking of the Frankish crown. Two years later, with the Lombards threatening Rome and the Byzantine emperor unwilling to send help, Pope Stephen II called upon Pepin, who successfully came to the defense of Rome. After this formation of a Frankish-papal alliance, the popes were never again dependent on the emperor in Constantinople. Western Europe became politically, culturally, and religiously independent of the East, through the alliance of the Frankish monarchy and the papacy. This alliance is one of the most important contributions to the birth of Europe.

INTELLECTUAL DEVELOPMENTS

Gregory of Tours, in the passge quoted above, was surely right when he described his age as one of general educational and intellectual decline. However, this should not be taken to mean that the era was without writers of sophistication and influence. Gregory the Great is only one of several writers in the three centuries following the end of the Roman Empire in the West who can be called, along with Jerome and Augustine, founders of the medieval world view.

Boethius (c.480–524), statesman and philosopher, was minister to the Ostrogothic King Theodoric. He fell into disfavor, lost his position, and later lost his life when he was accused of plotting against Theodoric. His most important work, the *Consolation of Philosophy,* is one of the central texts of the

early Middle Ages, a work remaining influential throughout the medieval period and beyond. More manuscripts of the *Consolation* survive than almost
any other work of the Middle Ages. It was translated into Old English by King
Alfred the Great; into German by Notker; into French by Jean de Meun, author of the *Romance of the Rose;* into Middle English by Geoffrey Chaucer;
and into Early Modern English by Queen Elizabeth I. Scarcely an educated
person in Europe from the sixth to the eighteenth centuries would have been
without a deep knowledge and love of the work. A good rule of thumb in the
late Middle Ages is that the greater the writer, the more profound the effect
of Boethius on his work. Consequently, an understanding of the *Consolation*
is essential for a proper understanding of Dante and Chaucer.

His subject, as one surmises from the title, is the kind of consolation that
philosophy can provide, a subject that no doubt springs from his experience
as an exile and prisoner. Although he was not under the immediate threat of
death when he wrote the *Consolation,* he writes about the fall of a statesman
from high position, and from his own fate he generalizes. The *Consolation* is
about the instability of fortune. Both in external and internal structure, the
work was highly influential. The *Consolation* was written in five books, each
consisting of alternating sections of verse and prose. The five-book structure
of Chaucer's *Troilus and Criseyde* is one example of a later work modeled on
the *Consolation*. The internal structure of the work is even more suggestive
to later writers; it can be charted by the growth of the speaker, Boethius the
exile and prisoner, as he laments his fate in Book 1, is educated by Lady Philosophy throughout the central books, and has gained an understanding of the
ways of God by Book 5. This movement from ignorance to knowledge resonates throughout the literature of the Middle Ages, establishing a pattern repeated over and over in narrative poetry. Lady Philosophy, comforting and
enlightening Boethius, performs for him the very function that Dante's guides
perform in the *Divine Comedy*. The seemingly overwhelming task of ap-
proaching the *Comedy* for the first time can be greatly simplified by seeing
there the same pattern as in the *Consolation*—of a man moving from ignorance to knowledge. Dante the pilgrim, no less than Boethius the exile, starts
out by asking the wrong questions, begins to ask the right ones, and finally
learns some answers. This movement is also the pattern of the saint's life, containing the conversion from self to God. It is also the pattern of the dream vision, in which the dreamer falls asleep and is enlightened by his dream. It is
also the pattern of first-person narratives such as *Piers the Plowman* and quest
romances such as *Sir Gawain and the Green Knight*. Even the writings of medieval mystics show the same movement of the speaker from ignorance to
knowledge.

The *Consolation*'s most well-known and influential image is that of Fortune and Fortune's wheel. An important step in Boethius's education is to learn
to move from immersion in what changes to contemplation of what is per-

manent. Explaining to Boethius why he should not lament the loss of his earthly fame and possessions, Lady Philosophy says to him:

> "What is it, my friend, that has thrown you into grief and sorrow? Do you think you have encountered something new and different? You are wrong if you think that Fortune has changed toward you. This is her nature, the way she always behaves. She is changeable, and so in her relations with you she has merely done what she always does. This is the way she was when she flattered you and led you on with false happiness. You have merely discovered the two-faced nature of this blind goddess. Although she still hides herself from others, she is now wholly known to you. If you like her, abide by her conditions and do not complain. But if you hate her treachery, ignore her and her deceitful antics. Really, the misfortunes which are now such a cause of grief ought to be reasons for tranquility. For now she has deserted you, and no man can ever be secure until he has been forsaken by Fortune.
>
> "You have put yourself in Fortune's power; now you must be content with the ways of your mistress. If you try to stop the force of her turning wheel, you are the most foolish man alive. If it should stop turning, it would cease to be Fortune's wheel."[32]

Fortune and her wheel imaginatively provide an image for the proper medieval attitude toward worldly goods. Anything material such as money or property, or any worldly pleasure, such as food or sex, is incapable of fully satisfying anyone because it is only partial. As the *Consolation* states at a later point:

> The good is defined as that which, once it is attained, relieves man of all further desires. This is the supreme good and contains within itself all other lesser goods. If it lacked anything at all, it would not be the highest good, because something would be missing, and this could still be desired.[33]

To see any of Fortune's goods—those subject to Fortune's wheel—as the highest good is seriously to misunderstand the nature of reality. What is subject to change is incapable of bringing full satisfaction. Or, to express this same idea in the language of Augustine, to put one's trust in worldly possessions is to mistake means for ends. Whenever the wheel of Fortune appears in medieval art or medieval literature, it suggests these related concepts: the instability of all earthly possessions and the folly of putting one's trust in them. The reference to Fortune's wheel at the beginning of *Sir Gawain and the Green Knight* provides a reminder of the instability and mutability of all attempts at governance in our unstable world, including Arthur's Round Table. Fortune's wheel is an image that dominates the structure of Chaucer's *Troilus and Criseyde*, whose movement from "wo to wele [happiness], and after out of joie" recreates one complete turning. The image is also responsible for medieval definitions of comedy and tragedy: when the wheel makes a downward turn, moving from good fortune to bad, it describes a tragedy; when the wheel makes an upward turn, moving from bad fortune to good, it is a comedy.

Boethius's education also consists of learning that people are responsible for their actions. The problem of fate and free will, a crucial philosophical concern during the Middle Ages, is explored at length in the *Consolation*. Lady Philosophy tells Boethius that humans have free will, but she adds that those who have been blinded by passion are unable to see clearly, and hence unable to choose clearly:

> "Human souls, however, are more free while they are in contemplation of the divine mind, and less free when they are joined to bodies, and still less free when they are bound to earthly fetters. They are in utter slavery when they lose possession of their reason and give themselves wholly to vice. For when they turn away their eyes from the light of supreme truth to mean and dark things, they are blinded by a cloud of ignorance and obsessed by vicious passions. By yielding and consenting to these passions, they worsen the slavery to which they have brought themselves and are, as it were, the captives of their own freedom. Nevertheless, God, who beholds all things from eternity, foresees all things in his providence and disposes each according to its predestined merits."[34]

This passage contains the substance of the central problem. If God sees all things, and if whatever he forsees must take place, how can one's will really be free? If the outcome of human events does indeed depend on humans' free choices, the outcome must be uncertain, or as Boethius would put it, not necessary. If this is so, how can God foresee them? Boethius's answer to this dilemma begins in the perception of the radical difference between two ways of knowing, human and divine:

> "This is an old difficulty about Providence," Philosophy answered. "It was raised by Cicero in his book on divination, and has for a long time been the subject of your investigation, but so far none of you had treated it with enough care and conviction. The cause of the obscurity which still surrounds the problem is that the process of human reason cannot comprehend the simplicity of divine foreknowledge. If in any way we could understand that, no further doubt would remain."[35]

The difference between what is above and what is below forms one of the major thematic concerns of the *Consolation*, and is responsible for some of its most memorable and influential imagery.

> Then, as though she were making a new beginning, Philosophy explained: "The generation of all things, and the whole course of mutable natures and of what is in any way subject to change, take their causes, order, and forms from the unchanging mind of God. This divine mind established the manifold rules by which all things are governed while it remained in the secure castle of its own simplicity. When this government is regarded as belonging to the purity of the divine mind, it is called Providence; but when it is considered with reference to the things it governs, it has from very early times been called Fate. . . .

"Some things, however, which are subject to Providence are above the force of Fate and ungoverned by it. Consider the example of a number of spheres in orbit around the same central point: the innermost moves towards the simplicity of the center and becomes a kind of hinge about which the outer spheres circle; whereas the outermost, whirling in a wider orbit, tends to increase its orbit in space the farther it moves from the indivisible midpoint of the center. If, however, it is connected to the center, it is confined by the simplicity of the center and no longer tends to stray into space. In a like manner, whatever strays farthest from the divine mind is most entangled in the nets of Fate; conversely, the freer a thing is from Fate, the nearer it approaches the center of all things."[36]

This difference between divine and human knowledge leads to the conclusion that divine foreknowledge is not really foreknowledge at all; since God exists out of time, it is more accurately described simply as knowledge. What humans see as past, present, and future is all present to God. This distinction helps to solve the problem of fate and free will, but Lady Philosophy also suggests that part of the problem is due to the limits of human reason.

A final way of suggesting the importance of Boethius to the Middle Ages is in other images from the *Consolation* that become commonplace in medieval literature. When Lady Philosophy first comes to Boethius, one of her complaints is that he has forgotten his "native country." He has, in other words, mistaken his life here on earth for his true home. This formulation, so close to the scriptural and Augustinian ideal of life as a pilgrimage, is repeated throughout the Middle Ages. In one of his short poems, Chaucer uses it practically word for word. Boethius's early questions about his condition are all so wide of the mark that Lady Philosophy is not convinced that he is capable of understanding her wisdom. Returning his questions with a question, she implies that he may be too gross to understand a spiritual message:

"Do you understand what I have told you," Philosophy asked, "have my words impressed you at all, or are you like the ass which cannot hear the lyre? Why are you crying? Speak out, don't hide what troubles you. If you want a doctor's help, you must uncover your wound."[37]

Another image in this passage is that of Lady Philosophy coming to Boethius as a physician to cure his malady, resonating with the New Testament portrayal of Christ as a spiritual physician. Throughout medieval literature, doctors are called upon to cure maladies that are not exclusively physical.

Lady Philosophy is one in a long line of illustrious allegorical ladies in medieval literature and history. The allegorical figures of Ecclesia and Synagoga, church and synagogue, appear frequently in medieval art and literature, as does Sophia, the allegorical personification of wisdom. Francis of Assisi will marry Lady Poverty in the thirteenth century. The use of a human figure to represent an abstract idea is also present in another work of the fifth century,

Sculpture of an Ass Playing a Harp. Church of Saint Paraize, France. Twelfth century. This is the visualization of an idea deriving from Boethius's Consolation of Philosophy. *A beast that can play the lyre but not understand the music thus became a powerful metaphor for spiritual deafness in the Middle Ages.*

Martianus Capella's *Marriage of Mercury and Philology* (c.430), a work similar to the *Consolation* not only in form (it also uses alternating prose and verse sections), but in the extent of its influence. The work is a treatise on the seven liberal arts, personified as characters in a mythological story. Following a classical tradition that can be traced back as far as Isocrates in the fourth century B.C.E., Martianus divides the seven into groups: the trivium, consisting of grammar, rhetoric, and logic; and the quadrivium, consisting of music, astronomy, arithmetic, and geometry. The liberal arts appear at the marriage of Mercury and Philology as the handmaidens of Mercury. The marriage was traditionally taken to symbolize the union of eloquence and learning, that is, the union of the trivium and the quadrivium. For the next thousand years, Martianus's work was to be one of the most widely read in Western Europe, ensuring that the seven liberal arts became the educational core of the medieval schools. Their centrality was further strengthened by the approval of Martianus's schema in the writings of Cassiodorus (c.485–c.580); he was an official at the court of Theodoric the Ostrogoth and later established a monastery at Vivarium, where classical as well as Christian texts were studied and copied. The revival of the seven liberal arts became the key to the educational reforms of the Carolingian Renaissance in the eighth century. Their study (with emphasis on the trivium, and especially on grammar and rhetoric) became the foundation of monastic education throughout the Middle Ages. They were central to the educational system developed in the cathedral schools in the twelfth century. From the time of the Carolingian Renaissance to the end of the Middle Ages, personifications of the liberal arts were also an important subject in art, their depiction on the facade of Chartres Cathedral being perhaps the best-known example.

We have already examined excerpts from the writings of the historians Gregory of Tours and Bede. Gregory (539–594), bishop of Tours, came from a Roman family and was an important advisor to the Merovingian kings. Though deploring much of their cruelty, he supported the Franks because of their orthodox Christianity. His long *History of the Franks*—about six hundred pages in the newest English translation—begins with creation but concentrates on the events of his own lifetime. By adopting this strategy, Gregory places the story of the Franks in a universal framework but also claims for his own time the heritage of both biblical and classical traditions. This practice is repeated throughout the Middle Ages whenever kingdoms and cities claim Trojan and Roman origins or visits from the apostles and other biblical saints from Joseph of Arimathaea (England) to Mary Magdalen (France). Gregory's *History of the Franks* is filled with palace intrigue, grotesque punishments, religious charlatans, miraculous cures, and rebellious nuns. His narrative and descriptive powers maintain the reader's interest and provide details of life in the early Middle Ages that are available from no other source. In the final analysis, however, he lacks the sophisticated organizational and analytical skills of his Anglo-Saxon counterpart.

Bede (673–735) spent part of his childhood and all his adult life as a monk of Jarrow in the north of England. His *History of the English Church and People* is perhaps the most significant piece of historical writing in the entire medieval period. The work focuses on England from the time of the arrival of the Roman missionaries and magnificently unfolds the story of the establishment of Christianity there. His descriptions of the most important events such as the conversion of King Ethelbert of Kent and the Synod of Whitby plus the sharply and sympathetically drawn portraits of kings, bishops, monks, and nuns are unforgettable. Bede was also the author of numerous scientific works, biblical exegesis, and hagiography, and his writings were widely known throughout Europe in the Middle Ages. He is, for example, the only English person Dante places in his *Paradiso*.

The Visigothic kingdom also produced an author of the greatest importance—Isidore of Seville (560–636). He was the historian of the Visigoths and an important compiler of church law, but he is most famous for his encyclopedia, called the *Etymologies*. Isidore attempted to assemble no less than all human knowledge. Drawing mostly from classical Latin authors, he put together what became a standard reference work for the Middle Ages. The table of contents gives a sense of the work's scope.

BOOK I: Grammar
BOOK II: Rhetoric and Dialectic
BOOK III: Arithmetic, Geometry, Music, Astronomy
BOOK IV: Medicine
BOOK V: Law; Divisions of Time and Chronology
BOOK VI: Books of the Bible and Their Interpreters; Canons; Ecclesias-
                 tical offices
BOOK VII: God; Angels; Saints
BOOK VIII: The Church and the Sects
BOOK IX: Languages; Races; Kingdoms; the Army; Citizens; Kingship
BOOK X: Etymological Word List
BOOK XI: Men and Fabulous Monsters
BOOK XII: Animals
BOOK XIII: The Universe and its Parts
BOOK XIV: The Earth and its Parts
BOOK XV: Buildings and Lands
BOOK XVI: Stones and Metals
BOOK XVII: Agriculture and Botany
BOOK XVIII: War; Games; Pastimes
BOOK XIX: Ships; Building Materials; Dress
BOOK XX: Food and Drink; Furniture[38]

The *Etymologies* was widely used for reference even where the Latin authors from whom Isidore derived his information survived; having so much in one book was convenient. For example, many of the fabulous creatures carved in the twelfth-century Church of Saint Mary Magdalen in Vézelay, which were originally described by the Roman nauralist Pliny, were probably known in Vézelay through Isidore. In some cases, Isidore's sources did not survive. Consequently he himself became an important source for the transmission of classical culture to the Middle Ages.

The *Etymologies* derives its name from the fact that Isidore provided the origins of the words and names he wrote about. The idea that the etymology of a word says something about the essence of the object or person it names remained a popular and forceful concept throughout the Middle Ages. The following example, fancifully explaining the origin and meaning of the name Gregory, comes from the thirteenth-century collection of saints' lives called the *Golden Legend:*

The name Gregory (Gregorius) is formed from *grex,* flock, and *gore,* which means to preach or say, and Saint Gregory was preacher to his flock. Or the name resembles *egregarius,* from *egregius,* outstanding, and *gore;* and Gregory was an outstanding preacher and doctor. Or Gregorius, in our language,

Detail of Sculpture of People from the Ends of the Earth. Church of Mary Magdalen, Vézelay, France. Twelfth century. The dog-headed men depicted here are part of a sculptural program showing Christ sending the apostles to convert all the world's people. Ideas about what people at the ends of the earth were like came from the Roman writer Pliny (first century C.E.). Isidore of Seville drew heavily from Pliny, and the artist at Vézelay probably had Isidore rather than Pliny as his direct source.

suggests vigilance, watchfulness; and the saint watched over himself, over God, and over his flock—over himself by virtuous living, over God by inward contemplation, over the flock by assiduous preaching—and in these three ways he merited the vision of God.[39]

One other author will complete our list of the seminal writers of the period. He has come to be known as the Pseudo-Dionysius (fifth century), since in the Middle Ages the writings of this anonymous Greek-speaking monk were wrongly attributed to Dionysius the Areopagite, an Athenian whom Paul converted to Christianity according to Acts 17:34. In order to appreciate these writings and their influence, it is necessary first to discuss the origins of Christian mysticism.

Mysticism assumes that the highest goal of humans is union with God through contemplation and that this goal is possible while we are still on earth. The achievement of this union is not dependent on striving toward God so much as on God opening up to us. This union is to be sought and found neither in intellectual activity nor by striving to learn and understand all that God has revealed, but rather by turning inward. People can at best ready themselves for this direct contact by emptying themselves of any desires, activities, and predispositions that prevent the total detachment in which God might make his presence known. The tradition of Christian mysticism in the Middle Ages can be traced to early Fathers such as Gregory of Nyssa (c.332–395), often considered to be the founder of Christian mysticism, and beyond that to those points in the scriptural tradition in which God's presence is directly encountered. Thus, Christ's apparition to Paul on the road to Damascus, together with Paul's statement that he journeyed to the third heaven (2 Cor. 12:2–4), become the most important examples of mystical experience in the New Testament, just as Moses seeing God directly on Mount Sinai becomes its exemplar in the Old. From the time of the Fathers the tradition then stretches forward through a whole line of thinkers and writers throughout the Middle Ages: Augustine, who devotes a great deal of his writings to the meaning of contemplation; the twelfth-century school of Saint Victor in Paris, whose most famous writers, Hugh and Richard, present the main tenets of Christian mystical tradition in both devotional and analytic terms; Bernard of Clairvaux, perhaps the most important and influential mystical writer of the Middle Ages; Bonaventure, who in the thirteenth century became the most important academic synthesizer of the Franciscan mystical tradition; and Julian of Norwich, a fourteenth-century English woman who is perhaps the most well known in the English-speaking world of a great many important medieval female mystical writers.

In the fifth century, most likely in Syria, the mystical works associated with the name Pseudo-Dionysius were in fact composed. They were first introduced in the West in the ninth century through Latin translations by John Scotus Eriugena (c.810–c.875). Pseudo-Dionysius was a speculative theologian whose writings were thought to be another embodiment of his mystical gifts. A thirteenth-century account of the life of Dionysius the Aeropagite, assumed to be the author of these works, connects his life and his works as follows:

It is said that Paul revealed to Dionysius what he, in ecstasy, had seen in the third heaven, as Dionysius himself seems to insinuate in more than one place. Hence, he discoursed upon the hierarchies of the angels, their orders, ranks, and functions, so brilliantly and clearly that you would not think he had learned all this from someone else, but that he himself had been rapt to the third heaven and there he had looked upon all he described.[40]

His description of the kinds and attributes of angels in his work *The Celestial Hierarchies* became standard for much of the Middle Ages, finding its way into such important later works as Bonaventure's *Mind's Road to God*, Dante's *Divine Comedy*, the mosaics of the dome of the Baptistry in Florence, and the portals of many Gothic cathedrals. His description of the universe as an emanation from God allowed him to see in all creation vestiges of divine attributes, and he develops from this what comes to be called the doctrine of analogy. According to this doctrine, the reality of a given entity can be described in terms of the kind and amount of Divine Being it possesses. Pseudo-Dionysius was a most important channel through which this aspect of Neoplatonic thought was transmitted throughout the Middle Ages. This doctrine was enormously influential in the development of the mystical tradition, but also in the thought of such an "unmystical" thinker as Thomas Aquinas, who wrote commentaries on the works of Pseudo-Dionysius and who incorporated the doctrine of analogy into his *Summa*.

In *The Divine Names*, Pseudo-Dionysius describes the knowledge that can be obtained from reading Scripture and proceeds from there to talk about the relation of the universe to its creator:

> We learn of all these mysteries from the divine scriptures and you will find that what the scripture writers have to say regarding the divine names refers, in revealing praises, to the beneficent processions of God. And so all these scriptural utterances celebrate the supreme Deity by describing it as a monad or henad, because of its supernatural simplicity and indivisible unity, by which unifying power we are led to unity. We, in the diversity of what we are, are drawn together by it and are led linto a godlike oneness, into a unity reflecting God.
>
> They also describe it as a Trinity, for with a transcendent fecundity it is manifested as "three persons." That is why "all fatherhood in heaven and on earth is and is named after it." They call it Cause of beings since in its goodness it employed its creative power to summon all things into being, and it is hailed as wise and beautiful because beings which keep their nature uncorrupted are filled with divine harmony and sacred beauty. But they especially call it loving toward humanity, because in one of its persons it accepted a true share of what it is we are, and thereby issued a call to man's lowly state to rise up to it. In a fashion beyond words, the simplicity of Jesus became something complex, the timeless took on the duration of the temporal, and, with neither change nor confusion of what constitutes him, he came into our human nature, he who totally transcends the natural order of the world.

This is the kind of divine enlightenment into which we have been initiated by the hidden tradition of our inspired teachers, a tradition at one with scripture. We now grasp these things in the best way we can, and as they come to us, wrapped in the sacred veils of that love toward humanity with which scripture and heirarchical traditions cover the truths of the mind with things derived from the realm of the senses. And so it is that the Transcendent is clothed in the terms of being, with shape and form on things that have neither, and numerous symbols are employed to convey the varied attributes of what is an imageless and supra-national simplicity. But in time to come, when we are incorruptible and immortal, when we have come at last to the blessed inheritance of being like Christ, then, as scripture says, "we shall always be with the Lord." [1 Thess. 4:17] In most holy contemplation we shall be ever filled with the sight of God shining gloriously around us as once it shone for the disciples at the divine transfiguration. And there we shall be, our minds away from passion and from earth, and we shall have a conceptual gift of light from him and, somehow, in a way we cannot know, we shall be united with him and, our understanding carried away, blessedly happy, we shall be struck by his blazing light. Marvellously, our minds will be like those in the heavens above. We shall be "equal to angels and sons of God, being sons of the resurrection." [Luke 20:36] This is what the truth of scripture affirms.

But as for now, what happens is this. We use whatever appropriate symbols we can for the things of God. With these analogies, we are raised upward toward the truth of the mind's vision, a truth which is simple and one. We leave behind us all our own notions of the divine. We call a halt to the activities of our minds and, to the extent that is proper, we approach the ray which transcends being. Here, in a manner no words can describe, preexisted all the goals of all knowledge and it is of a kind that neither intelligence nor speech can lay hold of it nor can it at all be contemplated since it surpasses everything and is wholly beyond our capacity to know it. Transcendently it contains within itself the boundaries of every natural knowledge and energy. At the same time it is established by an unlimited power beyond all the celestial minds. And if all knowledge is of that which is and is limited to the realm of the existent, then whatever transcends being must also transcend knowledge.[41]

One can extract from this passage the core of Dionysius's thought. The created universe is a ladder that leads humans back to God. In this, Dionysius is clearly in the Pauline-Augustinian tradition, seeing the visible universe as a means to reach its invisible creator. Much of Dionysius's work, like that of Augustine, can be seen as a gloss on Rom. 1:20; and this scriptural text is quoted, significantly, in *The Divine Names*. Within this framework, however, he emphasizes the radical and total separation between creature and creator. We have the traces of God through his creation; they should lead us back to God. But it is impossible to talk about God as he really is from what we know about these traces. We should be led to the contemplation of God as our ultimate goal, but this experience is not describable by humans while on earth. It is an experience that is so above anything here that it is both ineffable and incommunicable. Traces are left in the language we use so that we attribute certain qualities to God; but the actual experience of God is above even language itself since, as he implies in the last sentence, language belongs to the existing world, the world of being, and "that which is beyond all being must be transcendent above all knowledge." The paradox that Dionysius explores is that even while we are meant to take the attributes of God as far as we can, we must recognize that our journey toward God is accompanied by an infinitely large gap between what these attributes tell us and the reality of God that as finite creatures we cannot know. We affirm things about God only to deny their ultimate applicability. Hence, the way to God in this tradition is primarily a way of negation, what later is called "apophatic" theology. Dionysius also says in this passage that we are to use "whatever appropriate symbols we can for the things of God." Following Dionysius's lead, a whole taxonomy of mystical imagery developed in the Middle Ages, in which Christ was seen in such guises as a lover-knight (see Chapter 9), as a mother, and as a bridegroom.

Perhaps the most important of those words attributable to God is "illumination." God is illumination, for we know from John's Gospel that Christ is the light of the world, coming into the world and dispelling the darkness. In the Middle Ages, light becomes a most important source of order and value here on earth; by the doctrine of analogy, the more a substance is infused with light, the more it resembles God as an image of its creator. Though the reality of God's illumination is above human comprehension, light, the purest substance, is the most important trace that leads us back to God. The influence of Dionysius's thought was limited during the Early Middle Ages, in part because his Latin translator John Scotus Eriugena was also a figure of limited influence. But during the High Middle Ages the effect of this theology of light was of the highest importance. As Otto von Simson says in *The Gothic Cathedral*, "for the twelfth and thirteenth centuries, light was the source and essence of all visual beauty."[42] This beauty was not a quality independent of or added to a substance's other qualities, but was rather an insight into a substance's very nature because it suggested the degree to which that substance partook of Being itself. Thus, the luminosity that is the characteristic of medieval manuscript illuminations and stained glass windows is an attempt to recreate the celestial harmony. The beauty of light also explains why, again in von Simson's words, "in the philosophical literature of the time, as in the courtly epic, no attributes are used more frequently to describe visual beauty than 'lucid', 'luminous', 'clear'."[43] Most important, light is the key to the aesthetic of Gothic cathedrals and to another "cathedral" in light, Dante's *Paradiso*. Light shining through the windows of Gothic cathedrals portray the celestial city; the opening lines of the *Paradiso* prepare the reader for the visions of light to follow: "The Glory of the All-Mover penetrates through the universe and re-glows in one part more, and in another less."[44]

The first attempt to translate these principles of light aesthetics into architectural form was in the Abbey Church of Saint Denis, near Paris, under the direction of its famous abbot, Suger (c.1081–1151). It was believed in the Middle Ages that Dionysius, as the follower of Paul described above, came to France and was martyred by beheading. After the beheading, "Instantly, the body of Saint Dionysius stood up, took his head in its arms, and, with an angel and a heavenly light leading the way, marched two miles, from the place called Montmartre, the hill of martyrs, to the place where, by his own choice and by God's providence, he rests in peace."[45] That place, of course, was later the site of Suger's church; the relation between the place and the doctrine informing the building of the church was by no means considered accidental.

The period discussed in this chapter was clearly an end, but it was also a beginning. This era of destruction, chaos, and cultural decline was also one of creativity, synthesis, and even genius. The traditions that came together often clashed, bringing confusion and bloodshed. But the Roman Empire that disappeared in the West in 476 was not the empire of Augustus or of the second century; it was, rather, a totalitarian, oppressive, and inefficient empire whose demise was an opportunity to start over, to create a new civilization. Although that civilization did not begin to congeal and flourish until the reign of Charlemagne (r.768–814) or perhaps even later, without the experimentation, dedication, and inventiveness of people in the centuries immediately following the collapse of the Empire, it could never have come into being. More than most periods of history, this was indeed an age of transition, perhaps even *the* greatest age of transition in the history of Western civilization.

CHAPTER 6

MONASTICISM

Sometime around the year 269, an eighteen-year-old boy named Antony, a Christian in Egypt, entered a church while the priest was reading the gospel. This event symbolically marks the beginning of Christian monasticism. The story is told in the famous life of Saint Antony (251–356) written by Saint Athanasius (c.296–373):

> He went into the church pondering these things [the apostles selling their goods], and just then it happened that the Gospel was being read, and he heard the Lord saying to the rich man, "If you would be perfect, go, sell what you possess and give to the poor, and you will have treasure in heaven." It was as if by God's design he held the saints in his recollection, and as if the passage were read on his account. Immediately Antony went out from the Lord's house and gave to the townspeople the possessions he had from his forebears.[1]

Soon Antony went to live in the desert; and although he returned to "the world" several times later in his life, he essentially lived in solitude for the rest of his life—eighty-seven years—praying and supporting himself through manual labor. He became famous for his holiness, and men came in large numbers to live near him in imitation. As mentioned in Chapter 3, this ascetic movement flourished after the end of Christian persecution, when Christianity became a favored religion. People now could become Christians who were less than fully devoted to its teachings; consequently, many saw the kind of commitment that Antony made as a way of demonstrating the depth of their devotion now that martyrdom was no longer a daily possibility. Antony came to a similar understanding of his own life:

> When finally the persecution ended, and Peter the blessed bishop had made his witness, Antony departed and withdrew once again to the cell, and was there daily being martyred by his conscience, and doing battle in the contests of the faith. He subjected himself to an even greater and more strenuous asceticism, for he was always fasting, and he had clothing with hair on the in-

terior and skin on the exterior that he kept until he died. He neither bathed his body with water for cleanliness, nor did he wash his feet at all, and he would not even consent to putting them in water unless it was necessary. Neither did anyone ever see him undressed—indeed, no one saw the body of Antony naked, except when he died and was buried.[2]

Throughout the Middle Ages people continued to regard the monastic vocation as a particularly high calling because of its imitation through asceticism of Christ and the martyrs of the church, and the documents of early monasticism were therefore treated with special reverence throughout the Middle Ages. Antony brought to Christian, and especially monastic, imagery the concept of life as an inward journey:

> But do not be afraid to hear about virtue, and do not be a stranger to the term. For it is not distant from us, nor does it stand external to us, but its realization lies in us, and the task is easy if only we shall will it. Now the Greeks leave home and traverse the sea in order to gain an education, but there is no need for us to go abroad on account of the Kingdom of heaven, nor to cross the sea for virtue. For the Lord has told us before, the Kingdom of God is within you. All virtue needs, then, is our willing, since it is in us, and arises from us.[3]

This image of the inward journey is central to the writings of Augustine, all monastic literature of the Middle Ages, and a very great number of non-monastic works as well.

Antony believed that monks should deny themselves earthly pleasures, perform physical labor, pray, and also remain in the same place:

> Just as fish die if they remain on dry land so monks, remaining away from their cells, or dwelling with men of the world, lose their determination to persevere in solitary prayer. Therefore, just as the fish should go back to the sea, so we must return to our cells, lest remaining outside we forget to watch over ourselves interiorly.[4]

Antony was not a scholar. He understood the need to read, of course, because the word of God was contained in the Bible. Yet Antony saw that God "wrote" another book as well:

> A certain philosopher asked St. Antony: "Father, how can you be so happy when you are deprived of the consolation of books?" Antony replied: "My book, O philosopher, is the nature of created things, and any time I want to read the words of God, the book is before me."[5]

This passage, closely related to the movement from visible to invisible expressed in Rom. 1:19–20, describes a way of viewing the created world that will continue to be important for many centuries. For example, in the thirteenth century, Bonaventure describes creation as a book written by God, and John Calvin will elaborate on that way of understanding creation in the sixteenth century.

Although Antony was not a philosopher, his wisdom was said to exceed that of the great scholars of Alexandria. The following story illustrates this:

> Antony was also extremely wise. It was a marvel that although he had not learned letters, he was a shrewd and intelligent man. For example, once two Greek philosophers visited him, thinking they would be able to put him to the test. He was in the outer mountain at the time, and knowing what the men were from their appearance, he went out to them and said through an interpreter, "Why did you go to so much trouble, you philosophers, to visit a foolish man?" When they responded that he was not foolish, but quite wise, he said to them, "If you came to a foolish man, your toil is superfluous, but if you consider me wise, become as I am, for we must imitate what is good. If I had come to you I would have imitated you; but since you came to me, become as I am; for I am a Christian." In amazement they withdrew, for they saw that even demons feared Antony.[6]

People wise in things of the spirit overcoming those of worldly wisdom can be seen in countless works throughout the Middle Ages. The hermit who dispenses true wisdom to the worldly-wise is an important figure in medieval literature, especially in stories of the knights of King Arthur's round table.

One of the difficulties inherent in the ruggedly individualistic monasticism of Antony and his followers was that the monks in the desert were deprived of the sacraments of the church since they were not priests. Furthermore, the desert was dangerous, especially to those who were ill or too old to provide for themselves. In the fourth century it thus became common for monks to gather together, living in communities that shared the liturgy, meals, and necessary labor. The most famous of these was established in Egypt by Pachomius, whose rule for his monastery is the earliest to survive. Monasteries did not supercede the hermit life; instead, two kinds of monasticism coexisted in the desert, and many of those who later became hermits began their monastic lives in a monastery.

Although most of the hermits in the desert were men, there were also women who took up the monastic vocation in the Egyptian desert. In the collections of the sayings of these early monastic figures are the words of women as well as of men. The image of women as heroic ascetics and as dispensers of wisdom is thus part of the monastic tradition. The following wise statement from a female hermit named Syncletica is similar in kind to the "one-liners" of Antony quoted above, but it also is built on an image taken from traditional women's work:

> For those capable of [voluntary poverty], it is a perfect good. Those who can sustain it receive suffering in the body but rest in the soul, for just as one washes coarse clothes by trampling them underfoot and turning them about in all directions, even so the strong soul becomes much more stable thanks to voluntary poverty.[7]

Beginning in the fourth century, there were monasteries of women as well as men. Throughout the Middle Ages and until the present, the importance of monasticism as a religious vocation and as a place of relative autonomy for women has been of central importance.

Before looking at the development of monastic ideals and institutions, it is appropriate to ask why monks were perceived to be so profoundly Christian throughout the Middle Ages and beyond, since Christ and his apostles carried out active ministries and did not practice the rigid asceticism of the desert fathers and mothers. The idea of the Christian life as an imitation of the life of Christ is already present in New Testament texts. The key question, of course, is, what does it mean to imitate Christ? Once we dismiss the most literal possible interpretation—that the imitation of Christ means walking around Palestine in sandals, being nailed to a cross, etc.—we have to develop a more serious understanding not only of Christ's ministries but also of what Christ teaches about the most fundamental purpose of life. Today, it is easy for those who are married with children, own homes, and work in business to wonder how a monk can think he is imitating Christ since Christ was out in the world and did not live separate from society. Yet, to state the obvious, Christ was not married with children either. He did not own a home nor was he employed. For monks, the purpose and goal of life is to enter God's kingdom; and Christ spoke of the blessedness of those with purity of heart. Monks, in addition to the daily martyrdom described above, embraced a life of asceticism, prayer, and separation because they found these to be the elements central for them to achieve purity of heart. After all, Christ did pray alone, he apparently owned no personal property, he was celibate. Thus, monks choose certain key elements of Christ's life and teaching to imitate directly, just as Christians who are not monks do. As one modern monk has put it, monks prune some branches which are good in and of themselves in order for other branches to flourish. Monks believe that it is false to think that Christians "can have it all."

Both eremitic (individual) and cenobitic (communal) forms of monasticism spread from Egypt, first to the Holy Land and the East, and then also to the West, reaching the latter as early as the middle of the fourth century. For the development of Western monasticism, the most important writer of this era was John Cassian (c.360–435), who traveled to the Egyptian desert and wrote in Latin of conversations he had with monks, incorporating a great deal of early monastic lore and thought in his books. Later, Benedict recommended in his Rule (Ch. 73) that monks read both Cassian's *Institutes* and *Conferences*. In the former, Cassian attempts to catalogue the vices that monks were susceptible to, and later authors used his scheme to develop what later became known as the Seven Deadly Sins. It is easy to see how medieval authors, including Dante, who wrote about the deadly sins—lust, gluttony, avarice, sloth, anger, envy, and pride—are dependent directly or indirectly on Cassian:

These are, first, gluttony, which is understood as the desire to gormandize; second, fornication; third, filargyria, which means avarice or, better expressed, the love of money; fourth, anger; fifth, sadness; sixth, acedia, which is anxiety or weariness of heart; seventh, cenodoxia, which means vain or empty glory; eighth, pride.[8]

Of all the deadly sins, pride was the most serious. Just about every discussion of pride in medieval literature is indebted to what Cassian wrote about it in the *Institutes:*

> Our eighth struggle, which is the last, is against the spirit of pride. Although this disease is the final one in the combat with the vices and is placed last in order, it is nonetheless first in terms of origin and time [i.e., Lucifer's rebellion against God and Adam and Eve's sin in the Garden of Eden]. It is the most savage beast, fiercer than all those previously mentioned, greatly trying the perfect and ravaging with its cruel bite those who are nearly established in the perfection of virtue.[9]

Pride becomes a particularly important monastic concern because the monk who gives up so much can easily come to believe that he or she is superior to those who live in the world. It is an "occupational hazard" for one progressing toward perfection by ridding oneself of lust, gluttony, and sloth. Cassian wrote about the value of all the material sacrifices that a monk makes:

> Thus fasts, vigils, meditating on Scripture, and the being stripped and deprived of every possession are not perfection, but they are the tools of perfection. For the end of that discipline does not consist in these things; rather, it is by them that one arrives at the end.[10]

This distinction between means and ends is a familiar one. In this context Cassian warns that self-denial will be of no benefit unless it is a means to move toward God, together with prayer and the practice of virtue. This remains an important lesson to the monks of the Middle Ages.

Various ascetic practices free the monk in order than he or she may pray. It is from the desert experience of early monks that Christianity takes its basic teachings on the value and practices of prayer, and no writer in this tradition was of greater importance than Evagrius of Pontus, a desert ascetic who had a classical education. Although Evagrius's works were often misattributed in the Middle Ages, he is the foundational figure in the history of the theory and practice of prayer.

> Go, sell your possessions and give to the poor, and take up your cross so that you can pray without distraction.[11]

In this passage, Evagrius takes two of Christ's commands and sees them as means to the end of a life of prayer. For Evagrius, prayer must never simply become habit:

Whether you pray along with the brethren or alone, strive to make your prayer more than a mere habit. Make it a true inner experience.[12]

In order to achieve this inner experience, Evagrius counsels monks not to "fashion some image or visualize some form at the time of prayer."[13] There will be many discussions of the usefulness of images for prayer in the Middle Ages.

The sort of prayer that Evagrius describes has the appearance of cutting people off from the world and its problems. However, Evagrius emphasizes that prayer brings union not just between the one who prays and God but also between the one praying and the rest of creation:

A monk is a man who is separated from all and is in harmony with all. A monk is a man who considers himself one with all men because he seems constantly to see himself in every man.[14]

These ideas of prayer are not just for debate among monks. Francis of Assisi will seek the union that Evagrius advises but also finds a deeper unity with the most wretched of the earth and with all creatures because of his life of prayer. Even as "worldly" a man as Dante will attempt to describe his experience of God as a tie that binds him not just to heaven but also to his fellow creatures.

As monasticism entered the West it developed in numerous forms, including hermits, some of whom performed dramatic feats of asceticism, and early monastic communities with a wide variety of lifestyles. Furthermore, there were apparently some who sought the advantages of monasticism—respect and hospitality, for example—without seriously pursuing a path to God. The period in which monasticism first spread in Europe corresponded to the collapse of the Roman Empire in the West, and unstable conditions "in the world" were often mirrored in the cloister.

In the first half of the sixth century lived a man who was to become the most important influence on Western monasticism from his own time till the present. His name is Saint Benedict of Nursia (480–547); and his Rule, written primarily for his own monks at Monte Cassino in Italy, eventually spread all over Latin Christendom. Pope Gregory the Great's sixth-century life of Saint Benedict, one of the most important saints' lives of the early Middle Ages, was of greatest importance for the spread of the Rule. What follows is Gregory's description of one of Benedict's temptations after he gave up his study in Rome to become a hermit:

A greater temptation of the flesh than he had ever experienced overtook the holy man. For the evil spirit brought back before the mind's eye a certain woman whom he had once seen. So intensely did the Tempter inflame his mind by the sight of that woman that he could hardly control his passion. He was overcome by sensuality, and almost considered leaving his solitary retreat. Then suddenly God graciously looked upon him and he returned to himself. Since he saw that thickets of nettles and thorn bushes were growing

Fresco of Saint Benedict. Church of the Sacro Speco, Subiaco, Italy. Four-teenth century. This image of Benedict is painted in a church built over the cave where he lived as a hermit before founding Monte Cassino. This image is not a portrait in the modern sense—an attempt to represent what a person actually looked like. Instead it shows viewers what is important about the saint. As the father of Western monasticism, he is depicted as a wise, white-haired elder. He wears a monastic habit of the fourteenth century, when the fresco was painted. He carries his Rule and blesses the viewers with his right hand. The haircut of Benedict, called the tonsure, is a visible sign that he is a cleric and thus subject to the law of the church.

nearby, he stripped off his garments and flung himself naked upon those sting-ing thorns and burning nettles. He rolled about there for a long time, and came out with his whole body wounded by them. So through the wound of the skin he drew out from his body the wound of the mind by changing his lust to pain. Although he burned painfully on the outside, he had put out the forbidden flame within.[15]

After a rather unsuccessful attempt to reform a monastery that had asked for his help and a failed attempt to return to the solitary life of a hermit, Bene-dict tore down a pagan shrine and in its place founded a new monastery at Monte Cassino in central Italy. There Benedict combined older monastic sources with his own practical and commonsense approach to the cenobitic life to create the Benedictine Rule. In the preface he states the monk's and the monastery's prime purpose:

And so we are going to establish a school for the service of the Lord. In found-ing it we hope to introduce nothing harsh or burdensome. But if a certain strictness results from the dictates of equity for the amendment of vices or the preservation of charity, do not be at once dismayed and fly from the way of salvation, whose entrance cannot but be narrow. For as we advance in the religious life and in faith, our hearts expand and we run the way of God's commandments with unspeakable sweetness of love. Thus, never departing from His school, but persevering in the monastery according to His teaching until death, we may by patience share in the sufferings of Christ and deserve to have a share also in His kingdom.[16]

In addition to describing the monastery as a school and thus the monk as a pupil, Benedict also describes the monk as a soldier doing battle with the Enemy, a worker laboring for God, and a pilgrim on a journey. All of these require discipline and focus, and it is fair to say that the Rule provides monks with what they need to accomplish these tasks.

While many early Christian authors—Augustine is the most obvious example—prescribe a life for Christians that borrows from both biblical and classical models, Benedict's Rule contains only one classical reference, and Benedict probably got it from a Christian writer who had incorporated it into his work. Thus, one could describe the Rule as the first book to present a lifestyle derived entirely from the Bible. In the Prologue to the Rule, which is about four modern printed pages in length, there are no fewer than twenty quotations from the Old and New Testaments.

The Rule called for a strong abbot in the monastery, almost unlimited in his powers and answerable only to God. However, the abbot could not act completely on his own:

Whenever any important business has to be done in the monastery, let the Abbot call together the whole community and state the matter to be acted upon. Then, having heard the brethren's advice, let him turn the matter over in his own mind and do what he shall judge to be most expedient. The reason we have said that all should be called for counsel is that the Lord often reveals to the younger what is best.[17]

The sections of the Rule that deal with the role of the abbot are among the most influential passages of this seminal text. Abbots must teach more by example than precept and must also consider the needs of the individual when dealing with monks who have erred. It is clear from the passage quoted in the previous chapter from Gregory the Great's *Pastoral Care* that Gregory has incorporated principles of the Rule into his manual on Christian leadership.

Benedict passionately believed that a monastery cannot successfully be organized by the world's standards. Thus, he wanted to root out the worldly hierarchies such as privilege of birth or age or wealth. The only monks to be regarded as superior were those who achieved the rare combination of good works *and* humility. One prerequisite for eliminating the world's standards in the monastery was the elimination of private property. Benedict is uniquivocal and uncompromising on this matter in a chapter entitled "Monks and Private Ownership":

> Above all, this evil practice must be uprooted and removed from the monastery. We mean that without an order from the abbot, no one may presume to give, receive or retain anything as his own, nothing at all—not a book, writing tablets or stylus—in short, not a single item, especially since monks may not have the free disposal even of their own bodies and wills.[18]

A few lines later, he quotes Acts 4:32, which describes the earliest Christian community in Rome holding goods in common.

Food, drink, shelter, and clothing were all provided for the monk at the discretion of the abbot, but Benedict certainly intended a minimum of food and plain clothing:

> We think it sufficient for the daily dinner, whether at the sixth or the ninth hour, that every table have two cooked dishes, on account of individual infirmities, so that he who for some reason cannot eat of the one may make his meal of the other. Therefore let two cooked dishes suffice for all the brethren; and if any fruit or fresh vegetables are available, let a third dish be added.
>
> But if it happens, that the work was heavier, it shall lie within the Abbot's discretion and power, should it be expedient, to add something to the fare. Above all things, however, over-indulgence must be avoided and a monk must never be overtaken by indigestion; for there is nothing so opposed to the Christian character as over-indulgence, according to Our Lord's words, "See to it that your hearts be not burdened with over-indulgence." . . .
>
> We believe that a hemina of wine [about half a bottle] a day is sufficient for each. But those to whom God gives the strength to abstain should know that they will receive a special reward.
>
> If the circumstances of the place, or the work, or the heat of summer require a greater measure, the Superior shall use his judgment in the matter, taking care always that there be no occasion for surfeit or drunkenness. We read, it is true, that wine is by no means a drink for monks; but since the monks of our day cannot be persuaded of this, let us at least agree to drink sparingly and not to satiety, because "wine makes even the wise fall away." . . .
>
> We believe, however, that in ordinary places the following dress is sufficient for each monk: a tunic, a cowl (thick and woolly for winter, thin or worn for summer), a scapular for work, stockings and shoes to cover the feet.
>
> The monks should not complain about the color or the coarseness of any of these things, but be content with what can be found in the district where they live and can be purchased cheaply. . . .
>
> And in order that this vice of private ownership may be cut out by the roots, the Abbot should provide all the necessary articles: cowl, tunic, stockings, shoes, girdle, knife, pen, needle, handkerchief, tablets; that all pretext of need may be taken away.[19]

The principal activities of the monk were to pray and work, in Latin, *ora et labora*. Through the Rule of Saint Benedict, manual labor was given a dignity it never had in Roman times. The Rule established an elaborate schedule of services for prayer, called offices, beginning with vigils in the middle of the night and ending with compline in the early evening. In between were the offices of lauds, prime, tierce, sext, none, and vespers. At other times the monks remained busy because

> Idleness is the enemy of the soul. Therefore the brethren should be occupied at certain times in manual labor, and again at fixed hours in sacred reading. . . . And if the circumstances of the place or their poverty should require that they themselves do the work of gathering the harvest, let them not be discontented; for then are they truly monks when they live by the labor of their hands, as did our Fathers and the Apostles. Let all things be done with moderation, however, for the sake of the faint-hearted.[20]

A monk's life consisted of times of communal prayer, manual labor, and rest. The interweaving of these was a way to see all activity as God-centered and thus as a kind of prayer. Furthermore, the monastic day conformed to nature. The office of vigils, sung at night, had the theme of waiting for the Lord. Lauds, at daybreak, celebrated the coming of the Lord, symbolized by the light, while vespers came at the end of the working day as the sun was setting and was an office of Thanksgiving.

Study was not a main element of the monk's life for Benedict, although each monk was expected to be literate and had an obligation to read an entire book during Lent. Monte Cassino was first and foremost a place to win salvation rather than a place to advance knowledge of the world. However, often by default, monasteries were, especially in the early Middle Ages, centers of learning and scholarship because monasteries brought together literate people, books, and stability. Indeed, monasteries were *the* centers of learning in the early Middle Ages. Perhaps because learning was fostered almost exclusively in an environment in which monks and nuns lived according to a vow of chastity, one of the legacies of early medieval monasticism to the rest of the Middle Ages is the idea that the life of the mind can best be pursued in the absence of marriage and procreation. This idea was certainly not unique to monasticism. It was present in many of the church fathers and also present in the classical world. But monasteries were, significantly, the places where the church fathers were studied and classical learning was preserved. Monastic culture would have seen in this ideal of celibate learning a confirmation of its own theory and practice. Even though a connection between learning and celibacy is not much in evidence in Jewish biblical culture, it nevertheless becomes a theme that permeates medieval discourse.

Benedict wrote his Rule for Monte Cassino, never envisioning the creation of a religious order or its spread throughout Western Christendom. However, the Rule of Benedict spread rapidly. It became the norm in England in the seventh century and was firmly established in Germany and Gaul in the eighth century. By the ninth century the Rule had become almost universal in Latin Christendom, making it the most important document in the history of Western monasticism. There were two primary reasons for its success. One was the popularity of the cult of Saint Benedict, largely due to the writings of Pope Gregory the Great. Second was the genius of the Rule itself. It provided a stable structure with a strong abbot, and it provided a synthesis of the older desert tradition with a new moderation. The combination of moderation and strictness in Benedict's attitude toward the monks drinking wine, quoted above, is a good example of this synthesis.

Although the Rule became the constitution of hundreds, indeed thousands, of monasteries, like all constitutions it had to be interpreted and adapted to conditions quite different from its origins. To take two obvious examples, the clothing regulations were not adequate for a cold climate, and in some parts of northern Europe, wine was nonexistent. Thus, in the spirit of the Rule itself, different customs developed within the context of Benedictine monasticism throughout Western Europe. Some of these lists of practices, called customaries, survive from the tenth and eleventh centuries, although it is clear that the tradition of each community developing its own way of following the Rule began as soon as it spread from Monte Cassino.

Although Benedict wrote his Rule for men, it was adopted by and adapted for women from the early Middle Ages till the present. Women monastics could not be as separated from men as the monks were from women, in large part because of the need for a priest to say mass and carry out other sacramental functions. Yet in a world in which women had very little autonomy in law or practice, it was monasteries that provided women with opportunities for leadership, for administration of property, and for the creation of feminine forms of spirituality that have made important contributions to the development of Christian thought. Most of the female saints of the Middle Ages were cloistered women, and the stories of their lives were circulated outside their monasteries. In recent years, there has been a significant renewal of interest in the spirituality of medieval women living in Benedictine communities. The twelfth-century visionary, composer, and artist Hildegard of Bingen has received the greatest attention, but in fact there were many important women monastic writers. We rely heavily today on their voices to understand issues of gender in the Middle Ages. In the following passage, Hildegard develops the mother/child image in order to understand and experience human relationships with the Church. In doing this, Hildegard is adding to the ways that men as well as women can come to a fuller experience and understanding of their relationship with the means of salvation:

And as a baby is nourished in its body by milk and the food another grinds up for it, so also a baptized person must observe from his inmost heart the doctrine and the faith given to him in his baptism. But if the baby does not suck at its mother's breast or take the food ground up for it, it will die at once, and so also if a baptized person does not receive the nurturing of his most loving mother, the Church, or retain the words his faithful teachers proposed to him at baptism, he will not escape a cruel death for his soul, for he has refused his soul's salvation and the sweetness of eternal life. And as, when the baby cannot chew its bodily food with its teeth, someone else grinds it up for it to swallow lest it should die, so too in baptism, since it lacks words to confess Me [God], of necessity there are spiritual helpers for it, who provide it with the food of life, namely the Catholic faith, lest it fall into the snares of perpetual death.[21]

Hildegard did much to expand our ways of talking about God. Her writings make frequent use of female allegorical figures such as Ecclesia and Synagoga (church and synagogue, or New and Old Testaments). The illustrations she herself drew to accompany her writings are highly imaginative and play with some of the same allegorical concepts as the texts do. Moreover, she demonstrates a deep knowledge in so many fields of learning that it would be hard to come up with a male counterpart as versatile or as learned. In addition to recording her visions, whose imaginative power alone serves to make her one of the most interesting writers of the Middle Ages, Hildegard wrote an herbal and a lapidary—works dealing with the properties of herbs and stones—and several medical texts, all of which confirm her place as an important "scientific" writer of her day. She composed music that is currently enjoying a great deal of popularity, and her play, the "Ordo Virtutum" (Order of Virtues) is often considered the first liturgical drama in the medieval West. Nor was her influence limited to the cloister. Hildegard possessed enormous intellectual authority, so much so that Paris theologians often wrote to her to enlist her support in their debates, and her writings include responses to some pointed academic questions. (See Chapter 9.) And like the fourteenth-century mystic Catherine of Siena, she was deeply involved in the political currents of her day. (See Chapter 11.) She clashed with the emperor Frederick Barbarossa and with Church authorities at all levels. Hildegard's cult following did not prevent her convent from coming under papal interdiction because she insisted on allowing a local aristocratic patron to be buried in its cemetery. The pope later relented.

Like male Benedictines, cloistered women also played roles in society at large. Hildegard was also a preacher, although that was highly unusual and controversial. More commonly, people in need appealed to convents of nuns for material and spiritual help. Here is a story from the life of Saint Leoba, an eighth-century nun:

> There was a certain poor little crippled girl, who sat near the gate of the monastery begging alms. Every day she received her food from the abbess's

[Leoba's] table, her clothing from the nuns, and all other necessities from them; these were given to her from divine charity.[22]

Although in the eleventh, twelfth, and thirteenth centuries new religious communities and orders were formed that did not live under the Rule, for example the Franciscans and Dominicans (see Chapter 10), it did continue to be the fundamental law in hundreds of Benedictine houses (black monks) and Cistercian houses (white monks, a reform of the Benedictines established in 1098; see Chapter 8). Men and women in all walks of life in the Middle Ages knew the basic tenets of the Rule; thus there are many allusions to it in medieval literature. One immediately thinks of the Monk in the *General Prologue* to Chaucer's *Canterbury Tales,* who takes the tenets of the Rule and systematically turns them upside down. There is also an unmistakably monastic quality to Dante's *Purgatory,* which uses monastic discipline in its depiction of communal repentence.

Despite the overwhelming importance of Benedict for Western monasticism, he was not the only person who contributed to defining the lifestyle and work of monks. Were one to ask non-medievalists to describe a medieval monk, they would probably picture a scholar-scribe seated at his desk copying books. That would be right in part; yet as we have suggested, neither the desert fathers nor Benedict envisioned the monk primarily as a scholar. Such an emphasis on scholarship was the work of monks such as Cassiodorus (c.485–580), who established two monasteries at Vivarium in southern Italy where monks

Monastery of Saint Martin du Canigou, France, c.1000. This thousand-year-old monastery in the Pyrenees contains the most familiar elements of monastic life—isolated location, church, cloister, buildings for living and meeting.

attempted to combine pagan and Christian learning. Scholarly zeal in the monastic tradition also comes from another source, Irish monasticism. Since Ireland had not been part of the Roman Empire and thus its inhabitants did not read or write Latin, learning the language of the Bible required study. Thus, the Irish monks soon became the best classicists in Western Europe. Within two centuries of the arrival of Christianity there, monks from Ireland came to both England and the European continent, introducing new elements into monastic life as far away as Italy.

Although monks were people who removed themselves from the mainstream of medieval society, monasticism, paradoxically, permeated that society. Because of their value to the monastic vocation, both classical and early Christian writings were preserved, studied, and employed in monasteries; the earliest surviving manuscripts of almost all ancient texts are copies made by monks. It was in the monasteries of early medieval Europe that the first fully Christian culture developed—that is, in a monastic setting all was subordinated to the search for God and the achievement of salvation. With the brief exception of the reign of Charlemagne (768–814) and the years immediately following, monastic schools had a virtual monopoly on education until the twelfth century. Finally, many men who either were themselves monks or who were educated in monasteries served as advisors to secular rulers, became bishops, or even were elected pope (e.g., Gregory VII and Urban II; see Chapter 8), thus bringing monastic culture out of the cloister and into the world.

CHAPTER 7

THE FIRST
MEDIEVAL SYNTHESIS
The Carolingian World and Its Dissolution

CHARLEMAGNE

The Frankish alliance forged in 751 when, with the pope's approval, Pepin replaced the last Merovingian king of the Franks, was tested, strengthened, and made permanent in the next half-century. The creation of an axis of power that crossed the Alps and reached from Aachen to Rome in some significant way created Europe, more precisely a Western European civilization distinct from the Christian civilization centered in Constantinople and of course far different from the Muslim civilization that dominated half of the Mediterranean. That body of water was no longer the center of the world (the literal meaning of the word Mediterranean). In later centuries, the religion and culture of London and Paris and Trier would have more in common with Rome than Rome would with Athens, Constantinople, Antioch, and Carthage.

As medieval civilization developed in the West, a less fragmented and more integrated culture began to develop, primarily a blend of classical (primarily Latin), Christian, and Germanic elements. Although scholars usually refer to the thirteenth century as the era of *the* great medieval synthesis, it was during the reign of Charlemagne (768–814) that we find the first medieval synthesis. Although most of the achievements, political and intellectual, were attenuated or largely dismantled in the two centuries following Charlemagne's death, this period is important both for what it achieved and how those achievements, no matter how short-lived, were crucial building blocks for the period that followed, often called the Renaissance of the Twelfth Century.

The papacy did not wait long to call upon the new Frankish king Pepin for help, for the Lombards threatened Rome in 753. Pepin arrived in Italy, defeated the Lombards, and in 756 "donated" the conquered territory to the papacy. It is possible that Pepin knew of the forged Donation of Constantine (see Chapter 3), for it came into existence about this time.

Charlemagne, deservedly one of the best known figures of the Middle Ages, succeeded his father Pepin as king of the Franks. He not only ruled the Frankish kingdom from 768 to 814, but also conquered northern Italy from the Lombards and much territory to the east of the Frankish kingdom from the Saxons, Bavarians, and Hunnic Avars. Charlemagne's empire thus consisted of almost all of Western Christian continental Europe. Not all of Charlemagne's military campaigns were successful, most famously his skirmishes with Muslims in the area of the Pyrenees. However, Charlemagne was much more than a successful conqueror; his concept of empire and his sponsorship of a program of educational reform and religious uniformity, often called the Carolingian Renaissance, make his reign the most important in early medieval history. After his death, Charlemagne became a figure celebrated in song and legend, revered as a warrior and a saint.

By the end of the 780s, Charlemagne, in part under the influence of his trusted advisors, had begun to develop a concept of a Christian empire of which he was the head. He clearly perceived himself as the defender of the Church and consequently issued decrees on matters of ecclesiastical policy and even doctrine, which he expected clerics and laity alike to obey. It is no accident that his nickname at court was David, after the great Hebrew king. In his famous *Admonitio Generalis* of 789, he likened himself to another Old Testament king, Josias, the great religious reformer (2 Kings 22 ff.). In this decree, he used pastoral language reminiscent of Gregory the Great when describing the functions of the clergy:

> Accordingly it has pleased us to solicit your efforts, O pastors of the churches of Christ and leaders of His flock and distinguished luminaries of the world, to strive to lead the people of God to the pastures of eternal life by watchful care and urgent advice and stir yourselves to bring back the wandering sheep within the walls of ecclesiastical constancy on the shoulders of good example or exhortation, lest the wolf, plotting against anyone who transgresses the canonical laws or evades the fatherly traditions of the ecumenical councils— which God forbid!—find him and devour him. Thus they must be admonished, urged, and even forced by the great zeal of piety, to restrain themselves within the bonds of paternal sanctions with staunch faith and unrelenting constancy. Therefore, we have sent our missi [messengers and inspectors] who by the authority of our name are to correct along with you what should be corrected. And we append herewith certain chapters from canonical ordinances which seem to us to be particularly necessary.[1]

The following is among the many chapters that demonstrate that Charlemagne's legislation dealt with issues which in modern categories would be purely ecclesiastical matters:

And you are to see to it, chosen and venerable pastors and rulers of the church of God, that the priests whom you send through your dioceses for ruling and preaching in the churches to the people serving God, that they rightly and justly preach; and you are not to allow any of them to invent and preach to the people new and unlawful things according to their own judgment and not according to Holy Scripture. And you too are to preach those things which are just and right and lead to eternal life, and instruct others that they are to preach these same things.[2]

During the 790s, Charlemagne's concept of a Christian empire grew, and his position as protector of the papacy was tested when political rivals in Rome drove Pope Leo III from the city in 799. Three years earlier, Charlemagne had presented his views on the roles of temporal and spiritual authorities in a letter to the pope:

For it is our task, with the aid of divine goodness, to defend the holy church of Christ everywhere from the attacks of pagans without and to strengthen it within through the knowledge of the Catholic faith. And it is your duty, O Holy Father, with your hands raised high to God, after the manner of Moses, to aid our armies so that by your intercession with God, our leader and benefactor, the Christian people may always and everywhere be victorious over the enemies of His Holy Name, and the name of Our Lord Jesus Christ be proclaimed throughout the world.[3]

Charlemagne intervened directly on behalf of Leo III, and the pontiff's restoration to the throne of Saint Peter was probably the immediate cause of one of the most famous events of the Middle Ages—the coronation of Charlemagne as Roman emperor (often referred to by modern historians as the Holy Roman Emperor) by the pope in Saint Peter's on Christmas Day, 800. Undoubtedly there had been discussion between the pope and the Frankish king before that day concerning the revival of the Empire, and the idea of empire appears frequently in the writings of Charlemagne's advisor Alcuin (c.735–804) during the decade preceding the coronation. With this in mind, the account of the coronation written by Charlemagne's friend and biographer Einhard is surprising:

The truth is that the inhabitants of Rome had violently attacked Pope Leo, putting out his eyes and cutting off his tongue [Einhard is wrong about injuries to the pope], and had forced him to flee to the King for help. Charlemagne really came to Rome to restore the Church, which was in a very bad state indeed, but in the end he spent the whole winter there. It was on this occasion that he received the title of Emperor and Augustus. At first he was far from wanting this. He made it clear that he would not have entered the cathedral that day at all, although it was the greatest of all the festivals of the Church, if he had known in advance what the Pope was planning to do.[4]

Perhaps the explanation for Charlemagne's displeasure is not with the title but with the manner in which it was conferred. In ancient Roman imperial ceremony, acclamation by the people preceded the actual coronation; and it was the former that actually conferred power. However, Leo III's coronation preceded a well-rehearsed acclamation; this is clear from another contemporary account:

> On the most holy day of Christmas, when the king rose from prayer in front of the shrine of the blessed apostle Peter, to take part in the Mass, Pope Leo placed a crown on his head, and he was hailed by the whole Roman people: To the august Charles, crowned by God, the great and peaceful emperor of the Romans, life and victory! After the acclamations the pope addressed him in the manner of the old emperors. The name of Patricius was now abandoned and he was called Emperor and Augustus.[5]

The acclamation in unison plus the availability of a crown make clear that this was not a spontaneous act on the part of a grateful pontiff. Charlemagne probably disliked the prominence of the pope's role in the reconstitution of the Empire, something totally absent in the Roman imperial tradition, even after Constantine. However, it would be a long time before popes used this precedent as a demonstration of their right to make and unmake Roman emperors. Perhaps the most convincing sign of Charlemagne's displeasure with the way he became emperor is the fact that when he conferred the imperial title upon his son Louis, the ceremony took place in Germany; and Charlemagne placed the crown on his son's head without any ecclesiastical participation in the ceremony.

In 802, Charlemagne required his subjects—even those who had done so prior to his imperial coronation—to swear an oath of loyalty to him *as emperor,* for this was the one title that he held in all the territories he ruled:

> He [Charlemagne] has given instructions that in all his kingdom all men, both clergy and laity, and each according to his vows and way of life, who before have promised fealty to him as king, should now make the same promise to him as Caesar [synonymous with Emperor]; and those who until now have not made the promise are all to do so from 12 years old and upwards.[6]

Before 800, Charlemagne had established his permanent residence in Aachen (sometimes known by its French name, Aix-la-Chapelle) near Cologne in modern Germany, where his chapel, throne, and sarcophagus survive. In the years after his coronation, Aachen was the real center of his empire rather than Rome itself; and the court was still in essence Frankish in its customs despite the classical nicknames, the Roman-inspired architecture of the chapel, and the colossal statue of the fifth-century Emperor Theodosius II. After his coronation, Charlemagne never again set foot in Rome.

Charlemagne had planned to divide his territories among his three sons, following the custom of his Merovingian predecessors; but these kingdoms

were all to remain part of a single empire, with Louis holding the imperial title. However, all his sons but Louis predeceased him, and thus for another
generation the Empire remained more or less intact. In marked contrast to the
decentralizing tendencies of the Merovingian kings, Charlemagne strove to
bring about a high degree of uniformity to all the lands he governed. His imperial title was one key element of this unity; its importance is suggested in
the text of 802 quoted above. In that same document, Charlemagne described
some of the machinery he established for making a unified empire a reality:

> Our most serene and most Christian lord and emperor, Charles, has selected
> the most prudent and wise from among his leading men, archbishops and bish-
> ops, together with venerable abbots and devout laymen, and has sent them
> out into all his kingdom, and bestowed through them on all his subjects the
> right to live in accordance with a right rule of law. . . . And the missi them-
> selves, as they wish to have the favour of Almighty God and to preserve it
> through the loyalty they have promised, are to make diligent inquiry wher-
> ever a man claims that someone has done him an injustice; so everywhere,
> and amongst all men, in God's holy churches, among poor people, orphans
> and widows, and throughout the whole people they may administer law and
> justice in full accordance with the will and the fear of God. And if there be
> anything which they themselves, together with the counts of the provinces
> [appointed officials], cannot correct or bring to a just settlement, they should
> refer it without any hesitation to the emperor's judgment along with their
> reports. And in no way, whether by some man's flattery or bribery, or by the
> excuse of blood relationship with someone, or through fear of someone more
> powerful, should anyone hinder the right and proper course of justice.[7]

Despite Charlemagne's imperial titles, his missi, and his charisma, the uni-
fication of the Empire was far from complete and indeed may not have been
as extensive as the sources suggest. Moreover, the partial and fragile unity
and strong government that he did create did not long outlive him because of
internal weakness and foreign invasion but also because it took someone of
Charlemagne's personal qualities to keep the forces opposed to centralization
in check. Nevertheless, his idea of empire became a part of the medieval world
view.

Charlemagne's energy and genius were not limited to military and political affairs. The cultural revival and educational reform that he began and nourished are every bit as important as the other achievements of his reign. Charlemagne, a Germanic warrior chieftain, was also a man deeply committed to
learning, and to the study of theology in particular:

> He spoke easily and fluently, and could express with great clarity whatever
> he had to say. He was not content with his own mother tongue, but took
> the trouble to learn foreign languages. He learnt Latin so well that he spoke
> it as fluently as his own tongue; but he understood Greek better than he

could speak it. He was eloquent to the point of sometimes seeming almost garrulous.

He paid the greatest attention to the liberal arts; and he had great respect for men who taught them, bestowing high honours upon them. When he was learning the rules of grammar he received [tutoring] from Peter the Deacon of Pisa, who by then was an old man, but for all other subjects he was caught by Alcuin, surnamed Albinus, another Deacon, a man of the Saxon race who came from Britain and was the most learned man anywhere to be found. Under him the Emperor spent much time and effort in studying rhetoric, dialectic and especially astrology. He applied himself to mathematics and traced the course of the stars with great attention and care.[8]

This text documents Charlemagne's careful and successful search for the greatest scholars of Western Christendom to serve as tutors, teachers for his children, advisors, and ecclesiastical reformers, including men from Italy, Ireland, and Christian Spain as well as from the Frankish kingdom. By far the most important of these was Alcuin of York, the chief architect of the cultural revival known today as the Carolingian Renaissance. He expressed his enthusiasm for the revival of classical learning in somewhat exalted terms in a 799 letter to Charlemagne:

If many people became imbued with your ideas, a new Athens would be established in Francia—nay, an Athens fairer than the Athens of old, for it would be ennobled by the teachings of Christ, and ours would surpass all the wisdom of the ancient Academy. For this had only for its instruction the disciples of Plato; yet, moulded by the seven liberal arts, it shone with constant splendour. But ours would be endowed as well with the sevenfold fullness of the Spirit, and would surpass all secular wisdom in dignity.[9]

What precisely was this renaissance all about? Compared to the cultural revival of the twelfth century or the Italian Renaissance of the fifteenth, it was modest indeed. In order for Charlemagne to be a responsible defender and guide of those he ruled and in order for Christianity to be a (perhaps *the*) major element of unity in his territories, it was vital that both doctrine and liturgy be uniform. That would only be possible if accurate texts of Scripture and other authoritative Christian texts were available, which was in turn only possible if the clergy were educated. Consequently, Charlemagne ordered the production of accurate copies of texts and called upon Alcuin and others to plan a new educational system. This passage from the *Admonitio Generalis* make clear the importance Charlemagne attached to these enterprises:

And let schools be established in which boys may learn to read. Correct carefully the Psalms, the signs in writing, the songs, the calendar, the grammar in each monastery or bishopric, and the catholic books; because often some desire to pray to God properly, but they pray badly because of the incorrect books. And do not permit your boys to corrupt them in reading or writing.

If there is need of writing the Gospel, Psalter, and Missal, let men of mature age do the writing with all diligence.[10]

No doubt this order to found schools for boys in every monastery and cathedral remained unfulfilled, although many schools were established. Most of the cathedral schools disappeared during the ninth century; consequently, the monastic schools provided virtually all the education in the West from the ninth to the eleventh century. And in the eleventh century, it was the reestablishment of the cathedral schools—Charlemagne's educational ideals lived on—that was largely responsible for the developments in philosophy and learning that are usually called the Renaissance of the Twelfth Century.

For the curriculum of the monastic and cathedral schools, Alcuin employed the seven liberal arts, outlined by Martianus Capella in the fifth century. However, in reality the first two, grammar and rhetoric, dominated the Carolingian schools. Generally the texts used to teach these subjects were from late antiquity rather than from the Augustan Age (for example, the Christian historians of the fourth and fifth centuries such as Eusebius and Orosius were more popular than Livy or Tacitus); however, Virgil was well known and textbooks often included selected passages from the greatest Latin writers. The study of grammar and rhetoric was to prepare clerics to study Christian texts and to give them the necessary tools to correct poor manuscripts, make new editions, and write intelligent commentaries. The focus of this study, in addition to the Bible, was the Latin Fathers, including many lesser known figures of the fourth and fifth centuries, but also of course Jerome and Augustine. Charlemagne himself had a special affection for the works of Augustine; Einhard tells us that he liked to have the *City of God* read to him at dinner. One of the important "inventions" of the Carolingian Renaissance was the replacement of Merovingian handwriting with a new, legible script that made it much easier to make accurate copies of the Bible, the Fathers, and liturgical texts. This script, known today as Caroline miniscule, is the ancestor of our lower case alphabet thanks to its revival during the Italian Renaissance.

Charlemagne made important liturgical reforms, establishing the Roman liturgy throughout his empire in place of the variety of liturgical forms that had grown up in the kingdom of the Franks known as the Gallican rite. Alcuin, after receiving a copy of the Roman (i.e., Gregorian) rite, found it incomplete and inadequate; he revised it, adding a preface and a list of proper readings. In the preface, he explained the problems he encountered and what he did to solve them:

> The foregoing sacramentary, although marred by many a copyist's error, could not be reckoned to be in the condition in which it had left its author's hands, [so] it was our task to correct and restore it, for the benefit of all. Let a careful reader examine it, and he will promptly agree with this judgement, unless the work be again corrupted by scribes.

But since there are other materials which Holy Church necessarily uses, and which the aforesaid Father [Gregory], seeing that they had been already put forth by others, left aside, we have thought it worth while to gather them like spring flowers of the meadows, and collect them together, and place them in this book apart, but corrected and amended and headed with their [own] titles, so that the reader may find in this work all things which we have thought necessary for our times, although we had found a great many also embodied in other sacramentaries.[11]

The Roman rite as revised by Alcuin is the direct ancestor of the liturgy used in Roman Catholic churches today. The Roman rite was less flexible and less dramatic than the Gallican rite, which it replaced. Perhaps as an attempt to compensate for what was lost in the older tradition, dramatic set pieces were sometimes embedded in the liturgy of the Roman rite, especially at the important feasts, as in the following example from the introit for the Mass of Easter at the monastery of Saint Gall (c.950):

Question: Whom do you seek in the sepulchre, O followers of Christ?

Answer: Jesus of Nazareth, who was crucified, O heaven-dwellers. He is not here, he has risen as he had foretold; go announce that he has risen from the sepulchre.[12]

More elaborate versions of this scene of the visitation of the holy women to the sepulchre developed, especially in the eleventh and twelfth centuries; scholars have seen in this process the rebirth of drama in the West.

The broad purpose and goals of the Carolingian Renaissance are summarized in a letter of Charlemagne to Baugulf, abbot of the monastery of Fulda, written in the last decade of the eighth century:

We, Charles, by the grace of God king of the Franks and Lombards and patrician of the Romans, to Abbot Baugulf and all your congregation and our faithful teachers entrusted to your charge, send affectionate greeting in the name of Almighty God. Be it known to your devotion, most pleasing in the sight of God, that we, along with our faithful advisors, have deemed it useful that the bishoprics and monasteries which through the favour of Christ have been entrusted to us to govern should, in addition to the way of life prescribed by their rule and their practice of holy religion, devote their efforts to the study of literature and to the teaching of it, each according to his ability, to those on whom God has bestowed the capacity to learn; that, just as the observance of a rule gives soundness to their conduct, so also an attention to teaching and learning may give order and adornment to their words, and that those who seek to please God by living aright may not fail to please him also by rightness in their speaking. For it is written: "Either by your words shall you be justified, or by your words shall you be condemned (Matt. 12:37)." For although it is better to do what is right than to know it, yet knowledge comes before action. Thus each man must first learn what he wishes to carry out, so that he will know in his heart all the more fully what he needs to do, in order that his tongue may run on without stumbling into falsehood in the praise of Almighty God. . . . We began to fear that their [the monks'] lack of knowledge of writing might be matched by a more serious lack of wisdom in the understanding of holy scripture. We all know well that, dangerous as are the errors of words, yet much more dangerous are the errors of doctrine. Wherefore we urge you, not merely to avoid the neglect of the study of literature, but with a devotion that is humble and pleasing to God to strive to learn it, so that you may be able more easily and more rightly to penetrate the mysteries of the holy scriptures. For since there are figures of speech, metaphors and the like to be found on the sacred pages, there can be no doubt that each man who reads them will understand their spiritual meaning more quickly if he is first of all given full instruction in the study of literature.[13]

Charlemagne: a Germanic chieftain who gloried in arms and enjoyed raucous drinking bouts with his men but who also enjoyed hearing Augustine read at dinner in Latin; a Roman emperor who kept his court in the heart of Frankish territory; a Christian who loved the scriptures and the mass but who was almost constantly engaged in warfare. These contrasts are important because they so forcefully exemplify both the fusion and the unresolved conflicts of Germanic, Roman, and Christian cultures, which is one of the great themes of early medieval history. The most succinct statement of Charlemagne's synthesis of these traditions is found in Einhard's description of the Emperor's educational plans for his children:

Charlemagne was determined to give his children, his daughters just as much as his sons, a proper training in the liberal arts which had formed the subject of his own studies. As soon as they were old enough he had his sons taught to ride in the Frankish fashion, to use arms and to hunt.[14]

It is especially noteworthy that Charlemagne provided that his daughters be literate. We know very little about the education of laywomen in the early Middle Ages. One exception comes in the generation after Charlemagne. The noblewoman Dhouda, whose father perhaps imitated Charlemagne's plan for the education of his children, wrote a manual for her son William. In it, she shows familiarity not only with the writings of Alcuin but also of the Bible, Augustine, and other important Christian writers. The passage below is sprinkled with Old and New Testament references. In it, she calls upon William to arm himself with the seven gifts of the Holy Spirit, a theme popular in the writings of early Latin church fathers:

If you are humble and peaceful, my son, you will surely be able to receive, at least in part, the seven gifts of the grace of the Holy Spirit.... Then the good spirit of the Lord will rest upon you. In being humble and obedient, you will easily be able to exchange the yoke of evil spirits for the yoke of Christ. As he says, *For my yoke is sweet and my burden light* [Matt. 11:30]. Indeed, that man who bears the yoke and the burden of Christ is himself borne from the depths to highest heaven. The blessed apostle Peter said, when he ended his happy course in glorious suffering, "God, my master, raised to heaven on a tall cross, has also seen fit to transfer me from earth to heaven [a passage from the "Passion of the Holy Apostles Peter and Paul," a hagiographical work].

Therefore, my son, flee fornication and keep your mind away from any prostitute. It is written, *Go not after thy lusts, but turn away from thy own will* [Ecclus. 18:30]. *Do not give to thy soul* [Ecclus. 18:31] to fly away after her evil desires. Surely, if you attend to one or another of these ills and if you consent to them, they will make you fall onto the sword and into the hands of your enemies. They will say with the Prophet, *Bow down, that we may go over* you [Isa. 51:23]. May this not happen to you. But if those evils come and sting your mind through an angel of Satan sent against you [cf. 2 Cor. 12:7], fight them , pray, and say with the Psalmist, *Deliver not up to the beasts* [Ps. 73:19] of the earth my soul, I beseech you, and forget not the soul of thy poor servant; *give me not the haughtiness of my eyes* [Ecclus. 23:5]; *let not the lusts of the flesh take hold of me, and give me not over to a shameless and foolish mind* [Ecclus. 23:10].[15]

Charlemagne also desired to use the tools of Roman-Christian culture to preserve his people's Germanic heritage:

At the same time he directed that the age-old narrative poems, barbarous enough, it is true, in which were celebrated the warlike deeds of the kings of ancient times, should be written out and so preserved. He also began a grammar of his native tongue.[16]

If any of this was done, it has, alas, been lost. However, Charlemagne's efforts to preserve the Germanic heritage did lead to the recording of several law codes.

Charlemagne's attempt to fuse the cultural traditions in the West was personal and even to some extent superficial. Learned treatises written in generations following his death did more to merge Germanic kingship with the Roman imperium than Charlemagne's words or deeds. But without Charlemagne there would have been no reason to try to do so. It is not really until the twelfth century that one can talk of a cultural and institutional fusion into the more or less consistent world view that is suggested by the term *medieval*. However, the accomplishments of Charlemagne are a necessary step toward the formation of this view.

The political and cultural achievements of Charlemagne are only a part of his legacy to the remainder of the Middle Ages; the other major part is his legend. In the years of disintegration that followed his death, he began to take on mythic proportions. How different is Einhard's biography (c.830) from that of Notker the Stammerer (mid-880s), which borrows some of its literary devices from hagiography. The following text taken from Notker shows that the Charlemagne legend was already emerging in the century of his death:

Charlemagne, of all kings the most glorious, was standing by a window through which the sun shone with dazzling brightness. He was clad in gold and precious stones, and he glittered himself like the sun at its first rising. He rested his arm upon Heiro, for that was the name of the Bishop who some time previously had been sent to Constantinople. Around the Emperor, like the host of heaven, stood his three sons, the young men who were later to share the Empire; his daughters and their mother, adorned with wisdom, beauty and ropes of pearls; his bishops, unsurpassed in their virtue and their dignified posture, and his abbots, distinguished by their sanctity and their noble demeanour; his leaders, like Joshua when he appeared in the camp of Gilgal; and his army like that which drove back the Syrians and the Assyrians out of Samaria. Had David been in their midst he would have had every reason to sing: "Kings of the earth, and all people; princes, and all judges of the earth; both young men and maidens; old men, and children: let them praise the name of the Lord."[17]

By the twelfth century, there were legends of Charlemagne going to Jerusalem and driving the Muslims out of Spain, making him the exemplar of both crusader and pilgrim. He was even canonized by a twelfth-century imperially sponsored antipope; and although the Church does not now recognize him as a saint, he was widely venerated in the Middle Ages. Statues of Charlemagne are found on churches all over Western Europe.

Charlemagne's expedition into Spain in the late 770s provided material for important works of literature throughout the Middle Ages. Einhard wrote a historical account of it, stressing the ambush of Charlemagne's rearguard by the Basques at Roncesvalles in the Pyrenees.

[Charlemagne] marched over a pass across the Pyrenees, received the surrender of every single town and castle which he attacked and then came back with his army safe and sound, except for the fact that for a brief moment on the return journey, while he was in the Pyrenean mountain range itself, he was given a taste of Basque treachery. . . . At a moment when Charlemagne's army was stretched out in a long column of march, as the nature of the local defiles forced it to be, these Basques, who had set their ambush on the very top of one of the mountains, came rushing down on the last part of the baggage train and the troops who were marching in support of the rearguard and so protecting the army which had gone on ahead. The Basques forced them down into the valley beneath, joined battle with them and killed them to the last man. . . . In this battle died Eggihard, who was in charge of the King's table, Anshelm, the Count of the Palace and Roland, Lord of the Breton Marches, along with a great number of others. What is more, this assault could not be avenged there and then, for, once it was over, the enemy dispersed in such a way that no one knew where or among which people they could be found.[18]

By the twelfth century, this relatively unimportant incident at Roncesvalles had been transformed into an all-out apocalyptic confrontation between Christians and Muslims and given an important place within the whole scheme of salvation history. The best-known version of this story is the French *chanson de geste,* the *Song of Roland,* although versions exist in other vernacular languages and in the visual arts. In this poem Charlemagne is more than two

Tympanum Sculpture of Apostles and a Battle. Cathedral of Angoulême, France. Twelfth century. In the lintel (see detail), a battle scene from the Song of Roland is depicted. From its placement beneath the figure of Saint Peter and two other apostles, it is clear that the story of Roland is understood as a story about the spread of the faith, an important theme in the era of the crusades. Although a French story, it appears in stone and glass throughout Europe, including Italy, Spain, and Germany.

hundred years old, with the wisdom of Solomon and the courage of David; he carries the lance that pierced Christ's side; he has the authority to absolve a sinner; and he is the conqueror of Spain, England, and Constantinople. He is presented as a man who often and effectively communes with God:

> In a green meadow he gets down from his horse,
> Kneels on the ground and prays almighty God
> To make the sun stop moving through the sky,
> Delay the night, and let the day remain.
> And then an angel, who often spoke with him,
> Came in great haste to give him this command:
> "Charles, speed you on! The light won't fail you now.
> God knows that you have lost the flower of France.
> You'll have your vengeance on the vile Saracen!"
> Already Charles has mounted once again.
> For Charlemagne God worked a miracle:
> The sun stops moving, and stands still in the sky.
> The pagans flee, the Franks pursue them hard.[19]

In this poem the man who described himself to be like David and Josias now also becomes like Joshua. The Charlemagne of history and the Charlemagne of legend are two of the most important figures of the Middle Ages.

THE DISSOLUTION OF THE CAROLINGIAN EMPIRE

Louis the Pious (r.814–840), though ultimately lacking his father's military genius and vision, nevertheless tried to continue some of his father's policies, especially with regard to the protection and direction of the Church. His most successful effort was in the area of monastic reform. He established a model monastery at Inda near Aachen under the leadership of Benedict of Aniane (d.821). The following text, taken from Ardo Smaragdus's life of Benedict, explains the imperially sponsored reform program, including the goal of monastic uniformity:

> The emperor [Louis] placed him over all the monasteries in his kingdom so that as he had instructed Aquitaine and Gothia in the ways of salvation he might also by salutary example teach Francia. There were many monasteries which had at one time been regularly instituted, but gradually, with discipline slackening, the regular routine had almost disappeared. . . . [H]e discussed the rule [of Saint Benedict] anew and elucidated obscure matters for everyone, resolved doubts, rooted out former errors, and confirmed useful customs and usages. When opinions regarding the *Rule* and all doubts were resolved, with the consent of all, he explained those usages which the *Rule* does not present clearly. He presented a capitulary on these things to the emperor for his confirmation and so that he might order it observed in all monasteries in the kingdom. To this we refer the reader desirous of more information. The em-

Bust of Charlemagne. Aachen, Germany. Fourteenth century. This image was created centuries after Charlemagne's death to hold his skull. It is highly idealized and presents Charlemagne as both a great king and as a holy man since this type of shrine is traditionally associated with saints. Like the Song of Roland, *this bust provides evidence for the importance of the mythical Charlemagne.*

peror immediately assented to this and appointed inspectors for each monastery who were to see to it that all things which he had ordered were observed and to explain the proper procedures to those who were not informed. And so the work was carried out and speeded with the aid of divine mercy; and one established rule is universally observed by everyone and all monasteries brought to a standard of unity, as though they were instructed by one master in one place.[20]

Benedict of Aniane's interpretation of the Rule of his namesake significantly altered the development of Western monasticism. It is important to remember that over the course of several centuries, many monasteries had accumulated great amounts of land and other forms of wealth. Those nobles who could afford to do so often gave such gifts to monasteries in return for the monks' prayers both when they were living and when they faced judgment. Benedict of Aniane expanded the daily liturgical cycle so that it took up more time than the Rule had prescribed. Manual labor was mostly limited to housework, while tenant farmers did the agricultural labor. This was a logical change insofar as the men who became monks at this time had not been agricultural workers but rather came from landed families. However, the limitation of manual labor upset the balance between work and prayer that was central to the Benedictine Rule. Although Benedict of Aniane also tried strictly to limit the monks' contact with the outside world, it proved impossible because monasteries possessed great estates and political power and were the most important centers of literacy and education.

Monasticism generally declined in the ninth century as "extra" children of nobles were sent to monasteries although they had no vocation; many of these monks wanted to live as much like nobles as possible within the cloister, and hunting dogs and mistresses were not unknown within the monastic precincts. Some abbots and monks even fought in military campaigns. Several monastic reform movements developed in the tenth and eleventh centuries, most notably at Cluny; but these reforms began with the Rule as interpreted by Benedict of Aniane. It was only with the establishment of the Cistercian Order in the twelfth century that a significant reform of Benedictine monasticism attempted to return to a life based on a strict return to the precepts of the Rule (see Chapter 8).

Louis the Pious's reign was troubled by rebellious sons, among whom the Empire was finally divided. One became king of the West Franks; another, king of the East Franks; the eldest, Lothar, became king of Lotharingia, a territory containing both a corridor between the other two kingdoms and northern and central Italy. And it was the king of Lotharingia who also held the title of Roman emperor. There was still one empire, but there were three kingdoms that were de facto independent, the title of emperor counting for little. The disintegration of the Carolingian Empire did not stop here. The kings of these successor states declined in power as local magnates established virtual independence. Furthermore, when Lothar died, his kingdom was divided among his three sons; thus, Lotharingia did not survive its founder. For about a century, the title of Roman Emperor was usually held by the ruler of one of the Italian kingdoms that emerged from the disintegration of Lotharingia, although these emperors were little more than political pawns of the Italian nobility. For a period of forty-two years (920–962), no one even bothered to take the imperial title.

Other developments were equally important to the Empire's history. Louis the Pious crowned Lothar as Roman emperor in 817 in Aachen, following the pattern Charlemagne had established at Louis the Pious's coronation. However, Louis was deeply devoted to the Roman Church and agreed to a subsequent papal coronation for Lothar in Rome, renewing the close tie between the papacy and the Empire. Pope Nicholas I (r.858–867), one of the outstanding medieval popes, further sought to tie the Empire to papal policy; and after the coronation of Charles the Bald as Roman emperor in Rome on Christmas Day 875, there was no longer any doubt that it was the pope who performed imperial coronations.

Despite the weakness of their rulers, the kingdoms of the West and East Franks remained at least theoretically intact. The stronger, that of the East Franks (roughly, modern Germany), had a descendant of Charlemagne on the throne until 911, when the dynasty failed to produce an heir. Then the monarchy became elective, with the most powerful nobles choosing the king. The election of Otto I (the Great) in 936 was a turning point in the history of that kingdom and indeed all of Europe. His coronation is described by Widukind of Corvey:

> And when they had arrived, the dukes and the great lords with a force of the chief vassals gathered in the portico of the basilica of Charlemagne. They placed the new ruler on the throne that had been constructed there, giving him their hands and offering fealty; promising their help against all his enemies, they made him king according to their custom. . . .
>
> The king, dressed in a close-fitting tunic according to the Frankish custom, was escorted behind the altar, on which lay the royal insignia—sword with sword-belt, cloak with bracelets, staff with sceptre and diadem. . . .
>
> Going to the altar and taking from it the sword with swordbelt and turning to the king, he [Archbishop Hildibert of Mainz] said: "Accept this sword, with which you may chase out all the adversaries of Christ, barbarians, and bad Christians, by the divine authority handed down to you and by the power of all the empire of the Franks for the most lasting peace of all Christians." Then taking the bracelets and cloak, he clothed him saying, "These points [of the cloak] falling to the ground will remind you with what zeal of faith you should burn and how you ought to endure in preserving peace to the end."
>
> Then taking the sceptre and staff, he said: "With these symbols you may be reminded that you should reproach your subjects with paternal castigation, but first of all you should extend the hand of mercy to ministers of God, widows, and orphans. And never let the oil of compassion be absent from your head in order that you may be crowned with eternal reward in the present and in the future."[21]

This text shows the Church's deep involvement in royal as well as imperial coronations. Kingship was perceived to have a sacred character, and some considered the anointing of a king to be one of the Church's sacraments. It was common to refer to a monarch as both king and priest; this did not mean that a king could celebrate mass or hear confession, but it did suggest a special and unique status for him.

Otto faced attacks from the East and rebellion by his nobles, but he was able to overcome both foreign and domestic enemies largely because he received the support of the Church, from whose land most of his soldiers came. In turn, it was crucial for Otto to have loyal bishops and abbots. Thus, royal appointment and investiture of bishops was becoming common practice. Otto was crowned king of the East Franks at Aachen, and he probably planned to restore the Carolingian Empire from that time on. He found his opportunity when Pope John XII was driven from Rome and called on him for help. We have observed that as far back as Pepin's reign, the papacy had come to rely on Frankish kings north of the Alps for protection. However, during the ninth and tenth centuries, the weak successors of Charlemagne were unable to oversee and protect the papacy; and it fell victim to the Italian nobles who treated it as a political toy. Here was Otto's chance to prove his strength. Though John XII was no model of holiness, in 962 Otto I restored him to his throne, much as Charlemagne had restored Leo III more than a century and a half earlier, and received the imperial crown from him. Otto spent the remaining eleven years of his life in Italy, attempting to bring northern Italy under his control. His empire was smaller than Charlemagne's, consisting only of the kingdom of the East Franks and northern Italy. For the rest of the Middle Ages, the Empire essentially consisted of the territories of Otto rather than those of Charlemagne.

Otto arranged for his son and heir, Otto II (r.973–983), to marry the Byzantine princess Theophano. When Otto II died, she became the regent for their infant heir Otto III (r.983–1002). The third Otto grew up in Italy tutored by Greeks who had accompanied Theophano to the West. His vision of empire blended his Carolingian heritage with Byzantine imperial ideology. He even dreamed of reuniting East and West into one Roman Empire. But he died without heirs, bringing about a dynastic change. Although the imperial title continued, the Empire's center shifted once again to Germany.

During the reign of the Ottos, there was something of a cultural revival, sometimes called the Ottonian Renaissance. Several new cathedral schools were established, and Byzantine craftsmen influenced both sculpture and manuscript illumination. The most important element of this revival, however, was that it kept alive the achievements and goals of the Carolingian Renaissance.

Until the eleventh century, the kingdom of the West Franks was almost always weaker and less significant than that of the East Franks. From 887 to 987, the royal title went back and forth between Carolingians and the family of the counts of Paris. In 987, Count Hugh Capet became king; the dynasty he established—with two name changes—ruled what was soon thereafter called France until the execution of Louis XVI in 1793. Although the first Capetian kings exercised little power beyond the area around Paris, often referred to as the Ile-de-France, they had the support of the Church; and they consistently produced male heirs, two major factors that solidified their position as hereditary monarchs.

Detail of a Bronze Column with Lazarus at the Table of the Rich Man. Bern-
ward of Hildesheim, 1015–1022. Cathedral of Hildesheim, Germany. This col-
umn is one of the most important works of the Ottonian Renaissance. The
story, from Luke 16, is about a rich man who turned a poor man named
Lazarus away; dogs with long necks on the left lick Lazarus's sores according
to the gospel. The column, narrating a story from top to bottom, is modeled
on Trajan's Column in Rome, a work of the early second century C.E. *that*
narrates the Emperor Trajan's conquest of Dacia.

NINTH-CENTURY INVASIONS

One of the most serious problems Western Europe faced in the century and a
half after Charlemagne's death was a series of invasions by non-Christians. One
group of invaders, the Vikings, came from Scandinavia. The earliest Viking attacks took place in the kingdom of the Franks and England during Charlemagne's
reign. Einhard described the problem and how Charlemagne dealt with it:

> Charlemagne took upon himself the task of building a fleet to ward off the
> attacks of the Northmen. For this purpose ships were constructed near to the
> rivers which flow out of Gaul and Germany into the North Sea. In view of
> the fact that these Northmen kept on attacking and pillaging the coast of Gaul
> and Germany, Charlemagne placed strongpoints and coastguard stations at all
> the ports and at the mouths of all rivers considered large enough for the en-
> try of ships, so that the enemy could be bottled up by this military task force.[22]

The raids on Gaul became more serious during the reign of Louis the Pious. The following selections are from the story of the monks of the Monastery of Saint Philibert, originally located on the island of Noirmoutier at the mouth of the Seine River:

> The frequent and unfortunate attacks of the Northmen, . . . were in no wise abating, and Abbot Hilbodus had built a castle on the island for protection against that faithless people. Together with the council of his brothers, he came to King Pepin [a son of Louis the Pious] and asked His Highness what he intended to do about this problem. Then the glorious king and the great men of the realm—a general assembly of the kingdom was then being held— deliberated concerning the problem with gracious concern and found themselves unable to help through mounting a vigorous assault. Because of the extremely dangerous tides, the island was not always readily accessible to our forces, while all knew that it was quite accessible to the Northmen whenever the sea was peaceful. The king and the great men chose what they believed to be the more advantageous policy. With the agreement of the most serene king Pepin, almost all the bishops of the province of Aquitaine, and the abbots, counts, and other faithful men who were present, and many others besides who had learned about the situation, unanimously advised that the body of the blessed Philibert ought to be taken from the island and no longer allowed to remain there. . . .
>
> The number of ships grew larger, and the Northmen were beyond counting. Everywhere there were massacres of Christians, raids, devastations, and burnings. For as long as the world shall last, this will remain evident by manifest signs. Whatever cities the Northmen attacked, they captured without resistance: Bordeaux, Périgueux, Saintes, Limoges, Angoulême, and Toulouse; then Angers, Tours, and Orléans were destroyed. The remains of numerous saints were carried off. What the Lord warns through the prophet came close to fulfillment: "From the north shall an evil break forth upon all the inhabitants of the land" (Jeremias 1. 14). We also fled to a place which is called Cunauld, in the territory of Anjou, on the banks of the Loire, which the glorious king Charles [another son of Louis the Pious] had given us for the sake of refuge, because of the imminent peril, before Angers was taken. . . .
>
> The Northmen attacked Spain besides; they entered the Rhône River, and they devastated Italy. While everywhere so many domestic and foreign wars were raging, the year of the Incarnation of Christ 857 passed. As long as there had been in us some hope of returning to our own possessions (which, however, proved to be fruitless), the body of the blessed Philibert, as has been said, was left in his own soil. With evils surrounding us, we had not been able to obtain a definite place of security. But since a refuge was nowhere to be found, we did not permit the most holy body to be carried with us hither and yon. Now, it was more truly smuggled away from the grasp of the Northmen than carried with festive praises, and it was taken to the place we have mentioned, which is called Cunauld. This was done in such a way that, when

necessity required, it might be moved elsewhere. The year of the Lord's Incarnation was 862 when the body was carried from Cunauld to Messay.[23]

This story makes clear the seriousness and the scope of Viking raids. It is a long way by boat from Scandinavia to Italy. And Louis the Pious's helplessness is equally clear, for the Vikings raided quickly and were gone long before a royal army could be summoned.

By the middle of the ninth century, some Vikings began to winter in Gaul, establishing permanent bases for their raids. In 911, following military setbacks, the Viking leader Rolf (or Rollo) agreed to become a vassal of the West Frankish king and to accept Christianity. This was the beginning of the duchy of Normandy, the name deriving from "Northmen."

England faced the same problem as Gaul, for the Vikings (usually called Danes by English historians) began to settle down in the eastern part of Britain. In fact, several of the Anglo-Saxon kingdoms were destroyed. The most western of them, Wessex, produced one of the great heroes of English history, King Alfred the Great (r.871–899), who organized defenses against further Viking attacks and began the process of their conversion to Christianity.

> [In a battle in 878, Alfred] destroyed the Vikings with great slaughter, and pursued those who fled as far as the stronghold, hacking them down; then seized everything which he found outside the stronghold—men (whom he killed immediately), horses, and cattle—and boldly made camp in front of the gates of the Viking stronghold with all his army. When he had been there for fourteen days the Vikings, thoroughly terrified by hunger, cold and fear, and in the end by despair, sought peace on this condition: the king should take as many chosen hostages as he wanted from them and give none to them; never before, indeed, had they made peace with anyone on such terms. . . . When they had been handed over, the Vikings swore in addition that they would leave his kingdom immediately, and Gunthrum, their king, promised to accept Christianity and to receive baptism at King Alfred's hand [i.e., with Alfred as his godfather].[24]

Alfred and his successors were the first kings to be recognized by all the Anglo-Saxons; in the course of the tenth century, the Danes also accepted Anglo-Saxon rule while retaining their own law. However, in the eleventh century a successful second Scandinavian attack on England brought two Christian Danes to the English throne. In addition to Alfred's political and military achievements, he was a great supporter of learning and translated Boethius's *Consolation of Philosophy* into Anglo-Saxon.

In the ninth and tenth centuries, Western Europe was also attacked by Muslims. Einhard tells us that as early as Charlemagne's reign they had sacked cities on the Italian coast. These raids were essentially piratical in nature, not as serious a long-term threat to order as those of the Vikings. Nevertheless, Muslims from North Africa disrupted traffic on the Rhône and established pirate dens on the French Riviera and even in the Alps, where they attacked merchants and kidnapped them for ransom.

Beginning in the 860s, the East Frankish kingdom came under attack from a nomadic tribe of horsemen called the Magyars (Hungarians). For almost a century they wreaked havoc in the East Frankish kingdom, also occasionally venturing into the West Frankish kingdom and even Italy. In 955, Otto I (the Great) defeated them at the battle of Lechfeld. Soon afterward, they settled down in the middle Danube area, which Charlemagne had cleared of Hunnic Avars, and accepted Christianity. Their first Christian king, Stephen, received his crown from Pope Sylvester II in the year 1000.

While the East Franks were fighting with the Magyars, they were also engaged in war with pagan Slavs from time to time, especially the Bohemians and Poles. By 1000, both of these peoples had accepted Christianity from the West and had begun to absorb Latin culture; in fact, in the year 1000, Otto III made a pilgrimage to Poland to obtain relics of Saint Adalbert, the man most responsible for the Poles' conversion.

Taken together, these raids of Vikings, Muslims, and Magyars had disastrous short-term effects on both the continent and England. They were a main cause of the disintegration of royal authority because of royal impotence in fighting against the raiders. However, apart from the Muslims, the raiders eventually accepted Christianity and the Roman-Latin culture that went with it and became vital parts of Western Christendom. Furthermore, some Vikings settled in Iceland and Greenland and even explored America. They established Christianity in their settlements and also created an important literature, the Icelandic sagas—like so much else in medieval culture, a creative fusion of pagan and Christian. For example *Hrafnkel's Saga*, a work of the thirteenth century, tells a story set in pre-Christian Iceland. In it Hrafnkel swears an oath to a pagan god that he would kill anyone who rode his horse Freyfaxi. In describing the story of Hrafnkel's shepherd Einar riding the horse, there are clear allusions to the temptation of Adam and Eve in Genesis 3:

> [Hrafnkel said to Einar:] Some ten or twelve other horses go with Freyfaxi and you're free to use any of them, by day or night. [Hrafnkel confronts Einar after discovering that the shepherd has ridden Freyfaxi:] Why did you ride this one horse which was forbidden to you, when there were plenty of other horses for you to ride? . . . Then he [Hrafnkel] dismounted and killed Einar with a single blow.[25]

Riding the "one horse which is forbidden to you" is a clear allusion to Adam and Eve eating from the one forbidden tree in the Garden of Eden in Genesis. The punishment for that transgression was death, even as death is the punishment for Einar here. These biblical parallels shape the passage as much as the story itself.

That the Vikings continued to exert a dynamic influence on European history can be seen in the Norman conquest of England in 1066. The saintly Edward the Confessor, son of an Anglo-Saxon king and a Norman mother, had become king in 1042. However, he left no heir, and upon his death in 1066 the throne was claimed by both the leading Anglo-Saxon noble, Harold, and

*Embroidery of the Normans Sailing to England. From the Bayeux Tapestry,
Bayeux, France. Late eleventh century. The Normans have their military
equipment in their boats; to the far right are horses in a boat. The style of
the Norman ships is a reminder of the Normans' Viking heritage. The in-
scription at the top indicates that they landed in England at Pevesney.*

William, Duke of Normandy. With the support of the pope, William invaded
England, defeated and killed Harold at the battle of Hastings, and had himself
crowned king on Christmas Day, 1066, at Westminster Abbey, a Benedictine
monastery and Edward the Confessor's burial place.

William's conquest was a turning point in English history. The Anglo-
Saxon nobility and ecclesiastical hierarchy were replaced by Normans, who
superimposed their institutions upon those of the Anglo-Saxons rather than
starting from scratch, taking advantage of the fact that England before the conquest was the most centralized monarchy in Western Europe. Since William
continued to be Duke of Normandy, England became more directly involved
in continental and especially French politics. In fact, King Henry II of England
(r.1154–1189) ruled almost the entire western half of France, and England became deeply involved in his efforts to retain it. Though the English kings lost
most of their continental possessions early in the thirteenth century, they desired to reconquer them. In one sense, the Hundred Years War (1337–1453)
was about English possessions in France; thus, the English attachment to the
continent that was the result of the Norman conquest was central to the history of England for the remainder of the Middle Ages (see Chapter 11).

The English language also changed, for the Normans brought the French
language with them to England. In the centuries after the conquest the new

aristocracy spoke French while the lower classes continued to use Anglo-Saxon. These languages began to blend, a process essentially complete by the fourteenth century. The grammatical structure of English remains essentially Germanic, but the vocabulary is divided between French and Anglo-Saxon.

FEUDAL SOCIETY

We have already observed the division of Charlemagne's Empire and the decline in royal authority, partly due to internal strife and partly caused by the ninth-century invasions. It is important now to ask precisely what took the place of royal authority. To find the answer, we must return to Charlemagne and even to his predecessors. Both Roman and Germanic traditions contained certain hierarchical views of society, in part expressed respectively by relations such as patron-client and chieftain-warrior. In the instability of the Merovingian world, ties of dependence between freemen were common. One who needed help protecting his property and his person would attach himself to a powerful man who would agree to aid him in return for some kind of service. Those wishing to increase their power and status could do so by acquiring the service of freemen in return for providing for their needs, usually defense. During the Carolingian period, kings encouraged all freemen to establish such relationships, and a law of 847 issued jointly by Louis the Pious's three sons tried to require it: "We wish that every free man in our kingdom select the lord whom he prefers, us or one of our faithful subjects."[26]

The term *vassal* describes a person who binds himself to another freeman and pledges loyalty and service to him; *lord* refers to the one who accepts the vassal's service, usually in exchange for protection and support. One reason that Charlemagne and his successors encouraged vassalage was to make governing easier, since they required a lord to be responsible for his vassals. Charlemagne issued a law dated between 801 and 813 that suggests the importance of vassalage:

> If any vassal should wish to abandon his lord, he may do so only if he can prove that the lord has committed one of these crimes: first, if the lord should have unjustly sought to enslave him; second, if the lord plotted against his life; third, if the lord committed adultery with the wife of his vassal; fourth, if the lord willingly attacked him with drawn sword in order to kill him; fifth, if, after the vassal commended his hands into his, the lord failed to provide defense which he could have done. If the lord has committed any of these five offenses against his vassal, the vassal may abandon him.[27]

Usually, vassals were required to perform military service for their lords. Sometime during the eighth century, the character of military service changed rapidly. Until then, foot soldiers were the basic units of an army, and all freemen were expected to bear arms. But the introduction of the stirrup, an

Eastern invention, began to change all that by dramatically increasing the efficiency of mounted soldiers. To fight on horseback presumes a great deal of equipment, including a sword, shield, lance, protective suit, and several horses. Furthermore, a mounted warrior needs training and practice with this rather sophisticated equipment. Charlemagne and his successors sought vassals who would serve them in battle, as well as in nonmilitary capacities, but they had to provide for their support. There were several ways to do this, including housing them in their own palace; however, the most common practice was to give them lifetime grants of a piece of land with peasant cultivators, called a *fief*. Sometimes a fief was merely enough land to support one soldier, but other times a king granted a large fief to a vassal from whom he required the service of several soldiers. Such a vassal usually divided his fief into smaller ones, which were granted to men who became their vassals, a practice called *subinfeudation*.

The predominantly military character of vassalage is clear from another part of the 847 law quoted above:

> And we wish that the vassal of any one of us [Charles the Bald, Louis the German, and Lothar] should accompany his lord into the army in order to fulfill his services, in no matter whose kingdom he should be.[28]

While the military elements of vassalage were strictly men's work, it is vital to remember that while men were away at war, women often administered the fief which was the economic basis of warfare. The noblewoman Dhouda, writing in the 840s, illustrates this often forgotten element of feudal society:

> I acknowledge that, to defend the interests of my lord and master Bernard [her husband], and so that my service to him might not weaken in the [Spanish] March . . . I know that I have gone into great debt. To respond to great necessities, I have frequently borrowed great sums, not only from Christians but also from Jews.[29]

Land was not the only way Charlemagne provided for his subordinates. To some he gave the office of count. Within a defined section of his Empire, a count held military, judicial, and financial power. To most people, the count *was* the government, although Charlemagne did have his *missi* to check up on each count. These officials not only enjoyed great power but also became wealthy from the profits realized from the land that went along with their offices and from a portion of the fines collected.

Because of the decreasing effectiveness of imperial and royal governments after Charlemagne's death and the ineffectiveness of centralized defense in light of the Viking and Magyar raids, the counts, at least de facto, often became independent of those whom they theoretically served. They became virtually the only source of justice and military power in their counties, relying on their vassals to perform military service for them. Vassalage was not originally inherited since it was a personal bond between two men that ceased to exist when one died. The office of count was not inheritable either; in fact, a king would move counts rather frequently from one county to another. By the end of the ninth century, however, the succession of both vassalage and the office of count from father to son had become common, largely because it was easier to accept a son as a vassal or a count than to dispossess him. When Emperor Charles the Bald left his Frankish possessions for a military campaign in Italy in 877, he provided for the succession to office by sons of the counts who were with him in Italy should their fathers die when they were away.

An eleventh-century edict of the Emperor Conrad II illustrates the triumph of the inheritability of fiefs:

> We also command that when a vassal, great or petty, should die, his son shall receive his fief. If he has no son, but is survived by a grandson born of male issue, the grandson should in equal manner have the fief, while respecting the customs of the great valvassores [vassals] in giving horses and arms to their lords. If he does not have a grandson born from male issue and if he should have a legitimate brother from the side of his father, and if that brother, after offending the lord, is willing to make amends and become his vassal, he should have the fief which was his father's.[30]

Since a fief was granted to provide enough income to support at least one mounted soldier, there was a conflict with the Germanic custom of a father dividing his property equally among his sons. However, the practice of primogeniture—the eldest son inheriting all the land and titles—became standard on the continent by the eleventh century and in England by the twelfth.

The great counts often treated their fiefs as their own territory. One of the characteristics of the feudal period is the treatment of political power as a private possession and its division among a large number of people.[31] Until about 1000, this decentralizing trend did not normally go beneath the level of the count. However, in the eleventh century, many vassals of counts wrested political power from their lords just as those lords, the counts, had done from the kings in the ninth and tenth centuries.

The preceding description of vassalage and feudal relations is noticeable for the absence of a role for women. The formal ties were in fact virtually a male monopoly. However, women were essential to the functioning of feudal society, and not only as brides and mothers. When men were away from the manor, women were often at least the de facto administrators of the land and household. Furthermore, women were often witnesses for charters. The frequency with which women appear in such legal documents suggests that women's activities in feudal society were more complex and public than often imagined. Even in the fifteenth century, the noblewoman Christine de Pizan instructs women of her class about how to administer property, plan agricultural work, and administer charity since men were often away at war or at court (see Chapter 11).

The developments described above did not occur at the same time or to the same degree in all parts of Latin Christendom. Vassalage and the private possession of political power existed in northern and central Italy, but the papacy and the early development of cities there limited these developments. England is particularly difficult to characterize. It was not part of the Carolingian Empire, and its history is quite different despite such common problems as Viking raids. Although lordship and vassalage may have existed to a degree in preconquest England, these concepts were essentially imposed upon England by William the Conqueror. The Norman variety of lordship and vassalage checked rather than augmented the private possession of political power. Thus, England was "feudalized" as a matter of policy and not through a long period of gradual development. The same is true of southern Italy and Sicily when the Normans created a state there at the end of the eleventh century. Since the Norman variety of lordship and vassalage checked the private possession of political power, it did not lead to decentralized authority. The crusader states established in the Holy Land at the end of the eleventh century also became instantaneous feudal states.

Vassalage and the private possession of political authority occurred most completely in the heartland of the Frankish kingdom—north of the Loire and west of the Rhine. It was not nearly as prevalent in southern Gaul, for example, and decentralization was never as complete in the kingdom of the East Franks. Furthermore, within the Frankish heartland there were almost as many variations in the relationship of lord to vassal and in the ways and degree to which the counts ruled as there are surviving documents. There were some common elements, but there was nothing systematic or consistent about what is sometimes misleadingly called the "feudal system." In fact, the term *feudalism* came into use only in the seventeenth century and has lost much of its usefulness today because there are almost as many definitions as there are medieval historians. The following charter of 1110 lists the most common sorts of obligations of a vassal to his lord. The lord in this case is the abbot of a monastery, demonstrating that the Church, as well as the laity, took part in this kind of relationship:

> [S]ince lord Leo, abbot of the said monastery, has asked me, in the presence of all those above mentioned, to acknowledge to him the fealty and homage for the castles, manors, and places which the patrons, my ancestors, held from him and his predecessors and from the said monastery, as a fief, and which I ought to hold as they held, I have made to the lord abbot Leo acknowledgement and homage as I ought to do.
>
> Therefore, let all present and to come know that I the said Bernard Atton, lord and viscount of Carcassonne, acknowledge verily to thee my lord Leo, by the grace of God, abbot of St. Mary of Grasse, and to thy successors that I hold and ought to hold as a fief, in Carcassonne, the following: [a list of manors, castles, and villages] . . . for each and all of which I make homage and fealty

with hands and with mouth to thee my said lord Leo and to thy successors, and I swear upon these four gospels of God that I will always be a faithful vassal to thee and to thy successors and to St. Mary of Grasse in all things in which a vassal is required to be faithful to his lord, and I will defend thee, my lord, and all thy successors, and the monastery and the monks present and to come and the castles and manors and all your men and their possessions against all malefactors and invaders, at my request and that of my successors at my own cost; and I will give to thee power over all the castles and manors above described, in peace and in war, whenever they shall be claimed by thee or by thy successors.

Moreover I acknowledge that, as a recognition of the above fiefs, I and my successors ought to come to the said monastery, at our own expense, as often as a new abbot shall have been made, and there do homage and return to him the power over all the fiefs described above. And when the abbot shall mount his horse I and my heirs, viscounts of Carcassone, and our successors ought to hold the stirrup for the honor of the dominion of St. Mary of Grasse; and to him and all who come with him to as many as two hundred beasts, we should make the abbot's purveyance in the borough of St. Michael of Carcassone, the first time he enters Carcassone, with the best fish and meat and with eggs and cheese, honorably according to his will, and pay the expense of the shoeing of the horses, and for straw and fodder as the season shall require.

And if I or my sons or their successors do not observe to thee or to thy successors each and all the things declared above, and should come against these things, we wish that all the aforesaid fiefs should by that very fact be handed over to thee and to the said monastery of St. Mary of Grasse and to thy successors.[32]

The personal nature of the lord-vassal relationship is clear in this text, for the term *homage* comes from the Latin word for human and the term *fealty* comes form the Latin word for faithfulness. Furthermore, when the vassal dies, his successor must also pledge homage and fealty. The oath on the Gospels, or sometimes on relics of saints, became common and gave the Church a role in preserving feudal relations since the violation of oaths was considered an act against the Church.

In a famous letter of 1020, Bishop Fulbert of Chartres describes the duties of a lord and vassal, making clear that a significant part of those duties was negative—not to do harm, not to be unfaithful.

To William, most illustrious duke of the Aquitanians, Bishop Fulbert, the favor of his prayers:

Requested to write something regarding the character of fealty, I have set down briefly for you, on the authority of the books, the following things. He who takes the oath of fealty to his lord ought always to keep in mind these six things: what is harmless, safe, honorable, useful, easy, and practicable.

Harmless, which means that he ought not to injure his lord in his body; safe, that he should not injure him by betraying his confidence or the defenses upon which he depends for security; honorable, that he should not injure him in his justice, or in other matters that relate to his honor; useful, that he should not injure him in his property; easy, that he should not make difficult that which his lord can do easily; and practicable, that he should not make impossible for the lord that which is possible.

However, while it is proper that the faithful vassal avoid these injuries, it is not for doing this alone that he deserves his holding: for it is not enough to refrain from wrongdoing, unless that which is good is done also. It remains, therefore, that in the same six things referred to above he should faithfully advise and aid his lord, if he wishes to be regarded as worthy of his benefice [fief] and to be safe concerning the fealty which he has sworn. The lord also ought to act toward his faithful vassal in the same manner in all these things. And if he fails to do this, he will be rightfully regarded as guilty of bad faith, just as the former, if he should be found shirking, or willing to shirk, his obligations would be perfidious and perjured.[33]

Since it is clear in the two previous documents that the ceremony in which vassals did fealty and homage really defined the nature of relations and obligations in feudal society, it is important to see what one such ceremony consisted of. In the following passage, Galbert of Bruges describes such an event that took place in 1127:

On April 7, Thursday, homages to the count were again performed; they were carried out in this order in expression of faith and loyalty. First they did homage in this way. The count asked each one if he wished to become wholly his man, and the latter replied, "I so wish," and with his hands clasped and enclosed by those of the count, they were bound together by a kiss. Secondly, he who had done homage pledged his faith to the count's spokesman in these words: "I promise on my faith that I will henceforth be faithful to Count William and that I will maintain my homage toward him completely against every one, in good faith and without guile." And in the third place he swore an oath to this effect on the relics of the saints. Then the count, with a wand which he held in his hand, gave investiture to all those who by this compact had promised loyalty and done homage and likewise had taken an oath.[34]

Lords had obligations to their vassals. Most obviously, they provided the land that was the economic basis of knighthood. They were also required to defend their vassals' fiefs if they were attacked. Importantly, lords owed justice to their vassals—that is, they were to adjudicate between vassals if there was a conflict.

The practices described above, practical and to a great extent effective responses to the problems of the time, were formalized in the creation of ideals of lordship and vassalage. There was a desire to justify in theoretical terms power in the hands of the landed nobility and to establish a code of conduct for those

*Sculpture of Theophilus Doing Fealty to the Devil. Abbey Church of the Souil-
lac, France. Twelfth century. The story of Theophilus making a pact with the
devil was already old in the twelfth century. Here it is made relevant to a society that sees relationships in terms of lord and vassal, for Theophilus is performing the act of fealty to the devil, thus becoming his vassal.*

who held power. The following description from Odo of Cluny's life of Saint
Gerald of Aurillac (d.909), a powerful lord, clearly states the ideals of lordship:

> He therefore exerted himself to repress the insolence of the violent, taking care
> in the first place to promise peace and most easy reconciliation to his enemies.
> And he did this by taking care, that either he should overcome evil by good, or
> if his enemies would not come to terms, he should have in God's eyes the greater
> right on his side. And sometimes indeed he soothed them and reduced them to
> peace. When insatiable malice poured scorn on peaceful men, showing severity
> of heart, he broke the teeth of the wicked [Ps. 57:7], that, according to the say-
> ing of Job, he might snatch the prey from their jaws [Job 29:17]. He was not
> incited by the desire for revenge, as is the case with many, or led on by love of
> praise from the multitude, but by love of the poor, who were not able to pro-
> tect themselves. He acted in this way lest, if he became sluggish through indo-
> lent patience, he should seem to have neglected the precept to care for the poor.
> He ordered the poor man to be saved and the needy to be freed from the hand
> of the sinner. Rightly, therefore, he did not allow the sinner to prevail. But

sometimes when the unavoidable necessity of fighting lay on him, he commanded his men in imperious tones, to fight with the backs of their swords and with their spears reversed. This would have been ridiculous to the enemy if Gerald, strengthened by divine power, had not been invincible to them.

And it would have seemed useless to his own men, if they had not learnt by experience that Gerald, who was carried away by his piety in the very moment of battle, had not always been invincible. When therefore they saw that he triumphed by a new kind of fighting which was mingled with piety, they changed their scorn to admiration, and sure of victory they readily fulfilled his commands. For it was a thing unheard of that he or the soldiers who fought under him were not victorious. . . . Let no one be worried because a just man sometimes made use of fighting, which seems incompatible with religion. No one who has judged his cause impartially will be able to show that the glory of Gerald is clouded by this. For some of the Fathers, and of these the most holy and most patient, when the cause of justice demanded, valiantly took up arms against their adversaries, as Abraham, who destroyed a great multitude of the enemy to rescue his nephew [Genesis 14], and King David who sent his forces even against his own son. [2 Kings 18]. Gerald did not fight invading the property of others, but defending his own, or rather his people's rights. . . . It was lawful, therefore, for a layman to carry the sword in battle that he might protect defenceless people, as the harmless flock from evening wolves according to the saying of Scripture [Acts 20:29], and that he might restrain by arms or by the law those whom ecclesiastical censure was not able to subdue.[35]

For the ideals of vassalage, the *Song of Roland* is likewise a important source, although we need to remember that it reflects the time it was written (early twelfth century) rather than the time of its hero Charlemagne. Just before the battle of Roncesvalles, Roland states a vassal's obligations to his lord:

Here we will stand, defending our great king.
This is the service a vassal owes his lord:
To suffer hardships, endure great heat and cold,
And in a battle to lose both hair and hide.[36]

Ideals and historical realities are usually far apart. But the ideals of bravery and loyalty on the part of the vassal, and wisdom and justice on the part of the lord, were long-lasting measurements for those who governed and fought. Chaucer, for example, embodies them in his portrait of the knight in the *Canterbury Tales*, written shortly before 1400.

From the description of lordship and vassalage and the private possession of political power, feudal society would appear to be incompatible with strong monarchy. Yet since a powerful man such as William the Conqueror consciously "feudalized" England and the clever Emperor Frederick Barbarossa (r.1152–1190) extended lordship and vassalage as a way of increasing his power, it is necessary to reevaluate that analysis. The political and military structure of eleventh-century France was certainly not compatible with a powerful monarchy, but a resourceful king could use some elements of it while modifying others. For example, the practice of liege lordship developed: simply, however far down the feudal hierarchy a vassal might be (he could be a vassal of a vassal of a vassal of the king), his preeminent obligation was to the king rather than to his immediate lord. Kings and great nobles could not create new societies from scratch, but were forced to strengthen their offices by using elements of traditional relations already in existence.

The historian Joseph Strayer's analysis suggests three ways that the kings adapted existing relationships and institutions to their benefit in the eleventh and twelfth centuries.[37] First, they focused on the land itself, that is, the fief, rather than on a vassal's personal service. Kings thus became willing to replace personal service with money payments. They were able to use the revenues generated by the fiefs to hire full-time soldiers and other functionaries, who were more dependable and loyal than the independent-minded vassals. Second, the kings sought to systematize the various customs and traditions that had developed over centuries. In the period when local lords operated independently of their kings, they nevertheless continued to recognize that they were royal vassals, paying lip service to their obligations. They may have generally ignored their kings, but they never denied the monarchy's existence or their obligations to it. As kings began to try to enforce their vassals' neglected obligations, they also claimed that any judicial powers that their vassals exercised had originated from royal grants. Although this was not necessarily true, it laid the groundwork for kings to claim appellate jurisdiction and even to revoke earlier grants. Third, kings began to develop a bureaucracy. With the money they received from their vassals added to their other sources of income, they could hire efficient and loyal administrators trained in the law. By establishing courts over which these royal employees presided, kings were able to convince many lesser vassals in their realms that royal justice was superior to that offered by local lords, who often relied on such primitive methods of detecting guilt as trial by battle and the ordeal. Furthermore, if a fief became vacant because of the lack of an heir or through confiscation from a rebellious vassal, kings often chose not to grant it out again as a fief but rather had it administered by paid bureaucrats, who had no independent power base and whose office was not hereditary. This happened in 1206 when the king of France took away Normandy from its rebellious duke (King John of England). Although it is wrong to speak of a feudal system in the ninth, tenth, and eleventh centuries, it is proper to speak of feudal monarchies in the twelfth and thirteenth. These kingdoms are the real beginnings of the nation-states of Europe.

The ideas of lordship and vassalage came to be applied far beyond their original context, especially from the twelfth century on. For example, in the twelfth century, even though many vassals were paying their lords rather than fighting for them, writers began to apply the concept of vassalage to descriptions of relationships with women. The language of courtly literature is in part the language of lordship and vassalage, with the man as vassal pledging his service to a lady (see Chapter 9). Another example can be seen in the language and even the posture of prayer. Early Christians prayed with their arms extended to either side. The position that we associate with prayer, closed hands held together, is in fact the position of a vassal in the act of doing fealty (see the text of Galbert of Bruges and the sculpture from Souillac above). People during the feudal period expressed their relationship with God the way they expressed the relationship of vassal to lord. Furthermore, hymns written to God began to use this same language, as did hymns written to the Virgin Mary. The concept of dependent relationships that we often label "feudal" was of great importance long after the lord-vassal relationship changed radically from the time of its origins.

During the two centuries following the death of Charlemagne, several different authors both in England and on the continent developed the idea of the three orders of society—those who pray (oratores), those who fight (bellatores), and those who work (laboratores). One version of this social structure is found in the writings of Adalberto of Laon in the early eleventh century:

> The house of God, which is thought to be one is therefore triple. Now [some] pray, others fight, and others work. These three are together and they suffer no split: the workings of two thus stand on the office of one, [and] alternately they offer support to everyone. This triple connection is therefore single.[38]

The basic idea of this tripartite division of society is that each of the three groups carries out its function both for itself and for everyone else. Thus, the clergy, primarily monks, pray not just for themselves but are the pray-ers for everyone. Likewise, the feudal nobility defends everyone, not just those of this class, as illustrated in the passage from life of Saint Gerald. The great majority of people in this scheme belong to the so-called third estate—they were the producers of food. By the time of Adalberto, this social structure was understood as a reflection of the Trinity. Just as God the Son and God the Holy Spirit proceed from the Father (Nicene Creed, see Chapter 3), so do the two lay estates stand on the clerical estate. Of course, this social theory is a model and never fully included everyone in the society. Even the secular clergy are in a somewhat ambivalent position since they do not literally pray as their primary function. There were always some people who lived in cities and engaged in trade. In the later centuries of the Middle Ages, this social concept would be challenged by the development of urban life and would sometimes be adapted to try to fit everyone into it. If merchants, despite their wealth, cannot ever quite fit into this scheme, then some respond by trying to enter the feudal nobility and thus move from an ambiguous social status into a recognized place in society. This model, for all its inexactness, nevertheless provides an important summary of what could be called the theory behind feudal society.

PART 3

THE HIGH MIDDLE
AGES AND BEYOND

EUROPE IN THE
HIGH MIDDLE AGES

---- Approximate Boundaries of the
     Papal States

BLACK SEA

Constantinople

•Damascus
• Nazareth

Jerusalem •

TERRANEAN SEA

• Alexandria

CHAPTER 8

CHURCH, STATE,
AND SOCIETY

We often refer to the period of medieval history beginning in the eleventh century as the High Middle Ages. The eleventh, and even more the twelfth and thirteenth centuries were a time of recovery, of change, and of synthesis. In the next two chapters, we will treat this period in terms of these broad categories, with an emphasis in this chapter on change and development, and in the next chapter, "The Renaissance of the Twelfth Century," on synthesis. Hints of some of those changes have been presented in the last chapter, for example in the educational reforms established by Charlemagne and the development of feudal monarchy. To set the stage for changes in the political, religious, and cultural spheres, we will begin with an examination of demographic changes along with the development of long-distance trade and the renewal of urban life.

THE RISE OF CITIES

One of the most important phenomena of the tenth and, even more, the eleventh century was the renewal of long-distance trade and urban life. Commerce, of course, never ceased completely in the early Middle Ages, nor did cities disappear; but the Carolingian world was essentially agrarian, and its most important political and cultural centers were castles (fortifications) and monasteries rather than cities. In one sense, even the Roman Empire at its height was agrarian too, since the vast majority of its inhabitants tilled the soil, as was true of all preindustrial societies. Nevertheless, the Empire's political, economic, and cultural focal points were its cities. Consequently, the Church won its early converts and established its high priests, the bishops, in cities. However, during the Germanic invasions and the subsequent division of Western Europe into kingdoms, long-distance trade declined and so did cities as centers of commerce and culture. By the Carolingian period, the city as it was known in the ancient world essentially had ceased to exist. This does not mean that cities were completely abandoned, however, for they continued to function as ecclesiastical centers with cathedrals plus the clergy attached to them and the laypersons they employed. By the tenth century even Rome itself was little more than the seat of the pope, most of its great buildings deserted and crumbling.

By the end of the tenth century, Western Europe was relatively peaceful following the defeat and conversion of the Vikings and Magyars. And for a variety of reasons, most importantly the development of new agricultural practices and technologies, its population began to increase. However, the land could only support a certain number of people; sometimes younger sons of agricultural laborers had to leave their homes and fend for themselves, some becoming vagabonds and robbers, others obtaining a few goods, trading them wherever they were in demand. The twelfth-century *Life of St. Godric* describes such a young man. By Godric's time, some cities were already well established, but it is likely that his activities and motivation likewise describe ambitious individuals of earlier generations.

> Wherefore he chose not to follow the life of a husbandman, but rather to study, learn, and exercise the rudiments of more subtle conceptions. For this reason, aspiring to the merchant's trade, he began to follow the chapman's [peddler's] way of life, first learning how to gain in small bargains and things of insignificant price; and thence, while yet a youth, his mind advanced little by little to buy and sell and gain from things of greater expense. For, in his beginnings, he was wont to wander with small wares around the villages and farmsteads of his own neighborhood; but, in process of time, he gradually associated himself by compact with city merchants. Hence, within a brief space of time, the youth who had trudged for many weary hours from village to village, from farm to farm, did so profit by his increase of age and wisdom as to travel with associates of his own age through towns and boroughs, fortresses and cities, to fairs and to all the various booths of the marketplace, in pursuit of his public chaffer [barter]. He went along the highway, neither puffed up by the good testimony of his conscience nor downcast in the nobler part of his soul by the reproach of poverty. . . .
>
> The saint . . . roamed one day over stretches of foreshore [beach]; and, finding nothing at first, he followed on and on to a distance of three miles, where he found three porpoises lying high and dry, either cast upon the sands by the waves or left there by the ebb-tide.[1]

Godric was able to sell the porpoise fat, and hard work and great risk brought him success, for soon he was able to purchase a ship. In the end, Godric gave up his hard-earned wealth to become a hermit, but unlike him many other entrepreneurial people continued to increase and enjoy their fortunes.

Sometimes itinerant merchants formed groups for protection as well as to have a greater diversity of products to sell. They went on long-distance expeditions during the good weather months; but in the winter they needed places where they could collect goods, store them, and then prepare the year's business plans. They looked for secure places near surviving Roman roads, navigable rivers, or seacoasts. Often merchants sought permission to settle beneath the walls of a castle or an ecclesiastical center, in return for which they offered some of their goods. They sometimes built permanent dwellings, and the walls of the castles or ecclesiastical centers might then be extended to incorporate them. There were problems with this type of arrangement, however. The law administered by the lord of a castle or a bishop was not suited to the needs of merchants. These merchants wanted to live by their own law, and they often paid to free themselves from the jurisdiction of ecclesiastical or feudal courts and other obligations they had agreed to. In some cases, a group of merchants simply declared itself free from a protector's jurisdiction. To do this, they usually formed associations called communes. One of the best accounts of the origins of a commune is contained in the memoirs of Abbot Guibert of Nogent, describing events in the French city of Laon in the year 1112. Guibert was a monk living near Laon. He did not fully understand what was happening there, and he was unsympathetic to this innovation. His account thus reflects how many members of the nobility, the class from which Guibert came, viewed this new phenomenon:

> [T]he clergy, the archdeacons, and the nobles were looking for a way to extract money from the people, so they sent them messengers and made the following proposition: in exchange for a good offer the people could obtain authorization to create a commune. Now "commune" is a new and evil name for an arrangement by which all persons are subject to a yearly tax that they owe their lords as a result of their servitude. If they commit a crime they will be subject to a legal fine but all other forms of taxation that used to be inflicted on serfs are abolished. [Guibert's definition of "commune" is too narrow, ignoring its judicial dimension.] The people of Laon seized this opportunity to ransom themselves and contributed vast amounts of money to fill the gaping holes in these moneygrubbers' pockets. The moneygrubbers in turn were delighted to see so much money raining upon them so they confirmed under oath that they would respect the pact that had just been agreed upon.[2]

When the bishop returned, he was bribed to support the commune. However, he later decided to try to keep the money and his authority too and bribed the king to release him from his oath to uphold the commune. Within a week people were in the streets shouting "Commune," and violence followed:

Now the insolent crowd, which had been screaming before the walls of his [the bishop's] palace, attacked the bishop. [Bishop] Gaudry, along with those who had come to his aid, kept the enemy at bay by throwing stones and shooting arrows. In this as in other moments Gaudry showed the fierceness in battle that had always been his hallmark; but because he had unjustly and wrongly taken up that other [spiritual] sword, he perished by the sword. Unable to repel the fierce attacks of the people he took the clothes of one of his servants and fled to the cellar of the church where he hid himself in a small barrel. . . . [Soon, the people found the bishop hidden away.] Now Gaudry who, sinner though he was, was nevertheless the Lord's anointed, was pulled out of the barrel by the hair, repeatedly beaten, then dragged outside into a narrow street of the cloister, before the house of Godfrey the chaplain. There he began a most pathetic plea for his life, swearing that he would never again be their bishop, that he would give them immense sums of money, and that he would leave the country. The crowd jeered at him, their hearts being closed to all feeling. Finally a man named Bernard de Bruyères raised his axe over the head of this holy (though admittedly sinful) man and dashed his brains out. As they tried to hold him up, Gaudry fell between their hands; and then another blow, this one delivered sideways across the nose and under the eye sockets, finished him off. He died on the spot. They broke his legs and kept inflicting repeated blows on his corpse. Then Theudegaud saw the ring on the ex-bishop's finger; and as he was having a hard time trying to pull it off, he cut off the dead man's finger with his sword and seized the ring. The bishop's body was then stripped of its garments and thrown naked into a street corner. . . . [3]

As the passage demonstrates, establishing a commune was important enough for the leaders of the commune in Laon to slay their bishop. After the violence, it took several more years before Laon's commune was finally confirmed. Although many communes were established peacefully, Guibert shows just how passionate was the merchants' desire to be free. The freedom that communes paid and fought for gave cities the opportunity to develop their own institutions and eventually produced sophisticated urban governments and the great medieval trade guilds.

In Italy, cities began to reemerge somewhat earlier than they did north of the Alps. This is in part because Italy was more highly urbanized in Roman times than northern Europe, in part because Italy suffered less from the ninth-century invasions than the North, but primarily because of its position in the center of the Mediterranean. Venice, for example, was engaged in trade with Constantinople and the eastern Mediterranean from its foundation at the time of the dissolution of the Roman Empire in the West. By the eleventh century, cities such as Amalfi and Pisa also traded in the East and carried pilgrims to the Holy Land. Italian cities too threw off the yoke of the landed nobles and bishops and eventually dominated the surrounding countryside and its inhabitants. Otto of Freising, a monk and the biographer of the Emperor

Piazza del Campo, Siena, Italy. This magnificent urban space was the Forum of a small city in Roman times. The city hall with its tall tower was built at the beginning of the fourteenth century, when Siena was a prosperous independent state. Large open spaces such as the Campo of Siena were important for assemblies, festivals, and preaching.

Frederick Barbarossa, characterized the cities of northern Italy as he observed them in the 1150s:

> In the governing of their cities, also in the conduct of public affairs, they [the people of Lombardy, a region in northern Italy whose center is Milan] still imitate the wisdom of the ancient Romans. Finally, they are so desirous of liberty that, avoiding the insolence of power, they are governed by the will of consuls rather than rulers. There are known to be three orders among them: captains, vavasors [a term that sometimes means vassal but here apparently refers to people of substance who are subordinate to the captains], and commoners. And in order to suppress arrogance, the aforesaid consuls are chosen not from one but from each of the classes. And lest they should exceed bounds by lust for power, they are changed every year. The consequence is that, as practically that entire land is divided among the cities, each of them required its bishops to live in the cities, and scarcely any noble or great man can be found in all the surrounding territory who does not acknowledge the authority of his city. And from this power to force all elements together they are wont to call the several lands of each [noble or magnate] their contado. Also, that they may not lack the means of subduing their neighbors, they do not disdain to give the girdle of knight-

hood or the grades of distinction to young men of inferior station and even some workers of the vile mechanical arts, whom other peoples bar like the pest from the more respected and honorable pursuits. From this it has resulted that they far surpass all other states of the world in riches and in power.[4]

It is clear from Otto's complete account of the Italian cities that they were reluctant to accept imperial authority, and they formed a league to oppose Emperor Frederick Barbarossa. In 1176 at Legnano, the Italian cities defeated the emperor. From that time on they were able to grow without imperial intervention although they paid lip service to the Empire, and later emperors tried several times to reimpose control over them.

Bonvesin de la Riva, a teacher in Milan toward the end of the thirteenth century, wrote a description of his city. Even allowing for some exaggeration, we cannot but be impressed at how different Milan is from anything existing in Western Europe a few centuries earlier:

The houses with doorways onto public streets have been found to number about 12,500 in very many of which several families cohabit with a multitude of servants. . . . The courtyard of the commune . . . occupies an area of 10 square perches [about 6500 sq. meters]. . . . In the middle stands a marvellous palace, and in the same courtyard is a tower in which are the four bells of the commune. On the east side is the palace where the offices of the podestà [mayor] and judges are, at the end of which is the podestà's chapel built in honour of our patron saint Ambrose. . . . On the south side is a loggia where judicial sentences convicting the guilty are read out. . . . A ditch of admirable beauty and which circles right round the city, containing not a swamp or putrid standing water, but fresh spring-water, [is] full of fish and crabs. The ditch runs between a marvellous wall and an internal embankment. Beyond the walls are so many suburban dwellings that they form a city by themselves. The main gates of the city are very strong and number six, the secondary gates, called posterns, are ten. . . . The main gates each have a pair of towers. . . . The saints' shrines . . . number about 200 in the city alone, with 480 altars . . . and it is wonderful to note how and how much the Virgin Mary is venerated in the city, for there are thirty-six churches built in worship of her alone.

There are in the city alone 120 lawyers in civil and canon law, and their college is believed to have no equal in the world for size and learning. . . . There are more than 1,500 notaries . . . [and] 28 expert medics, commonly called physicians . . . [and] over 150 surgeons of various kinds . . . [and] eight grammar teachers, each with a crowd of pupils under their rods . . . [and] over 70 teachers of elementary reading. The book-scribes, though there is no university in the city, exceed 40 in number, who earn their daily bread by copying books in their own hands. The ovens in the city, cooking bread for the citizens, are 200, as can be seen from the communal registers. . . . The retail wine-merchants, selling a wonderful wine of all kinds, are without doubt over one thousand . . . [and] the butchers are over 440. . . . [5]

Clearly, life in a city such as Milan in the late thirteenth century would have been unimaginable three centuries earlier, when the population of most Italian cities consisted of relatively few people, mostly associated with the Church, living among the ruins of a much larger Roman city. Milan, to continue the example, had been the seat of the Roman Empire in the fourth century and was the city to which Augustine was drawn and in which he was baptized.

Medieval cities grew in size, wealth, and sophistication. Although the urban population of Europe in the High Middle Ages probably never exceeded 15 percent of the total population, it was a disproportionately wealthy and influential minority. The centers of education—cathedral schools and later the universities—were located in cities. The great Gothic cathedrals dominated the urban skylines. Both Dante and Chaucer were men of the cities, products of a sophisticated urban culture. Eventually even the monarchs and their increasingly complex bureaucracies established permanent seats of government in cities such as Westminster, adjacent to medieval London and part of modern London, and Paris.

THE BEGINNINGS OF CHURCH REFORM

Since the Church in the early Middle Ages had come to control a great deal of land and since land was the chief source of wealth and warriors, lay rulers often sought and obtained control over bishoprics and even abbacies, either to bestow on trustworthy persons—often relatives—or to sell to the highest bidder. Parish priests were generally semiliterate at best, usually serfs or peasant farmers; many were married and passed on the job to their sons. Monasteries had become rather wealthy and were often lax in their observance of the Rule of Saint Benedict. These problems had their beginnings as early as the Merovingian period but intensified following the collapse of the centralized authority that Charlemagne had established.

In the post-Carolingian world, the papacy also suffered; the tenth and first half of the eleventh centuries were perhaps the bleakest times in its history. The potential for corruption came with the development of papal temporal power in central Italy, which had been accelerated with the Donation of Pepin (Chapter 7). Pope Leo III had been expelled from Rome in 799, but Charlemagne restored him when he journeyed to Rome for that purpose. With the demise of the Carolingian Empire, however, there was no longer a temporal power able and willing to rescue the papacy from local, essentially political squabbles. The depths to which the papacy had sunk can be symbolized by the example of Pope Formosus. When he died in 896, a member of the family opposed to his political policies was elected pope and convened a synod that exhumed Formosus's body, put him on trial, and convicted him of usurping the papal office. His corpse was stripped of the papal garments; the fingers on the right hand, used in giving the benediction, were broken; and his body was thrown into the Tiber. Clearly, the sacred and the secular, temporal and spiritual power, were thoroughly mixed and confused. From the parishes and monasteries to the great prelates and the papacy, the Church was in need of a reform in both head and members.

A harbinger of the great reform movements in the Church during the eleventh century and the beginning of important monastic reform was the foundation of the Burgundian monastery of Cluny in 910. Its foundation charter declared that the monastery was to be completely free of lay control and even from local episcopal jurisdiction. Cluny was placed directly under papal authority. In essence, this was a declaration of complete independence since the bishops of Rome at this time cared little about exercising control over a monastery far away and had no means to do so anyway. The monks of Cluny were not exactly like the Benedictines on Monte Cassino four hundred years earlier. Their observance was based on the reforms of Benedict of Aniane in the ninth century (see Chapter 7), and included elaborate liturgical practices, the use of splendid works of art, and virtually no manual labor. The Cluniacs had a class of monks called lay brothers and/or serfs to do manual labor while the choir monks spent as much as seven hours a day singing the monastic offices. Cluny's independence from lay control and its way of observing the Rule of Saint Benedict struck a responsive chord in monasteries throughout Western Europe. Even in the century of its foundation, Cluny established daughter houses and sent its monks to established monasteries desiring reform. Although there was no such thing as a Cluniac Order with a central governing authority, Cluny's form of monasticism spread to all parts of Latin Christendom. Abbot Hugh the Great (r.1049–1109) began the building of the great Romanesque abbey church at Cluny. For four hundred years it was the largest church in Christendom. After the building of the new Saint Peter's in Rome in the sixteenth century, it remained second largest until its destruction during the French Revolution.

In the second half of the eleventh century came the reform of the papacy and its reemergence as an important political as well as ecclesiastical institution throughout Europe. The year 1046 was one of particular scandal in Rome. Pope Benedict IX sold his office to a sincere reformer named Gregory VI; then Benedict reclaimed it. To add to the confusion and degradation, a rival Roman faction claimed that one of its members was the true pope. Thus, there were three claimants to the throne of Peter. The concerned Holy Roman Emperor Henry III called a synod that deposed all three, and Henry appointed a new pope. That pope and the one who succeeded him quickly died in suspicious circumstances. Henry's third appointment, however, Leo IX (r. 1049–1054), initiated the great papal renewal called the Gregorian Reform, after Leo's most famous successor in the reform tradition, Gregory VII (r.1073–1085). Leo recognized the encroachment of the secular on the sacred as the great evil of his day. He sought to prohibit clerical marriage, perceived as a conflation of religious and lay functions and thus as a symbol of the general problem. However, the chief ill that he tried to cure was the practice of simony—the buying and selling of Church offices—named after Simon Magus, whose story is told in Acts 8:9–24. The elimination of simony became the chief concern of Leo's pontificate both because of its intrinsic seriousness and because it epitomized the Church's corruption. Leo brought trustworthy men to Rome to help in the reform movement and gave them the liturgical title of cardinal. These included important figures in the history of medieval Christianity in their own right such as the monk Hildebrand, the future Gregory VII; the coldly intellectual and inflexible Humbert; and the ascetic theologian Peter

Capital depicting the Fall of Simon the Magician. Cathedral of Saint Lazare, Autun, France. Twelfth century. This capital depicts the story of the Fall of Simon Magus (the Magician), who appears in Acts 8:9–24. In the story related there, Simon tried to buy the gifts of the Holy Spirit and was rebuked by Peter. According to a popular post-biblical legend, Simon later met Peter in Rome and flew over the city to demonstrate his magical powers. However, when Peter prayed, Simon fell out of the sky. In this sculpted capital, the devil on the right is in contrast with Saint Peter, keys in hand, on the left. The wings on Simon's arms and legs are useless. The popularity of this story in art attests to the Church's concern with the problem of simony (named for Simon) during the High Middle Ages. Simon is an important figure in later medieval literature.

Damian. Leo was faced with the difficult problem of enforcing his reform decrees throughout Christendom. He wrote letters, appointed legates (men given his authority in a specific geographical area or in a specific matter), held synods, and traveled with an impressive entourage literally to show Europe the reformed papacy. His activity at the dedication of the new Monastery of Saint Remigius at Reims illustrates his method. After processing through the city with the relics of its patron, Remigius, he demanded that all bishops take an oath in the presence of the relics that they did not buy their office. Several refused. One was deposed on the spot, and the archbishop of Reims himself was ordered to appear later in Rome. Leo meant business. His attempts to enlarge the scope of papal power also had their tragic element, however. During a mission in 1054 to establish the pope's authority in the East, the overzealous Cardinal Humbert placed a bull of excommunication on the altar of Santa Sophia in Constantinople. The strong-willed and politically oriented Patriarch of Constantinople, Michael Cerularios, reciprocated by excommunicating the pope. This schism proved to be long lasting despite serious attempts to heal it in the 1270s and 1430s. Only in 1965 did Pope Paul VI and the Greek Patriarch Athenagoras rescind these bulls; however, the Roman Catholic and Eastern Orthodox communities remain separated even today.

A series of reformers in the tradition of Leo succeeded him on the papal throne. In 1059 Nicholas II issued a decree establishing a procedure for papal election by the cardinals; although this was altered somewhat about a hundred years later by Alexander III, it is still the basis for papal election. The purpose of this decree was to keep the election of the pope out of the hands of laypersons, including the Holy Roman Emperor. Since it was a Holy Roman Emperor who appointed the first reform pope, there is a certain irony here.

The election of Cardinal Hildebrand in 1073 as Gregory VII brought to the throne of Saint Peter the most experienced man in the curia (the papal court). His pontificate is pivotal in understanding the subsequent history of medieval Europe. Within the curia of Leo IX, two schools of thought had developed on the relationship of spiritual to temporal authority. Peter Damian had called for real cooperation between secular and ecclesiastical leaders and was willing to be flexible in dealing with thorny matters that came before the pope. For example, he saw simony as a terrible sin but nevertheless accepted the validity of ordinations performed by simoniac bishops. Humbert on the other hand stood for ecclesiastical supremacy over the state and rejected the validity of simoniac bishops, thus coming close to the old heresy of Donatism (see Chapter 3). Gregory VII ardently supported Humbert's position.

Within two years of his accession to the papal throne, Gregory was in open conflict with the Holy Roman Emperor-elect Henry IV. The specific issue was lay investiture—the practice of a layperson, such as the Holy Roman Emperor, investing a bishop with the spiritual symbols of his office. Henry knew that to control his empire in fact as well as theory he needed loyal bishops, for they controlled vast amounts of land, the means for providing him with an army. The only way to ensure the bishops' loyalty was to have complete control over their selection and investiture. This was obviously in clear opposition to the principles of the papal reform movement to which Gregory was heir. The conflict that broke out in 1075 after Henry invested the bishop of Milan was about much more than simply who was to present a ring and staff to a bishop: it was a struggle for the leadership of Latin Christendom. The struggle had several melodramatic and tragicomical episodes before Gregory died in exile in 1085. However, Henry's apparent victory was short-lived as he faced rebellion even within his own family and died in the midst of a struggle against a major coalition of opposition in 1106.

In the year 1122, the issue of lay investiture was settled by a compromise, the Concordat of Worms. Bishops were to be elected only by clergy, but an imperial representative could be present at the election. Investiture of the spiritual symbols of office was to be performed by other bishops but only after investiture of the temporal symbols had been performed by the emperor or his representative. However, the larger question of the leadership of Christian society was far from being decided. The Empire was severely weakened, both in theory and practice. The emperor no longer had sole control over the selection of bishops, and the bitter struggle between popes and emperors destroyed the papacy's support of the Empire. Furthermore, the theory of theocratic kingship, an important buttress of the emperor's position that developed in the Carolingian period, was swept away by the sharp distinctions between priesthood and kingship made by advocates of the papal position.

THE CRUSADES

The era of papal reform gave birth to one of the most important, interesting, and yet tragic phenomena of the Middle Ages, the Crusades—wars to win back the Holy Land from the Muslims. The idea of a holy war against the enemies of Christendom was not new at the end of the eleventh century. Something like it existed as early as the ninth century in England during the invasion of the pagan Danes. A more clearly conceived idea of holy war developed in Spain in the eleventh century, as the surviving Christian kingdoms in Iberia began the *Reconquista* to free the rest of the peninsula from Muslim rule. However, the Crusades were the culmination of the idea of the holy war, since they were also regarded as pilgrimages to the holiest shrines of Christendom, to the land where Jesus lived, to Jerusalem, the earthly model of the heavenly city.

The immediate stimulus for the Crusades came from the East. The Byzantine Emperor, Alexius Comnenus, sought help from the West to win back the Holy Land. Pope Urban II responded, and in 1095 he called the First Crusade at a council held in the French city of Clermont-Ferrand. Urban saw this as an opportunity to continue the papal reform program and to restore the papacy's dignity in the aftermath of Gregory VII's death in exile, by rallying the forces of Western Europe for a great military and moral enterprise. Thus, the First Crusade cannot be understood apart from its context as a part of papal assertion of leadership in the West. The plan was to send an army by land through the Byzantine Empire into the Holy Land, which Muslims had controlled since the mid-seventh century. Although the emperor in Constantinople had sought papal help in forming an army to liberate Palestine, the crusaders were by and large not as willing to submit to imperial authority as he had hoped.

For those who were willing to go on the Crusade, Urban offered forgiveness of sins:

> I address those present; I proclaim it to those absent; moreover Christ commands it. For all those going thither there will be remission of sins if they come to the end of this fettered life while either marching by land or crossing by sea, or in fighting the pagans. This I grant to all who go, through the power vested in me by God.[6]

The crusaders also were given badges marking them as pilgrims, albeit special ones. The most important chronicler of the First Crusade, Fulcher of Chartres, describes the badge and provides an Augustinian interpretation of it:

> Oh how fitting, and how pleasing it was to us all to see those crosses made of silk, cloth-of-gold, or other beautiful material which these pilgrims whether knights, other laymen, or clerics sewed on the shoulders of their cloaks. They did this by command of Pope Urban once they had taken the oath to go. It was proper that the soldiers of God who were preparing to fight for His honor should be identified and protected by this emblem of victory. And since they thus decorated themselves with this emblem of their faith, in the end they acquired from the symbol the reality itself. They clad themselves with the outward sign in order that they might obtain the inner reality.[7]

After the crusaders arrived in territory under Muslim control, they found themselves ill-equipped to fight in the desert; often they were discouraged and even desperate. Fulcher gives a gruesome description of one such moment:

> Those two leaders with their men seized the two cities of Barra and Marra in an attack showing great bravery. They very quickly captured the former, killed the citizens to a man, and confiscated everything. Then they hastened to the other city and besieged it for twenty days. Here our men suffered from excessive hunger. I shudder to say that many of our men, terribly tormented by the madness of starvation, cut pieces of flesh from the buttocks of Saracens [Muslims] lying there dead. These pieces they cooked and ate, savagely devouring the flesh while it was insufficiently roasted. In this way the besiegers were harmed more than the besieged.[8]

The crusaders often acted with brutality, even when entering Jerusalem itself:

> Many of the Saracens who had climbed to the top of the Temple of Solomon [the building referred to here is actually the famous mosque, the Dome of the Rock] in their flight were shot to death with arrows and fell headlong from the roof. Nearly ten thousand were beheaded in this Temple. If you had been there your feet would have been stained to the ankles in the blood of the slain. What shall I say? None of them were left alive. Neither women nor children were spared.[9]

Even allowing for the exaggeration typical in this sort of narrative, it is clear that the crusaders often forgot that they came to reclaim the land on which the Prince of Peace had once walked. Despite the cruelties and the violence, the crusaders were hailed as heroes in Western Europe, especially with the capture of Jerusalem and the establishment of a Latin kingdom centered in the Holy City.

Fortunately, the deeds of the crusaders are described in Muslim as well as Christian chronicles. Reading Muslim "coverage" of the same events is a valuable reminder that often in the study of medieval history, we only have one side of the story—the history of groups declared heretical immediately comes to mind. Consider two versions of the First Crusade's capture of Antioch. The two versions agree that someone inside the city allowed the crusaders to enter it, but that is where the agreement ends. Here is Fulcher of Chartres's account:

> Our Lord appeared to a certain Turk, chosen beforehand by his grace, and said to him: "Arise, thou who sleepest. I command thee to return the city to the Christians." [Shortly after this vision, he gave aid to the crusaders.] In a loud voice, altogether the Turk shouted: "God wills it! God wills it!"[10]

Ibn Al-Athir recounts the same event quite differently:

> After the siege had been going on for a long time, the Franks made a deal with one of the men who were responsible for the towers. He was a cuirass-maker named Ruzbih whom they bribed with a fortune in money and lands. . . . The Franks sealed their pact with the cuirass-maker, God damn him! and made their way to the water gate.[11]

The First Crusade was only one of a series of papally sponsored expeditions to the Holy Land. The Second Crusade was called in 1147, largely through the urging of the Cistercian monk Bernard of Clairvaux, because one of the cities which the First Crusade had captured had fallen to the Muslims. Though unlike the earlier expedition its head was a ruling monarch, Louis VII of France, this crusade accomplished nothing militarily.

In 1187 the city of Jerusalem fell to the Muslims because of political problems in the kingdom and the tactics of a brilliant Muslim leader named Saladin. In response, the Third Crusade was launched, with the three most powerful monarchs in Europe participating—Frederick I (Barbarossa), the Holy Roman Emperor; Richard I (the Lion-hearted) of England; and Philip II (Augustus) of France. Again, the Crusade accomplished very little. Pope Innocent III (r.1198–1216) called the Fourth Crusade, a naval expedition that began in Venice. The crusaders did not have enough money to pay the Venetians for their transportation, so they agreed to attack the Christian city of Zara (in modern Croatia) for Venice as payment. From there they proceeded to Constantinople, still by far the largest Christian city in the world. The crusaders reestablished a recently deposed emperor who promised them aid; but when he could not provide it, they captured the city and sacked it, dividing the European parts of the Byzantine Empire between themselves and the Venetians. There were later Crusades to recapture the Holy Land, most notably two led by the pious King Louis IX of France (d. 1270 in Tunis in modern Tunisia while on Crusade). However, the scandal of the Fourth Crusade really marked the end of the most important era of crusading history.

The effects of the Crusades were enormous. They probably reduced the level of violence in Western Europe, for many younger sons of nobles or small landholders greedy for more land went to the Holy Land instead of making war within Europe. Urban himself had stated that one of his reasons for calling the First Crusade was to take these violent men and turn their energy toward the Muslims both for the good of Christendom and their souls. The crusades hardened religious divisions in the Mediterranean region. The religious enthusiasm which the First Crusade created led to an outbreak of violence against Jews in Europe. Some popular preachers argued that the Crusades should start at home, since "Christ-killers," that is, the Jews, were living among them. The following describes a massacre in the Holy Roman Empire:

> At the beginning of summer in the same year in which Peter and Gottschalk, after collecting an army, had set out, there assembled in like fashion a large and innumerable host of Christians from diverse kingdoms and lands; namely, from the realms of France, England, Flanders, and Lorraine. . . . I know not whether by a judgement of the Lord, or by some error of mind, they rose in a spirit of cruelty against the Jewish people scattered throughout the cities and slaughtered them without mercy, especially in the Kingdom of Lorraine, asserting it to be the beginning of their expedition and their duty against the enemies of the Christian faith. This slaughter of Jews was done first by citizens of Cologne. These suddenly fell upon a small band of Jews and severely wounded and killed many; they destroyed the houses and synagogues of the Jews and divided among themselves a very large amount of money. When the Jews saw this cruelty, about two hundred in the silence of the night began flight by boat to Neuss. The pilgrims and crusaders discovered them, and after taking away all of their possessions, inflicted on them similar slaughter leaving not even one alive.[12]

Except in Spain and Sicily, contact between Western Christendom and the Islamic world had been mostly indirect. However, the creation of a bitter enmity between Christians and Muslims as a result of the Western assault in the Middle East during the crusading era led to a distrust between the Islamic East and the Christian West that continues to exist to this day.

A third effect was to bring the West into closer contact with Constantinople and the Byzantine Empire. Crusaders were awed by the size and beauty of the capital and not a little greedy for its riches, including the luxury goods manufactured there or brought from the East. The experience of crusaders in the Empire created a market for Eastern goods in the West, contributing to the development of international commerce and the growth of Italian cities. The Crusades stimulated trade in other ways as well. There was a constant flow of pilgrims and soldiers from West to East. Furthermore, the crusading states established in the Holy Land needed goods from the West, weapons and supplies, for example. For both men and material, the sea was the easiest and safest route, again contributing to the wealth of Italian cities.

The idea of the Crusade came to be applied in the thirteenth century to wars within Europe itself. Innocent III launched a Crusade against Albigensian heretics in southern France. Innocent IV (r.1245–1254) organized a Crusade against the Holy Roman Emperor Frederick II and his family, applying the idea of a holy war to heretics or even political enemies of the papacy. This kind of "crusade" continued into the fifteenth century, most notably against a group of "heretics," the Hussites, in Bohemia. After the fall of Constantinople to Muslim Turks in 1453, there was renewed papal interest in launching a Crusade against the infidels that lasted into the sixteenth century.

Finally, the Crusades had a significant impact on the literature and art of the twelfth century. The *Song of Roland,* composed between the First and Second Crusades, is a literary representation of ideals of the Crusades. The tympanum of the Church of Saint Mary Magdalen in Vézelay, under which Bernard of Clairvaux preached the Second Crusade, embodies a Crusade ideology. Both works place the Crusades in the scriptural context of completing the task Christ gave to the Church as a precondition to his return—the preaching of the Gospel to the ends of the earth. The zeal of the crusading spirit, the goals of crusading for both the Church and individual crusaders, and the theology of the Crusades are well summed up in a letter of Bernard of Clairvaux to England to recruit men for the Second Crusade:

> Now is the acceptable time, now is the day of abundant salvation. The earth is shaken because the Lord of heaven is losing his land, the land in which he appeared to men, in which he lived amongst men for more than thirty years; the land made glorious by his miracles, holy by his blood; the land in which the flowers of his resurrection first blossomed. And now, for our sins, the enemy of the Cross has begun to lift his sacrilegious head there, and to devastate with the sword that blessed land, that land of promise. Alas, if there should

be none to withstand him, he will soon invade the very city of the living God, overturn the arsenal of our redemption, and defile the holy places which have been adorned by the blood of the immaculate lamb. They have cast their greedy eyes especially on the holy sanctuaries of our Christian Religion, and they long particularly to violate that couch on which, for our sakes, the Lord of our life fell asleep in death. . . .

Your land is well known to be rich in young and vigorous men. The world is full of their praises and the renown of their courage is on the lips of all. Gird yourselves therefore like men and take up arms with joy and with zeal for your Christian name, in order to "take vengeance on the heathen, and curb the nations." For how long will your men continue to shed Christian blood; for how long will they continue to fight amongst themselves? You attack each other, you slay each other and by each other you are slain. What is this savage craving of yours? Put a stop to it now, for it is not fighting but foolery. Thus to risk both soul and body is not brave but shocking, is not strength but folly. But now, O mighty soldiers, O men of war, you have a cause for which you can fight without danger to your souls; a cause in which to conquer is glorious and for which to die is gain.[13]

THE NEW MONASTIC ORDERS

The period of papal reform and conflict between the Roman Church and Holy Roman Empire was also important for the development of monasticism. The Cluniac reform did not satisfy those who longed for the simplicity and rigor of early monasticism and who believed that the Cluniacs had not "retreated" far enough from secular involvement. In the eleventh century several new orders of hermits emerged, including the Camaldolese in Italy and, more important, the Carthusians in France. The Cistercian Order was founded in 1098 as a reform of cenobitic monasticism, returning much more closely to the practice of the Rule as Benedict had intended it to be lived.

Bruno of Cologne founded a hermit order of monks with the establishment of La Grande Chartreuse in the wilderness near Grenoble in 1084. The ideal to which Bruno looked was that of the desert fathers such as Saint Antony (see Chapter 6). Although Bruno soon was called to Italy and died there, the monastery nevertheless grew and daughter houses (called charterhouses in English, a term which roughly translates "Chartreuse") sprang up. By the middle of the twelfth century, the *Consuetudines*, a Carthusian Rule, had been established. The order remained small, and few Carthusians played important roles in church politics, but Carthusian monks were highly respected. In the fourteenth century, cities all over Europe encouraged the Carthusians to make a foundation in their city in order to ward off the bubonic plague. Ruling families in Burgundy and Lombardy endowed huge Carthusian houses, which were also the families' burial grounds. By reputation, the Carthusians retained the purity of the founders: "Never reformed because never deformed." Their desire to return to the spirituality of the early monks of the desert and to find God in solitude is carefully explained in the *Golden Epistle*, a work written by a Cistercian monk, William of Saint Thierry, to a fledgling Carthusian community:

> The man who has God with him is never less alone than when he is alone. It is then he has undisturbed fruition of his joy, it is then he is his own master and is free to enjoy God in himself and himself in God. It is then that in the light of truth and a serenity of a clean heart a pure soul stands revealed to itself without effort, and the memory enlivened by God freely pours itself out in itself. Then either the mind is enlightened and the will enjoys its good or human frailty freely weeps over its shortcomings.[14]

The essence of Carthusian spirituality is embodied in a letter written by Guigo, fifth prior of La Grande Chartreuse:

> But the poor and lonely life, hard in its beginning, easy in its progress, becomes, in its end, heavenly. It is constant in adversity, trusty in hours of doubt, modest in those of good fortune. Sober fare, simple garments, laconic speech, chaste manners. The highest ambition, because without ambition. Often wounded with sorrow at the thought of past wrong done, it avoids present, is wary of future evil. Resting on the hope of mercy, without trust in its own merit, it thirsts after heaven, is sick of earth, earnestly strives for right conduct, which it retains in constancy and holds firmly for ever. It fasts with determined constancy in love of the cross, yet consents to eat for the body's need. In both it observes the greatest moderation, for when it dines it restrains greed and when it fasts, vanity. It is devoted to reading, but mostly in the scripture canon and in holy books, where it is more intent upon the inner arrow of meaning than on the spume of words. But you may praise or wonder more at this: that such a life is continually idle yet never lazy. For it finds many things indeed to do, so that time is more often lacking to it than this or that occupation. It more often laments that its time has slipped away than that its business is tedious.[15]

The Cistercian Order was founded at Cîteaux (Cistercium in Latin) in 1098 by Robert of Molesmes. Like Bruno, he soon left his foundation, but it grew and flourished; within a century more than a thousand Cistercian foundations for men and women had been established in Europe. The Cistercian ideal was a strict return of the simplicity of Benedict's Rule. There was to be no ornate sculpture or painting, no elaborate liturgy, no rich vestments, and monks were to perform manual labor. However, there were also elements of Cistercian monasticism that had no precedent in the Rule. First, monks were divided into two classes—choir monks, who sang the entire Divine Office prescribed by the Rule and did only light physical work, and lay brothers, who sang an abbreviated Divine Office and did most of the manual labor. These two groups of monks within one monastery had separate living quarters and even separate sets of choir stalls in church. The second departure from the Rule was that the Cistercians had a constitution and a centralized government for all of their monasteries, described in a document called the *Charter of Charity:*

> It seems proper to us, that all our monasteries should have the same usages in chanting, and the same books for the divine office day and night and the celebration of the holy sacrifice of the Mass, as we have in the New Monastery; that there may be no discord in our daily actions, but that we may all live together in the bond of charity under one rule, and in the practice of the same observances. . . .
>
> The Abbot of a mother-house shall visit annually, either in person or by one of his co-abbots, all the filiations of his own monastery. And if he should visit the brethren more frequently than this, let it be to them a subject of joy. The four abbots of La Ferte, Pontigny, Clairvaux and Morimond, shall visit in person, unless prevented by sickness, once in the year, and on the day which they shall appoint, the monastery of Citeaux, besides their attendance at the General Chapter, unless one of them is prevented by grave illness. . . .

Monastery of Paray-le-Monial, France. Twelfth century. This splendid church is a smaller version of the Third Abbey Church at Cluny, which was destroyed during the French Revolution. Like Cluny, this church was elaborate in both its architecture and decoration.

But all the abbots of our Order shall meet each year in General Chapter, without excuse, except they are prevented by grievous sickness; and then they shall depute a proper representative. An exception is made also in the case of those who live in too distant countries, which shall be decided by the Chapter.[16]

Clearly there was a uniformity in the Cistercian Order, extending even to architecture and general monastic layout, that was foreign to Benedict or the network of monasteries affiliated with Cluny.

The order's popularity in the twelfth century was largely due to the genius and energy of one man—Bernard, abbot of Clairvaux (d. 1153). He was an advisor to popes and kings; a mystic, theologian, and poet; and one of the great literary figures and saints of the Middle Ages. He also became the relentless foe of the philosopher Peter Abelard (see Chapter 9) as well as the moving force behind the Second Crusade. He was also quite a showman, which he demonstrated when he preached the Second Crusade at Vézelay in 1147. He worked up such fervor for the Crusade that men began to cut crusaders' badges out of available cloth to pin on themselves; when the cloth ran out, Bernard took off his habit so that more badges could be made.

Bernard has been called "the last of the Fathers." Well versed in classical rhetoric, he displayed little interest in the development of Scholastic method,

Cistercian Abbey of Pontigny, France. Twelfth century. This church illustrates the solidity and simplicity of the architecture of the Cistercian Order. The many towers of Cluny and churches modeled on it contrast sharply with the unadorned lines of Pontigny. The visual comparison of Cluniac and Cistercian churches is a useful symbol of differences between the two forms of Benedictine monasticism.

which was the preoccupation of contemporaries such as Peter Abelard; and he doubted the value of Aristotle's writings as a means to illuminate the faith. His concern, deeply rooted in the mystical tradition, was with the direct experience of God rather than with what dialectic could say *about* God. The Cistercian quest for experiential knowledge of God is embodied in one of Bernard's most important works, the eighty-six sermons on the Song of Songs. The following passage from sermon three exemplifies Bernard's method:

> Today the text we are to study is the book of our own experience. You must therefore turn your attention inwards, each one must take note of his own particular awareness of the things I am about to discuss. I am attempting to discover if any of you has been privileged to say from his heart: "Let him kiss me with the kiss of his mouth." [Song 1:1] Those to whom it is given to utter those words sincerely are comparatively few, but anyone who has received this mystical kiss from the mouth of Christ at least once, seeks again that intimate experience, and eagerly looks for its frequent renewal. I think that nobody can grasp what it is except the one who receives it. For it is "a hidden manna" [Rev. 7:17] and only he who eats it still hungers for more. [Sir. 24:29] It is "a sealed fountain" [Song 4:12] to which no stranger has access; only he who drinks still thirsts for more. [Sir. 24:29] Listen to one who has had the experience, how urgently he demands: "Be my saviour again, renew my joy." [Ps. 50:14] But a soul like mine, burdened with sins, still subject to carnal passions [2 Tim. 3:6], devoid of any knowledge of spiritual delights, may not presume to make such a request, almost totally unacquainted as it is with the joys of the supernatural life.
>
> I should like however to point out to persons like this that there is an appropriate place for them on the way of salvation. They may not rashly aspire to the lips of the most benign Bridegroom, but let them prostrate with me in fear at the feet of a most severe Lord. Like the publican full of misgiving, [Luke 18:13] they must turn their eyes to the earth rather than up to heaven. Eyes that are accustomed only to darkness will be dazzled by the brightness of the spiritual world, [Prov. 25:27] overpowered by its splendor, repulsed by its peerless radiance and whelmed again in a gloom more dense than before. All you who are conscious of sin, do not regard as unworthy and despicable that position where the holy sinner laid down her sins, and put on the garment of holiness. There the Ethiopian changed her skin, [Jer. 13:23] and, cleansed to a new brightness, could confidently and legitimately respond to those who insulted her: [Ps. 118:42] "I am black but lovely, daughters of Jerusalem." [Song 1:4] You may ask what skill enabled her to accomplish this change, or on what grounds did she merit it? I can tell you in a few words. She wept bitterly, [Luke 22:62] she sighed deeply from her heart, she sobbed with a repentance that shook her very being, till the evil that inflamed her passions was cleansed away. The heavenly physician came with speed to her aid, because "his word runs swiftly." [Ps. 147:15] Perhaps you think the Word of God is not medicine? Surely it is, a medicine strong and pungent, testing

the mind and the heart. [Ps. 7:10] "The Word of God is something alive and active. It cuts like any double-edged sword but more finely. It can slip through the place where the soul is divided from the spirit, or the joints from the marrow: it can judge the secret thoughts." [Heb. 4:12] It is up to you, wretched sinner, to humble yourself as this happy penitent did so that you may be rid of your wretchedness. [Luke 7:37ff] Prostrate yourself on the ground, take hold of his feet, soothe them with kisses, sprinkle them with your tears and so wash not them but yourself. Thus you will become one of the "Flock of shorn ewes as they come up from the washing." [Song 4:2] But even then you may not dare to lift up a face suffused with shame and grief, until you hear the sentence: "Your sins are forgiven," [Luke 7:48] to be followed by the summons: "Awake, awake, captive daughter of Sion, awake, shake off the dust." [Isa. 52:1–2][17]

This passage well illustrates important aspects of Bernard's thought. In his allegorical reading, the kiss of the lips of the Song of Songs becomes union between the soul and Christ, the direct experience with God himself. Bernard suggests that the movement toward this ecstatic experience with God is an inward and thus intensely personal one. One finds God within oneself since humans are made in God's image. However, in order to discover this true self, one must strip away the sin that separates one from God and keeps one from God's image within oneself. The sermon starts with what Bernard calls the book of experience, which is essentially this experience of self. From there, the movement toward ultimate union is in three stages, which Bernard calls the three kisses. The first stage, the kiss of the feet, is repentance; the kiss of the hand is perseverance; the kiss of the lips is the union itself. In describing this process Bernard brings together more than fifty scriptural references in this one sermon, which by no means come exclusively from the Song of Songs. Bernard, proceeding almost associatively, brings in Scripture wherever he thinks it will fit. A reading of this passage in fact shows that all of Scripture is such an immediate part of Bernard's own experience that he sees it as a unity; he draws on his immense, almost spontaneous knowledge of it to give meaning to the most diverse attitudes. Bernard thinks scripturally and thus is able to draw freely from all parts of Scripture. However, his primary interest is not in giving a systematic exegesis of each verse of the Song of Songs; in fact, there are sermons in this collection that are not really commentaries on any specific passage of the Song but instead are insights Bernard has had while reading the book.

Bernard maintained a lively correspondence with Peter the Venerable, abbot of Cluny from 1122 to 1156. In those letters, Bernard criticized elements of the Cluniac observance, and clearly influenced reform at Cluny, although Peter vigorously defended many of Cluny's practices against Bernard's invectives. Bernard was especially strong in his condemnation of laxity in the monastery. In a diatribe immediately directed against the Cluniacs, but in reality intended to reach anyone living under the Benedictine Rule, Bernard brings considerable gifts for satire and invective to his burning desire for reform. Perhaps Bernard's most quoted passages deal with the artistic splendor of Cluny and its dependencies:

> What excuse can there be for these ridiculous monstrosities in the cloisters where the monks do their reading, extraordinary things at once beautiful and ugly? Here we find filthy monkeys and fierce lions, fearful centaurs, harpies, and striped tigers, soldiers at war, and hunters blowing their horns. Here is one head with many bodies, there is one body with many heads. Over there is a beast with a serpent for its tail, a fish with an animal's head, and a creature that is horse in front and goat behind, and a second beast with horns and the rear of a horse. All round there is such an amazing variety of shapes that one could easily prefer to take one's reading from the walls instead of from a book. One could spend the whole day gazing fascinated at these things, one by one, instead of meditating on the law of God. Good Lord, even if the foolishness of it all occasion no shame, at least one might balk at the expense. I shall say nothing about the soaring heights and extravagant lengths and unnecessary widths of the churches, nothing about their expensive decorations and their novel images, which catch the attention of those who go in to pray, and dry up their devotion. To me they seem like something out of the Old Testament; but let them be since it is all to the glory of God.[18]

Bernard's literary gifts are apparent here. As in so much of medieval humor, the comic aspects of the passage are intended forcefully to heighten the reader's awareness of deviation from an ideal, in this case the ideal of Benedictine austerity. This same combination of zeal and literary talent characterizes much of Bernard's writing, which accounts for his subsequent influence on such advocates of reform as Dante and even Martin Luther.

Some have seen in the above passage evidence that Bernard was an iconoclast without aesthetic sensibility, but they have misread the text. Firmly in the tradition of Augustine, Bernard, carefully distinguishing between means and ends, strongly criticizes an art that he believes has come dangerously close to being an end in itself. For Bernard, no less than for Augustine, the purpose of art is to lead viewers from the visible to the invisible. The excessively decorative art that Bernard decries here is dangerous because its details can easily command attention in and for themselves, waylaying the viewers and keeping them from moving to the deeper realities that art should point toward. This is seen as an especial danger in a monastery, where the Rule demands a unique kind of austerity and where deviation from this austerity could destroy monastic harmony. Throughout his writings Bernard recognizes that different demands are made by different vocations; what is totally out of place in the austerity of a monastery may well have its place in other vocations. He recognizes, as did Gregory the Great before him (see Chapter 5), that works of art can be books for the layperson; but for monks, who can read, they should not be necessary. The kind of piety that art can excite ought to be in a monk to begin with:

> It *is* not the same for monks and bishops. Bishops have a duty toward both wise and foolish. They have to make use of material ornamentation to rouse devotion in a carnal people, incapable of spiritual things. But we no longer belong to such people. For the sake of Christ we have abandoned all the world holds valuable and attractive. All that is beautiful in sight and sound and scent we have left behind, all that is pleasant to taste and touch. To win Christ we have reckoned bodily enjoyments as dung. (Phil. 3:8)[19]

Despite the differences between the Cluniacs and the Cistercians in the twelfth century, it is important to remember that they shared the common inheritance of the Rule, the Fathers, and a long tradition of monastic spirituality. When one compares the writings of Cluniac and Cistercian monks with non-monastic authors, for example those engaged in the revival of Aristotle in the cathedral schools, the essential unity of monastic culture becomes clear. There are important analogies to be made between monastic writers such as Bernard and the great monastic art and architecture of the period called Romanesque, notwithstanding Bernard's objections to some of its excesses. As

Interior of the Church of Mary Magdalen, Vézelay, France. Twelfth century. The nave of this church is the finest surviving example of a Cluniac church with its decorative architecture and many sculpted capitals. The choir (east end) of the church, in the Gothic style, was added later and appears much lighter.

the great monastic scholar Jean Leclercq writes in his seminal work *The Love of Learning and the Desire for God*: "Just as the cathedrals of the thirteenth century have been compared to theological *summas*, monastic writings of the Romanesque period may be likened to the abbey churches of the period: the same simplicity, the same solidity, the same vivacity of biblical imagination."[20]

SECULAR AND ECCLESIASTICAL AUTHORITY

By the middle of the twelfth century, the papacy had found that ecclesiastical or, more properly, canon law was the best means by which to exert the Church's authority throughout Latin Christendom. Gratian's collection of canons and the study of church law at the emerging University of Bologna (see Chapter 9) provided both a body of law and able practitioners and interpreters of it. In the century and a half beginning c.1150, canon lawyers dominated the papal office and the curia. For the next century and a half, popes were almost always chosen from among those trained in canon law. Increasingly, the popes understood their office largely as the head of a system of ecclesiastical courts, and many of the cases adjudicated in these courts involved property settlements rather than strictly moral judgments. One of those most concerned with this new orientation of the papacy was Bernard of Clairvaux. When one of his former novices at Clairvaux was elected pope as Eugenius III in 1145, he wrote to tell his former charge exactly what he thought of the turn the papacy had taken:

> I ask you, what is the point of wrangling and listening to litigants from morning to night? And would that the evil of the day were sufficient for it, but the nights are not even free! Your poor body scarcely gets the time which nature requires for rest before it must rise for further disputing. . . . What is more servile and more unworthy, especially for the Supreme Pontiff, than every day, or rather every hour, to sweat over such affairs for the likes of these. Tell me this, when are we to pray or to teach the people? When are we to build up the Church or meditate on the law? Oh yes, every day laws resound through the palace, but these are the laws of Justinian, not of the Lord.[21]

Despite this frank language, Bernard, clearly distinguishing between the person and the office, spoke of the theoretical power of the pope in the most exalted terms.

The use of canon law to enforce and advance papal policy was partly responsible for conflicts with secular authorities. The powerful Holy Roman Emperor Frederick I (Barbarossa) (r.1152–1190) created a schism by renouncing his allegiance to Pope Alexander III (r.1159–1181), one of the first trained canon lawyers to occupy to throne of Saint Peter, and choosing his own claimant to the papal office. The issues between pope and Empire were their legal relationship and the question of the pope's right to intervene in the Em-

Detail of the Last Judgment: Entrances into Heaven and Hell. Church of Sainte Foi, Conques, France. Twelfth century. These details come from the façade sculpture of Sainte Foi, an important medieval pilgrimage church. They show the stark contrast between reward and punishment, the essence of the theme of judgment. The serenity of the saved souls being ushered through the gate of paradise by an angel contrasts with the anguish of the damned about to be pushed through the gaping jaws of hell's mouth by a devil. We can see the legs of a sinner sticking out of the mouth.

pire's affairs. Although Frederick ultimately submitted to Alexander's authority, largely due to defeat on the battlefield, the issue was by no means settled. Another conflict between the Church and a secular ruler at this time took place in England over the right of the king to try clerics in royal courts. The protagonists were the Archbishop of Canterbury Thomas à Becket (d.1170) and King Henry II (r.1154–1189). The most dramatic event in this conflict, of course, was Becket's murder. The specific dispute in England was settled in a compromise that preserved the Church's demand that clergy be tried in ecclesiastical courts. At the time of the Protestant Reformation more than three centuries later, the issue of secular jurisdiction over clerics still generated great passion.

In the last part of the twelfth century, the papal curia moved somewhat cautiously in its relations with the monarchies, on the heels of its dramatic conflicts with Frederick Barbarossa and Henry II. The popes toward the end of the century sought to consolidate the achievements of such predecessors as Alexander III rather than to seek confrontation or assert new claims. However, in 1198 the thirty-seven-year-old Cardinal Lothario dei Segni was elected pope, taking the name Innocent III. His pontificate (1198–1216) saw the apex of papal political power and influence, the development of a strong though somewhat eclectic theory of papal supremacy, and several attempts to reform the Church and define doctrine.

Innocent III held the position that the pope received both spiritual and temporal authority from God. His exalted notion of papal power can be seen in two of his early statements after assuming the throne of Peter:

> You see then who is this servant set over the household, truly the vicar of Jesus Christ, successor of Peter, anointed of the Lord, a God of Pharaoh, set between God and man, lower than God but higher than man, who judges all and is judged by no one. . . .
>
> Just as the founder of the universe established two great lights in the firmament of heaven, a greater one to preside over the day and a lesser to preside over the night, so too in the firmament of the universal church, which is signified by the word heaven, he instituted two great dignities, a greater one to preside over souls as if over day and a lesser one to preside over bodies as if over night. These are the pontifical authority and the royal power. Now just as the moon derives its light from the sun and is indeed lower than it in quantity and quality, in position and in power, so too the royal power derives the splendor of its deity from the pontifical authority. . . . [22]

Innocent was a brilliant statesman more interested in shaping the development of Christian Europe than in winning theoretical battles. When he dealt with matters in which there was some question of his right to intervene, he used whatever argument would meet least resistance. From Innocent, therefore, we get no fully developed, carefully argued theory of papal supremacy but rather a patchwork of statements and actions. In one case he would claim the right to intervene because an oath was involved and the Church was the guardian of oaths; in another he would claim the right because sin was involved. Innocent found grounds to intervene in the affairs of Europe whenever he wanted, although he never claimed the right to do so simply because as pope he was lord of the world.

Innocent faced two major outbreaks of heresy centered in southern France. In 1174, a merchant of Lyons named Valdes (sometimes written Waldo or even Peter Waldo) sold all of his goods and dedicated himself to a life of poverty. He wished to preach but could not get a license from his bishop. He and his followers publicly attacked the wealth of the Church and the priests' abandonment of their pastoral role. Valdes and his followers, called Waldensians, were condemned by a synod in 1184; after this, they became more radical, attacking the priesthood in more fundamental ways. At about the same time a widespread heretical movement known by the names Albigensian (after the city of Albi) and Cathar (meaning "pure ones") was developing. The belief system of this movement was based on a dualist world view related to that of the earlier Gnostics and Manichees (see Chapter 3). The Albigensians attracted many followers, the ascetic lives of their leaders contrasting favorably with the Catholic clergy. By the time of Innocent III, the Waldensians and Albigensians posed a serious threat to Catholicism, especially in southern France but also in northern and central Italy. Innocent first sought to put an end to these heresies peacefully. He sent preachers into the strongholds of the Albigensian movement to try to win its followers back to the Roman fold. He approved the founding of the Franciscans and Dominicans (collectively called mendicants), preaching orders that combined poverty and simplicity with loyalty to the pope and the Church (see Chapter 10). He welcomed back those heretics who were willing to submit to the papacy. However, after preaching failed to win over the leaders, and after a papal legate was murdered in Toulouse, Innocent launched a Crusade against the Albigensians, a Crusade that eventually eliminated them as a threat to the unity of Latin Christendom. The pope saw the Waldensians as less of a threat and did not pursue them with the same vigor; they survived the thirteenth century attacks on heresy and exist even today.

Innocent was genuinely interested in reform. In addition to approving the Franciscan and Dominican orders, he called the Fourth Lateran Council, which met in Rome in 1215. It limited the number of new orders, tried again to eliminate simony, and defined dogma more carefully both in response to heretical movements and to differences of opinion among theologians. Four actions by the Fourth Lateran Council were particularly important. First, the number of sacraments was clarified. In the early Middle Ages, the Church had not spoken authoritatively about the number of sacraments. Before and during the investiture contest, for example, many believed that the anointing of a king was a sacrament, a notion discredited after the Concordat of Worms. The theology that was developing with the rediscovery of Aristotle emphasized order and classification. Theologians now wanted to define precisely what a sacrament was and how many there were. The definition of a sacrament as "an outward and physical sign of an inward and spiritual grace" became authoritative at about this time. The Fourth Lateran Council named seven sacraments: baptism, confirmation, penance, Eucharist, extreme unction (now called sacrament of the sick), holy orders (ordination), and marriage. Second, Innocent's council defined the nature of the sacrament of the Eucharist through the doctrine of transubstantiation. Using Aristotelian categories, the council spoke of the eucharistic bread and wine as consisting of substance (what they are by nature) and accidents (their appearance). Accidents can change without a substance ceasing to exist. The accidents of bread include its texture, color, shape, and size, all of which can change without bread ceasing to exist. According to the Council, when the bread and the wine are consecrated at Mass, the accidents of the bread and wine remain, but their substance is changed into the substance of the body and blood of Christ. Thus, the sacrament is in its nature—substance—Christ's body and blood.

Third, the council decreed that only the clergy could receive the transubstantiated wine at communion. Laypeople were to receive the Eucharist only under one kind or species (transubstantiated bread). This decree, modified only by the Second Vatican Council in the 1960s, symbolizes a development in the Church beginning with the investiture contest. The clergy, in stressing their rights and their differences from the laity, sometimes had come to treat the laity as almost peripheral to the Church. Several developments in the twelfth century embody this: masses were often celebrated without the presence of the laity despite the fact that their presence had once been considered essential. Altars were often moved against the east walls of churches, and thus priests consecrated the bread and wine with their backs to the congregated people. Sometimes screens were built between the nave, where the laity stood, and the choir so that the consecration could not even be seen. Laypeople were not encouraged to take communion frequently, often receiving the host only once a year at Easter. In sum, the laity were being excluded from an integral place in the Church. Fourth, the council mandated that Catholics receive the sacrament of penance—that is, go to Confession—at least once during the liturgical year. Among other important effects of this mandate, it allowed the Church in the guise of its confessors to implement the Lateran Reform movement after the close of the council.

Although the needs of laypeople in the thirteenth century were primarily addressed by the mendicant orders (see Chapter 10), the papacy did encourage everyone to venerate the Eucharist through the institution of the feast of Corpus Christi (Latin for "the body of Christ"). This celebration usually consisted of a procession through the streets with the local bishop carrying the consecrated host for the veneration of the people. This feast became an important motif in late medieval art, as well as an important stimulus to the development of vernacular drama, since these elaborate processions were both inherently dramatic in themselves and offered a time and a place for even more elaborate dramatic representations. The great biblical cycle dramas of late medieval England are often called Corpus Christi cycles.

After the death of Innocent III in 1216, the papacy gradually began a long period of decline and decay. In part this was due to the all-out struggle that developed between the papacy and the Holy Roman Emperor Frederick II (r.1220–1250). Frederick was also king of Sicily, which included southern Italy as well as the island of Sicily. Thus, Frederick's two crowns made him lord of both northern and southern Italy, leaving the pope pinched in the papal states between his holdings. Furthermore, Frederick was a brilliant politician who desired and enjoyed the use of power. Caring little about adherence to the doctrines of Western Christianity, he created a court at Palermo that was a mixture of Roman Catholics, Eastern Orthodox, Muslims, and Jews. When open war came between the pope and the emperor, more and more of the Church's money was diverted to hire mercenaries to defend the pope's temporal possessions. The Church's reputation suffered as popes became preoccupied with eliminating Frederick and his family, the Hohenstaufens. The papacy was largely successful, thanks to the timely death of Frederick II in 1250 and the efforts of its French mercenaries commanded by Charles of Anjou. Charles became king of Sicily while the emasculated office of Holy Roman Emperor remained vacant for twenty-three years. However, this papal victory was short-lived. In 1282 a revolt in Palermo led to the expulsion of the French from the island of Sicily, although Charles continued to rule the rest of southern Italy from his court in Naples. The Holy Roman Empire was revived beginning in 1273 with the election of Rudolf of Habsburg. In the beginning of the fourteenth century, the Emperor Henry VII pursued plans to reestablish de facto as well as de jure control over northern Italy, which had become a series of essentially independent city-states since 1176, when a league of Italian cities defeated Frederick Barbarossa at the battle of Legnano. Dante was one of the supporters of Henry's attempt to re-create the Holy Roman Empire and has an empty throne waiting for Henry in heaven at the end of the *Paradiso*.

Political activities were only one cause of the demise of the papacy. Popes sought, often high-handedly, to centralize their ecclesiastical power in Rome. This involved taking cases out of the hands of bishops and either conducting trials directly in Rome or sending papal legates to conduct them. Furthermore, the new mendicant orders, the Franciscans and Dominicans, were directly under the authority of the pope and thus in some ways free from episcopal control (see Chapter 10). In the thirteenth century these mendicants began to carry out some of the traditional functions of the secular clergy. They built huge churches in cities and preached to enormous crowds, luring many laypeople away from their parishes; they also heard confessions and buried the dead. Hence, the alms they collected were divided between the orders and Rome; the bishops and secular clergy got none. Thus, there was a great struggle within the Church between the secular clergy on one side and the pope and mendicants on the other. Some bishops began to turn to their secular lords to form a united front against papal centralization.

Another strong element in the decline of the papacy in European society stems from the development of nation-states. The revival of Roman law in the twelfth century (see Chapter 9) was beneficial to secular rulers because with it they could provide better justice, weakening the control over judicial matters that the nobility had acquired during the disintegration of the Carolingian Empire. Kings such as Henry II (r.1154–1189) and Edward I (r.1272–1307) in England and Louis VII (r.1137–1180), Philip Augustus (r.1180–1223), Louis IX (r.1226–1270), and Philip IV (r.1285–1314) in France were effective in molding their monarchies into strong, politically viable states. Both monarchies established royal courts as courts of last appeal; both hired Roman lawyers, men loyal to their paymasters, to function as judges and as bureaucrats throughout the kingdoms. England's common law developed from the time of Henry II; and Edward I, who strove for greater royal power through the use of law, is sometimes referred to as the English Justinian. The French kings had to work to limit the power of independent vassals. The most significant victory for the monarchs came when Philip Augustus regained, at the expense of the unstable King John (r.1199–1216), most of the land in France controlled by the English monarchy, virtually the entire west of France. These lands were not granted to other nobles as fiefs but governed directly by the crown through royal bureaucrats.

With the rediscovery of Aristotle in the thirteenth century, kings were able to construct viable theoretical arguments for their existence independent of the ecclesiastical hierarchy. As we have seen, Augustine viewed the state as a necessary result of sin; thus the state's main function is essentially negative—to police. This concept dominated the early Middle Ages, and the popes of the Gregorian era based their argument for papal supremacy in part on the inherent superiority of Church over state. However, Aristotle's idea of the state was different. To him the state is a positive and creative force; people are by nature, says Aristotle, political beings. Although Thomas Aquinas (d.1274) was by no means a royal propagandist, short selections from his writings show how the Aristotelian view of the state became incorporated into medieval political thought:

> The ultimate end of the whole universe is considered in theology which is most important without qualification. He [Aristotle] says that it belongs to political science to treat the ultimate end of human life.
>
> And, since the things that come to man's use are ordained to man as to their end, and the end takes precedence over the things that are for the end,

it is therefore necessary that this whole, which is the state, take precedence over all wholes that may be known and constituted by human reason.

A free man may be ruled by another when the latter directs him to his own good or to the common good. And such government over man by man would have existed, for two reasons, in the state of innocence. First, because man is a naturally social animal; man even in the state of innocence would have lived in society. Social life among many could not exist, however, unless someone took the position of authority to direct them to the common good.[23]

This last statement shows the contrast between Thomas and Augustine. The passage also shows that there is nothing in Thomas to imply that secular power is derived from or commanded by the ecclesiastical authorities.

The revival of Roman law coupled with the rediscovery of Aristotle's writings provided the theoretical underpinning for the emerging states in their struggle with the ecclesiastical hierarchy. This development of the "lay thesis" combined with the politicization and centralization of the Church resulted in still another major church-state controversy, one that ended in a crushing defeat for the pope. A struggle between the politically ambitious Pope Boniface VIII (r.1294–1303) and the wily King Philip IV of France (r.1285–1314) broke out at the end of the thirteenth century over the king's claim to the right to tax the French clergy. Philip began to levy taxes on the clergy because he was involved in war with England and therefore in need of money. Boniface demanded that he stop. Philip responded that if he were not allowed to tax the clergy, he would not allow any money to leave France, including all the money collected by ecclesiastical authorities for the pope. Boniface backed down by conceding that Philip could tax the clergy without papal permission in an emergency and that Philip was the one who could define an emergency. Philip, who clearly had won, then picked another fight with Boniface. After several threats and counterthreats, Boniface published the bull *Unam Sanctam* in 1302, which said little that popes had not said before, but made clear his uncompromising belief in papal authority over all facets of society and summarized a century of papal propaganda:

> Certainly anyone who denies that the temporal sword is in the power of Peter has not paid heed to the words of the Lord when he said, "Put up thy sword into its sheath" (Matt. 26:52). Both then are in the power of the church, the material sword and the spiritual. But the one is exercised for the church, the other by the church, the one by the hand of the priest, the other by the hand of kings and soldiers, though at the will and sufferance of the priest. One sword ought to be under the other and the temporal authority subject to the spiritual power. . . .
>
> Therefore, if the earthly power errs, it shall be judged by the spiritual power, if a lesser spiritual power errs it shall be judged by its superior, but if the supreme spiritual power errs it can be judged only by God not by man,

as the apostle witnesses, "The spiritual man judgeth all things and he him-self is judged by no man" (1 Cor. 2:15). Although this authority was given to a man and is exercised by a man it is not human but rather divine, being given to Peter at God's mouth, and confirmed to him and to his successors in him, the rock whom the Lord acknowledged when he said to Peter himself "Whatsoever thou shalt bind" etc. (Matt. 16:19). Whoever therefore resists this power so ordained by God resists the ordinance of God unless, like the Manicheans, he imagines that there are two beginnings, which we judge to be false and heretical, as Moses witnesses, for not "in the beginnings" but "in the beginning" God created heaven and earth (Gen. 1:1). Therefore we declare, state, define and pronounce that it is altogether necessary to salvation for every human creature to be subject to the Roman Pontiff.[24]

Philip did not lay down and play dead with the publication of *Unam Sanctam*. He waged a propaganda campaign accusing Boniface of every crime from heresy to sodomy. Philip sent a mission to Boniface at his residence in Anagni, south of Rome; and although accounts vary, there is reason to think that Philip's men assaulted him physically as well as verbally. At any rate, Boniface died soon afterward. His successor (following the brief pontificate of Benedict XI) was a Frenchman, Clement V (r.1305–1314), who sought to placate the French monarchy by trying to explain away some of Boniface's stronger statements. In spite of this, the king prevented Clement from going to Rome, keeping him on the other side of the Alps. Clement settled down in the city of Avignon, which belonged at the time to the king of Naples. By the 1330s it became clear that the popes would remain in Avignon indefinitely; and a magnificent papal palace, which still stands today, was built there. During this period, often called the Babylonian Captivity, the papacy definitively lost its struggle to control European society, sometimes appearing to be little more than a plaything of the French monarchy. It was not until 1377 that the papacy returned to Rome, ending three quarters of a century in which the bishop of Rome did not set foot in Italy, let alone the city of Rome.

About the time of the conflict between Boniface VIII and Philip IV, an important political treatise was written by the Dominican John of Paris, who argued that God gave some power directly to kings and some power directly to the pope. It was obvious to John that the papacy could not have instituted royal power because there were monarchies before the papal office was established. John recognized that the popes could control property and have political authority, but only insofar as they had been granted it. Even then the pope was viewed primarily as an administrator. In essence the pope governed souls and had no jurisdiction over bodies; kings on the other hand ruled bodies but could not bind and loose souls. This concept of the separation of powers, which had existed in germ since the time of the investiture contest, became more widely accepted in Europe, in part because of the powerful arguments of its advocates but primarily because it was the theory that was closest to the de facto relationship between temporal and ecclesiastical powers and consequently appealed to thinkers sympathetic to the Aristotelian reliance on empirical reality as a starting point.

However, although the Holy Roman Emperor was no longer the de jure or de facto secular head of Western Christendom by 1300, there were those who clung to the notion that only a universal rule on earth by the Roman Emperor would defeat papal claims to supremacy in secular matters and bring peace to Europe. The most important writer to hold this view was Dante (1265–1321) in his *On World Government:*

> Since it appears that the whole of mankind is ordained to one end, as we proved above, it should therefore have a single rule and government, and this power should be called the Monarch or Emperor. And thus it is plain that for the well-being of the world there must be a single world-rule or empire. . . .
>
> Therefore mankind in submitting to a single government most resembles God and most nearly exists according to the divine intention, which is the same as enjoying well-being, as was proved at the beginning of this chapter.
> . . .
> And so I maintain that though Peter's successor may loose or bind in performing the duties of the office entrusted to Peter, it does not follow that he can therefore loose or bind imperial laws or decrees, as they maintain, unless it can be proved that this is related to the power of the keys; and it is the contrary of this which I shall prove.[25]

As monarchies such as France and England developed effective institutions of government, they needed increasing resources to hire officials, for example highly trained lawyers. Since kings' vassals originally owed their lords only their service, we must ask where monarchs got the funds to pay these lawyers. As we have already seen, one source of revenue was from the newly developing cities, which were willing to pay for the right to govern themselves in certain matters. The other source was from the vassals themselves; it became common for the king to commute their obligations from fighting and hospitality to money payments. Kings benefited from this innovation because they could hire lawyers, but also soldiers who would fight for them not just for forty days but all year, and who were loyal to them as long as they were being paid. Commutation of services was usually for a fixed sum in perpetuity; however, inflation meant that the amounts paid did not long suffice. The kings of Europe could not "live on their own." A king could ask his vassals for more money, but the vassals had to approve extra payments. The need for more money came about the time that Roman law was being seriously studied in Western Europe for the first time in several centuries. The Justinian Code contained a significant amount of corporation law, which came to be applied to monasteries, cathedral chapters, the Church as a whole, cities, guilds, and even nations. Roman law created fictitious personalities, corporations as legal entities that were treated like persons. Corporations such as guilds and monasteries increasingly found themselves parties in adjudication. Using a Roman legal formula, many of these corporations came to appoint permanent officials called procurators who would be given *plena potestas* (full power) to speak for the entire corporation.

Soon kings found that it was sometimes valuable to negotiate, not with individual cities, but rather with their representatives, who would have *plena potestas* to speak for and bind those whom they represented. Furthermore, kings could ask these representatives to come together to talk about affairs of the entire nation (including but not limited to money) and to give their consent. In doing so, monarchs often cited another piece of Roman law that originally applied to corporations: "What touches all must be approved by all." In the late twelfth and thirteenth centuries, rulers honored this principle and began to call assemblies of representatives with *plena potestas;* these are what we call representative institutions or parliaments. The latter name immediately calls to mind the English Parliament, which had developed into the most powerful representative institution in Europe by the end of Middle Ages, though it was neither the first nor was it necessarily clear in the thirteenth century that it was to become the strongest representative institution in Europe. The Cortes of the Spanish kingdom of Aragon was meeting before the end of the twelfth century; and Pope Innocent III, as temporal ruler of the papal states, called a representative assembly at the beginning of the thirteenth century. Even the Fourth Lateran Council's summons sounded much like those of rulers calling together representatives. By the end of the thirteenth century there were also representative assemblies in the kingdoms of Sicily, England, and the Holy Roman Empire; and Philip IV called the first Estates General during his quarrel with Boniface VIII. In this brief and schematic discussion of the origin of representative institutions, it is important to remember that they evolved slowly from the lord-vassal relationship, the rise of cities, the centralization of authority, and the revival of Roman law.

The controversy concerning the right relationship between secular and spiritual authorities—or church and state—reached a new level of intensity in the eleventh through thirteenth centuries. This tension was at times destructive, as the struggles we have just described indicate; but at other times it was responsible for much that was creative and vital during the period. Neither the pagan classics nor the Bible dealt with the conflict, which was a unique product of medieval society. Thus, although thinkers continued to look to those old texts, they had to use them in creative new ways, since it was impossible simply to copy past arguments or practices. Thus, the innovations in government that we have just discussed happened in much the same way that the apparently unrelated areas of theology and literature developed: creatively mixing the classical and biblical traditions and doing so with an awareness of a new context that had different problems and needed different answers than those available in their sources.

CHAPTER 9

THE RENAISSANCE OF
THE TWELFTH CENTURY

During the Carolingian period, there was a cultural revival, a renaissance, which quite consciously looked to both the Bible and classical antiquity for models and inspiration. Much of this classical revival, however, was dependent on late Latin writers and collections of passages anthologized from the earlier Latin writers. Furthermore, most of the great figures of the Carolingian Renaissance were educated in a monastic setting, where the study of the classics was clearly subordinate to the goals of the Christian and more specifically the monastic life. Since the revival of the ninth century was sponsored by the Carolingian rulers, their failures made its influence beyond the imperial court rather limited. Nevertheless, the achievements of the Carolingian Renaissance were significant; and they were not forgotten or completely abandoned even during the years of political disintegration, monastic corruption, and invasion that followed.

Scholars today generally regard the cultural and intellectual revival of the twelfth century (more accurately c.1050–c.1250) as *the* medieval renaissance, referring to it as the Renaissance of the Twelfth Century. During this time, there was an intense interest in Latin and Greek authors who had been either unknown or ignored in the West for centuries. Beginning in schools established in Carolingian times, scholars building on the Carolingian heritage discovered new sources, tools, and methods for the study of theology, using, but significantly altering, the dominant Augustinianism of early medieval Europe. Achievements sparked by discoveries from classical antiquity also occurred in law, science, and medicine, achievements that had an impact on every facet of intellectual activity, as well as on the development of papal power and the building of nation-states. To transmit this new knowledge, the institution known as the university emerged. Because this movement was not the product of a particular court and took place largely in dynamic urban settings, it

212

was broader in its scope and deeper in its penetration throughout Western Europe than its Carolingian predecessor.

In the millennial year 1000, Sylvester II (Gerbert of Aurillac) was pope. That he was pope at the beginning of the second millennium is prophetic of the intellectual changes that were to sweep Europe since Gerbert himself was one of the initiators those changes. He was well versed in the first part of the trivium—grammar—and was one of the first thinkers since the Carolingian age to seriously study the other parts—rhetoric and logic. In a letter dated 985, he explained the relationship between good living and good speaking:

> Since philosophy does not separate ways of conduct and ways of speaking, I have always added the fondness for speaking well to the fondness for living well, although by itself it may be more excellent to live well than to speak well, and if one be freed from the cares of governing, the former is enough without the latter. But to us, busied in affairs of state, both are necessary. For speaking effectively to persuade and restrain the minds of angry persons from violence by smooth speech are both of the greatest usefulness. For this activity, which must be prepared beforehand, I am diligently forming a library.[1]

Gerbert was also interested in the quadrivium and constantly sought out manuscripts of classical works on all the liberal arts. He also either invented or spread the knowledge of several mathematical and scientific devices, such as the abacus. The consequences of Gerbert's intellectual activities were greater than he could possibly have realized. To pursue the study of rhetoric required the close study of Latin writers such as Cicero. To learn logic meant the careful examination of that small portion of the writings of Aristotle that Boethius had translated into Latin, as well as other works by Greek philosophers. Thus, some writings of the ancient Greeks soon also became indispensable to medieval students.

One of the most influential texts for the philosophical upsurge in the generations following Gerbert was written by the Greek Neoplatonist Porphyry (c.232–303) and existed in a Latin translation. The following excerpt raised a question that engaged philosophers for the rest of the Middle Ages, the so-called problem of universals:

> Next, concerning genera and species, the question indeed whether they have a substantial existence, or whether they consist in bare intellectual concepts only, or whether if they have a substantial existence they are corporeal or incorporeal, and whether they are separable from the sensible properties of the things (or particulars of sense), or are only in those properties and subsisting about them, I shall forbear to determine. For a question of this kind is a very deep one and one that requires a long investigation.[2]

This text, which authors such as Boethius had already commented on, stimulated debate and aroused passions from the eleventh century on. Porphyry has outlined three possible positions on the question of universals. One, following Plato, is that universals (genera) have a real existence independent of any individual examples (species) of them. For those who hold this position, individual objects are real to the degree that they partake of the universal. For example, an individual person exists because he or she is a part of humanity, the universal. This position is usually called extreme realism. When this concept was applied to Christian theology, problems arose. Universals were thought to have their existence in God and since individuals were real only inasmuch as they were part of the universal, extreme realists were open to the charge of pantheism, a belief destructive of the basic Judaeo-Christian distinction between creator and creature. In the eleventh century, William of Champeaux and others came very close to a pantheistic view of the universe. Extreme realism continued to have its adherents for the rest of the Middle Ages, most notably the English theologian John Wyclif (d.1384).

The opposite of extreme realism is nominalism. Adherents of this position argue that universals have no real existence but are only names we use to categorize individuals. Humanity, for a nominalist, exists only as a name, as a sound, or as a series of marks on a piece of paper to represent a group of individuals, which are the only real things. This position also caused trouble for its extreme adherents when applied to Christian teachings, for it seemed to force them to deny either the plurality or the unity of the Trinity. In 1093, a regional synod forced a nominalist named Roscelin to repudiate his nominalist teachings on the Trinity. Nevertheless, nominalism survived and had many notable adherents in the late Middle Ages, including William of Ockham (c.1300–c.1349) and John Gerson (1363–1429). Between these two extremes falls a position, essentially that of Aristotle, called moderate realism or conceptualism. Its followers assert that universals are real but not independent of individual examples. Thus, "humanity" is real, referring to those qualities shared by all individual persons and discovered through the observation of individuals. Some of the most important medieval philosophers, including Thomas Aquinas, adhered to this middle-of-the-road position.

Some of the eleventh-century scholars who tried to apply these pagan classical philosophical categories to Christian theology got themselves in trouble with the ecclesiastical authorities, and many pious people doubted the value of trying to use classical philosophy for the purpose of illuminating Christianity. The man who did the most to make the application of ancient philosophy to Christian revelation respectable was a monk, later archbishop of Canterbury, named Anselm (c.1033–1109). No rationalist, he was steeped in Augustinian theology and monastic spirituality. However, as Anselm explains at the beginning of his famous treatise *Why God Became Man*, reason has a role to play in understanding and explaining faith:

> Both by word of mouth and by letter I have received many earnest requests that I should commit to writing the proofs of a particular doctrine of our faith,

as I usually present them to inquirers. I am told that these proofs are thought to be both pleasing and adequate. Those who make this request do not expect to come to faith through reason, but they hope to be gladdened by the understanding and contemplation of the things they believe, and as far as possible to be "ready always to satisfy everyone that asketh" them "a reason of that hope which is in" them. . . . And since investigations that are carried on by means of question, and answer are clearer to many (especially to slower) minds, and so are more acceptable, I shall take one of those who discuss this subject . . . to debate with me, so that in this way Boso may ask and Anselm answer.[3]

Anselm also developed a proof for the existence of God, the so-called ontological proof:

And certainly this being [God] so truly exists that it cannot even be thought not to exist. For something can be thought to exist that cannot be thought not to exist, and this is greater than that which can be thought not to exist. Hence, if that-than-which-a-greater-cannot-be-thought can be thought not to exist, then that-than-which-a-greater-cannot-be-thought is not the same as that-than-which-a-greater-cannot-be-thought, which is absurd. Something-than-which-a-greater-cannot-be-thought exists so truly then, that it cannot be even thought not to exist.

And You, Lord our God, are this being. You exist so truly, Lord my God, that You cannot even be thought not to exist. And this is as it should be, for if some intelligence could think of something better than You, the creature would be above its creator and would judge its creator—and that is completely absurd. In fact, everything else there is, except You alone, can be thought of as not existing. You alone, then, of all things most truly exist and therefore of all things possess existence to the highest degree; for anything else does not exist as truly, and so possesses existence to a lesser degree. Why then did "the Fool say in his heart, there is no God" [Ps. Xiii 1, lii 1] when it is so evident to any rational mind that You of all things exist to the highest degree? Why indeed, unless because he was stupid and a fool?[4]

The text of Anselm's argument has probably been commented upon more than any other philosophical text of comparable size from the Middle Ages. Even without attempting to engage the numerous philosophical issues this argument presents, one can see from the text how Anselm proceeds by means of a number of clearly articulated logical steps. If God is by definition the greatest thing that can be conceived of, then God must exist, for something that exists is greater than something that does not exist. Thus, if God does not exist, anything that does exist is greater; but that contradicts our definition of God.

Anselm was a monk trained in monastic schools. However, by the time of his death, several important schools attached to cathedrals rather than monasteries had developed in France, with teachers who were clerics but not monks. Some of the greatest teachers and students traveled from school to school. The rapidity of this important change in medieval education is testified to in the memoirs of Guibert de Nogent, written about 1115:

> In the recent past, and even partly during my childhood, there had been such a shortage of teachers that you could find hardly any in the towns and rarely any in the cities. When one did happen to find some, they knew so little that they couldn't even be compared to the wandering scholars of the present day.[5]

The most famous teacher to emerge from the French cathedral schools of the early twelfth century was Peter Abelard (1079–1142). He is chiefly known in modern times because of his adventures and misadventures with Heloise, strikingly told in his autobiographical *History of My Misfortunes*. But this story fails to do justice to either of these two figures. Heloise is an important figure in her own right. As her letters reveal, she was well educated in the classics, in the Bible, and in theology, as well as the traditions of courtly literature. Her letters also provide useful insights into everyday life in a twelfth-century convent. Abelard's role in the intellectual developments of the twelfth century is especially important. His most famous work was the *Sic et Non* (Yes and No). In the preface, strongly influenced by both classical philosophy and the biblical scholarship of Jerome, he explains the need for a scholarly, logical examination of the writings of the Christian Church, including Scripture itself:

> Why should it seem surprising if we, lacking the guidance of the Holy Spirit through whom those things were written and spoken, the Spirit impressing them on the writers, fail to understand them? Our achievement of full understanding is impeded especially by unusual modes of expression and by the different significances that can be attached to one and the same word, as a word is used now in one sense, now in another. Just as there are many meanings so there are many words. Tully [Cicero] says that sameness is the mother of satiety in all things, that is to say it gives rise to fastidious distaste, and so it is appropriate to use a variety of words in discussing the same thing and not to express everything in common and vulgar words. . . .
>
> We must also take special care that we are not deceived by corruptions of the text or by false attributions when sayings of the Fathers are quoted that seem to differ from the truth or to be contrary to it; for many apocryphal writings are set down under names of saints to enhance their authority, and even the texts of divine Scripture are corrupted by the errors of scribes. That most faithful writer and true interpreter, Jerome, accordingly warned us, "Beware of apocryphal writings . . . "
>
> In view of these considerations we have undertaken to collect various sayings of the Fathers that give rise to questioning because of their apparent contradictions as they occur to our memory. This questioning excites young read-

ers to the maximum of effort in inquiring into the truth, and such inquiry sharpens their minds. Assiduous and frequent questioning is indeed the first key to wisdom. Aristotle, that most perspicacious of all philosophers, exhorted the studious to practice it eagerly, saying, "Perhaps it is difficult to express oneself with confidence on such matters if they have not been much discussed. To entertain doubts on particular points will not be unprofitable." For by doubting we come to inquiry; through inquiring we perceive the truth, according to the Truth Himself. "Seek and you shall find," He says, "Knock and it shall be opened to you."[6]

The body of *Sic et Non* consists of 158 questions, such as, "Is God all powerful, or no?" and "Is God the author of evil, or no?" For each, Abelard assembled appropriate texts from Scripture and the Fathers for both sides of the question. He did not give the correct answer himself but suggested rather that it is to be attained by applying reason to the assembled texts.

Abelard wrote an important ethical treatise with the subtitle "Know Thyself." In it, again using elements drawn from classical philosophy, Abelard proposes that the essence of morality is intent and not deed. He would say, for example, that if a person helped someone in need only to get good publicity which he could then turn into personal gain, then that person did not act morally despite the good that came out of the deed itself:

> Indeed we call an intention good (that is, right) in itself. We don't however say that a "doing" takes on any good *in itself*, but that it proceeds from a good intention. Hence even if the same thing is done by the same person at different times, nevertheless because of the diversity of the intention, his doing it is called now good, now bad. So it appears to shift between good and bad, just as the proposition "Socrates is sitting" (or the understanding of it) shifts between true and false according as Socrates is now sitting, now standing. Aristotle says this alteration, the shift between true and false, occurs in these cases not in such a way that the things that shift between true and false take on anything in their changing, but rather that the subject thing, namely Socrates, is in himself moved from sitting to standing or conversely.[7]

The following passage makes clear the radical possibilities inherent in this doctrine:

> [I]f someone should ask whether the martyrs' persecutors, or Christ's, sinned in doing what they believed was pleasing to God, or whether without sin they could have given up what they thought shouldn't be given up, then insofar as we earlier described sin to be scorn for God or consenting to what one believes shouldn't be consented to, we certainly can't say they were sinning. No one's ignorance is a sin, and neither is the disbelief with which no one can be saved.[8]

Abelard is introducing his readers to an ethical realm that deeply challenges the prevailing view, expressed in the Irish penitentials quoted in Chapter 5, that deeds define virtue and vice. Abelard is not suggesting that the killing of Christ was a good thing. In fact, one conclusion to draw from his ethical theory is the value of reason and knowledge precisely so that one can do the right thing as well as have good intentions. Nevertheless, we can imagine how distressing and threatening Abelard's ideas were to many serious thinkers who could not imagine that Christ's executioners acted without sin.

Abelard, stressing the role of human reason in attaining Christian truth, came into conflict with Bernard of Clairvaux (d.1153; see Chapter 8), whose approach to such truth was quite different. Bernard pursued Abelard, who ultimately found refuge at the monastery of Cluny, with a fervor almost resembling that of later inquisitors. At Bernard's instigation, some of Abelard's writings were condemned by a French synod. Despite his attack, the use of the principles of Aristotelian logic to deal with theological questions continued. Peter Lombard (c.1100–1160), for example, wrote the *Four Books of Sentences* in Abelard's dialectical style, and his work became the basic textbook for the study of theology for the rest of the Middle Ages. Almost every great theologian, including Thomas Aquinas, wrote a commentary on this important book.

The cathedral schools not only promoted the study of logic but also the other liberal arts. The importance of grammar and rhetoric in the educational programs of the cathedral schools is best seen in the description of Bernard of Chartres, a famous teacher of that city's cathedral school, by his pupil John of Salisbury (c.1115–1180):

> Bernard of Chartres, the greatest font of literary learning in Gaul in recent times, used to teach grammar in the following way. He would point out, in reading the authors, what was simple and according to rule. On the other hand, he would explain grammatical figures, rhetorical embellishment, and sophistical quibbling, as well as the relation of given passages to other studies. He would do so, however, without trying to teach everything at one time. On the contrary, he would dispense his instruction to his hearers gradually, in a manner commensurate with their powers of assimilation. And since diction is lustrous either because the words are well chosen, and the adjectives and verbs admirably suited to the nouns with which they are used, or because of the employment of metaphors, whereby speech is transferred to some beyond-the-ordinary meaning for sufficient reason, Bernard used to inculcate this in the minds of his hearers whenever he had the opportunity. In view of the fact that exercise both strengthens and sharpens our mind, Bernard would bend every effort to bring his students to imitate what they were hearing. In some cases he would rely on exhortation, in others he would resort to punishments, such as flogging. Each student was daily required to recite part of what he had heard on the previous day. . . . He [Bernard] would also explain the poets and orators who were to serve as models for the boys in their introductory exercises in imitating prose and poetry. Pointing out how the dic-

tion of the authors was so skillfully connected, and what they had to say was so elegantly concluded, he would admonish his students to follow their example. And if, to embellish his work, someone had sewed on a patch of cloth filched from an external source, Bernard, on discovering this, would rebuke him for his plagiary, but would generally refrain from punishing him. After he had reproved the student, if an unsuitable theme had invited this, he would, with modest indulgence, bid the boy to rise to real imitation of the [classical authors], and would bring about that he who had imitated his predecessors would come to be deserving of imitation by his successors. He would also inculcate as fundamental, and impress on the minds of his listeners, what virtue exists in economy; what things are to be commended by facts and what one's choice of words, where concise and, so to speak, frugal speech is in order, and where fuller, more copious expression is appropriate; as well as where speech is excessive, and wherein consists just measure in all cases. Bernard used also to admonish his students that stories and poems should be read thoroughly, and not as though the reader were being precipitated to flight by spurs. Wherefor he diligently and insistently demanded from each, as a daily debt, something committed to memory. At the same time, he said that we should shun what is superfluous. According to him, the works of distinguished authors suffice. . . .

A further feature of Bernard's method was to have his disciples compose prose and poetry every day, and exercise their faculties in mutual conferences, for nothing is more useful in introductory training than actually to accustom one's students to practice the art they are studying. Nothing serves better to foster the acquisition of eloquence and the attainment of knowledge than such conferences, which also have a salutary influence on practical conduct, provided that charity moderates enthusiasm, and that humility is not lost during progress in learning.[9]

The emphasis on the study of the writings of classical antiquity, the Bible, and the Fathers that is so clear in the works of Abelard and John of Salisbury is explained in a famous metaphor of Bernard of Chartres:

> Bernard of Chartres used to compare us to dwarfs perched on the shoulders of giants. He pointed out that we see more and farther than our predecessors, not because we have keener vision or greater height, but because we are lifted up and borne aloft on their gigantic stature.[10]

All of the writers examined so far had only small portions of the writings of Aristotle at their disposal, those translated by Boethius. In the second half of the twelfth century and the beginning of the thirteenth, Latin translations were made of virtually all the extant writings of Aristotle. Generally, the earliest translations came not from Greek manuscripts available in Constantinople but rather from Arabic translations in Sicily and Muslim Spain. Along with the works of Aristotle came commentaries from Jewish and especially Islamic philosophers on these works that were to be crucially important guides

to "The Philosopher"—as Aristotle came to be known to the Middle Ages—
for theologians such as Thomas Aquinas. These commentaries were useful because their authors had already wrestled with the question of how adherents
of a revealed, monotheistic religion could make use of Aristotle. Muslim
philosophers such as Avicenna and Averroes were later used by groups declared heretical, such as the so-called thirteenth-century Latin Averroist
philosophers in Paris.

Given Aristotle's basic argument that knowledge begins with sense perception, it is not surprising that scholars in Western Europe desired not just
Aristotle's writings on science but similar writings of other Greek thinkers.
Hence, in addition to Aristotle's works, those of authors such as Euclid (geometry), Ptolemy (astronomy), and Galen (medicine) also appeared in Latin translation. Just as with Aristotle's writings, these often came together with works
of Muslim thinkers who had developed and improved the treatises of antiquity. Even some things that the Muslims learned from people beyond their
eastern frontier, such as a kind of mathematics that they called algebra, entered into the Western tradition at this period.

Given the variety of subject matter about which Aristotle wrote (including logic, metaphysics, physics, ethics, political theory, literary criticism, and
biology), one can begin to imagine the impact of the return of the Aristotelian
corpus to Western Europe. The writings of Aristotle together with the other
Greek scientific works gave to Western Europe a philosophy that argued that
knowledge comes from sense perception as well as a great deal of scientific
data to complement that philosophy. As this material came to be absorbed into
Europe, philosophers conceived of ways to arrange it comprehensively. They
began to organize well-ordered series of questions that attempted to deal with
all human knowledge in a systematic way, employing Abelard's method in his
Sic et Non. This type of work is called a *summa*. In the thirteenth century
several were written, most importantly the *Summa Theologiae* of Thomas
Aquinas.

The towering figure of Thomas Aquinas (c.1224–1274) most often comes
to mind when a modern student thinks of philosophy in the Middle Ages. And
without doubt, there is justice to this association. Thomas's works, and in particular his *Summa Theologiae*, stand among the most impressive achievements
of the Middle Ages, alongside the *Divine Comedy* and Chartres Cathedral,
works to which they are very often compared. Yet seeing Thomas in this exalted position can lead to a distortion, obscuring the real similarities that he
shares with other thinkers of the Middle Ages. Thomas's importance has much
to do with the long tradition of which he is a part. Like so much else that is
best in medieval culture, his very originality lies in his ability to assimilate
the available resources of his milieu. In his absolutely thorough familiarity
with Scripture, he is one with every important writer, thinker, or artist of the
Middle Ages. Next to Scripture, Augustine, the very theologian to whom his

system is usually contrasted, is his most frequently quoted source. In addition, Thomas's thought is also heavily dependent on many other Fathers of the Church, particularly Pseudo-Dionysius, Boethius, and Gregory the Great. Thomas was neither immediately nor universally recognized as a great thinker, especially outside his Dominican Order. In fact, some of his ideas were scrutinized by church officials to see if they contained heretical teachings. Even though Thomas was canonized, that is, formally declared a saint, in 1323, it was not until the sixteenth century that his thought became the quasi-official theology of the Roman Catholic Church (see Chapter 11).

Many of Thomas's works are themselves commentaries on the writings of others. The writing of commentaries was an essential part of the philosophical training in medieval universities; Thomas differs from the other scholars who learned according to this method only in that several of his commentaries are acknowledged masterpieces, among which are those on Peter Lombard, Boethius, Pseudo-Dionysius, and, most important, Aristotle.

The rediscovery of Aristotle in the West was a sensational event because of its implications in almost every field of knowledge. But it was a sensational event in another sense as well—because of the controversy it aroused. In many important areas, such as the origin and creation of the world, there is an incompatibility between Aristotelian and Christian thought. From the twelfth century on, there was continual, strong objection to the study of Aristotle. Even though the entire Aristotelian corpus was put into the curriculum at the University of Paris in 1255, the fight for legitimacy was by no means over. In one sense, Thomas's use of Aristotle brings to fruition a revolution in thought that had begun with twelfth-century thinkers. In another sense, Thomas must be seen as a revolutionary because he took upon himself the task not simply of using this Aristotelianism in an uneasy peace with Christian thought but of having Christian thought assimilate Aristotelianism. Thomas's achievement is to have assimilated Aristotle into a larger tradition, a vaster framework, and to have shown that there is no essential conflict between the approach through faith and the approach through reason. His ability to bring together so many seemingly disparate sources into a harmonious balance is perhaps unmatched in any thinker.

For a philosopher, one test of importance is a concern with large questions rather than small ones. By this criterion, Thomas is an important philosopher because he writes about the large questions—about God, humanity's place in the universe, and the relation between all the different parts of the universe—with a tenacious thoroughness. What characterizes Thomas, however, is not only that he deals with the large questions but that he sees them in a certain order, in a relationship to each other. His synthesis is an achievement in ordering both the large questions and the intellectual traditions that have dealt with them. What the Scholastics developed, and what Thomas as the greatest of the Scholastics perfected, was a method of examining and commenting on reality as they saw it, through logic and discipline and organization. The form of Scholasticism, as much as its content, was one of the significant intellectual achievements of the Middle Ages.

The basic building block in Thomas's system is the *article*. In principle its form is very simple. In the tradition of dialectic, which was given impetus by Abelard and by Peter Lombard, Thomas divides the arguments concerning any proposition into *sic et non* and lists the arguments on each side. When these arguments have been given, he presents a conclusion, a synthesis. One result of this technique is that it allows him to find a systematic way of bringing together all the various opinions on a given issue. Here, for example, is one of the articles in which Thomas deals with whether we can know God by our natural reason in this life:

1. It seems that we cannot in this life know God by natural reason. For Boethius says, "The reason cannot grasp simple forms." Now God, as has been shown, is supremely a simple form. Therefore natural reason cannot attain a knowledge of him.

2. According to Aristotle the soul understands nothing by natural reason without images. But since God is incorporeal there can be no image of him in our imagination. So then he cannot be known to us by natural reason.

3. Natural reason is common to the good and the bad, for human nature is common to both. Knowledge of God, however, belongs only to the good, for Augustine says, "The weak eye of the human mind is not fixed on that excellent light unless purified by the justice of faith." Therefore God cannot be known by natural reason.

On The Other Hand we read in Romans, "What may be known about God is manifest to them," i.e. what can be known about him by natural reason.

Reply: The knowledge that is natural to us has its source in the senses and extends just so far as it can be led by sensible things; from these, however, our understanding cannot reach to the divine essence. Sensible creatures are effects of God which are less than typical of the power of their cause, so knowing them does not lead us to understand the whole power of God and thus we do not see his essence. They are nevertheless effects depending from a cause, and so we can at least be led from them to know of God that he exists and that he has whatever must belong to the first cause of all things which is beyond all that is caused.

Thus we know about his relation to creatures—that he is the cause of them all; about the difference between him and them—that nothing created is in him; and his lack of such things is not a deficiency in him but due to his transcendence.

Hence: 1. The reason can know *that* a simple form is, even though it cannot attain to understanding of *what* it is.

2. God is known to the natural reason through the images of his effects.

3. Knowledge of God in his essence is a gift of grace and belongs only to

the good, yet the knowledge we have by natural reason belongs to both good and bad. Augustine says, "I do not now approve what I said in a certain prayer, 'O God who hast wished only the clean of heart to know truth' for it could be answered that many who are unclean know many truths," i.e., by natural reason.[11]

The schematic form apparent in the method makes clear that a primary aim of the procedure is to reduce all the work that was required to raise, discuss, and solve this question to simple elements. Nevertheless, the method is much more subtle than a first glance at the procedure might suggest. First of all, even though articles in the *Summa* invariably begin with *sic* and *non* statements, for and against the question that is being argued, they are not brought together simply to find an immediate answer to the question; nor are they brought together to set up straw men to be knocked down in the synthesis that follows; nor are these arguments simply opposed to one another. They are brought together rather so that the mind can begin to consider all the possibilities inherent in the question. They represent different possibilities that need to be tried out in order to explore the question fully, to push the possibilities for inquiry to their limit. The entire process, starting from the beginning of a question and working through to the end, becomes a dialectical process whose intention is to enable the mind to work at its highest level. The third part of the article, the synthesis, either attempts to solve the problem (as in this example) or attempts at least to give the principles by means of which the problem might be solved. The solution proposed will almost always agree more with one side of the argument presented in the *sic et non* than in the other. However, the arguments that Thomas does not agree with are not simply rejected. Instead he analyzes them in order to show how their position is founded on partial truth and then attempts to embody this truth within a wider framework. In this example, the *non* arguments are true as far as they go, but as the synthesis shows they do not go far enough.[12]

One sees in every step of the argument a strict logical development, each point following from another. And if one steps back to view the development, not of a single argument, but of the *Summa* as a whole, the same logic is evident. There is a movement from the large, comprehensive outline of the work as a whole, to the major divisions of this outline, to smaller subdivisions within the major divisions, down to individual articles. One could reasonably argue that every writer carefully organizes the relationship between the parts and the whole. In Augustine's *Confessions*, for example, the individual incidents are all related to the major thematic consideration—the story of Augustine's own conversion as an exemplar. What differentiates Scholasticism, as exemplified by Thomas, is that the organization is made explicit. There is no attempt made to hide the outline; in fact, the outline and structure, almost independent of content, are themselves embodiments of order. After Thomas, concern for form would sometimes all but overwhelm concern for significant content. But during the thirteenth century, Thomas exemplified a method of thinking and writing that was a very powerful tool for assimilating and describing reality.

Scholasticism was a way of thinking that resonated in many other areas. Erwin Panofsky, in his book *Gothic Architecture and Scholasticism,* suggests that the characteristic features of Scholasticism are embodied in another *"summa"* of medieval thought, the Gothic cathedral.[13] One of the distinguishing features of Gothic architecture that sets it apart from the earlier Romanesque is that it aims to be complete and comprehensive in its sculptural programs and its stained glass windows. The central truths of Christianity are embodied in stone and glass in each cathedral: creation; Old Testament history and prophecy; the mysteries of the Incarnation, Passion, and Resurrection; the story of the Church; and especially the Last Judgment. To achieve this comprehensive vision, it is necessary, no less than in a Scholastic treatise, to establish very clearly the relationship between the parts and the whole. In Gothic, clear principles of subordination are always present, so that each figure, statue, or story must not be seen simply in itself, but in terms of its place-

Façade of Amiens Cathedral, France. Begun 1220. The front view gives a sense of the architectural and decorative splendor of this great Gothic edifice. It took about two hundred years to complete the building. The asymmetry of the towers reminds us that later architects did not always follow the earlier design.

Detail of the Sculpture of the Façade of Amiens Cathedral. Beneath the jamb statues decorating the left portal of the cathedral are the twelve signs of the zodiac and the agricultural labors appropriate to each. In this detail is the sign of Scorpio, a fall season, accompanied by someone trampling the grapes that had been harvested. The cycle of the year needs to be seen in relation to events outside of time, for the Last Judgment is the subject of the sculpture over the central portal.

ment, and thence as it is related to the comprehensive sculptural arrangement in the cathedral as a whole. Specifically, a statue sculpted near one of the portals of a Gothic cathedral is invariably part of a larger group. If this group is a depiction of Old Testament figures, it will be balanced by a grouping of New Testament figures. Both groupings will be related to the sculptural programs in the *tympanum,* the arch over the doorway. And this entire grouping will have its place in the totality, as part of a clearly articulated design. Moreover, as in Scholastic writings, the architects of Gothic cathedrals make no attempt to conceal the outlines of their structures. Just as the Scholastic document is put together by means of a logical method that at all points is evident to the reader, so also are the "outlines"—the structure—of the cathedral evident: that typically Gothic structural device, the flying buttress, is on the outside of the cathedral, and hence clearly evident. The pillars, supporting the vaulting on the inside, are similarly evident. Thus, the form of the cathedral, how it is put together, stands independently of its content, what it is expressing, in a way that is analogous to the relationship between form and content in scholastic theology and philosophy

It would be naive to suggest that the builders of the Gothic cathedrals had a scholastic Summa in one hand and their blueprints in the other. Indeed, the closer one looks, the more one sees that there are differences as well as similarities; there are always inherent dangers in suggesting such analogies. But the analogy between Gothic architecture and Scholasticism helps establish the shared point of view of the age; in the thirteenth century this clearly includes a tendency toward order and comprehensiveness, and the explicit organization of form.

Another significant point of contact between Scholasticism and the Gothic cathedral is the Aristotelian reliance on the senses. For Thomas, following Aristotle, philosophy begins with sense experience. In the Gothic cathedral, and in artistic representations more generally, this can be seen in a more re-

Cathedral of Notre Dame, Paris. Twelfth and Thirteenth centuries. These elegant flying buttresses provided the support for the roof, which allowed Gothic cathedrals to soar to great heights while also letting a great amount of light into the church. The Gothic cathedral was thought of as an earthly model of the Heavenly City. From this angle, it is easy to see that the church itself is built in the shape of a cross.

Left: The Visitation of Mary to Elizabeth (Luke 1:39–56). Monastery of Saint Benoit-sur-Loire. Eleventh century. Right: The Visitation. Façade of the Cathedral of Reims, France. Thirteenth century. These two depictions of the same story show the movement toward an increased realism from Romanesque to Gothic art.

alistic representation of figures in sculpture. This is not to say that these works lost their iconographic significance; rather, this significance was now expressed in figures that looked more like real people and animals and plants than was true of Romanesque. These Scholastic elements can also be found in the literature that was written during and after this time. Dante's *Divine Comedy*, written at the beginning of the fourteenth century, is often called a literary *summa*. Some useful sense of the *Comedy* can be gained by this rough analogy: It is a work of comprehensive scope, taking for its subject matter an account of nothing less than the states of souls after death, and the relationship of God to all creation, living and dead; it is a work that depends on a great many other sources from classical antiquity through the Middle Ages—as Aristotle is to Aquinas, so is Virgil to Dante, who is his first guide to the afterlife. Like Thomas, Dante is a supreme master of assimilation. And the *Comedy*, too, is clear and explicit in its outline, and in articulating the relationship between the parts and the whole. In addition, Dante draws heavily on the philosophy of Thomas for many of the underpinnings of the *Comedy*. Moreover, in the *Comedy*, characters clearly achieve a greater degree of verisimilitude, becoming much more recognizably lifelike than in previous literature. Some of these elements are also present in works that are not so obviously dependent on a Scholastic milieu. In Chaucer's late-fourteenth-century poem *Troilus and Criseyde*, for example, the way in which the action of the story is outlined in advance by the narrator can be related to the concern with an explicit rendering of the relationship between the parts and the whole that is one of the heritages of Scholasticism.

The revival of philosophy in the twelfth and thirteenth centuries was paralleled by a revival in law. One of the most important rediscoveries from the past was the Code of Justinian, the corpus of Roman law compiled during the reign of the Byzantine Emperor Justinian (527–565). The exact means of discovery is still disputed among historians, but by the early twelfth century the code was known and studied in Italy, especially at Bologna. It contains the laws of the Roman Empire, a society quite different from twelfth-century Europe. Much of its municipal, corporate, and trade law would appear on the surface to be largely irrelevant to medieval society. Nevertheless, Italian communes and medieval kings began to make use of certain relevant parts of the code, although they "modernized" it, just as a medieval artist would portray the Roman soldiers at Christ's tomb as medieval knights. Passages that had one meaning in the ancient world took on a very different significance in feudal Europe. Perhaps as much as its specific sections, monarchs were interested in the idea of a unified code of law for their kingdoms that recognized the authority of the ruler as the origin of the law. King Philip Augustus of France (r.1180–1223) used Roman law and lawyers to try to consolidate his authority over his independent-minded vassals. The Holy Roman Emperor Frederick Barbarossa (r.1152–1190) used certain texts from the Justinian Code to try to justify his claim of independence from the pope. Even the development of English common law under King Henry II (r.1154–89) was affected by the renewed interest in the law of the Roman Empire.

Not only did secular rulers realize the value of Roman law and an organized body of legal material, but the Church did too. One thing that kept the eleventh-century Gregorian reform from achieving greater success in its attempt to centralize ecclesiastical authority was the lack of an authoritative and organized body of canons (laws of the Church). At the beginning of the twelfth century, canon law was a confused and often contradictory mixture of Scripture, patristic writings, papal letters and bulls, and conciliar and synodal decrees. Several attempts had been made at collecting canons, but none was complete enough or widely enough accepted to be authoritative. Thus, the law of the Church was in fact quite different in one part of Europe than in another.

At Bologna between 1140 and 1150, a Camaldolese monk named Gratian published a book entitled *A Concord of Discordant Canons*, usually known as the *Decretum*. It was a collection of canons profoundly influenced in form by the revival of Aristotelian dialectic. Much of the material was organized around a series of hypothetical situations. For example, one can see how many different legal principles and problems Gratian could explore from the following:

> Gratian: A certain noblewoman was informed that she was sought in marriage by the son of a certain noble. She gave her consent. But one who was not a noble and who was of slave condition offered himself in the name of the first man and took her as a wife. The one who had first pleased her finally came and sought her in marriage. She complained that she was deceived and wanted to be joined to the first man. It was first asked here: was there marriage between them? Secondly, if she first thought that he was a free man and afterwards learned that he was a slave, is it lawful for her to withdraw at once from him?[14]

The superiority of the *Decretum* over other collections of canons was quickly recognized. Thus, the *Decretum* and later collections of decrees made after its publication came into widespread use throughout Europe in ecclesiastical courts and became the basic textbooks of canon law, much as the Code of Justinian was to civil law and Peter Lombard's *Sentences* was to theology. Many commentaries were written on the *Decretum*, often making use of new hypothetical questions such as, "What if the pope invents a new heresy?" or even, "What is to be done if the pope fornicates on the altar of St. Peter's?" One question discussed in many commentaries was the familiar one of the relationship between spiritual and temporal authorities. The twelfth-century canonist Alanus writes:

> But in truth, and according to the Catholic faith, he [the Emperor, meaning secular rulers in general] is subject to the pope in spiritual matters and also receives his sword from him, for the right of both swords belongs to the pope. This is proved by the fact that the Lord had both swords on earth and used both as is mentioned here, and he established Peter as his vicar on earth and all Peter's successors. Therefore today Innocent [II] has by right the material sword. If you deny this you are saying that Christ established a secular prince as his vicar in this regard. Again Peter said to the Lord, "Behold, here are two swords" [Luke 22:38], so the material sword too was with Peter. Again if the emperor was not subject to the pope in temporalities he could not sin against the church in temporalities. Again the church is one body and so it shall have only one head or it will be a monster.[15]

This text is a good example of how lawyers no less than theologians used Scripture and its exegesis as their fundamental authority. The text from Luke involving the two swords was universally believed to refer to the secular and ecclesiastical powers. However, the text was subject to more than one interpretation. Here is the analysis of another twelfth–century canonist, Huguccio of Pisa:

> Here it can clearly be gathered that each power, the apostolic and imperial, was instituted by God and that neither is derived from the other and that the emperor does not have the sword from the apostle. . . . Again the words, "Behold, here are two swords" [Luke 22:38] were spoken to symbolize the fact that the two powers, namely the apostolic and imperial, are distinct and separate.[16]

Commentaries written on the *Decretum* became important authorities in themselves, cited in legal disputes for centuries. Furthermore, virtually all of the popes from the mid-twelfth to the fourteenth century on were Bologna-trained canon lawyers who had studied and written commentaries on the *Decretum*. Pope Innocent IV (r. 1245–1254), for example, was probably the most significant legal commentator of his generation.

The renewed interest in logic and law that was such an integral part of the Twelfth-Century Renaissance led to the development of new educational institutions. The monastic schools were not concerned with these subjects, and the cathedral schools generally remained wedded to the seven liberal arts, emphasizing grammar and rhetoric, as described above in the writings of John of Salisbury. By the end of the twelfth century, a university had been established at Bologna; it was the great center for the study of law, both civil and canon. Its students and later its faculty formed corporations (the word "universitas" means "corporation" or "guild") for protection and were granted monopolies by the city government. The faculty set the curriculum and gave certificates of membership in the guild of teachers to students who completed their study—the origin of the degree system. In Paris, a university was in existence by 1200; its specialties were the undergraduate arts curriculum (mostly Aristotle) and theology; for hundreds of years the faculty of theology at Paris was an important voice in the Church. In form and curriculum, the other medieval universities took their lead from Bologna and Paris. Northern universities such as Oxford, Cambridge, and Prague followed the Parisian model while southern universities such as Montpellier, Salamanca, Valladolid, Coimbra, and Padua were patterned after Bologna. For the rest of the Middle Ages, the most important theologians and members of the church hierarchy came from the universities. As mentioned previously, most popes of the High Middle Ages were trained canon lawyers; and many of the great theologians, including Thomas Aquinas and Bonaventure, taught at the University of Paris. On the other hand, the seven liberal arts, with the exception of dialectic, were not taught in the universities and thus were reduced to being the preliminaries to the university curricula.

The Renaissance of the Twelfth Century changed the course of the intellectual history of the West. The creation of the university as a new institution for the transmission and generation of knowledge signaled a shift in the intellectual centers from the monasteries to the cities. There was also a shift from the experiential theology of the cloister to something much more like a modern academic subject: scholastic theology emphasized organization, definition, and description rather than experience and exhortation to the good life. The literary quality of monastic writing gave way to the precise structure and technical, well-defined vocabulary of the *Summa*. Some saw this as progress while others such as Bernard of Clairvaux deplored the change. But none denied the importance of the shift.

The cultural changes that began in the twelfth century were not limited to philosophy and law. Literature too was transformed during this period. The major centers of literary activity, however, were the courts, not the universities, and its most impressive achievements were written in the vernacular languages, not Latin. A vernacular tradition in literature certainly existed earlier than the twelfth century, especially in the Germanic languages; and Latin literature did not die out at this time, continuing in both university and monastic settings. For example, Latin lyric poetry, a product of the schools, was an important genre. Alan of Lille (c.1116–1203), whose major works, the *Complaint of Nature* and the *Anticlaudianus*, creatively fuse Platonism with Christianity, was an important narrative poet who greatly influenced subsequent literature. Latin Church drama, elaborately staged and sung works usually presented in connection with the liturgical cycle, flourished under the direct auspices of school and monastery. But it was the vernacular literature beginning in the courts of France which established themes and patterns that have continued to influence European writers until the present. From the end of the twelfth century until the close of the Middle Ages, the most important literary monuments of European culture were written in vernacular languages, including the Arthurian romances of Chrétien de Troyes and the *Romance of the Rose* of Guillaume de Lorris and Jean de Meun in French, Wolfram von Eschenbach's *Parzival* in German, Dante's *Divine Comedy* in Italian, and Chaucer's *Canterbury Tales* in English.

The shift to the vernacular had several important consequences. First, it ensured a wider audience, since knowledge of Latin was basically limited to those with a clerical education. Significantly, this new audience included women, who not only became consumers of the new literature, but also producers of it as well. The courts of Marie de Champagne and Eleanor of Aquitaine were important centers of literary production during the twelfth century, and Marie de France was one of the new movement's most innovative figures, writing important short romances called Lais. Second, the shift made for an uneasy relationship between philosophy and theology on the one hand, and literature on the other. The later clerical culture of the university tended to be suspicious and somewhat dismissive of vernacular literary culture. Imaginative writers had to defend not only their use of the vernacular, but literature itself, which was often seen as a less noble and important enterprise by the schoolmen. Marie de France takes note of this tension in the Prologue to her *Lais*. She addresses an audience of presumed philosophers with a self-deprecation that is typical of medieval women writers, even religious authors of the stature of Hildegard of Bingen. She refers to herself—as does Hildegard—as "only a little woman." This modesty topos suggests both the hostility that women often incurred when they claimed an authority that was officially reserved for men and a strategy for dealing with that hostility. The presence of women writers as an important aspect of courtly literature may also help to explain some of the hostility directed against it on the part of the dominant clerical culture.

The late twelfth century saw an important change in subject matter in narrative poetry. Stories were generally told in verse rather than prose in classical antiquity, in the Middle Ages, and until the rise of the novel in the eighteenth century. When Western Europe had been under siege from Muslims and Norsemen, its literature understandably reflected a militant spirit. One kind of story that the people of the early Middle Ages especially enjoyed hearing—in addition to how a saint reached heaven—was that of a brave warrior fighting against overwhelming odds, finally meeting a glorious death in battle, as in *Beowulf* and the *Song of Roland*. Toward the end of the twelfth century, the emphasis shifts to stories of courtly quests and adventures that a knight undertakes, often to win the love of a lady.

This extremely significant shift, often described as the change from epic to romance, embodies the new leisure of a society no longer primarily concerned with self-preservation: tournaments, feasts, and entertainments at court, all presented with great color and splendor, idealized society's new self-awareness. The new literature greatly enhances the role of women. The most striking thing about women in the *Song of Roland* is their absence. They fare somewhat better in *Beowulf*, but because the heroic ideal is bravery in battle, they are nonetheless "second-class citizens." In the romance, by contrast, women often are the focal point for the action. Heroes, often motivated in their actions by the powerful and sometimes all-consuming emotion of romantic love, must now be courteous as well as brave; and a new language develops to describe the ideal of courtesy. The relationship between love, courtesy, and adventure is embodied in the following passage from Chrétien de Troyes's (fl.1160–1190) *Erec and Enide:*

> Now that Enide was very happy and had everything she desired, her great beauty returned to her; for her great distress had affected her so much that she was very pale and wan. Now she was embraced and kissed, now she was blessed with all good things, now she had her joy and pleasures; for unadorned they lie in bed and each enfolds and kisses the other; nothing gives them so much joy. They have had so much pain and sorrow, he for her, and she for him, that now they have their satisfaction. . . . But now they must go on their way; so they asked his leave to depart from Guivret, in whom they had found a friend indeed.[17]

In this passage the love between Erec and Enide is both a reward for past deeds and a spur to the deeds the hero is about to perform.

A corresponding change in style accompanies the change in subject matter from epic to romance, for which the change from Romanesque to Gothic style in the visual arts provides a rough analogy. The monsters of Romanesque art allow easy identification between good and evil. In Gothic, however, the style achieves a uniformity of elegance that precludes such easy identification. For example, on the facades of several Gothic cathedrals—Strasbourg and Paris to name two—are allegorical figures who represent the Old and New Testaments. However, these figures cannot be identified on the basis of style, one being almost identical with the other to the viewer following the elegantly flowing rhythms of each body. It is only by a consideration of the iconographic attributes of each figure that the viewer can identify them: the Old, blindfolded, carries the tablets of the mosaic law and represents the Synagogue; the New carries the chalice of the New Covenant. A similar example on the facade of the Cathedral of Amiens shows the kings who were prefigurations of Christ in the Old Testament sharing a stylistic identity with Herod, his persecutor in the New. In the romance, as in Gothic art, stylistic elegance does not imply moral approval, as the following passage from *Erec and Enide* illustrates. An evil count, wishing to kill Erec and seduce Enide, speaks as follows:

> I ask a favor of you, and may it not displease you. As an act of courtesy and as a pleasure, I would fain sit by yonder lady's side. With good intent I came to see you both, and you should see no harm in that. I wish to present to the lady my service in all respects. Know well that for love of you I would do whatever may please her.[18]

Herod (L) and one of the Magi (R). Cathedral of Amiens, France. Thirteenth century. The new subtlety and elegance of Gothic are demonstrated in these two adjacent statues on the façade of Amiens Cathedral. Herod is a persecutor of Christ and the magi are the first Gentiles to recognize Christ as the Son of God. Yet they look remarkably similar.

The immediate context of his speech makes the count's treacherous intentions clear to the reader, if not to Erec, contradicting the grace and eloquence with which it is presented. To engage the moral concerns that are often central to the romance, the reader must be aware of both the context and the possible iconographic significance of an action.

The increased knowledge of classical antiquity that was the catalyst for the achievements in philosophy and law during the Twelfth-Century Renaissance played a significant part in its literary achievement as well. Learned authors looked to the past to give distance and dignity to the romance, and at the same time to serve as a model for the present. They saw themselves as the heirs of a storytelling art that had passed from Greece to Rome to France. This *translatio*—translation in the literal sense of being moved from one place to another—is illustrated by a passage from the beginning of Chretien's *Cliges:*

> Our books have informed us that pre-eminence in chivalry and learning once belonged to Greece. Then chivalry passed to Rome, together with that highest learning which now has come to France. God grant that it may be cherished here, and that it may be made so welcome here that the honor which has taken refuge with us may never depart from France: God had awarded it as another's share, but of Greeks and Romans no more is heard, their fame is passed, and their glowing ash is dead.[19]

Not surprisingly, many romances retell stories and legends of classical antiquity, most often stories set in Troy or Thebes (generically though somewhat misleadingly called the "Matter of Rome" by some modern scholars). Others go back to another "past" for their setting. The adventures of King Arthur and his knights of the round table were the material for folklore and legend in the early Middle Ages. They were incorporated into a historical work, Geoffrey of Monmouth's *History of the Kings of Britain*, in 1147. They were turned to specifically literary use in five romances written in French by Chrétien de Troyes in the 1170s *(Erec and Enide, Cliges, Yvain, Lancelot,* and *Percival)*. From the time of Chrétien until Edmund Spenser at the end of the sixteenth century, Arthurian romance was a central focus for European narrative literature, and it continues as a subject matter for contemporary writers. Whether the setting be Troy or Britain (Arthurian material is often called the "'Matter of Britain"), writers of romance make extensive use of the Latin poets, especially Ovid, in their works, often achieving a sophistication that supports their claims for the "translation" of knowledge from ancient Rome to their own time.

One of the most significant aspects of romance is its emphasis on interior description—debates and monologues that take place within the mind of the speaker. The earlier epic emphasizes forceful action and descriptions of changeless, static values: life is a battle between good and evil. In the romance the image of life as a journey comes to dominate; and the battlefield is now also in the mind of each character, whose inner movement, change, and growth the reader is allowed to observe. In the following excerpts, the description of Charlemagne from the *Song of Roland* and the description of the hero of Chrétien's *Lancelot* are juxtaposed to exemplify this change:

> The Emperor Charles is jubilant and gay;
> The lofty walls of Cordres are torn down,
> His catapults have laid its towers low;
> His knights rejoice, for great is their reward
> Silver and gold, and costly gear for war. . . .
> A throne is placed—it's made of purest gold.
> There sits the king, the ruler of sweet France;
> White is his beard, and silver streaks his hair,
> Handsome his form, his bearing very proud:
> No stranger needs to have him pointed out.
> The Saracens dismount and come on foot
> To greet the king, as friendly envoys would.[20]

> It was unlucky for him that he shrank from the disgrace and did not jump in at once, for he later regretted the delay. Reason, which is inconsistent with the dictates of love, bids him refrain from getting in, warning him and counseling him not to do or undertake anything for which he may reap shame and dishonor. Yet reason which dares thus to speak to him reaches only his lips, not his heart; for love is enclosed within his heart, urging him to mount at once into the cart. So he jumps in, since love will have it so, feeling no concern about the shame; he is prompted by love's commands.[21]

In the passage from *Roland*, action and description are simple and straightforward, expressing the differences between Christian and pagan as forcefully as possible; that struggle, as embodied in the attitude of the militant Christian, is what the poem is most fundamentally about. In Chrétien's work there is a struggle too, but it is experienced inside the hero's heart. The conflict between reason and love described in the passage is presented by suspending the external action of the poem to present an account of an internal debate. This inward turning undoubtedly reflects the influence of monastic spirituality. Bernard of Clairvaux begins his Third Sermon on the Song of Songs by exhorting those in his audience to turn inward, to examine their own spirituality, a spiritual self-analysis that characterizes the essence of the Cistercian monastic search (see Chapter 8). The habit of examining spiritual states, which developed in the monasteries, spread beyond the cloister and became part of the storytelling art that flourished in the courts and then moved to the cities.

Throughout the Middle Ages, the short poem or lyric was an important genre in Latin literature. The twelfth century saw the rise of the lyric in the vernacular languages as well, an important development that began in the south of France, the result of a group of professional poets known as troubadors, writing in a Romance language called Provençal. The lyrics—which were written to be sung, sometimes by the troubadors themselves and sometimes by traveling entertainers called jongleurs—are intensely emotional; and by far the most important emotion they express is love. The speaker of the poem is usually a knight–errant expressing his feelings toward his lady and, perhaps more important, the results of her actions on his feelings. The love is usually unfulfilled: longing, separation, and departure are all standard themes. Christianized forms of this lyric poetry, in which the speaker addresses his poem to the Blessed Virgin or to Christ in the guise of a lover-knight, were also quite popular. The poems are also very skillfully wrought, as if the poet takes the themes of love for granted, but must then decide the most ingenious and skillful way to express them. Thus, many elaborate formal patterns were developed, with very complicated stanzaic structures and rhyming patterns, as well as elaborate plays on words. The following stanza, the beginning of a poem by Bernart de Ventadorn (fl.1140–1180), shows how love becomes the source of poetic inspiration:

> A song cannot in any way have value
> If the singing doesn't spring from the heart,
> And the singing cannot well from the breast
> Unless its source is fine, true love.
> And so my verse looms high,
> For I have joy from love, devoting there
> My mouth and eyes, my heart and mind.[22]

Many of the important lyric forms in the subsequent history of European poetry grow out of forms that the troubadours originally developed. The sonnet, for example, is a variation that was developed in Sicily, one of the places where troubadour songs flourished. This influence was felt in the flowering of the lyric all over Europe, in Italy, in France, and in Germany. Indirectly, and much later, it entered English poetry as well, through translations from Italian during the Renaissance.

The changes that developed during the Twelfth-Century Renaissance were both significant achievements in their own right and changes that have helped to chart the course of Western society and thought down to our own time. If we consider the reemergence of autobiography, the interiority of the vernacular literature, the deep expressions of romantic love, the new ethical theory of intent, and the close observation of the physical world which in turn led to differentiation and distinction, we can describe the period discussed in this chapter as the "discovery of the individual."[23] Since we usually associate the development of the concept of the individual with Europe in the fifteenth and sixteenth centuries, we can understand better why the intellectual developments of the twelfth century are indeed properly referred to as a Renaissance.

The culture that was emerging at the end of the twelfth century was centered more in urban areas than earlier medieval culture had been. The rise of universities created a different sort of scholar from the great intellects of previous centuries. The meaning of courtliness was reexamined to make it relevant to an increasingly urban culture. Much of the new vernacular literature dealt with secular subjects, with an implied threat to the church's teachings, authoritatively expressed in Latin. If we add to these changes the threat of heresy, the conflict between church and state, and the popes' centralization of ecclesiastical authority, we can appreciate the uncertainty and instability that were the consequences. Although the issues raised by this new world that was emerging were addressed by many people in a variety of ways, the person who most successfully responded to them was a man from a small town in Italy named Francis of Assisi.

CHAPTER 10

FRANCIS OF ASSISI
AND THE MENDICANTS

The developments in Europe in the eleventh and twelfth centuries described in the last two chapters brought enormous changes to everyone, from the the poorest peasants to the greatest nobles and prelates. These changes were uneven and not necessarily all for the good. The popular heresies that developed in the most dynamic parts of Europe are one clear indication that traditional institutions and value systems were no longer universally accepted. The Catholic Church, even after the institutionalization of many tenets of the Gregorian Reform, was deeply anchored in the political, economic, and social values of the world in which it existed. The development of cities and the beginnings of capitalism magnified problems that could no longer be ignored. The gap between rich and poor may not have been much greater in 1200 than in 1000, but it was surely more visible. Cities in Italy, for example, contained members of the great landed aristocracy and newly wealthy merchants, but also those who were desperately poor and often diseased and disfigured. Even in the twenty-first century it is easier to notice poverty in urban than in rural areas.

Some responded to these new or at least increasingly visible problems by retreating from them, hence part of the attractiveness of new monastic forms, both cenobitic and eremetical, in the eleventh and twelfth centuries. But new forms of spiritual life, which responded at least in part to the new realities of the twelfth century, were modestly successful in addressing the needs of Europe's population. One example were the Augustinian canons, clergy living communally, largely in cities and towns, under a rule that was derived from some of the letters of Saint Augustine. Other responses included religious groups such as the Humiliati in Italy. Often suspected of being heretical, even after Pope Innocent III approved their form of life, they did not develop over all of Western Europe. Another religious group were the Beguines, religious women who often lived in their own homes and took no formal vows, but who came together communally to do good deeds and also to share their prayer life. They too were often regarded with suspicion. At the beginning of the thirteenth century, a new form of religious life, anchored in the past but also genuinely original, developed in Europe beginning in Italy. Just as the new realities of life in Europe affected every element of medieval society, so did this new movement participate in the transformation of life and thought in Europe in everything from art to zoology. In 1182 in Assisi a man was born who transformed medieval spirituality. His name was Francesco di Bernardone, Francis of Assisi.

From several accounts of his life written shortly after his death (1226) by those who knew him or had access to people who knew him, a picture of Francis as a figure unique in the history of the Church emerges. Like the Gospels themselves, which present the meaning of Jesus' life and teaching rather than biographies of Jesus in any modern sense, these hagiographical accounts display the variety that Francis's life had for his own time. The one by Bonaventure (published in 1263) is most important because just after its appearance the

Image of Saint Francis of Assisi. Margarito d'Arezzo, Museum of Medieval and Modern Art. Arezzo, Italy, c.1240. Although this painting was made just a few years after Francis died, it is not a portrait in the modern sense. However, it does capture Francis's poverty, humility, and simplicity.

governing body of the Franciscan Order demanded that the earlier lives be destroyed. Today these early lives survive in a small number of manuscripts, providing us with valuable information and insight. This is especially true of the two early official lives by the Franciscan Thomas of Celano. However, they were of little direct influence after the appearance of Bonaventure's life, although they were the most important sources for it. Bonaventure's life of Francis survives in about a thousand manuscripts from the end of the Middle Ages and was well known to virtually every friar. Furthermore, many copies of the life circulated outside the order, and stories from it were painted in countless Franciscan churches, to be seen by all who entered them. It was from Bonaventure that people from the mid-thirteenth century on, learned and unlearned, have known the events and meaning of the life of Saint Francis of Assisi.

Until he was almost twenty-five Francis lived the typical life of a wealthy merchant's son, helping in the family business, frolicking with his friends, and dreaming of being skilled and brave at arms. After an illness, however, he began to experience deep religious feelings. He would go off by himself to pray, wear ragged garb and give away money from the family business to the poor, understandably irritating his father, who summoned Francis before the court of the bishop of Assisi to get back all his possessions. Francis stood before his father and the bishop, stripped himself naked, and returned his clothes to his father, declaring that he would now speak only of his Father in heaven. Bonaventure's account of this extraordinary event is prefaced by a description and interpretation of several visions Francis had had. The first occurred shortly after he had given his cloak to a poverty-stricken knight:

> The following night, when he had fallen asleep, God in his goodness showed him a large and splendid palace full of military weapons emblazoned with the insignia of Christ's cross. Thus God vividly indicated that the compassion he had exhibited toward the poor knight for love of the supreme King would be repaid with an incomparable reward. And so when Francis asked to whom these belonged, he received an answer from heaven that all these things were for him and his knights. When he awoke in the morning, he judged the strange vision to be an indication that he would have great prosperity; for he had no experience in interpreting divine mysteries nor did he know how to pass through visible images to grasp the invisible truth beyond. Therefore, still ignorant of God's plan, he decided to join a certain count in Apulia, hoping in his service to obtain the glory of knighthood, as his vision seemed to foretell.[1]

As Bonaventure explains, Francis fails to understand this first divine summons. He takes the vision quite literally, immediately wanting to go and become a soldier; Bonaventure tells the reader that what Christ intended rather was to show Francis how to become a spiritual soldier—a soldier of Christ. In a subsequent vision he again receives a command from Christ, this time to repair his Church:

One day when Francis went out to meditate in the fields (Gen. 24:63), he walked beside the church of San Damiano, which was threatening to collapse because of extreme age. Inspired by the Spirit, he went inside to pray. Prostrate before an image of the Crucified, he was filled with no little consolation as he prayed. While his tear-filled eyes were gazing at the Lord's cross, he heard with his bodily ears a voice coming from the cross, telling him three times: "Francis, go and repair my house which, as you see, is failing completely into ruin."

Trembling with fear, Francis was amazed at the sound of this astonishing voice, since he was alone in the church; and as he received in his heart the power of the divine words, he fell into a state of ecstasy. Returning finally to his senses, he prepared to obey, gathering himself together to carry out the command of repairing the church materially, although the principal intention of the words referred to that Church which Christ purchased with his own blood (Acts 20:28), as the Holy Spirit taught him and as he himself later disclosed to the friars.[2]

Once again, Francis understands and acts upon the letter of the command but not its spirit. Only later does he come to understand its full meaning. Francis's whole life, as recorded by Bonaventure, follows this movement to deeper and deeper levels of spiritual understanding.

After Francis rejected his earthly father and accepted his Father in heaven—the first event in his life showing that he has learned to move from the letter to the spirit—he settled at a small church dedicated to Mary called the Portiuncula. A few men from Assisi and its vicinity sold all their earthly possessions and came to live with him, doing good deeds and menial work, living in poverty, and even ministering in Christ-like fashion to lepers. When the number of followers grew to be about twelve, Francis went to Pope Innocent III and asked permission to found an order (1209). According to legend, Innocent dreamt that the Lateran Basilica (the cathedral of Rome) was falling until a man dressed in a coarse tunic with a cord for a belt propped it up. He saw Francis, recognized him as the man in the dream, and approved a simple rule made up largely of biblical quotations for this new order, the Friars Minor. When one thinks of the splendor and high politics of Innocent's pontificate, it seems remarkable that he would agree even to see Francis, let alone give him, an uneducated layperson, permission to found an order dedicated to absolute poverty and the preaching of repentance. Perhaps Innocent saw that this order could show Christendom that the Church still held to the ideals of the Gospel and that one did not have to join a heretical sect to practice them. Perhaps Innocent was genuinely moved by Francis and the poor men from Assisi. In any case, it is impressive both that Innocent in his splendor recognized the validity of the ideal of Francis and that Francis in his poverty recognized the validity of the authority of Innocent, Christ's vicar and Peter's successor. In a sense these two great men complemented each other. In Innocent III one saw an imitation of Christ in all his splendor and glory and power, in Francis an imitation of Christ in his humanity—poor and humble.

After Innocent's approval of the order, it grew rapidly. Soon there were Franciscans everywhere. A governing structure was established, the center of which was an annual chapter. Francis was instrumental in establishing a female branch of the movement called the Poor Clares, named after Clare of Assisi, the first woman converted to Francis's way of life. Clare, who died in 1253, was an extremely important part of the Franciscan movement. Although she and her sisters came to live a cloistered life at the church of San Damiano, the church Francis had repaired, and although she remained devoted to Francis and turned to him for guidance and support while he was still alive, the spirituality and lifestyle that she developed there had its own unique stamp, and exerted a long and powerful influence within Christianity. It combined a traditional monastic spirituality with a rigorous insistence on Franciscan poverty. A "third order" was also established for those in secular life who could not fully practice Franciscan poverty but who held Franciscan ideals and

Saint Clare's Hair Is Cut by Saint Francis. Panel painting by the Master of Santa Chiara. Church of Santa Chiara, Assisi, c.1280. In this story, Clare has fled from her home to meet Francis in a small church just outside Assisi. Francis cuts her hair, effectively declaring her to be part of his Order.

practiced certain elements of that ideal, such as simplicity and poverty of spirit. One way of understanding the ideals of the early Franciscans is to see them as a kind of offshoot of Benedictine monasticism, another attempt to return to monastic simplicity. A life interweaving prayer and works practiced by the early followers of Francis was similar in principle to that prescribed by Benedict. However, the significant difference is that for Francis and his followers their monastery became the world all around them, and their work was ministering to the world's needy, primarily in the cities.

Francis himself continued to live a life of utmost poverty and simplicity. He traveled a great deal, working and begging for what he needed. (The word *mendicant* means "beggar.") He spent periods of time alone in caves or hermitages for prayer. He desired to convert Muslims to Christianity and sought martyrdom in this venture. He went to Egypt but made no significant conversions. What was significant about the journey is that Francis went to the Islamic world as a peacemaker. His gesture offered an alternative to the ideology of the Crusades.

As the order increased in size, some of the brothers desired to study, but Francis discouraged this. Once the friars asked him whether he was pleased that learned men, who had by that time been received into the order, should devote themselves to the study of sacred Scripture. He replied: "I am indeed pleased, as long as they do not neglect application to prayer, after the example of Christ, of whom we read that he prayed more than he read, and as long as they study not only in order to know what they should say but in order to practice what they have heard and when they have put it into practice themselves to propose it to others likewise."[3] Clearly, Francis envisioned the Friars Minor as men of simplicity, humility, and, most of all, poverty, for poverty was at the very center of this movement, as it was the center of Francis's life:

> One day when he was devoutly hearing a Mass of the Apostles, the Gospel was read in which Christ sends forth his disciples to preach and explains to them the way of life according to the Gospel: that they should not keep gold or silver or money in their belts, nor have a wallet for their journey, nor two tunics, nor shoes, nor staff (Matt. 10:9). When he heard this, he grasped its meaning and committed it to memory. This lover of apostolic poverty was then filled with an indescribable joy and said: "This is what I want; this is what I long for with all my heart." He immediately took off his shoes from his feet, put aside his staff, cast away his wallet and money as if accursed, was content with one tunic and exchanged his leather belt for a piece of rope. He directed all his heart's desire to carry out what he had heard and to conform in every way to the rule of right living given to the apostles. . . .
>
> When the friars asked him at a gathering what virtue does more to make one a friend of Christ, he replied as if opening up the hidden depths of his heart: "Know, brothers, that poverty is the special way to salvation, as the stimulus of humility and the root of perfection, whose fruit is manifold but

hidden. This is the Gospel's treasure hidden in a field (Matt. 13:44); to buy this we should sell everything, and in comparison to this we should spurn everything we cannot sell."[4]

Poverty for Francis and his followers, as this passage indicates, was not an end in itself so much as the means of aligning themselves by direct imitation with the Christ of the Gospels. Here, as in so much of Franciscan writing, the language of Scripture provides the basic iconography. Francis not only insisted that each friar give up all his individual property, he also wanted the order to have no money or property collectively. According to Franciscan imagery, Francis was said to have married Lady Poverty. A story from a thirteenth-century work called the *Mirror of Perfection* perhaps best sums up Francis's attitude toward money:

> While this true friend of God completely despised all worldly things he detested money above all. From the beginning of his conversion, he despised money particularly and encouraged his followers to flee from it always as from the devil himself. He gave his followers this observation: money and manure are equally worthy of love.
>
> Now, it happened one day that a layman came to pray in the church of Saint Mary of the Portiuncula, and placed some money by the cross as an offering. When he left, one of the brothers simply picked it up with his hand and threw it on the windowsill. What the brother had done reached the saint, and he, seeing he had been caught ran to ask forgiveness, threw himself to the ground and offered himself to be whipped. The saint rebuked him and reprimanded him severely for touching coins. He ordered him to pick up the money from the windowsill with his own mouth, take it outside the fence of that place, and with his mouth to put it on the donkey's manure pile. While that brother was gladly carrying out this command, fear filled the hearts of all those who heard it. From then on, all of them held in even greater contempt what had been so equated with manure and were encouraged to despise it by new examples every day.[5]

As the order grew, it became necessary to have a more carefully drawn up and comprehensive rule than that earliest set of principles that Innocent III had agreed to in 1209. Thus, in 1221 the so-called Earlier Rule was completed; it is clearly Francis's in spirit though no doubt he had help in the precise language. However, even this rule was soon seen as inadequate because of its lack of legal terminology and its strictness in certain areas, and the Later Rule was promulgated in 1223. Pope Honorius III gave his seal of approval, and the rule of 1223 remains to this day the rule for Franciscan friars. Francis, helped and perhaps at times cajoled by the order's official protector, Cardinal Hugolino (the future Pope Gregory IX), made some concessions in this rule. Two emphases in this 1223 rule are the order's obedience to the pope—there was going to be no straying of these friars into heresy—and the friars' restraint from condemning those who do not live in poverty. There were concessions to those friars who were priests with regard to possessing books. Furthermore, the increasingly elaborate governing structure of the order was spelled out. Despite these concessions, which Francis probably agreed to only reluctantly, there was still a strong statement with regard to money:

> I strictly command all my brothers not to receive coins or money in any form, either personally or through intermediaries. Nevertheless, the ministers and custodians alone may take special care through their spiritual friends to provide for the needs of the sick and the clothing of the others according to places, seasons and cold climates, as they judge necessary, saving always that, as stated above, they do not receive coins or money.[6]

Francis's last years saw friars begin to relax the original rigor of the order. Reacting against what he saw as an excessive reliance on property, he ordered a house of studies that had been erected for the friars in Bologna to be torn down. On his deathbed, he dictated a last testament, recalling his first years in the religious life and imploring the friars to preserve the simplicity and poverty of those happy times:

> [In the beginning] those who came to receive life gave whatever they had to the poor and were content with one tunic, patched inside and out, with a cord and short trousers. We desired nothing more. We clerical [brothers] said the Office as other clerics did; the lay brothers said the Our Father; and we quite willingly remained in churches. And we were simple and subject to all.
>
> And I worked with my hands, and I still desire to work; and I earnestly desire all brothers to give themselves to honest work. Let those who do not know how to work learn, not from desire to receive wages, but for example and to avoid idleness. And when we are not paid for our work, let us have recourse to the table of the Lord, begging alms from door to door. The Lord revealed a greeting to me that we should say: "May the Lord give you peace."
>
> Let the brothers be careful not to receive in any way churches or poor dwellings or anything else built for them unless they are according to the holy poverty we have promised in the Rule. As pilgrims and strangers, let them always be guests there.
>
> I strictly command all the brothers through obedience, wherever they may be, not to dare to ask any letter from the Roman Curia, either personally or through an intermediary, whether for a church or another place or under the pretext of preaching or the persecution of their bodies. But, wherever they have not been received, let them flee into another country to do penance with the blessing of God. . . .
>
> And I strictly command all my cleric and lay brothers, through obedience, not to place any gloss upon the Rule or upon these words saying: "They should not be understood in this way." But as the Lord has given me to speak and write the Rule and these words simply and purely, may you understand them simply and without gloss and observe them with a holy activity until the end.[7]

Toward the end of his life, Francis grew deeper in contemplation with special devotion to the Christ crucified, the Christ who spoke to him from the Cross in San Damiano, whom he finally was able to accept with full spiritual understanding. This devotion culminated, according to tradition, in Francis's receiving the very wounds of Christ, the stigmata, while in contemplation on the mountain of La Verna in 1224. Bonaventure describes this taking on of the wounds of Christ:

> By the Seraphic ardor of his desires, he was being borne aloft into God; and by his sweet compassion he was being transformed into him who chose to be crucified because of the excess of his love (Eph. 2:4). On a certain morning about the feast of the Exaltation of the Cross, while Francis was praying on the mountainside, he saw a Seraph with six fiery and shining wings descend from the height of heaven. And when in swift flight the Seraph had reached a spot in the air near the man of God, there appeared between the wings the figure of a man crucified, with his hands and feet extended in the form of a cross and fastened to a cross. Two of the wings were lifted above his head, two were extended for flight and two covered his whole body. When Francis saw this, he was overwhelmed and his heart was flooded with a mixture of joy and sorrow. He rejoiced because of the gracious way Christ looked upon him under the appearance of the Seraph, but the fact that he was fastened to a cross pierced his soul with a sword of compassionate sorrow (Luke 2:35).
>
> He wondered exceedingly at the sight of so unfathomable a vision, realizing that the weakness of Christ's passion was in no way compatible with the immortality of the Seraph's spiritual nature. Eventually he understood by a revelation from the Lord that divine providence had shown him this vision so that, as Christ's lover, he might learn in advance that he was to be totally transformed into the likeness of Christ crucified, not by the martyrdom of his flesh, but by the fire of his love consuming his soul.
>
> As the vision disappeared, it left in his heart a marvelous ardor and imprinted on his body markings that were no less marvelous. Immediately the marks of nails began to appear in his hands and feet just as he had seen a little before in the figure of the man crucified. His hands and feet seemed to be pierced through the center by nails, with the heads of the nails appearing on the inner side of the hands and the upper side of the feet and their points on the opposite sides. The heads of the nails in his hands and his feet were round and black; their points were oblong and bent as if driven back with a hammer, and they emerged from the flesh and stuck out beyond it. Also his right side, as if pierced with a lance, was marked with a red wound from which his sacred blood often flowed, moistening his tunic and underwear.[8]

The story of the stigmata vividly embodies two themes central to Francis's life—his imitation of Christ and his singular devotion to Christ crucified.

One of the most striking qualities of Francis was his great joy. Throughout all his privation and tears he could and did continue to sing praises to God

Stigmatization of Saint Francis. Panel painting by Bonaventura Berlinghieri of Lucca. Church of San Francesco, Pescia, Italy. 1235. This is the earliest image of Francis receiving the stigmata. The model the artist used for this "new story" was Christ's agony in the garden of Gethsemani.

and rejoice in all creation. Francis loved nature, seeing all things, whether human, animal, or inert, as his brothers and sisters, all created by the same loving God. Some of the most famous stories of the life and miracles of Francis involve animals:

> When he was approaching Bevagna, he came to a spot where a large flock of birds of various kinds had come together. When God's saint saw them, he quickly ran to the spot and greeted them as if they were endowed with reason. They all became alert and turned toward him, and those perched in the trees bent their heads as he approached them and in an uncommon way directed their attention to him. He went right up to them and solicitously urged them to listen to the word of God, saying: "Oh birds, my brothers, you have a great obligation to praise your Creator, who clothed you in feathers and gave you wings to fly with, provided you with the pure air and cares for you without any worry on your part." While he was saying this and similar things to them, the birds showed their joy in a remarkable fashion: They began to stretch their necks, extend their wings, open their beaks and gaze at him at-

tentively. He went through their midst with amazing fervor of spirit, brushing against them with his tunic. Yet none of them moved from the spot until the man of God made the sign of the cross and gave them his blessing and permission to leave; then they all flew away together.[9]

The following story is taken from a popular collection of Franciscan stories compiled at the beginning of the fourteenth century called *The Little Flowers:*

At the time that Saint Francis was staying in the city of Gubbio, in the district of Gubbio there appeared a very big wolf, fearsome and ferocious, which devoured not only animals but even human beings, so that all the citizens were in great fear, because many times he came near the city. All would go armed when they went out of the city as if they were going to combat, yet with all this, those who were alone and encountered him could not defend

Francis Preaching to the Birds. Panel Painting by Guido di Graziano, c. 1280. National Gallery, Siena, Italy. In the paintings of the life of Saint Francis this story not only tells of Francis's love of and intimacy with nature but also depicts him as a great preacher.

themselves from him. And out of fear of this wolf it came to the point that no one dared to leave that town.

For this reason Saint Francis had compassion on the people of the town, and decided to go out to this wolf, even though all the citizens advised against it. Making the sign of the most holy cross, he went out of the town, he and his companions, placing all his confidence in God. As the others hesitated to go any further, Saint Francis took the road toward the place where the wolf was. Then that wolf, seeing many citizens who had come to see this miracle, ran toward Saint Francis with his mouth open. Drawing close to him, Saint Francis made the sign of the most holy cross on him and called him to himself and said this: "Come here, Brother Wolf. I command you on behalf of Christ that you do no harm to me or to anyone." An amazing thing to say! Immediately, when Saint Francis had made the sign of the cross, the fearsome wolf closed his mouth and stopped running; and once the command was given, it came meekly as a lamb, and threw itself to lie at the feet of Saint Francis. . . .

And once all the people were fully assembled Saint Francis got up and preached to them, saying, among other things, that God allows such things and pestilences because of sins; and the flame of hell, which lasts forever for the damned, is much more dangerous than the fierceness of the wolf, which can only kill the body. "How much should the mouth of hell be feared when the mouth of a little animal holds such a great multitude in fear! Dear people, return to God, therefore, and do fitting penance for your sins, and God will free you from the wolf in the present, and hell's fire in the future."[10]

Francis's love for nature and God's creatures was never an end in itself. As this story demonstrates, Francis's taming of the wolf becomes an opportunity for him to preach repentance to people more concerned with the bodily harm a wolf can cause than the spiritual harm caused by their own sin. Also, because all creatures reflect the glory of the creator, Francis here uses the wolf to let others see this same glory. His love for nature becomes a sermon to be read by the people so that they too can see in nature a sign that will help them move from visible creation to the creator himself, even as Francis embodies this same movement in his own life. Thus, his life can be seen as a sequence of dramatic gestures that vividly recreated the essence of the Gospel message for the people of his own time. Francis's peacemaking extended beyond humans and wild animals. He helped to make peace between violent factions in Bologna and Siena. In one typically Francis-like dramatic gesture he brought about a reconciliation between secular and ecclesiastical officials in Assisi by writing a song to be sung to them.

Bonaventure takes Francis's great love of God's creatures and portrays it in a language different from Francis's own but intelligible to the learned friars of his day:

Aroused by all things to the love of God, he rejoiced in all the works of the Lord's hands and from these joy-producing manifestations he rose to their life-giving principle and cause. In beautiful things he saw Beauty itself and through his vestiges imprinted on creation he followed his Beloved everywhere, making all things a ladder by which he could climb up and embrace him who is utterly desirable. With a feeling of unprecedented devotion he savored in each and every creature—as in so many rivulets—that Goodness which is their fountain-source. And he perceived a heavenly harmony in the consonance of powers and activities God has given them, and like the prophet David sweetly exhorted them to praise the Lord.[11]

The last line of the text probably refers to the fact that shortly before his death, Francis wrote a poem in Italian—the earliest surviving piece of Italian literature—usually called the "Canticle of the Creatures." In it, Francis the poet shows that his love for all creatures, even "Sister Bodily Death," comes from his understanding of the relation between God and all of his creation. Francis added the second stanza to bring peace to Assisi and composed the third as he lay near death:

Most High, all-powerful, good Lord,
   Yours are the praises, the glory, and the honor, and all blessing,
To You alone, Most High, do they belong,
   and no human is worthy to mention Your name.
Praised be You, my Lord, with all Your creatures,
   especially Sir Brother Sun,
   Who is the day and through whom You give us light.
And he is beautiful and radiant with great splendor;
   And bears a likeness of You, Most High One.
Praised be You, my Lord, through Sister Moon and the stars,
   in heaven You formed them clear and precious and beautiful.
Praised be You, my Lord, through Brother Wind,
   and through the air, cloudy and serene, and every kind of weather,
   through whom You give sustenance to Your creatures.
Praised be You, my Lord, through Sister Water,
   who is very useful and humble and precious and chaste.
Praised be You, my Lord, through Brother Fire,
   through whom You light the night,
   and he is beautiful and playful and robust and strong.
Praised be You, my Lord, through our Sister Mother Earth,
   who sustains and governs us,
   and who produces various fruit with colored flowers and herbs.

Praised be You, my Lord, through those who give pardon for Your love,
   and bear infirmity and tribulation.
     Blessed are those who endure in peace
     for by You, Most High, shall they be crowned.

Praised be You, my Lord, through our Sister Bodily Death,
   from whom no one living can escape.
     Woe to those who die in mortal sin.

Blessed are those whom death will find in Your most holy will,
    for the second death shall do them no harm.

Praise and bless my Lord and give Him thanks
    and serve Him with great humility.[12]

Francis died in his beloved Portiuncula in 1226; he was perhaps the best-loved man in Europe at the time. It was only two years later that he was can-onized by his friend and former protector Pope Gregory IX; in 1230 his relics were placed in the newly begun Basilica of Saint Francis, soon to be adorned with frescoes by Cimabue, Simone Martini, and Pietro Lorenzetti, plus others whose names we do not know—collectively a who's who of late medieval Ital-ian painting. On Francis's last journey, the vicar of the order sent bodyguards with Francis so that if he died, his body could be returned to Assisi, which would then become a center of pilgrimage. The fight for Francis's body and the splendor of his final resting place hardly seem appropriate to the ideals of Francis himself. There was a paradox inherent in his popularity, for in the very act of preserving his legacy for future generations, his followers appeared to do violence to the spirit of his teaching. Soon after his death there was a turning away from a strict interpretation of the rule of 1223, a turning that Francis himself saw the genesis of and strongly opposed. Once again, his very popularity was in some sense responsible. Many were those who were led to follow him; but Francis was surely a unique figure, and there were few who could follow his teaching in all its uncompromising rigor.

The problem of how Francis's followers were to preserve his message re-mained a burning issue in the subsequent generations of Franciscan history, and forms an important chapter in the history of medieval society. The early legends and biographies of Francis made his ideals of poverty and humility clear to all of Europe; yet how his followers were to carry out these ideals was not so clear. The brotherhood that grew up almost spontaneously around Francis had few outward signs of community organization in the beginning. But its growth from a spontaneous brotherhood to a large order was accompanied by a process of institutionalization that changed its outward look in many ways. The absolute poverty that Francis demanded of his followers was to be realized by working or by begging alms from day to day. But this was simply not as practical for thousands as it had been for a dozen eager men. The ideal of poverty had to be balanced against the need for security. In order to further the ideal of humility, Francis insisted that no distinction be made within the order be-tween those who were priests and those who were not. Yet as more and more priests entered the order, it was simply not possible to treat them in exactly the same way as laymen. They needed altars on which to say Mass and litur-gical books with which to say the Divine Office. Francis insisted that his fol-lowers avoid excessive contact with learning, believing that it interfered with both poverty and humility. Yet more and more learned men joined the order. And when Franciscan preaching began to include the correction and conversion of heresy, it became increasingly evident that some accommodation to learning was necessary. So Franciscans found their way to the universities. Were these changes the necessary condition for an organic continuation of the spirit of Francis, or were they a repudiation of his ideals, a total break with the past?

In the thirteenth century, the majority of Franciscans accepted modifications of the absolute poverty, the simplicity, and the nonacademic tone of early Franciscanism; they eventually came to be called Conventual Franciscans. One significant exception to this relaxation of early rigor were the Clares at San Damiano. Thanks to the courage and tenacity of their founder, they maintained both the letter and spirit of poverty which they had received from Francis. Moreover, among the male Franciscans, a small group (who later came to be called the Spirituals) fought all modifications to the original simplicity and absolute poverty that Francis himself had prescribed in the Rule of 1223 and the Testament.

As early as about 1250, some friars of the strict party made use of the writings of the twelfth-century Cistercian abbot, prophet, and apolcalyptic thinker Joachim of Fiore (d.1202) to further their cause. Joachim had divided history into three ages, each age corresponding to one of the persons of the Trinity. He declared that the third and final age, the Age of the Holy Spirit, was to be ushered in by "new spiritual men." A friar named Gerard of Borgo San Donnino took over this Joachite scheme, identifying the new spiritual men with Francis and his followers (that is, with themselves). One of those who became a follower of Gerard was John of Parma, minister general of the order. Like other radical followers of Joachim, they believed that in this Age of the Holy Spirit the institutional Church, which from the beginning had supported modifications of Francis's ideals, would be unnecessary. They believed that the Antichrist was already alive, identifying him first with the Holy Roman Emperor Frederick II and then with several popes who strongly supported the Conventual position. When Bonaventure was elected minister general to replace John of Parma in 1257, one of his chief tasks was to suppress the extreme followers of Joachim within the Franciscan order.

One of the greatest thinkers and writers of the Middle Ages, Bonaventure used his extraordinary talents as a philosopher and theologian to translate the ideals of Francis into a more permanent form. In addition to his *Life of St. Francis*, he wrote such quintessentially Franciscan works as the *Defense of the Mendicants* (his examination of the poverty question) and the *Soul's Journey into God* (a mystical treatise inspired by Francis's reception of the stigmata) as well as many important theological and philosophical works. These writings, together with his codification of Franciscan legislation, earned him the not inappropriate title of "second founder of the Franciscan order." Bonaventure himself was certainly sympathetic with the less extravagant claims of the Spirituals. He too saw Francis as a figure unique in history and somehow identified with apocalyptic expectations (see Chapter 4), identifying him specifically with the Angel of the Sixth Seal from the Book of Revelation. But he was also rigorous in his condemnation of their excesses. Bonaventure died in 1274, but the struggle between the Spirituals and the Conventuals continued and intensified in the 1320s. Pope John XXII condemned the Spirituals, and several prominent adherents were imprisoned. Three Franciscan writers, Peter John Olivi (c.1248–1298), Angelo Clareno (d.c.1323), and Ubertino da Casale (1259–c.1338), among the most important apocalyptic thinkers of the late Middle Ages, were among those who came under suspicion for their Spiritual leanings. Another figure who suffered for his Spiritual leanings was the poet Jacopone da Todi (d.1306), after Francis himself perhaps the greatest poet to wear the Franciscan habit. Imprisoned by Pope Boniface VIII, Jacopone turned that experience into a powerful subject for his poetry, which combined mysticism with papal politics, and autobiography with apocalyptic denunciation. Writing in his Umbrian dialect, he decried the increasingly academic tenor of the order with his famous line, "Paris has destroyed Assisi."

The Franciscan movement influenced all forms of expression. In their attempt to preach the Gospel to the widest possible audience, the Friars greatly extended the techniques of medieval preaching and transformed and vernacularized popular piety, influencing such literary forms as lyric poetry and drama in the process. Their influence on art was if anything even more significant. Cycles of the life of Francis portrayed on walls and panels what the early lives and legends had described in words. Francis's devotion to Christ Crucified and to the humanity of Christ provided a new focus for art; an increased realism in depicting the Crucified Christ developed in the wake of the movement. The Franciscan emphasis on the created universe in all its variety as a road leading the soul to God greatly changed the style of the visual arts. Together with the revival of Aristotle, whose medieval adherents began with sense perception and argued toward God as the cause of creation, it helped fashion the new realism that is one of the marks of the period. The influence of Franciscan spirituality spread far beyond the friars and even the members of the Third Order. Confraternities of lay people were formed, especially but not only in Italian cities. Those who focused on imitating Francis by praising God developed an important form of song called Lauds. Those who sought to imitate Francis's austerity sometimes practiced flagellation. Many others followed Francis's ministry to the poor and outcast, performing countless acts of compassion.

Women as well as men consciously sought ways to imitate Francis, some entering the Third Order and some becoming important penitential figures and mystical writers. Margaret of Cortona (d.1297) and Angela of Foligno (d.1309) are two important mystical figures among the many remarkable female followers of Francis. These two figures, Margaret and Angela, are illustrative of two important trends in the spirituality that begins with the figure of Francis and continues through the late Middle Ages and beyond. Many of the most important mystics of the late Middle Ages were laypeople, which allowed for a more public dimension to mystical experience. It would not be wrong to think of this trend as a kind of democratization of mysticism, possible now because of the change from Latin to the vernacular in religious discourse that Francis and the mendicants did so much to usher in. And a large percentage of these mystics were women. The voices of women, though still suspect in many quarters, gained a measure of authority that they did not have previously because of the fame and authenticity of such important mystical writers as Hadewijch (d. mid-thirteenth century), Mechtild of Magdeburg (d.c.1282–1294), and Julian of Norwich (d.1423).

The Franciscans were not the only new order to be established at this time. A contemporary of Francis's from Spain named Dominic de Guzman founded the other major mendicant order, the Dominicans. Concerned with the Albigensian heresy that was raging in southern France, Dominic went there to attempt to win people back to Roman Catholic orthodoxy. He came to realize that one reason heresy had infected the area was that ignorant clergy were not properly and persuasively preaching the word of God. He decided to found an order of preachers loyal to Rome that would be able to win people back from heresy. The Fourth Lateran Council (1215) had decreed that there would be no more new rules. However, in 1216 Dominic incorporated his preaching order by using one already in existence, the rule of Saint Augustine. Dominic, inspired by the ideals of Francis, also wished his friars to practice individual and collective poverty. Like the Franciscans, the Dominicans grew rapidly. In addition to the preaching for which they were founded (their official name is the Order of Preachers), they later often held positions in the Inquisition.

Unlike the Franciscans, the Dominicans had a need for education from the start because of their function as preachers of doctrine. They desired to study theology at the emerging universities; however, theology was a graduate course to which students were admitted only after completing the arts course, usually about six years. The Dominicans wanted to begin theology directly, without taking the arts course, causing tremendous struggles within the universities between themselves and the secular clergy, especially in Paris. Generally, the Dominicans won and they established their own schools in university cities to prepare members of the order for the study of theology. It is no accident that many of the greatest theologians of the thirteenth century belonged to the Order of Preachers, including Albertus Magnus and most importantly Thomas Aquinas. The Franciscans soon desired similar theological training for themselves; thus, at the universities of Europe in the thirteenth century, one also finds Franciscans such as Roger Bacon and Bonaventure. In fact, the Franciscan Bonaventure and the Dominican Thomas were contemporaries at the University of Paris.

Several other orders were created in the thirteenth century, which to various degrees imitated the basic tenents of the Franciscans and the Dominicans. Carmelites and Augustinians played important roles within Christianity for many centuries. The Augustinian Martin Luther and the Carmelites Theresa of Avila and John of the Cross were more important figures than any Franciscan or Dominican in the sixteenth century. However, the proliferation of orders became a problem and sometimes an embarrassment for the Church. In 1274, several of the new orders were surpressed, and no new orders developed for the remainder of the Middle Ages.

While the Dominican zeal was involved in the elimination of heresy in Western Europe, the Franciscan missionary spirit (recalling that Francis himself had gone to convert Muslims) took friars into North Africa and all the way to China. Franciscans carried out missions to the Mongols, and a Christian community was established in Beijing under a Franciscan archbishop. All the mendicant orders, working primarily in cities, preached, taught, and often operated hospitals, homes for reformed prostitutes, schools, and other charitable enterprises. Because of their popularity, the new orders received many gifts from pious donors and soon became wealthy, which often made them desirous of still more wealth. As the mendicant orders continued to change and to grow away from the ideals of Francis and Dominic, they came under severe attack from several quarters. Stories from Franciscan and Dominican lore, which had very quickly become part of the iconography depicting the ideals of Christianity for the late Middle Ages, were now seen in a new context. Although both orders continued to produce such saints as the Dominican mystical theologian Catherine of Siena (d.1380), and the Franciscan preacher Bernardino of Siena (d.1444), the veneration paid to Francis and Dominic, to Franciscans such as Anthony of Padua, Bonaventure, and Louis of Toulouse, and to Dominicans such as Peter Martyr and Thomas Aquinas, was soon contrasted with the degeneration of later times. An anti-fraternal tradition developed. Poets of the stature of Dante and Chaucer portrayed the decline from original purity to the corruption of their own times. In the *Paradiso*, Dante has the great mendicant theologians Thomas and Bonaventure praise the founders of each other's order, but they lament the degeneracy of their own. Chaucer, likewise, paints a lurid picture of the mendicants of his day in the *Friar's Tale* and the *Summoner's Tale*. Both authors articulated the tension that exists when reformers are in need of reform. It was a tension that continued into the late Middle Ages and beyond.

It would not be an exaggeration to refer to the thirteenth century as the "mendicant century." What had begun as a local movement of humble penitents in the first decades of the century became a set of values and institutions that reshaped the medieval world. In almost every area of thought and experience from ethics to mystical theology to painting to poetry, the friars either made or were the direct inspiration of those who made the most important contributions. Moreover, the world was a bigger place at least as much because of the missionary activities of the friars as because of the travels of Marco Polo. The friars also played a significant role in the shaping of both ecclesiastical and secular institutions. In 1288, a Franciscan was elected as Pope Nicholas IV. One of his achievements was to repair the cathedral of Rome, Saint John Lateran, thus literally bringing about the vision that Pope Innocent III had at the beginning of the century in his dream of Francis supporting that very building when it was in danger of collapse. King Louis IX of France, Saint Louis, was probably a member of the Third Order and certainly a lover of the mendicants. He invited the poor to dine with him regularly, and also included Thomas Aquinas as one of his frequent guests. In 1298, the heir to the crown of Sicily renounced his title and entered the Franciscan Order. Within a few years of his death, he became the highly venerated Saint Louis of Toulouse (better known in the United States by the Spanish version of his name, San Luis Obispo).

Even after the "mendicant century" ended, the new orders remained in the forefront of developments in late medieval society and beyond. Historians who study medieval wills have shown how laypeople continued to patronize the mendicant orders for centuries. In Florence, for example, Cosimo de' Medici (d.1464) sponsored the building of a new Dominican house, San Marco, which is still one of the great repositories of art there. Girolomo Savonarola, whose prophetic denunciations of secular folly and clerical corruption led to his burning in the main square of Florence, was a Dominican preacher. It was even a mendicant, the Augustinian Martin Luther, who ushered in the Protestant Reformation.

CHAPTER 11

THE FOURTEENTH CENTURY

The medieval synthesis of the thirteenth century symbolized by the *Summa* of Thomas Aquinas and the Gothic cathedrals of northern France has seemed to many the apex of medieval achievement. Some medievalists have even gone so far as to refer to the thirteenth as the greatest of centuries. By contrast, it was followed by what one writer has called "the calamitous fourteenth century," the most calamitous features of which are the Hundred Years War fought between England and France and the Black Death. Yet the fourteenth century was also clearly a period of great achievements, producing the most important vernacular writers of the Middle Ages, Dante (d.1321) and Chaucer (d.1400), as well as pictorial artists such as Duccio (d.1319) and Giotto (d.1337), now regarded among the greatest in European history. To add to the difficulty of trying to categorize the period, the most famous Italian writers of the second half of the fourteenth century, Petrarch (d.1374) and Boccaccio (d.1375), are more often associated with the Renaissance than the Middle Ages. So another label is often added to the fourteenth century: an age of transition. In this chapter, we will attempt to sort out some of the confusion associated with the fourteenth century, by demonstrating the value and the limits of these labels, by discussing achievements as well as calamities, and by showing continuity as well as transition.

It is important to remember that the numerical markers that define time periods are by their nature arbitrary and artificial. For example, let us take the concept of "the Sixties" in American history. In terms of the cultural markers that define the period, 1972 was much more "the Sixties" than 1962 was. The same is true with the fourteenth century in that no real boundary was crossed when 1299 became 1300 or 1399 became 1400. Furthermore, to return to our analogy, not every place in America became part of "the Sixties" at the same time. Defining the term by the same cultural markers, it was "the Sixties" in Berkeley long before it was "the Sixties" in rural Indiana. So too do scholars generally agree that there were cultural currents developing in Italy before they became widely known or accepted in northern Europe. The "Renaissance" Italian authors Petrarch and Boccaccio wrote their works before the "medieval" English author Chaucer. We must also keep in mind that definitions are not universal. Not everyone means the same thing when referring to "the Sixties," to the Renaissance, or to the Middle Ages, for that matter. Furthermore, the way people define the changes that took place in "the Sixties" depends on how they understand the characteristics of "the Fifties." Similarly, definitions of the Renaissance vary in part because those doing the defining have different ideas about the Middle Ages.

Our plan in this chapter is to examine aspects of church, state, and society in the fourteenth century as previous chapters have done for earlier periods, suggesting in our analysis areas of both continuity and change. Then we will look at the cultural developments that are beginning to challenge at least some elements of the medieval world view, though once again with an eye to both change and continuity.

Although there were dramatic and to some extent unprecedented events that occurred in the institutional Church in the fourteenth century, they were in significant ways continuations of problems and conflicts that had existed for centuries. Beginning in 1305, the papacy relocated from Rome to Avignon, in southern France. Although nothing quite like this had happened before, it was in fact the playing out of another chapter in the crisis of Church and State that we examined as far back as the time of the Investiture Contest in the eleventh century. In particular, the so-called Babylonian Captivity of the papacy described in Chapter 8 was the aftermath of the conflict between the French monarchy and Pope Boniface VIII at the end of the thirteenth century. Although many factors contributed to Gregory XI's decision to return to Rome in 1377, one of them was the powerful and public call of two female mystics, Bridget of Sweden and Catherine of Siena. Catherine, in modern times the first woman to be named a Doctor of the Church, made her plea to the pope in person in Avignon and later became an important supporter of Gregory's successor, Urban VI. Catherine was not afraid to criticize the pope for his tepid behavior and toleration of corruption in the Church, as illustrated in this passage from a letter she wrote to Gregory:

> If till now you haven't been very firm in truth, I want you, I beg you, for the little time that is left, to be so—courageously and like a brave man, following Christ, whose vicar you are. And don't be afraid, father, no matter what may happen, of these blustery winds that have descended upon you—I mean those rotten members [of the body of Christ] who have rebelled against you. Don't be afraid, for divine help is near. Just attend to spiritual affairs, to appointing good pastors and administrators in your cities, for you have experienced rebellion because of bad pastors and administrators.[1]

Another dramatic and disturbing event in the history of the institutional Church was the Great Schism. Beginning in 1378 and continuing for the next forty years, there were two and sometimes even three claimants to the papal

Palace of the Popes. Avignon, France. Fourteenth century. The palace built for the popes during the seventy-two-year stay of the papacy in Avignon is testimony to their wealth and power. It is the largest palace that survives from the Middle Ages.

office. However, political groups supporting different papal claimants was hardly a new phenomenon. During the conflict between papacy and the Holy Roman Emperors in the eleventh and twelfth centuries, the emperors Henry IV and Frederick I (Barbarossa) had their "own" popes. Of course, the schism of the fourteenth and early fifteenth centuries lasted longer, with the major political entities choosing sides, and the loss of confidence in the institutional Church was probably correspondingly greater. Nevertheless, the nature of the conflict between the rival claimants in Avignon and Rome was rooted in the fact that the papal office was both spiritual and secular, and that was hardly new.

The schism was settled by an ecumenical council, the Council of Constance (1414–1418). In its work, the council made some startling proposals for the future governance of the Church, one of which was that councils should meet every ten years and thus have a regular "constitutional" role. Yet a church council was a traditional way of resolving disputes in the Church, beginning with Nicaea in 325, and of announcing bold reforms, such as occurred at the Fourth Lateran Council of 1215. Furthermore, many of those bold reforms advanced at Constance were formulated from ideas that had developed in the writings of the great canon lawyers of the twelfth century in their commentaries on Gratian's *Decretum*.

Important heresies developed in the fourteenth and early fifteenth centuries. At the risk of oversimplifying, we can divide the older medieval heresies into two groups—scholarly and popular. Thus, for example, Eucharistic heresies of the eleventh century were essentially confined to academic discourse, while the Waldensian and Albigensian heresies encompassed large numbers of people, many of whom had little or no understanding of church doctrine. By contrast, the most important heretical movements of the late Middle Ages often combined these two sorts of heretical movements, making them stronger and more threatening to the Church and, especially when combined with the effects of war and plague mentioned above, creating a sense of crisis that led many authors to speak of the times with apocalyptic urgency. Although John Wyclif (d.1384) was essentially a scholar, the Lollard movement that developed after his death produced both learned treatises at Oxford and popular movements in London and other parts of England that threatened both orthodoxy and social stability. One important element of the Lollard movement was its support of female literacy and preaching, something the ecclesiastical hierarchy increasingly suspected was heretical in and of itself. Wyclif challenged church doctrine by rejecting transubstantiation and the prevailing structure of church government by rejecting the bases of papal supremacy. Even more significant was the Hus-

Bethlehem Chapel. Prague, Czech Republic. Beginning of the fifteenth century (largely reconstructed). The Hussite movement began as a program of moral and spiritual reform in Prague, center of the Kingdom of Bohemia. The Bethlehem Chapel was built for preaching, and the young scholar John Hus became well known for his reform sermons preached there.

site movement in Bohemia. John Hus was both an academic at Charles University in Prague and a vernacular preacher who called for moral reform. He borrowed from the writings of Wyclif, especially applying his criticisms of papal authority in the era of the Great Schism. Following Hus's execution at the Council of Constance in 1415, primarily on the trumped-up charge that he accepted Wyclif's heretical eucharistic theology, there was a rebellion in Bohemia against both king and Church. The Church responded by calling a series of Crusades against the Hussites, but they all failed. The precedent for this had been set as early as 1209, when Innocent III called a Crusade against the Albigensian heretics in France. With the failure of the Crusades, the Church agreed to listen to the Hussites' arguments in 1433 at the Council of Basel, but agreements that were reached there were never carried out. In some ways, the Hussite movement was a precursor of Martin Luther's challenge to the Church a century later. Luther knew Hussite history and teachings and learned from both.

The political map of Europe did not change a great deal in the late Middle Ages. Where developing monarchies existed at the beginning of the fourteenth century, they continued to develop. Despite wars and dynastic struggles, England, France, Aragon, Castile, Naples, Sicily, and some smaller national monarchies existed and continued to be prominent beyond the medieval period, though certainly the Kingdom of Sicily, ruled by a Spanish dynasty from the end of the thirteenth century, became less important politically, economically, and culturally in the late Middle Ages. In was in the second half of the fifteenth century that the monarchies of Aragon and Castile merged, forming the nation of Spain.

While some nations in existence today were developing in Europe in the Middle Ages, others were not. Germany was the heart of the Holy Roman Empire since Otto I redefined it in the tenth century and Frederick Barbarossa largely surrendered rule over northern Italy in the twelfth. However, Germany was hardly developing into a nation. There were literally hundreds of jurisdictions in Germany; and although several lords, both secular and ecclesiastical, emerged as major political powers within the Empire, they were constantly working to protect their autonomy rather than developing anything resembling a viable imperial government.

Despite the fact that the Holy Roman Empire's direct rule over northern Italy was essentially over after the battle of Legnano in 1176, emperors in the thirteenth and fourteenth centuries and beyond still dreamed, sometimes planned, and even occasionally acted to take back control. In 1310, for example, Henry VII brought an army to Italy. Although he had some allies, and some success in this venture, his death in 1313 brought an end to any real hope for imperial rule in Italy. One of Henry's supporters was Dante, by that time an exile from Florence. In his treatise on politics, *On World Government*, Dante wrote a defense of world government headed by the Holy Roman Empire, and in the *Divine Comedy* he saved a throne for Henry in Paradise.

The Italian peninsula was also a patchwork of political jurisdictions in the late Middle Ages. Like Germany, Italy would wait until the nineteenth century for nationhood despite Dante's call for uniting this piece of land "surrounded by a moat and a wall"—the Mediterranean and the Alps. In very rough terms, Italy was divided into three parts. The northern third of Italy was divided into sovereign city-states. Some, such as Pisa and Siena, which had earlier emerged as great powers in Italy, were already in political decline by the beginning of the fourteenth century. Eventually, Milan, Florence, and Venice emerged as the "superpowers" of the region. Central Italy was governed by the popes, although some areas within the papal states were able to act more or less independently of the pontiff. Moreover, papal absence from Rome for most of the fourteenth century, followed by the Great Schism, made it difficult for the pope to rule his Italian lands effectively. Nevertheless, the papacy was always a major player in the political developments of Italy. The southern third of Italy was a monarchy centered in Naples and, in the fourteenth century, ruled by a French dynasty. This kingdom was far less urban than northern Italy; although an important political force on the peninsula, it was less in the forefront culturally and economically, especially after the middle of the fourteenth century.

The dominant military conflict of the late Middle Ages was the so-called Hundred Years War, fought between England and France. Although this label is an umbrella that covers three separate wars fought in the fourteenth and fifteenth centuries (1337–1360, 1369–1396, 1414–1453), it is best seen as part of a larger conflict that can be traced back to the Norman Conquest of England in 1066. After William the Conqueror, Duke of Normandy, was crowned king of England, English kings were sovereigns of England in their own right while at the same time vassals to the king of France for Normandy. In the twelfth century, English kings were also vassals of the French kings for other parts of western France, including Anjou and Aquitaine. During the reign of the French king Philip Augustus (1180–1223), there were attempts to straighten out all of this mess. Indeed, before the end of the thirteenth century the English had effective rule only over a fairly small portion of southwestern France. Although there were immediate causes of the Hundred Years War, the big picture is that this series of conflicts was about the French kings' desire to rid France of English territorial claims of any kind and the English kings' attempt to maintain and expand their power base there.

It was not only the issues of the war that were old: it has often been said that the Hundred Years War was the last to be fought by the "old rules," the rules of chivalry, the code of conduct that had developed in the feudal society of earlier centuries. Of course, chivalry was never a precise set of rules for the feudal aristocracy, but was rather an idealized code of conduct that always fell short in practice. The war's principal historian was Jean Froissart, a Frenchman who supported the English cause (d.c.1410); he wrote about the war to a large extent in terms of the chivalric code. For example, he concluded that at the Battle of Poitiers in 1356 had died the "finest flower of French chivalry." Nor was Froissart without reason in seeing the struggle between England and France as a chivalrous war. At Poitiers, King John of France was taken captive. Hostages were held in England until ransom was paid. When one of John's hostages escaped, John surrendered, went to England, and in fact died there.

King Edward III ruled England during the first forty years of the Hundred Years War. His sense of chivalry is well captured in Froissart's description of the establishment of the Order of the Garter.

> At that time [1344] King Edward of England conceived the idea of altering and rebuilding the great castle of Windsor, originally built by King Arthur, and where had first been established the noble Round Table, from which so many fine men and brave knights had gone forth and performed great deeds throughout the world. King Edward's intention was to found an order of knights, made up of himself and his sons and the bravest and noblest in England and other countries too. There would be forty of them in all and they would be called the Knights of the Blue Garter and their feast was to be held every year at Windsor on St. George's day. To institute the feast, the King called together the earls, barons, and knights of the whole country and told them of his intentions and of his great desire to see them carried out. They agreed with him wholeheartedly, because they thought it an honorable undertaking and one which would strengthen the bonds of friendship among them.[2]

This passage is a good indication that at least the ideal of chivalry was alive and well not only when the event occurred but when Froissart composed it about a half century later. Writers of the period also noted the failure to live up to the ideal. Partly because of an obvious desire for economic gain on the part of English knights, there were observers during the time of the Hundred Years War who decried the lack of chivalric conduct on the part of members of the knightly aristocracy, who after all were privileged in law at least in part because it was their job to be protectors of everyone. One of these was Geoffrey Chaucer. At the beginning of the *General Prologue* to *The Canterbury Tales*, he pointedly contrasts the old and the new, the ideal of chivalry depicted in his portrait of the Knight and the lack of chivalry depicted in his son, the Squire.

The Hundred Years War produced the most famous female saint of the Middle Ages, Joan of Arc (although she was not formally canonized until the twentieth century). A peasant girl endowed with extraordinary courage and seized with a desire to free all France from English occupation, she played a significant role in turning the war around in France during a period of English occupation of a good deal of northern France, including Paris. Captured by the English, she was convicted of heresy in a trial that was obviously political. She was executed in 1431 and immediately considered a martyr by the French.

Another important woman during the period of the Hundred Years War was the writer Christine de Pizan (1365–c.1430). Perceived as a major literary figure only recently, Christine wrote on a wide variety of topics, including warfare. However Christine described warfare not from the point of view of the knights fighting pitched battles, but from the "home front" where crops had to be planted and harvested, workers had to be attended to, and homes had to be defended. Although an aristocratic woman who largely accepted the social structures of her society, she is an incisive commentator on a part of reality that male writers ignored. In the following passage, she describes the role of the wife of an important noble. Even in time of peace, he will be away a great deal, but that situation will be exacerbated during prolonged conflicts. Here are some samples of her advice:

> Now his [a baron's] lady and companion stays behind and she must take his place. Although there may be enough bailiffs, provosts, administrators and governors, there has to be someone in charge of them all, and therefore it is proper that she should take on this responsibility. She should conduct herself with such skill that she may be feared as well as loved. . . . She should be well informed and apprised of the legal aspects and local customs. . . . We have also said that she should have the heart of a man, that is, she ought to know how to use weapons and be familiar with everything that pertains to them, so that she may be ready to command her men if the need arises. She should know how to launch an attack or defend against one, if the situation calls for it. She should take care that her fortresses are well garrisoned. . . . She should devote some thought to how she will be able to provide for the household until her husband comes back, and what financial measure she has and can find in order to do this.[3]

How often women were in a position to act as Christine counseled is not known, but her writing allows us to view society from a quite distinct point of view and thus to ask questions and pursue issues that are easy to ignore when reading works such as Froissart's *Chronicles.*

Christine was one of the most versatile writers of the later Middle Ages, male or female. She translated and made additions to one of the most widely read treatises on warfare, creatively combining classical and medieval sources. She wrote a conduct manual for women of all classes and vocations. She wrote a life of Joan of Arc. And in the *Book of the City of Ladies* she constructed an allegorical edifice—drawing inspiration from Dante—in which she directly confronted the antifeminism of her culture both through argument and by presenting exemplars of female virtue throughout history.

Sometimes scholars view late medieval thought, especially in the areas of philosophy and theology, as rather sterile and uncreative. This reputation is in no small measure due to the scorn that some humanists and religious reformers writing in the sixteenth century had for late medieval thought. Erasmus criticized scholastic theology generally and later scholastic writers in particular for their triviality. In part based on his searing criticism, later scholars often wrote off late medieval philosophy as much ado about nothing. "How many angels can dance on the head of a pin" has become an emblem of the silliness and self-indulgence of late medieval schoolmen. In a famous passage from his *Praise of Folly* (1511), Erasmus mocks the scholastics of his own day.

> In addition, they [scholastics] interpret hidden mysteries to suit themselves: how the world was created and designed; through what channels the stain of sin filtered down to posterity; by what means, in what measure, and how long Christ was formed in the Virgin's womb; how, in the Eucharist, accidents can subsist without a domicile. But this sort of question has been discussed threadbare. There are others more worthy of great and enlightened theologians (as they call themselves) which can really rouse them to action if they come their way. What was the exact moment of divine generation? Are there several filiations in Christ? Is it a possible proposition that God the Father could hate his Son? Could God have taken on the form of a woman, a devil, a donkey, a gourd, or a flintstone? If so, how could a gourd have preached sermons, performed miracles, and been nailed to the cross? And what would Peter have consecrated if he had consecrated when the body of Christ still hung on the cross? Furthermore, at that same time, could Christ have been called a man? Shall we be permitted to eat and drink after the resurrection? We're taking due precaution against hunger and thirst while there's time.[4]

Although Erasmus has gleefully put his finger on one tendency of scholastic practice, we need to realize that while he is exaggerating some developments at the universities, he is ignoring others. While it is true that scholastic theology did sometimes become a game of clever argument that was often divorced from leading Christians toward salvation, its adherents also addressed many serious issues. Furthermore, we often discover and explicate important principles by examining extreme cases through a *reductio ad absurdum*. In the twelfth century, for example, canon lawyers used the seemingly silly question, "What if the pope fornicated publicly on the altar of St. Peter's?" as a way of struggling with the nature of papal power and the possible recourses of the Church if the pope should fall into grave sin or heresy.

As with the humanists, so too with the great Protestant reformers. Martin Luther, for example, rejects much of Thomas Aquinas's work and *a fortiori* the work of later and lesser theologians whose writings start with Thomistic premises. Luther objected not only to the methodology of the scholastics but also to their extensive reliance on Aristotle. In writing about university reform in 1520, he stated:

> [L]ittle is taught of the Holy Scripture or the Christian faith; the blind pagan teacher, Aristotle, is of more consequence than Christ. . . . In his book, *On*

the Soul, which is one of his best, the wretched fellow [Aristotle] teaches that the soul dies with the body; and many have tried, in vain, to defend him. It is as if we did not possess the Holy Scriptures where we find a superabundance of teaching on the whole subject, of which Aristotle has not the faintest inkling. Yet this defunct pagan has attained supremacy. . . . On the same principles, his book on *Ethics* is worse than any other book, being the direct opposite of God's grace, and the Christian virtues; yet it is accounted among the best of his books.[5]

Later the same year, Luther referred to current Catholic teaching as those of the "Thomist or Aristotelian Church." Once again, there is truth to Luther's critique of scholastic thought, but it is a partial truth. Thomas Aquinas (and many who were deeply influenced by him) certainly did make extensive use of Aristotle, but Thomas made more extensive use of the Bible and the biblical tradition, and of earlier Christian thinkers such as Augustine. Those Aristotelian thinkers whose work ignored the biblical tradition were few and their teachings declared heretical. Luther and others speak as if every theologian and church official after Thomas Aquinas was anchored in Thomistic theology, but that does not do justice to the variety of theological and philosophical thought in the fourteenth and fifteenth centuries, a period when serious alternatives were developed. It is ironic that the position of preeminence that Thomistic thought holds among Catholics began only after the Council of Trent (1545–1563), where it was seen as the most potent theology to counter Luther and the other reform traditions. That position was later solidified in the Thomist revival of the nineteenth and twentieth centuries.

Because in later centuries, especially after the Protestant Reformation, Catholic thought is frequently equated with Thomist thought, people often read this dominance back to the time of Thomas himself and assume that the moment he put his pen down, the Catholic world immediately proclaimed his superiority as a thinker. However, that was not the case. For one thing, the criticisms that humanists and reformers in the sixteenth century leveled at Thomas had been made with equal vehemence at the University of Paris in the 1250s by some of Thomas's own contemporaries (see Chapter 9).

Although his greatness was recognized soon after his death—one should note his importance as a spokesman in Dante's *Paradiso* and his canonization in 1323—he was still only one of several preeminent thinkers or, perhaps more accurately, the great representative of *one* of the major schools of thought at the time. One could make the argument that Bonaventure—who died the same year as Thomas and is an equally prominent presence in the *Paradiso*—was of similar importance and influence. And the approaches to truth of these two great mendicant theologians, Thomas the Dominican and Bonaventure the Franciscan, were not the only ones.

The theological pluralism that characterizes the thirteenth century is even more pronounced in the fourteenth. Thomas and Bonaventure were both philosophical realists who were deeply reliant, though in somewhat different ways, on both Aristotle and Augustine. In the fourteenth century there were thinkers who operated within this framework. There were also thinkers, John Wyclif being a prime example, who took an extreme realist position philosophically, though they were hardly disciples of Aquinas or Bonaventure. And there were those who rejected the realist framework altogether: the Nominalists, a school that included William of Ockham (d.1350) and several other important thinkers of the fourteenth century. Starting with the belief that only individual things are real will lead one quite far from Thomas Aquinas. In the passage from the *Summa* quoted in Chapter 9, Thomas argues that one can know about God by beginning with sense perception; in fact, this is the necessary beginning in the quest for knowledge of God. Although that position contributed to a more careful examination of the physical world, there were important consequences deriving from the assumption that the examination of the physical world was subsumed within a theological goal: the examination of the physical world was the means to an end—knowledge of God. Thus, it was theology that determined both the methods and the goals of the study of material reality.

Nominalists argued that such a "leap" from knowledge of the material world to knowledge of God was not possible. Knowing God was not a matter of investigating God's vestiges in creation. One long-term consequence of the Nominalist challenge to the realism of Thomas and others was the examination of the physical world as an autonomous activity and not as subordinate to theology. If the goals of such inquiry were limited to knowledge about physical reality, then the rules for investigation need no longer be dictated by the goals of theology. Of course, it took quite a long time for all the implications of this claim to become dominant in Western culture in the form of the scientific revolution; the Realists, after all, did not concede the field to these Nominalist claims. The clash between these two views of methods and goals ontinued through the scientific revolution of the seventeenth century. Galileo's difficulties when he argued for a heliocentric rather than a geocentric universe had as much to do with what constitutes proper methodology as with his conclusions.

A different emphasis on the material world was paralleled by a different emphasis on the qualities of God. Nominalist thinkers were concerned with preserving the absolute power and freedom of God. They believed that God could not be "figured out" in the way that some earlier philosophers had attempted. Anselm, for example, wrote a book explaining the logic of the Incarnation, the logic behind God's becoming human to save humankind. Nominalists claimed that God could have saved humans any way that God desired. We cannot, they argued, limit God's activities to what is logical for humans. One consequence of this line of thought was to emphasize God saving humankind rather than humans striving to please God. God can save anyone, independent of a person's actions. Theology must start with what God had done, as known through revelation, rather than what God ought to do or reasonably should do.

As in so many other areas of thought and endeavor in the fourteenth and fifteenth centuries, philosophy and theology contained a good deal that was innovative, but also much that was traditional in both method and content. There were, as we have suggested, important philosophers in the fifteenth century and beyond who can best be described as scholastic and specifically Thomist thinkers. Equally important, many of the humanists of the Renaissance who rebelled against and made fun of scholastic thought and thinkers were also, more than they realized or were willing to admit, rooted in the achievements of medieval thought.

One of the events that is often highlighted as responsible for the end of the Middle Ages is the calamity known as the Black Death. Many contemporary descriptions of the suffering and death caused by the Black Death appear to describe the symptoms of bubonic plague, although there are modern scholars who doubt that the plague was solely or even primarily responsible for this demographic disaster. Exactly how many people died is far from certain, but the common assertion that about one-third of Europe's population died in a two- to three-year period is probably as close as we can get. The Black Death did not take its toll equally in all parts of Europe, but its total effect on every aspect of European life is certainly undeniable. The plague remained a part of life in Europe for more than three centuries; and although its later manifestations were less widespread and less virulent, it kept populations relatively low and kept people invoking God and the saints to spare them from it.

This was not the first time that disease had a major impact on Europe's history. As early as the end of the second century C.E. there was a decline in the population of the Roman Empire from which it never recovered. In recent studies, the decline in population is often listed among the major causes for the fall of the Roman Empire in the West in the fifth century (see Chapter 5). Furthermore, the bubonic plague arrived in Western Europe in the sixth century and further reduced the population. Historians have probably underestimated the effects that this first attack of bubonic plague had on European society because of a lack of sources. Beginning in the eleventh century, however, Europe's population began to rise quite rapidly. By 1300 there was probably more land under cultivation in Western Europe than there is today. The horrendous effects of famine in the early fourteenth century in Northern Europe are a reminder of the dangers of Europe's high population.

Some of the early responses to the Black Death are typical of medieval responses to crises. A common explanation for the great devastation was that God was punishing people because of their sins. In parts of Europe, there developed movements of flagellants, people who were trying through their sometimes grotesque self-inflicted wounds to persuade God to withdraw this pun-

Image of Death Riding a Horse. Church of the Sacro Speco, Subiaco, Italy. Second half of the fourteenth century. Artists created many new images, often quite grotesque, to explain and contextualize the Black Death. Certain saints who were believed to be powerful advocates in heaven against the bubonic plague became enormously popular. The image of Saint Sebastian in Chapter 4 is probably meant at least in part to encourage prayers to the most important saintly intercessor against the disease.

ishment. However, flagellation as a penitential act was already well established in Europe, especially after the eleventh century. In the latter part of the thirteenth century, numerous penitential confraternities that practiced ritual flagellation, usually under the sponsorship of the mendicant orders, became commonplace in European cities.

Another response to the grave situation was to blame "out" or marginal groups. In particular, fingers were pointed at the Jews, who were sometimes accused of poisoning the wells. Since the Jews relied on the same wells as Christians did, it is easy to see the patent absurdity of such a claim. However, the theory of a Jewish conspiracy was believed to provide some explanation for an otherwise inexplicable phenomenon. The Jews were of course already under considerable suspicion since they were generally regarded as collectively responsible for the death of Christ. As a consequence, they were distrusted, persecuted, and expelled from communities and countries for centuries. As we have already seen, there were attacks on Jews at the time of the First Crusade.

University faculties weighed in on the causes of the Black Death. Following from the medieval notion that medicine first and foremost is a theoretical science, explanations focused on the positions of the planets and the resulting mixture of corrupt vapors in the air and the imbalance of humors in the body. The medieval conviction that the universe was an integrated system with corresponding parts that affected one another helped people find order in a chaotic-appearing universe. However, some of the consequences of this disease and its continued presence in Europe led to challenges to accepted understandings. Pope Clement VI specifically forbade persecution of the Jews, although his decrees were not particularly effective. After the middle of the fourteenth century, changes occurred in the practice of medicine and health care. Since quite a few people survived this disease, hospitals gradually evolved into places to seek treatment rather than simply places to die. Furthermore, rather than relying totally on theoretical models derived from Greek and Arabic textbooks, doctors also began to rely on the findings of experimental medicine.

In the decades following the Black Death there was serious political unrest in Europe, the most significant examples of which were the Jacquerie in Paris (1356), the Ciompi revolt in Florence (1378), and the Peasants' Revolt in England (1381). Although each event has its own specific causes, in some general way they all are rooted in the social confusion and unrest caused by the plague. Economic and social relations were seriously disrupted. For example, England enacted *maximum* wage laws because the relationship of the demand to the supply of labor had changed so radically. Certain social "givens" in the society were challenged. The feudal nobility claimed a set of economic, social, and legal privileges. However, the combination of the Black Death and the ongoing debilitating war between England and France raised questions about the necessity and the justification of such privileges. Even traditional sources could be used to justify new ways of looking at social relations. Turning to Genesis, some of those in the Peasants' Revolt used as their slogan: "When Adam delved and Eve span, who was then the gentleman?" When Adam and Eve were expelled from the Garden of Eden, the argument goes, they were required to dig and to spin. Since they are the ancestors of us all, why do some of their "children" today never have to dig or spin, but rather live off the digging and spinning of others, their fellow descendents?

Important as the dislocation and unrest caused by the Black Death undoubtedly was, it was not the only cause for the questioning of traditional social thought that is one of the characteristics of the period. The rise of cities, which had begun centuries before the plague, eventually led to a challenge of the threefold division of an essentially agricultural society into those who prayed, those who fought, and those who worked. Where, for example, were the great merchants and bankers in this scheme? They were not part of the feudal aristocracy, yet they were not much like laborers either. One reason that writers such as Chaucer and Dante are so concerned with social structures is that they were both urban middle-class men who did not quite "fit" into traditional categories. The disruptions that were the result of the Black Death certainly exacerbated and expanded challenges to traditional modes of social organization and were a stimulus to new ways of thinking about social categories.

There is virtually unanimous agreement among scholars that something happened in Italy in the fourteenth century that challenged medieval precepts, institutions, and aesthetic sensibilities. The changes brought about by these challenges, when solidified in the fifteenth century, have come to be known by the name *Renaissance*. To make the case for these changes, it is certainly possible to draw dramatic contrasts between ideas and art forms from 1300 and from 1500. A Botticelli (d.1510) Madonna is quite different from a Madonna painted two hundred years earlier by Cimabue (d.1302). And Machiavelli's political thought is quite different from that of his fellow Florentine Dante two hundred years earlier. Such comparisons can be misleading, however. A Cimabue Madonna is likewise quite different from one made in 1100. And the papacy under Sylvester II in 1000 was quite a different institution than under Innocent III two hundred years later. Yet despite these differences, everyone agrees that the eleventh and the thirteenth were both medieval centuries.

Right: Virgin Mary. Cimabue. Uffizi, Florence. Late thirteenth century. Left: Virgin Mary. Sandro Botticelli. Uffizi, Florence. Late fifteenth century. These two Florentine paintings, created about two centuries apart, show the stylistic development in Italian painting that is often referred to as the movement from the Middle Ages to the Renaissance. Nevertheless, paintings of the Virgin were as popular during the Renaissance as they were in the Middle Ages, thus reminding us that there is also deep continuity between these two stylistically different periods.

The Renaissance as an intellectual movement was rather narrowly based both socially and in terms of its centers in certain northern Italian cities. Today, people often assume that everyone in Europe or at least in places such as Florence was admiring the work of Leonardo da Vinci and Michelangelo and engaging classical texts, or at least that they were a little cleaner and more "civilized" than their forebears. However, workers, peasants, and all but aristocratic women during the period we call the Renaissance were not significantly different than their medieval counterparts.

Though there are few people who still openly view the Renaissance as the reemergence of civilization in Europe after a thousand years of barbarism and superstition, the argument to that effect which Jacob Burckhardt elegantly made in his 1860 book *The Civilization of the Renaissance in Italy* still subtly casts its long shadow over our understanding of the Middle Ages.[6] Just to cite one element of his thesis, he claimed that people in the Middle Ages were unable to conceive of themselves as individuals but were subsumed into various collective identities. It was the Italian Renaissance, according to Burckhardt, that discovered and honored the individual. But as we have already argued in Chapter 9, "the rise of the individual" is at least as much a product of the twelfth century as it was of the fifteenth.[7] Moreover, Burckhardt overlooks the degree to which communal values likewise underpin the Renaissance, especially when compared to Enlightenment and post-Enlightenment thought and practice. In the Renaissance, individuals were embedded in communities essentially, not accidentally.

Medieval scholars have challenged other traditional markers for the Renaissance. The Renaissance has often been seen as *the* time of recovery of classical texts. No doubt there were significant discoveries. However, many have inferred from this that classical texts were either largely ignored, or that there were no major discoveries of classical texts in the Middle Ages. Both of these inferences are patently false, as we have shown in detail in our chapters on the Classical Heritage and on the Renaissance of the Twelfth Century. From the reliance on Roman poets in early monastic schools to the rediscovery of Aristotle in the twelfth and thirteenth century to Dante's reliance on Virgil at the beginning of the fourteenth, the Middle Ages was dependent throughout on the texts of classical culture.

If we assume the newness of the Renaissance, then it will of course be new. But we have tended to believe a story told by people who, for whatever reasons, wanted to emphasize its newness and who therefore played down, or perhaps did not see, the much greater degree of continuity. This not only distorts what comes before, but it also misinforms us of the nature of the change. In Burckhardt's reading, for example, the Holy Roman Emperor Frederick II (d.1250) is seen as a man of the Renaissance before his time. For Burckhardt, implicitly assuming that anything good about the Middle Ages must be an anticipation of the Renaissance, Frederick becomes an exception to his generalizations about the Middle Ages (and about the Renaissance). Rather than seeing Frederick as Burckhardt does, as a kind of enlightened time traveler, however, it is far more logical to see him as an example of continuity between the periods, since much that Burckhardt sees as new is already implied in the old.

Developments that took place in Italy in the fourteenth century with respect to the texts of classical antiquity provide a way of discussing what was new and what was continuous with the medieval world. A good starting point is Dante's *Divine Comedy*. When Dante the poet visits Limbo, he meets the five greatest poets of all time. All were classical writers, four Latin poets plus the Greek Homer, who is ranked there as the greatest of them all. However, as we have already seen in Chapter 2, although he knew the poet's reputation and the basic stories of the *Iliad* and the *Odyssey*, Dante had never read Homer. The pilgrim is also introduced here to Plato. Plato's *Timaeus*, which was available in a Latin translation, is mentioned by name in the *Paradiso*, and is a text of fundamental importance there. But Dante had not read the *Republic* or the *Symposium* or the *Apology*. Nor had he read such Greek authors as Sophocles, or Thucydides, or Plutarch. During the fourteenth century, the process of recovering these and other Greek texts began in Italy, and this was a significant change. Like Dante, who makes the case for Homer, and like Thomas Aquinas, who recognized the centrality of Aristotle, scholars of the fourteenth century did not need to be convinced of the greatness or the usefulness of the Greeks. Thus, the recovery of Greek literature and philosophy that was taking place in Italy in the fourteenth century was both a continuation of the medieval search for wisdom and an introduction of new texts and new ideas that would significantly advance and expand Western thought.

A good example to use in trying to locate the nature of the change is the Latin writer Cicero. We have seen how medieval writers used Cicero's *Dream of Scipio* as a means of emphasizing the immortality of the soul and how virtue in this life will be rewarded by a heavenly vision. We have seen how Augustine used Cicero in book three of his *Confessions* when he explained that reading his work *Hortensius* had begun the process of turning Augustine toward the love of wisdom that was ultimately to lead to God—a God that Cicero of course knew nothing of. We have seen how the twelfth-century Cistercian monk Aelred of Rievaulx reworked Cicero's treatise *On Friendship* to deal with monastic ideals of friendship. To these examples, we could add Dante, who goes to a story in *On Friendship* to find a character to illustrate the sin of flattery in circle eight of the *Inferno*. Or we could point to medieval manuscript illuminations of Cicero in a monk's garb, suggesting him as a model of the contemplative life. We have insisted that all of these are legitimate uses of the texts. But none of these writers was reluctant to use Cicero for primarily un-Ciceronian ends.

Beginning in the fourteenth century in Italy, Cicero was more likely to be used in ways that were closer to his own agenda. Some used him as a guide to living well in this world, for example as a guide for making and nurturing friendships. But Cicero offered so much more. He was a master of persuasive speech in a republic where being able to speak well was a means to power and influence. He was a "philosopher" and an active politician and thus came more and more to be seen as someone who was able to balance the active and the contemplative life. As a lover and defender of the Roman republic, his writings were perceived to be directly applicable to the needs of the Florentine republic whose leaders found his political thought to speak directly to them. Cicero did not need rediscovering, because his writings were never lost. They were read and used throughout the Middle Ages, although it is also true that some texts of Cicero that had for all practical purposes been lost were in fact rediscovered in the fourteenth and fifteenth centuries. But there was an important shift in the way Cicero was read and applied.

Generalizing from the example of Cicero, two conclusions appear to be appropriate. The first is that classical writers began to be used more for themselves than for specifically Christian purposes in the fourteenth century and afterward. The second is that in the Renaissance there was a greater emphasis on this world as an autonomous sphere of concern than as primarily a prelude to an eternal life in heaven or hell. We need to be very cautious, however, in pushing these conclusions, recognizing that here too, we need to look at continuity as well as change. For the first, it is certainly true that medieval writers looked at other classical writers in the same way that they looked at Cicero, that is, as part of a Christian agenda that took those writers in directions different from their original intent, sometimes even picking and choosing excerpts at the expense of the meaning of the entire text. One could argue that even Thomas Aquinas, in an extraordinarily sophisticated way to be sure, made use of Aristotle in this same way. However, Dante's appropriation of Virgil and Virgil's *Aeneid* appears to be different in degree and perhaps even in kind. Virgil is introduced to the reader in the first canto of the *Inferno* as himself, and he pretty much retains that identity throughout the *Divine Comedy*. For the second, it is certainly true that one can find examples throughout the Middle Ages to suggest that life is little more than a "valley of tears" in preparation for the next life. But that tradition, that strand of Christianity, hardly ends with the Middle Ages. One can easily find similar examples in the texts of Reformation authors, not to mention Christian writers from the earliest Fathers up to the present day. Similarly, one can find a delight and appreciation for the "here and now" in such diverse medieval figures as Irish monks, Hildegard of Bingen, Francis of Assisi, Dante, and Chaucer; and to ignore this, or to consider these writers as somehow atypical of the Middle Ages, is simply to beg the question with respect to the differences between the Middle Ages and the Renaissance.

One of the writers often considered a founder of the new set of values that we call Renaissance is Petrarch (1300–1374). Although he was an Italian, born near Florence, he spent much of his adult life near Avignon, where the papal court was located. In his zeal for the classics, Petrarch appears in his poems and other writings to be someone who has broken out of some of the widely held cultural values of the Middle Ages. However, he also remains deeply attached to many ideals and values that we have found dominant in the Middle Ages. In the letter that he wrote describing his Climb of Mont Ventoux, a mountain in southern France, Petrarch demonstrates both something old and something new. The following passages bring together elements of Petrarch's thought and suggest something of its complexity:

> Today I climbed the highest mountain in the region. . . . The only motive for my ascent was the wish to see what so great a height had to offer. . . . The impulse to make the climb actually took hold of me while I was reading Livy's *History of Rome* yesterday.[8]

Livy's narrative of King Philip of Macedon climbing a mountain makes Petrarch curious about the experience of climbing a high mountain and he decides to duplicate the feat. Petrarch uses Livy as a guide to living well here on earth.

> When I thought about looking for a companion for the ascent, I realized, strangely enough, that hardly any of my friends were suitable—so rarely does one find, even among those most dear to one, the perfect combination of character and purpose. . . . So, with only my own pleasure in mind, with great care I looked about weighing the various characteristics of my friends against one another. . . .

Although Petrarch does not tell us the source of his thoughts on friendship, it is clearly Cicero. And Cicero is used to suggest that friends are a source of pleasure in this life rather than as an aid in the journey toward God.

Petrarch arrives at the summit of Mont Ventoux:

> I could see the clouds under our feet, and the tales I had read of Athos and Olympus [mountains in Greece] seemed less incredible as I myself was witnessing the very same things from a less famous mountain. I turned my eyes toward Italy, the place to which my heart was most inclined. The great and snowcapped Alps seemed to rise close by, though they were far away—those same Alps through which that fierce enemy of the Roman name [Hannibal] once made his way, splitting the rocks, if we can believe the story, by means of vinegar.

Petrarch knows about Athos and Olympus from classical texts, and the story of Hannibal is to be found, once again, in Livy. Even when turning to his homeland, his first focused thought is not some detail of his home town but on what the Roman historian Livy had written more than thirteen hundred years earlier. However, this "worldly" thought, rooted in the Latin Classics, is not all that occupies Petrarch as he climbs Mont Ventoux. On the way up, he tries to find the easiest, least steep way to the summit. Discovering that he was falling behind, he does more than change climbing strategy.

> After being misled this way a number of times, I finally sat down in a hollow and my thoughts quickly turned from material things to the spiritual, and I said to myself more or less what follows: "What you have experienced so often today in the ascent of this mountain certainly happens to you as it does to many others in their journey toward the blessed life. But this is not so easily perceived by men, for the movements of the body are out in the open while those of the soul are invisible and hidden. The life which we call blessed is to be sought on a high level, and straight is the way that leads to it. Many, also, are the hills that stand in the way that leads to it, and we must ascend from virtue to virtue up glorious steps. At the summit is both the end of our struggles and the goal of our journey's climb. Everyone wishes to reach this goal, but, as Ovid says: 'To wish is not enough; you must yearn with ardent eagerness to gain your end.'"

Petrarch turns from visible to invisible concerns, from this life to eternal life. He reads his climbing failures as an allegory of spiritual weakness. His mention of hills standing in his way is a borrowing from the beginning of Dante's *Inferno* and his image of ascending from virtue to virtue resonates with Dante the Pilgrim's climb up the mountain of Purgatory. Petrarch's use of Ovid in this passage is almost homiletic and significantly different from his use of Livy.

After Petrarch looks toward Italy for a while from the top of Mont Ventoux he turns toward the west.

> I could not see the tops of the Pyrenees, which form the barrier between France and Spain, not because of any intervening obstacle that I know of but simply because of the inadequacy of mortal vision. . . . While my thoughts were divided, now turning my thoughts to some worldly object before me, now uplifting my soul, as I had done my body, to higher planes, it occurred to me to look at Augustine's *Confessions*. . . . I opened the little volume, small in size but infinitely sweet, with the intention of reading whatever came to hand, for what else could I happen upon if not edifying and devout words. Now I happened by chance to open it to the tenth book. . . . As God is my witness and my brother [who also climbed the mountain] too, the first words my eyes fell on were: "And men go about admiring the high mountains and the mighty waves of the sea and the wide sweep of rivers and the sound of the ocean and the movement of the stars, but they themselves they abandon." I was ashamed, and asking my brother, who was anxious to hear more, not to bother me, I closed the book, angry with myself for continuing to admire the things of this world when I should have learned a long time ago from the pagan philosophers themselves that nothing is admirable but the soul beside whose greatness nothing can be great.

It is interesting that Petrarch's trail reading is Augustine's *Confessions*. Once again he turns from earthly to spiritual concerns. His account of this turn, this "conversion," as he himself explains in a later part of this letter, is a close imitation of Augustine's conversion in Book 8 of the *Confessions*. Whether what occurred next was exactly as Petrarch described it is probably the wrong question, just as we suggested for the Augustinian passage that is the source of Petrarch's meditation. What is important is how Petrarch understands and structures his meditation. In the last sentence of the passage, Petrarch recognizes the power of classical texts to lead one to contemplation of the highest things, which he conceives in explicitly Christian terms, once again deliberately echoing Augustine in form and content. Augustine is every bit as important for Petrarch as he is for Aquinas and Dante.

Petrarch, through his description of the ascent of Mont Ventoux, can be seen as emblematic of the transition between the Middle Ages and the Renaissance. There is no conscious break with or rejection of inherited tradition, but rather a desire to enlarge it and to go beyond it. Yet that desire is not new either, as we have seen throughout the Middle Ages. Some have suggested that the *rate of change* increased at the end of the Middle Ages, and the rapidity of change is well dramatized in the development of various artistic media during this time. But it would be wrong to see the Renaissance as a dismissal of the preceding thousand years of social, political, and intellectual development in Western Europe.

If we compare the opening and closing of the Middle Ages, there are some interesting parallels. One of the principal causes for the decline of Rome were the diseases that lowered the population so that Rome as an empire simply could no longer function in its traditional ways. Another obvious cause were the wars that Rome fought to defend its borders and later even its core. The end of the Middle Ages was marked, at least on the surface, by parallel phenomena: the natural disaster of the Black Death that cut Europe's population by about one-third, and the Hundred Years War, as well as smaller but nonetheless serious wars in other parts of Europe.

Yet these parallels can be misleading. While Rome's population was already spread thin before the arrival of diseases in the second half of the second century C.E., Europe's population on the eve of the Black Death was too high given the available resources. The decline in the population of the Roman Empire led to all sorts of problems that in turn led to more oppressive imperial edicts, for example, freezing people on their land or in their professions whether or not they could eke out a living. On the other hand, despite social and economic dislocation, the reduction of Europe's population in the fourteenth century led to new opportunities and allowed for social and cultural change and experimentation.

The "barbarian" invasions of the fourth and fifth centuries led to the dissolution of imperial power in the West and a radical redefinition of ideas such as "sovereignty" and "state." Certainly, as our earlier chapters have shown, there was significant continuity between ancient and medieval Europe, but the political and social changes were profound and disorienting. An Empire with fixed borders, a central government, and a body of written law was challenged by Germanic tribes which had none of these. In the long run, it was probably easier for the Roman Empire to fight the Persian Empire than to fight Goths and Vandals and Huns. The Persians, though an enemy, were more like Rome than the Germanic tribes were. Rome knew how empires worked and what sort of diplomacy was effective when dealing with them, but the invaders from the north played by different rules. One could argue that the same principle applies today with the breakup of the Soviet Union. The United States could deal with the Soviet Union more easily than it can deal with international terrorists at present. The Soviet Union was a nation with all of the attributes of a nation—borders, a central government, a diplomatic corps, and so on. Non-state terrorists have none of these, and the American government is often ineffective in dealing with powers who do not play by an agreed upon set of rules.

The situation in Rome and the situation in America today contrast with the wars at the end of the Middle Ages. The Hundred Years War involved two nation-states, quite different from nation-states today but nevertheless part of the structure of Western Europe. Despite a good deal of lawlessness and a change in the "rules of war" that was one of the war's results, there was at least some common ground on which the two sides operated. Without minimizing the horrors and destruction of the late medieval conflict between England and France, it did not destroy either state or the "system" of which they were part.

We have tried to show in Chapter 5 that the early Middle Ages was a time of creativity and synthesis as well as of destruction and chaos. It is nevertheless true that it took Europe centuries to equal and supersede the accomplishments of its Roman past in such areas as literacy, urban life, long distance trade, culture, and monumental architecture. However, out of the transformation of medieval society at the end of the Middle Ages, the passage to modernity came without similar dislocation and chaos. That is certainly one of the achievements for which we can give credit to the Middle Ages.

NOTES

CHAPTER 1. THE BIBLE

1. All quotations from the Psalms are from the version for singing of Joseph Gelineau (New York: Paulist Press, 1966). All other biblical quotations are from the New Revised Standard Version. The NRSV is a standard modern translation. We indicate some of the ways in which modern translations differ from the Latin Vulgate Bible in the text of this chapter.

CHAPTER 2. THE CLASSICAL HERITAGE

1. David Knowles, *The Evolution of Medieval Thought* (New York: Random House, 1962), pp. 3–4.

2. Ibid., p. 11.

3. Ibid., p. 13.

4. Moses Hadas, ed., *Basic Works of Cicero* (New York: Random House, 1951), p. 162.

5. Ibid., p. 168.

6. Virgil, *Aeneid*, trans. W. F. Jackson Knight (Baltimore: Penguin, 1956), pp. 160–61.

7. J. W. Mackail, trans., *Virgil's Works* (New York: Random House, 1950), p. 274.

8. Ovid, *Metamorphoses*, trans. Mary M. Innes (Baltimore: Penguin, 1955), pp. 231–32.

9. *Aeneid*, pp. 172–73.

CHAPTER 3. EARLY CHRISTIANITY

1. Maxwell Staniforth, trans., in *Early Christian Writings* (Baltimore: Penguin, 1968), pp. 89–90.

2. The story of these last Cathars, based on a local bishop's inquiry, is retold in Emmanuel LeRoy Ladurie, *Montaillou: The Promised Land of Error*, trans. Barbara Bray (New York: Random House, 1979).

3. From "The Epistle to the Trallians," in *Early Christian Writings*, p. 95.

4. From "Against Heresies," in *Early Christian Fathers*, trans. and ed. Cyril C. Richardson (New York: Macmillan, 1970), p. 372.

5. Leo the Great, *Letters and Sermons*, in *Library of Nicene and Post-Nicene Fathers XII*, 2nd series, trans. Charles Lett Feltoe (Grand Rapids: William B. Eerdmans, rpt. 1952), p. 117.

6. See "The First Apology" of Justin Martyr in Richardson, esp. p. 272.

7. "Letter of Origen to Gregory," in *Ante Nicene Fathers* X, ed. Alexander Roberts and James Donaldson (Grand Rapids: William B. Eerdmans, rpt. 1955), p. 295.

8. From "On First Principles," in *Documents in Early Christian Thought,* ed. Maurice Wiles and Mark Santer (Cambridge: Cambridge University Press, 1975), pp. 144–45.

9. From "On the Objections of the Heretics," in *The Records of Christianity* v. 1, ed. David Ayerst and A. S. T. Fisher (Oxford: Basil Blackwell, 1971), pp. 95–96.

10. See Henry Chadwick, *The Early Church* (Baltimore: Penguin, 1967), pp. 90–93.

11. Ayerst and Fisher, p. 16.

12. From "The epistle to the Romans," in Staniforth, pp. 104–5.

13. From "The Martyrdom of Polycarp," in Staniforth, p. 162.

14. Jacobus de Voragine, *The Golden Legend,* v. 2, trans. William Granger Ryan (Princeton: Princeton University Press, 1993), pp. 66–67.

15. From "The Martyrdom of Felix the Bishop," in *The Acts of the Christian Martyrs,* ed. and trans. Herbert Musurillo (Oxford: Clarendon Press, 1972), pp. 267–69.

16. International Committee on English in the Liturgy, trans., *Latin Mass Booklet* (Alcester: C. Goodliffe Neale, 1975), pp. 3–4.

17. Lewis Thorpe, trans., *The History of the Franks* (Baltimore: Penguin, 1974), pp. 107–8.

18. From "Life of St. Ambrose," in *Early Christian Biographies* in *The Fathers of the Church,* v. 15, ed. Roy J. Defarrari (Washington, DC: Catholic University of America Press, 1952), pp. 46–47.

19. In J. Stevenson, ed., *Creeds, Councils, and Controversies: Documents Illustrative of the History of the Church* A.D. 337–461 (London: SPCK, 1966), p. 161.

20. Dante, *Inferno,* ed. and trans. Charles Singleton (Princeton: Princeton University Press, 1970), p. 201.

21. From "On Simony," in *Advocates of Reform* in *Library of Christian Classics,* ed. Matthew Spinka (London: SCM, 1953), p. 224.

CHAPTER 4. THE LATIN FATHERS: JEROME AND AUGUSTINE

1. St. Jerome, *Letters,* in *Library of Nicene and Post-Nicene Fathers* VI, 2nd series, trans. W. H. Fremantle (Grand Rapids: William B. Eerdmans, rpt. 1952), p. 35. This and the following quotation from Jerome can be found in Brian Tierney, ed., *The Middle Ages: Sources of Medieval History* (New York: Alfred A. Knopf, 1970), pp. 31–33.

2. Fremantle, p. 149.

3. The Latin title of this book, *De Doctrina Christiana,* is translated in several different ways. Often known in English as *On Christian Doctrine,* we will use the title as it is rendered in the translation that we quote.

4. An important pioneering work is Emile Mâle, *The Gothic Image: Religious Art in France of the Thirteenth Century* (New York: Harper and Row, 1958).

5. Augustine, *On Christian Teaching,* trans. R. P. H. Green (Oxford: Oxford University Press, 1997), pp. 9–10.

6. Ibid., pp. 37–38.

7. Ibid., p. 81.

8. Ibid., pp. 32–33.

9. D. W. Robertson, "Introduction," in *On Christian Doctrine* (Indianapolis: Bobbs-Merrill, 1958), p. xv.

10. *On Christian Teaching,* p. 27.

11. Ibid., pp. 64–65.

12. Augustine, *Confessions,* trans. Henry Chadwick (Oxford: Oxford University Press, 1991), pp. 143–44.

13. Ibid., pp. 100–1.

14. Ibid., p. 3.

15. Jacobus de Voragine, *The Golden Legend,* v. 2, trans. William Granger Ryan (Princeton: Princeton University Press, 1993), pp. 230–31.

16. *Confessions,* p. 145.

17. Ibid., pp. 152–53.

18. Dante, *Inferno,* trans. Charles Singleton (Princeton: Princeton University Press, 1970), p. 54.

19. *Confessions,* p. 88.

20. Augustine, *Concerning the City of God Against the Pagans,* trans. Henry Bettenson (Baltimore: Penguin, 1972), p. 859.

21. Ibid., pp. 447–48.

22. Ibid., pp. 549–50.

23. Ibid., p. 553

24. Ibid., p. 596.

25. Ibid., p. 875.

26. Ibid., p. 213.

27. Ibid., p. 1091.

CHAPTER 5. THE TRANSITION FROM ANCIENT TO MEDIEVAL

1. *Complete Works of Tacitus,* trans. Alfred John Church and William Jackson Brodribb, ed. Moses Hadas (New York: Random House, 1942), p. 712.

2. Ibid., p. 715.

3. Ibid., pp. 715–16.

4. Katherine Fischer Drew, trans. and ed., *The Lombard Laws* (Philadelphia: University of Pennsylvania Press, 1973), p. 62.

5. Katherine Fischer Drew, trans. and ed., *The Burgundian Code* (Philadelphia: University of Pennsylvania Press, 1949), p. 23.

6. *Sidonius: Poems and Letters II, Loeb Classical Library,* trans. W. B. Anderson, (Cambridge: Harvard University Press, 1965), p. 287.

7. Gregory of Tours, *The History of the Franks,* trans. Lewis Thorpe (Baltimore: Penguin, 1974), p. 63.

8. Ibid., pp. 167–68.

9. Ibid., p. 154.

10. "Anonymous Vatesianus," trans. John C. Rolfe, in *Ammianus Marcellinus III, Loeb Classical Library* (Cambridge: Harvard University Press, 1939), pp. 545, 547.

11. Gregory of Tours, pp. 143–44.

12. Ibid., p. 144.

13. Gregory of Tours, *Glory of the Confessors,* trans. Raymond Van Dam (Liverpool: Liverpool University Press, 1988), p. 19.

14. Bede, A *History of the English Church and People,* trans. Leo Sherley-Price (Baltimore: Penguin, 1955), pp. 86–87.

15. Ibid., p. 76.

16. Ibid., p. 77.

17. Ibid., p. 69.

18. Ibid., p. 85.

19. Ibid., pp. 236–37.

20. Ibid., p. 206.

21. Trans. William C. McDermott in *Monks, Bishops, and Pagans: Christian Culture in Gaul and Italy, 500–700*, ed. Edward Peters (Philadelphia: University of Pennsylvania Press, 1975), pp. 79–80.

22. Ludwig Bieler, trans. and ed., *The Irish Penitentials* (Dublin: The Dublin Institute for Advanced Studies, rpt., 1975), pp. 113, 115.

23. Ibid., pp. 131, 133.

24. Ibid., p. 131.

25. *The Letters of Saint Boniface*, trans. and ed. Ephraim Emerton (New York: W. W. Norton, rpt., 1976), pp. 48–49. (Originally in the *Columbia University Records of Civilization*.)

26. Ibid., pp. 115–16.

27. Ibid., p. 92.

28. Gregory the Great, *The Book of Pastoral Rule and Selected Epistles*, in *Library of Nicene and Post-Nicene Fathers XII*, 2nd series, trans. and ed. James Barmby (Grand Rapids: William B. Eerdmans, rpt. 1952), pp. 228–29.

29. Gregory the Great, *Selected Epistles*, in *Library of Nicene and Post-Nicene Fathers* XIII, 2nd series, trans. and ed. James Barmby (Grand Rapids: William B. Eerdmans, rpt. 1952), p. 53.

30. Gregory the Great, *Pastoral Care*, in *Ancient Christian Writers*, trans. Henry Davis (New York: Newman Press, rpt. 1978), pp. 23–24, 51–52.

31. Gregory the Great, *Morals on the Book of Job*, in *Library of Fathers of the Holy Catholic Church*, trans. John Henry Parker (Oxford, 1847), Pt. 5, book 23, pp. 1–2. An excerpt is available in Robert Brentano, ed., *The Early Middle Ages, 500–1000* (New York: The Free Press of Glencoe, 1964), pp. 104–6.

32. Boethius, *The Consolation of Philosophy*, trans. Richard Green (Indianapolis: Bobbs-Merrill, 1962), pp. 21–22.

33. Ibid., p. 43.

34. Ibid., p. 104.

35. Ibid., p. 109.

36. Ibid., pp. 91, 92.

37. Ibid., p. 9.

38. Adapted from M. L. W. Laistner, *Thought and Letters in Western Europe A.D. 500 to 900* (Ithaca: Cornell University Press, 1931), p. 123.

39. Jacobus de Voragine, *The Golden Legend*, v. 1, trans. William Granger Ryan (Princeton: Princeton University Press, 1993), p. 171.

40. *Golden Legend*, v. 2, p. 239.

41. Pseudo-Dionysius, *The Divine Names*, in *The Complete Works*, trans. Colm Luibheid (Mahwah, NJ: Paulist Press, 1987), pp. 51–53.

42. Otto von Simson, *The Gothic Cathedral* (New York: Harper and Row, 1962), p. 50.

43. Ibid., p. 50.

44. Dante, *Paradiso*, trans. Charles Singleton (Princeton: Princeton University Press, 1975), p. 3.

45. *Golden Legend*, v. 2, p. 240.

CHAPTER 6. MONASTICISM

1. Robert C. Gregg, trans. and ed., *Athanasius: The Life of Antony and the Letter to Marcellinus*, in *The Classics of Western Spirituality* (New York: Paulist Press, 1980), p. 31.

2. Ibid., pp. 66–67.

3. Ibid., p. 46.

4. Saint Antony, *The Wisdom of the Desert*, trans. Thomas Merton (New York: New Directions, 1960), p. 29.

5. Ibid., p. 62.

6. *Athanasius*, pp. 83–84.

7. *The Sayings of the Desert Fathers: The Alphabetical Collection*, trans. Benedicta Ward (Kalamazoo: Cistercian Publications, 1975), p. 194.

8. John Cassian, *The Institutes*, trans. Boniface Ramsey (New York: Newman Press, 2000), p. 117.

9. Ibid., p. 255.

10. John Cassian, *The Conferences*, trans. Boniface Ramsey (New York: Newman Press, 1997), p. 46.

11. Evagrius Ponticus, *Praktikos: Chapters on Prayer*, trans. John Eudes Bamberger (Spencer, MA: Cistercian Publications, 1970), p. 58.

12. Ibid., p. 61.

13. Ibid., p. 74.

14. Ibid., p. 76.

15. Gregory the Great, *Dialogues*, trans. Myra L. Uhlfelder (Indianapolis: Bobbs-Merrill, 1967), pp. 6–7.

16. Leonard J. Doyle, trans., *Saint Benedict's Rule for Monasteries* (Collegeville, MN: The Liturgical Press, 1948), pp. 5–6.

17. Ibid., pp. 12–13.

18. Ibid., pp. 20–21.

19. Ibid., pp. 57–59, 76–77.

20. Ibid., pp. 67–68.

21. Hildegard of Bingen, *Scivias*, trans. Columbia Hart and Jane Bishop (Mahwah, NJ: Paulist Press, 1990), p. 183.

22. Rudolf of Fulda, "The Life of Saint Leoba," in *Carolingian Civilization: A Reader*, ed. Paul Edward Dutton (Peterborough, Ontario: Broadview Press, 1993), p. 319.

CHAPTER 7. THE FIRST MEDIEVAL SYNTHESIS: THE CAROLINGIAN WORLD AND ITS DISSOLUTION

1. Charlemagne, "Admonitio generalis," in *Christianity through the Thirteenth Century*, trans. and ed. Marshall W. Baldwin (New York: Harper & Row, 1970), pp. 115–16.

2. Ibid., pp. 117–18, 119.

3. Ibid., pp. 119–20.

4. Einhard, *The Life of Charlemagne*, in Two *Lives of Charlemagne*, trans. Lewis Thorpe (Baltimore: Penguin, 1969), p. 81.

5. Bernhard Walter Scholz, trans., *Royal Frankish Annals*, in *Carolingian Chronicles* (Ann Arbor: University of Michigan Press, 1970), p. 81.

6. "General Capitulary for the *missi*," trans. H. R. Loyn and J. Percival, in *The Reign of Charlemagne* (London: Edward Arnold, 1975), pp. 74–75.

7. Ibid., p. 74.

8. *Two Lives of Charlemagne*, p. 79.

9. Robert Folz, trans., *The Coronation of Charlemagne* (London: Routledge and Kegan Paul, 1974), p. 68.

10. *Christianity through the Thirteenth Century*, p. 117.

11. Ibid., p. 146.

12. David Bevington, ed., *Medieval Drama* (Boston: Houghton Mifflin, 1975), p. 26.

13. *The Reign of Charlemagne*, pp. 63–64.

14. *Two Lives of Charlemagne*, p. 74.

15. Dhouda, *Handbook for William*, trans. Carol Neel (Lincoln: University of Nebraska Press,1991), pp. 47, 51–52.

16. *Two Lives of Charlemagne*, p. 82.

17. Ibid., pp. 141–42.

18. Ibid., pp. 64–65.

19. Patricia Terry, trans., *The Song of Roland* (Indianapolis: Bobbs-Merrill, 1965), ll. 2448–60.

20. *Christianity Through the Thirteenth Century*, p. 132.

21. Boyd H. Hill, trans. and ed., *Medieval Monarchy in Action: The German Empire from Henry I to Henry IV* (New York: Barnes & Noble, 1972), pp. 113–15.

22. *Two Lives of Charlemagne*, pp. 71–72.

23. David Herlihy, trans. and ed., *The History of Feudalism* (New York: Walker, 1970), pp. 10, 11–13.

24. Asser's *Life of King Alfred*, in *Alfred the Great*, trans. Simon Keynes and Michael Lapidge (Harmondsworth: Penguin, 1983), pp. 84–85.

25. *Hrafnkels's Saga*, in *Hrafnkel's Saga and Other Icelandic Stories*, trans. Hermann Pálsson (London: Penguin, 1971), pp. 40, 42–43.

26. *History of Feudalism*, p. 87.

27. Ibid.

28. Ibid., pp. 87–88.

29. *Handbook for William*, pp. 51–52.

30. *History of Feudalism*, pp. 108–9.

31. Joseph R. Strayer, "The Two Levels of Feudalism," in *Life and Thought in the Early Middle Ages*, ed. Robert S. Hoyt (Minneapolis: University of Minnesota Press, 1967), p. 51.

32. Trans. in *Pennsylvania Translations and Reprints Series*, vol. 4, no. 3, and reprinted in *Medieval History: A Sourcebook*, ed. Donald A. White (Homewood, IL: Dorsey Press, 1965), pp. 268–70.

33. F. A. Ogg, trans. and ed., *A Sourcebook of Medieval History* (New York: American Book Company, 1907), pp. 220–21 and reprinted in *The History of Feudalism*, p. 97.

34. Galbert of Bruges, *The Murder of Charles the Good, Count of Flanders*, trans. James Bruce Ross (New York: Harper & Row, 1967), pp. 206–7.

35. Gerald of Aurillac, *St. Odo of Cluny*, trans. Dom Gerard Sitwell (New York: Sheed & Ward, 1958), pp. 99–101.

36. *The Song of Roland*, ll. 1009–12.

37. Strayer, "The Development of Feudal Institutions," in *Twelfth-Century Eu-*

rope and the Foundations of Modern Society, ed. Marshall Clagett et al. (Madison: University of Wisconsin Press, 1965), pp. 76–88. This essay and the other Strayer essay cited above are both reprinted in Medieval Statecraft and the Perspectives of History: Essays by Joseph R. Strayer (Princeton: Princeton University Press, 1971).

38. Quoted in Giles Constable, Three Studies in Medieval Religious and Social Thought (Cambridge: Cambridge University Press, 1995), p. 284.

CHAPTER 8. CHURCH, STATE, AND SOCIETY

1. G. G. Coulton, trans. and ed., Social Life in Britain from the Conquest to the Reformation (Cambridge: Cambridge University Press, 1918), pp. 415 and reprinted in Medieval Europe, ed. William H. McNeill and Schuyler O. Houser (New York: Oxford University Press, 1971), pp. 91–92.

2. John F. Benton, trans., Self and Society in Medieval France: The Memoirs of Abbot Guibert of Nogent (New York: Harper & Row, 1970), p. 167.

3. Ibid., pp. 155–156.

4. Otto of Freising, The Deeds of Frederick Barbarossa, trans. Charles C. Mierow (New York, W. W. Norton, rpt. 1966). (Originally in the Columbia University Records of Civilization.)

5. The Towns of Italy in the Later Middle Ages, trans. Trevor Dean (Manchester: Manchester University Press, 2000), pp. 12, 14.

6. Fulcher of Chartres, A History of the Expedition to Jerusalem, 1095–1127, trans. Frances Rita Ryan (New York: W. W. Norton, rpt., 1973), p. 66.

7. Ibid., p. 68.

8. Ibid., p. 117.

9. Ibid., pp. 121–22.

10. Edward Peters, ed., The First Crusade (Philadephia: University of Pennsylvania Press, 2nd. edition, 1998), p. 75.

11. Francesco Gabrieli, ed., and E. J. Costello, trans., Arab Historians of the Crusades (New York: Dorset Press, rpt. 1989), p. 6.

12. Albert of Aix, Chronicle, in The First Crusade: The Accounts of Eye-Witnesses and Participants, trans. A. C. Krey (Princeton: Princeton University Press, 1921) and reprinted in Edward Peters, ed., The First Crusade (Philadelphia: University of Pennsylvania Press, 1971), p. 102.

13. Bruno Scott James, trans. and ed., The Letters of St. Bernard of Clairvaux (Chicago: Henry Regnery, 1953), pp. 461–62.

14. William of St. Thierry, The Golden Epistle: A Letter to the Brethren at Mont Dieu, in Cistercian Fathers Series v. 12, trans. Theodore Berkeley, OCSO (Kalamazoo: Cistercian Publications, 1970), pp. 19–20.

15. Thomas Merton, trans., The Solitary Life: A Letter of Guigo (Worcester: privately printed, 1963), pp. 7–9.

16. A Monk of Gethsemani, trans., Compendium of the History of the Cistercian Order (Gethsemani, KY: Order of Cistercians of the Strict Observance, 1944), pp. 356, 357.

17. On the Song of Songs I, in Cistercian Fathers Series v. 4, trans. Kilian Walsh, OCSO (Kalamazoo: Cistercian Publications, 1971), pp. 16–17.

18. In Bernard of Clairvaux, Treatises I, in Cistercian Fathers Series v. 2, trans. Michael Casey, OCSO (Kalamazoo: Cistercian Publications, 1970), pp. 63–64, 66.

19. Ibid., p. 64.

20. Jean Leclercq, *The Love of Learning and the Desire for God* (New York: Fordham University Press, 1974), p. 306.

21. Bernard of Clairvaux, *Five Books on Consideration: Advice to a Pope*, in *Cistercian Fathers* v. 13, trans. John D. Anderson and Elizabeth T. Kennan (Kalamazoo: Cistercian Publications, 1976), pp. 29, 31–32.

22. Pope Innocent III, "Sermon on the consecration of a pope," and "Letter to the prefect Acerbus and the nobles of Tuscany," in *The Crisis of Church and State 1050–1300*, trans. Brian Tierney (Englewood Cliffs: Prentice-Hall, 1964), pp. 132–33.

23. Mary Clark, trans. and ed., *An Aquinas Reader* (New York: Doubleday, 1972), pp. 363, 364–65, 367.

24. Pope Boniface VIII, "Unam Sanctam," in Tierney, pp. 188–89.

25. Dante, *On World Government*, trans. Herbert W. Schneider (Indianapolis: Bobbs-Merrill, 1957), pp. 9, 11, 64.

CHAPTER 9. THE RENAISSANCE OF THE TWELFTH CENTURY

1. Harriet Pratt Lattin, trans. and ed., *The Letters of Gerbert*, in *Columbia University Records of Civilization* (New York: Columbia University Press, 1961), p. 90.

2. Quoted in Nathan Schachner, *The Medieval Universities* (New York: A.S. Barnes and Company, 1962), p. 19.

3. Eugene R. Fairweather, trans. and ed., *Why God Became Man*, in *A Scholastic Miscellany: Anselm to Ockham*, in *Library of Christian Classics* X (New York: The Macmillan Company, rpt. 1970), pp. 101–02.

4. M. J. Charlesworth, trans., (Notre Dame: Notre Dame University Press, 1979), p. 119.

5. *A Monk's Confession: The Memoirs of Guibert de Nogent* (New Park, PA: The Pennsylvania State University Press, 1996), pp. 14–15.

6. Brian Tierney, trans. and ed., *The Middle Ages: Sources of Medieval History*, 3rd ed. (New York: Alfred A. Knopf, 1978), pp. 168–69.

7. Paul Vincent Spade, trans., *Ethics* in *Ethical Writings by Peter Abelard* (Indianapolis: Hackett, 1995), p. 23.

8. Ibid., p. 84.

9. Daniel D. McGarry, trans., *The Metalogicon of John of Salisbury* (Gloucester, MA: Peter Smith, 1971), pp. 67–70.

10. Ibid., p. 167.

11. Thomas Aquinas, *Summa Theologiae* Vol. I, trans. Thomas Gilby (Garden City: Doubleday, 1969), pp. 191–92.

12. M.-D. Chénu, *Toward Understanding St. Thomas* (Chicago: Henry Regnery & Company, 1964), esp. Chs. 4 and 5, gives a cogent analysis of Thomas's method.

13. Erwin Panofsky, *Gothic Architecture and Scholasticism* (New York: World Publishing Company, 1957).

14. Gratian, *Decretum*, trans. John T. Noonan, in *The Records of Medieval Europe*, ed. Carolly Erikson (Garden City: Doubleday, 1971), p. 206.

15. Alanus, "Commentary on DIST 96 c.6," in *The Crisis of Church and State 1050–1300*, trans. Brian Tierney (Englewood Cliffs: Prentice-Hall, 1964), p. 123.

16. Ibid., p. 122.

17. Chrétien de Troyes, *Erec and Enide*, in *Arthurian Romances*, trans. W. W. Comfort (New York: Dutton, 1914), p. 68.

18. *Arthurian Romances*, p. 93.

19. Ibid., p. 91.

20. Patricia Terry, trans., *The Song of Roland* (Indianapolis: Bobbs-Merrill, 1965), ll. 96–100, 115–21.

21. *Arthurian Romances*, p. 203.

22. James J. Wilhelm, trans. and ed., *Medieval Song* (New York: Dutton, 1971), pp. 141–42.

23. Colin Morris, *The Discovery of the Individual 1050–1200* (Toronto: University of Toronto Press, 1972, rpt. 1987).

CHAPTER 10. FRANCIS OF ASSISI AND THE MENDICANTS

1. Ewert Cousins, trans. and ed., *Bonaventure: The Soul's Journey into God: The Tree of Life, The Life of Francis*, in *The Classics of Western Spirituality* (New York: Paulist Press, 1978), pp. 187–88. This is also the translation used in the new and definitive collection of Franciscan sources in English, Regis J. Armstrong, Wayne Hellmann, and William Short, eds., *Francis of Assisi: Early Documents. Vol. I: The Saint; Vol. II: The Founder; Vol. III: The Prophet* (New York: New City Press, 1999–2001).

2. Ibid., pp. 191–92.

3. Ibid., pp. 280–81.

4. Ibid., pp. 199–200, 239–40.

5. Thomas of Celano, *The Remembrance of the Desire of a Soul*, in *Early Documents Vol. II*, p. 290.

6. "The Later Rule (1223)," in *Early Documents Vol. I*, p. 102.

7. "The Testament (1226)," in *Early Documents Vol. I*, p. 125.

8. *Bonaventure*, pp. 305–6.

9. Ibid., pp. 294–95.

10. *The Little Flowers of Saint Francis*, in *Early Documents Vol. III*, pp. 601–3.

11. *Bonaventure*, pp. 262–63.

12. "The Canticle of the Creatures (1225)," in *Early Documents Vol. I*, pp. 113–14.

CHAPTER 11. THE FOURTEENTH CENTURY

1. *The Letters of Catherine of Siena*, trans. Suzanne Noffke (Tempe, AZ: Arizona Center for Medieval and Renaissance Studies, 2000), vol.I, p. 248.

2. Jean Froissart, *Chronicles*, trans. Geoffrey Brereton (New York: Penguin, 1968), p. 66.

3. Christine de Pizan, *The Treasure of the City of Ladies*, trans. Sarah Lawson (New York: Penguin, 1985), pp. 128–29.

4. Erasmus, *The Praise of Folly*, in *The Erasmus Reader*, ed. Erika Rummel (Toronto: University of Toronto Press, 1990), p. 158.

5. "An Appeal to the Ruling Classes of German Nationality as to the Amelioration of the State of Christendom," in *The Reformation Writings of Martin Luther Vol. I: The Bases of the Protestant Reformation*, trans. Bertram Lee Wolff (London: Lutterworth Press, 1953).

6. Burckhardt is available in a number of English editions, including that of Ben-

jamin Nelson and Charles Trinkaus, eds., *The Civilization of the Renaissance in Italy*, 2 Vols. (New York: Harper and Row, 1958).

7. Colin Morris, *The Discovery of the Individual* (Toronto: University of Toronto Press, rpt. 1987). Charles Taylor, in his important study *Sources of the Self* (Cambridge: Harvard University Press, 1986), would see the key figure in the development of the individual to be Augustine.

8. All of the quotations of Petrarch are from Petrarch, *Selections from the Canzoniere and Other Works*, trans. Mark Musa (New York: Oxford University Press, 1985), pp. 11–19.

BIBLIOGRAPHY

This bibliography is an entry into the world of medieval sources and scholarship. Although it cannot serve as a list of all available materials, even in English, for the study of the Middle Ages, those wishing to go more deeply into the material covered in this book, or to pursue research in medieval studies, will be able to find the relevant primary sources and scholarship that they need as they start.

PRIMARY SOURCES

As we state in the Introduction, we think that it is vitally important for anyone interested in the Middle Ages to turn first to primary sources, to those works that were created during the medieval (and premedieval) period. For the most famous writers whom we quote in this book, multiple English editions of at least their most famous works are generally available (although there remain a few notable exceptions). For instance, there are about a half dozen different English translations of Augustine's *Confessions* currently in print and quite a few older ones can be found in libraries and on the Internet. We recommend that those who want to see such works in their entirety begin with the relevant notes in this book, for we have used modern, easily accessible translations of these texts whenever possible. Works by authors such as Thomas Aquinas are often available, usually in out of copyright translations, on the Internet; but almost every year there are new translations and editions being published. Thus, browsing through bookstores and catalogues is a good way to find the newest presentations of such works. We urge readers to find out about a translation before committing to it. Older translations may be out of date because they are based on flawed texts of the original language, but they are just as likely to be out of date because of changes in English usage since the time of the translation. Readers should know whether they are reading a complete translation or an edited one. Readers should also ask themselves whether an edited version is sufficient for the purpose for which they are studying the text.

Ongoing Projects

There are several large translation projects that have been in progress for years and have produced multiple volumes of primary sources in modern English translation. The following is a partial list, indicating the sorts of translation projects that are currently underway. Some individual volumes in the series listed below will appear later in this bibliography.

Cistercian Fathers Series. Kalamazoo, MI: Cistercian Publications. This series contains multiple volumes of the work of Bernard of Clairvaux and many other early Cistercian writers.

Documents of Medieval History. London: Edward Arnold. R. I. Moore's *The Birth of Popular Heresy,* containing an excellent collection of documents concerning medieval dissent, is a volume in this series.

Manchester Medieval Sources Series. Manchester: Manchester University Press. The volume in this series edited by Rosemary Horrox, *The Black Death,* is the fullest and best organized collection of texts for this important topic.

The Pontifical Institute of Medieval Studies Sources in Translation: Toronto: Pontifical Institute of Medieval Studies. John of Paris's *On Royal and Papal Power* is an important volume in this series.

Saint Augustine for the Twenty-First Century. New York: New City Press. There are already about twenty-five volumes of new translations available in this series, including Augustine's most famous works such as *Confessions* and *The Trinity,* as well as works such as his sermons and his writings against the Palagians.

TEAMS: Medieval English Texts Series. Kalamazoo, MI: Medieval Institute Publications. Although this series of texts is in Middle English (as opposed to modern English translation), the works in this series are specifically tailored to a student audience, with detailed vocabulary and editorial help. More than forty volumes have been published thus far.

Since those interested in the Middle Ages need to be familiar with classical and early Christian texts, it is important that they know about collections of premedieval materials. Some series devoted to this material also include works from what we normally think of as the early Middle Ages. Thus, Boethius and Gregory the Great sometimes are included in classical and early Christian collections.

Loeb Classical Library. Cambridge: Harvard University Press. This is the standard, comprehensive collection of Greek and Latin classics. These volumes contain both the original text and a facing translation. All but the most obscure and fragmentary classical texts are also available in inexpensive editions. Two series that contain most major classical works are Oxford University Press, *World's Classics* and the older *Penguin Classics,* both of which we mention later.

Ancient Christian Writers. Mahway, NJ: Paulist Press. Volumes include the standard works of Augustine, Ambrose, Gregory the Great, and new and complete translations of the works of John Cassian.

Fathers of the Church. Washington: Catholic University of America Press. In addition to standard works, this series contains some hard to find sources such as Orosius's *Seven Books Against the Pagans,* an important source of ancient lore for writers in the Middle Ages, including Dante.

A Select Library of the Nicene and Post-Nicene Fathers of the Christian Church. Grand Rapids: Eerdmans (rpt.). Although volumes are nineteenth-century translations, they are the most extensive collection of the Christian writings of the fourth and fifth centuries.

There are many series of sources in translation that are not exclusively medieval but include the scope of Western and even world civilization. The ones listed below contain important medieval texts.

Cambridge Texts in the History of Political Thought. Cambridge: Cambridge University Press. Among important medieval volumes are works of John of Salisbury and William of Ockham and an excellent edition of Dante's *Monarchy (On World Government)*.

Classics of Western Spirituality. Mahway, NJ: Paulist Press. More than half of the volumes of the more than a hundred published so far in this important series are of interest to those studying the Middle Ages. For example, there are volumes of the works of Origen, Pseudo-Dionysius, Richard of St. Victor, Hildegard of Bingen, Bonaventure, Julian of Norwich, and Catherine of Siena, as well as volumes on apocalyptic thought (including works of Joachim of Fiore) and Dominican spirituality. Of use also to those interested in the Middle Ages are the many volumes in this series devoted to Islamic spirituality. The volumes devoted to authors such as Augustine and Aquinas are less useful because they are anthologies rather than complete works.

Columbia University Records of Civilization. New York: Columbia University Press. Examples of medieval texts include letter collections of Saint Boniface and Gerbert.

English Historical Documents. New York: Eyre and Spottiswoode. There are four medieval volumes in this series, and they contain many charters and other legal documents that are translated nowhere else.

Everyman Library. New York: Dutton. Medieval texts in this series include the writings of Chrétien de Troyes and Marie de France.

Library of Christian Classics. Philadelphia: Westminster Press. This series is largely centered on the Protestant Reformation, but it has a valuable volume for medievalists, *Late Medieval Mysticism*.

The Library of Liberal Arts. Indianapolis: Bobbs-Merrill. There are several medieval works including Boethius's *Consolation of Philosophy*.

Norton Critical Editions. New York: Norton. This series presents primary texts in translation accompanied by relevant critical works. Sample titles of use to medievalists are *Middle English Lyrics* and Boccaccio's *Decameron*.

Penguin Classics. New York: Penguin. This is an invaluable collection of sources, and many volumes are now the standard translations. Two examples are Gregory of Tours, *History of the Franks*, and Froissart, *Chronicles*. There are also some valuable collections of texts in this series including *The Age of Bede*.

World's Classics. New York: Oxford University Press. This is a relatively new series that has published excellent new translations of Augustine's *Confessions*, Bede's *Ecclesiastical History*, Dante's *Vita Nuova*, and selected Icelandic sagas, just to name four.

Websites

Many medieval authors and artists have websites devoted to their work and influence. Similarly, using a search engine with a key word such as "feudalism" yields many websites, some of which will have primary source materials. Thus, the following are only a few examples of medieval websites that include texts written during the medieval period

Internet Medieval Sourcebook: ⟨http://www.fordham.edu/halsall/sbook.html⟩. Contains legal texts, saints' lives, and a variety of historical topics with indices. Also has maps and images. Sometimes a password is necessary to log on.

The Online Catholic Encyclopedia: ⟨http://newadvent.org/cathen/⟩. Contains the text of Thomas Aquinas's *Summa* and many other religious works.

The Online Medieval and Classical Library: ⟨http://sunsite.berkeley.edu/omacl⟩. Full online texts of many classical and medieval works.

Two Thousand Years of Catholic Writings: ⟨http://www.cs.cmu.edu/afs/cs.cmu.edu/misc/mosaic/common/omega/Web/People/s pok/catholic/writings.html⟩. Provides links to documents concerning the Church Fathers and saints as well as documents concerning the history of the Church generally.

Other resources include audio and video tapes produced for both classroom and general use. Those produced by the Teaching Company, to give one example, include a wide variety of medieval subjects, with "courses" on Dante, Chaucer, medieval history, Byzantium, Augustine, Thomas Aquinas, and Francis of Assisi, among others. These courses come with elaborate explanatory booklets which include bibliographies and glossaries

Sources in Translation

Speculum, the journal of the Medieval Academy of America, periodically publishes a list of translation projects that are underway. Although somewhat dated, the following bibliographies of medieval sources in translation are helpful in finding lesser known works that were translated before 1967 and have not been re-translated. They are also helpful in locating texts that are included in larger collections of sources.

Farrar, Clarissa, and Austin Evans. *Bibliography of English Translations from Medieval Sources*. New York: Columbia University Press, 1946.

Ferguson, Mary Ann. *Bibliography of English Translations from Medieval Sources 1943–1967*. New York: Columbia University Press, 1974.

There are many focused collections of medieval source materials. Those researching a particular topic should look for collections whose titles and tables of contents indicate that they contain relevant texts. Some of the collections listed below are definitive for a particular topic, for example the three-volume edition of materials relating to Saint Francis and the Franciscans. Others are illustrative of the sorts of collections that exist.

Amt, Emilie, ed. *Women's Lives in the Middle Ages: A Sourcebook*. New York: Routledge, 1993.

Aquinas, Thomas. *Selected Writings*. Ed. and trans. Ralph McInerny. London: Penguin, 1998.

———. *Summa of the Summa*. Ed. Peter Kreeft. San Francisco: Ignatius Press, 1990.

Bartlett, Anne Clark, and Thomas H. Bestul, eds. *Cultures of Piety: Medieval English Devotional Literature in Translation*. Ithaca and London: Cornell University Press, 1999.

Bevington, David, ed. *Medieval Drama*. Boston: Houghton Mifflin, 1975.

Brentano, Robert, ed. *The Early Middle Ages, 500–1000*. New York: Free Press, 1964.

Brooke, Rosalind, ed. *The Coming of the Friars*. New York: Barnes and Noble, 1975. A valuable collection of texts that help people understand what "gaps" the friars filled and thus why they were so successful.

Brundage, James, ed. *The Crusades: A Documentary Survey*. Milwaukee: Marquette University Press, 1962.

Cassian, John. *The Conferences*. Trans. Boniface Ramsey. New York: Newman Press, 1997.

——. *The Institutes*. Trans. Boniface Ramsey. New York: Newman Press, 2000.

Davis, Raymond, trans. *The Book of Pontiffs (Liber Pontificalis)*. 3 volumes. Philadelphia: University of Pennsylvania Press, 1989 ff. These three volumes contain early biographies of almost all of the popes before 891.

Dawson, Christopher, ed. *Mission to Asia*. New York: Harper and Row, 1966. This work contains chronicles of Europeans journeying to China in the thirteenth century.

Dean, Trevor, ed. *The Towns of Italy in the Later Middle Ages*. Manchester: Manchester University Press, 2000.

Delany, Sheila, trans. *A Legend of Holy Women: Osbern Bokenham*. Notre Dame: University of Notre Dame Press, 1992.

Dhouda. *Handbook for William: A Carolingian Woman's Counsel for Her Son*. Trans. Carol Neel. Lincoln: University of Nebraska Press, 1991.

Dutton, Paul, ed. *Carolingian Civilization: A Reader*. Peterborough: Broadview, 1993.

Erikson, Carolly, ed. *The Records of Medieval Europe*. Garden City: Doubleday, 1971.

Francis of Assisi: Early Documents. Ed. Regis Armstrong et al. Vol.1: *The Saint*; Vol.2: *The Founder*; Vol.3: *The Prophet*. New York: New City Press, 1999–2001. The definitive collection of sources for the study of Francis and the Order that he founded.

Geary, Patrick, ed. *Readings in Medieval History*. 2d ed. 2 volumes. Peterborough: Broadview, 1997.

Goldberg, P. J. P., ed. and trans. *Women in England 1275–1325: Documentary Sources*. Manchester: Manchester University Press, 1995.

Gratian. *The Treatise on Laws*. Trans. Augustine Thompson. With the *Ordinary Gloss*. Trans. James Gordley. Washington: Catholic University of America Press, 1993.

Herlihy, David, ed. *Medieval Culture and Society*. New York: Harper and Row, 1968.

——, ed. *The History of Feudalism*. New York: Walker and Company, 1970.

Hennecke, E., and W. Scheemelcher, eds. *New Testament Apocrypha*. 2 vols. Philadelphia: Westminster Press, 1963. Although these works originated before the beginning of the Middle Ages, these non-canonical texts were important sources during the Middle Ages for stories about Jesus and the apostles and especially for stories concerning the Virgin Mary.

Hill, Boyd, ed. *Medieval Monarchy in Action: The German Empire from Henry I to Henry IV*. New York: Barnes and Noble, 1972.

Horrox, Rosemary, ed. *The Black Death*. Manchester: Manchester University Press, 1994. A very good collection of documents dealing with the coming of the bubonic plague, excellently organized.

Horstmann, C. *The Yorkshire Writers: Richard Rolle and His Followers*. Rochester, NY: D. S. Brewer, 1999.

Hyman, Arthur, and James Walsh, eds. *Philosophy in the Middle Ages*. Indianapolis: Hackett, 1973.

Jacopus de Voragine. *The Golden Legend*. Trans. William Granger Ryan. 2 vols. Princeton: Princeton University Press, 1993.

Lerner, Ralph, and Mushin Mahdi, eds. *Medieval Political Philosophy*. Ithaca: Cornell University Press, 1963.

McGinn, Bernard, ed. *Visions of the End: Apocalyptic Traditions in the Middle Ages*. New York: Columbia University Press, 1979.

McNeill, John, and Helena Gamer. *Medieval Handbooks of Penance*. New York: Columbia University Press, rpt. 1990.

Miller, Joseph, et al.,eds. *Readings in Medieval Rhetoric*. Bloomington: Indiana University Press, 1973.

Minnis, A. J., and A. B. Scott, eds. *Medieval Literary Theory and Criticism c.1100–c.1375: The Commentary Tradition*. Cambridge: Cambridge University Press, 1988.

Murray, Alexander, ed. *From Rome to Merovingian Gaul: A Reader*. Peterborough: Broadview, 1999.

Murray, Jacqueline, ed. *Love, Marriage, and Family in the Middle Ages: A Reader*. Peterborough: Broadview, 2001.

Nederman, Cary, and Kate Langdon Forhan, eds. *Medieval Political Theory—A Reader*. London: Routledge, 1993.

Noble, Thomas, and Thomas Head, eds. *Soldiers of Christ: Saints and Saints' Lives from Late Antiquity and the Early Middle Ages*. University Park, PA: Pennsylvania State University Press, 1995. Contains the earliest written accounts of the lives of Saint Martin, Saint Augustine, and others.

Peters, Edward, ed. *The First Crusade*. 2d ed. Philadelphia: University of Pennsylvania Press, 1998. This edition, in addition to containing a large body of Crusade narrative material from the West, contains Muslim and Jewish sources for the First Crusade.

———, ed. *Heresy and Authority in Medieval Europe*. Philadelphia: University of Pennsylvania Press, 1980.

———, ed. *Monks, Bishops, and Pagans: Christian Culture in Gaul and Italy, 500–700*. Philadelphia: University of Pennsylvania Press, 1975.

RB 1980. Ed. Timothy Fry. Collegeville, MN: Liturgical Press, 1981. This translation of the Rule of Saint Benedict is published as an inexpensive paperback and in a hardcover edition with Latin and English texts.

Salimbene de Adam. *Chronicle*. Trans. Joseph Baird. Binghamton, NY: Medieval & Renaissance Texts & Studies, 1986. This chronicle from thirteenth-century Italy written by a Franciscan contains narratives of some of the most important events of the era plus interesting commentary and gossip from a well-traveled friar.

Shapiro, Herman, ed. *Medieval Philosophy*. New York: Modern Library, 1964.

Shinners, John, ed. *Medieval Popular Religion 1000–1500: A Reader*. Peterborough: Broadview, 1997.

Strunk, Mary-Ann, ed. *Medieval Saints: A Reader*. Peterborough: Broadview Press, 1999.

Strunk, Oliver, ed. *Source Readings in Music History. Antiquity and the Middle Ages*. New York: Norton, 1965.

Wakefield, Walter, and Austin Evans, eds. *Heresies of the High Middle Ages*. New York: Columbia University Press, 1969.

White, Donald, ed. *Medieval History: A Sourcebook*. Homewood, IL: Dorsey Press, 1965.

Wilson, Katharina M., ed. *Medieval Women Writers*. Athens, GA: University of Georgia Press, 1984.

Winstead, Karen A., ed. *Virgin Martyrs: Legends of Sainthood in Late Medieval England*. Ithaca: Cornell University Press, 1997.

Wogan-Browne, Jocelyn, et. al., eds. *An Anthology of Medieval English Literary Theory, 1280–1520*. University Park, PA: Pennsylvania State University Press, 1999.

REFERENCE WORKS

The most important bibliographies for those interested in the Middle Ages can be found on the Internet through medieval websites or in on-line library catalogues. Using the websites cited below together with the simplest of search engines will produce good results. One time-tested way to find bibliography relating to a specific subject is to find a recent book about the subject and examine the author's footnotes and/or bibliography. *Speculum* publishes a long list of "Books Received" in each volume, keeping readers informed about the most recent books in the field. *Speculum* also publishes numerous book reviews, usually one to two years after the publication date; they are helpful in assessing the usefulness of a book for a specific project. In addition, *Speculum* publishes tables of contents of edited collections of essays. Thus, one can often find a useful article in a book with a very general title or a collection of presentations at a conference or essays in honor of a famous scholar (known as a *Festschrift*) where the title itself gives no clue about the contents. Other journals in the field of medieval studies and more general journals such as *Church History* and *The American Historical Review* also publish articles and book reviews.

Still occasionally useful are the following guides to scholarly studies about the Middle Ages.

Paetow, Louis. *A Guide to the Study of Medieval History*. Millwood, NY: Kraus International, rpt. 1980. This work contains items published before 1930.

Boyce, Gray. *Literature of Medieval History 1930–1975*. Millwood, NY: Kraus International, 1981. This work continues Paetow's work.

The University of Toronto Press has published a series, *Toronto Medieval Bibliographies*. Although the earlier volumes are a quarter-century old, they remain valuable starting places because they are thorough and well organized. These are the works of major scholars in their fields. Two examples follow:

Constable, Giles. *Medieval Monasticism: A Select Bibliography*. 1976.

Kaske, Robert. *Medieval Christian Literary Imagery: A Guide to Interpretation*. 1988.

The following websites are of use for people pursuing almost any sort of research on a medieval topic:

Additional References: Print and Web Sources: ⟨http://www.syr.edu/digital/collections/ m/MedievalManuscripts/shared_files/additional_references.html⟩. Contains a useful bibliography, especially on medieval manuscripts, and many Internet resources.

Argos Limited Area Search of the Ancient and Medieval Internet: ⟨http://argos.evansville.edu⟩. Allows a search for websites on ancient and medieval topics, and screens out irrelevant sites. Contains links.

Medieval History Homepage: ⟨http://historymedren.miningco.com/homework/historymedren/⟩ Extensive index, e.g., Byzantium Crusades, Arthurian Romances, daily life of peasants, archaeology, military history. Lots of online articles and easy to navigate. Links aplenty.

ORB: Online Reference Book for Medieval Studies: ⟨http://orb.rhodes.edu/default. html⟩. A major site with extensive links, resources for teaching, online books and course syllabi, and an encyclopedia.

WWW Medieval Resources: ⟨http://ebbs.english.vt.edu/medieval/medieval.ebbs.html⟩. Links to texts, history, architecture, sciences, libraries, and music. Specializes in Gregorian Chant.

WWW Virtual Library History Index—Medieval Europe: ⟨http://www.mus.edu/
~georgem1/history/medieval.html⟩. Links to images, literature, history, architecture, and reference pages

Certain subdisciplines of medieval studies have bibliographies. One of the most complete and important is the annual bibliography issue of the *Revue d'histoire ecclésiastique.* It fills hundreds of pages and looks intimidating, especially since most of the entries are not to English language publications. However, it is extremely well organized in an almost scholastic scheme of divisions and subdivisions; thus, it is useful even for the beginning researcher. *Dante Studies,* a periodical published annually, contains a well-annotated bibliography of translations of Dante's works and writing about Dante done in the United States. The *Publication of the Modern Language Association (PMLA)* publishes a yearly bibliography of work done in the field of languages and literature. Among specialized Internet resources for special areas and subdisciplines are the following:

Arthurian Resources on the Internet: ⟨http://jan.ucc.nau.edu/~jjd23/arthur/⟩. Extensive listings and links to texts and criticism. FAQ section explains elements of the legends. Discusses Arthurian movies and appearances in pop culture.
The Camelot Project: ⟨http://www.lib.rochester.edu/camelot/cphome.stm⟩. Contains online images, bibliography, and general information as well as links to other Arthurian websites.
The Canterbury Tales Project: ⟨http://www.cta.dmu.ac.uk/projects/ctp/⟩. Contains information about Chaucer e-texts and manuscripts and extensive collection of links to Chaucer websites on a variety of topics.
Gawain and the Green Knight Homepage: ⟨http://www.luminarium.org/medlit/gawain.htm⟩. Texts, links, essays, and articles by both scholars and students relating to *Sir Gawain and the Green Knight.*
Images of Medieval Art and Architecture: ⟨http://www.pitt.edu/~medart/⟩. Contains glossary of terms, images and floor plans of buildings (mostly castles and cathedrals), and maps. Focuses on France and Britain.
The Medieval Feminist Index: ⟨www.haverford.edu/library/reference/mschaus/mfi/mfi/html⟩. Bibliography of books and articles. Links to related sites.
The Medieval Science Page: ⟨http://members.aol.com/mcnelis/medsci_index/html⟩. Designed for students and nonspecialists. Collection of links to alchemy, biology, medicine, et al. Contains material on Greek and Roman antecedents.
The Medtext Database: ⟨http://www.mun.ca/mst/medtext/⟩. Archives of a medieval discussion group. Lots of topics addressed, generally by professors and others exchanging opinions and ideas.
Piers Plowman Electronic Archive: ⟨http://jefferson.village.virginia.edu/piers/archive.goals.html⟩. Addresses problems arising from the multiple texts of this work. Features manuscript descriptions and a Piers Plowman search engine.

Standard Textbooks

Although *The Medieval World View* provides a good historical introduction to the basic events and personalities of the medieval period, there is value in consulting more traditional medieval history texts or general introductions.

Hollister, C. Warren. *Medieval Europe: A Short History*. 5th ed. New York: Wiley, 1982.

Hoyt, Robert, and Stanley Chodorow. *Europe in the Middle Ages*. 3d ed. New York: Harcourt, Brace and Jovanovich, 1976.

Lopez, Robert. *The Birth of Europe*. New York: Evans, World, 1967.

Oakley, Francis. *The Medieval Experience*. New York: Scribners, 1974.

Peters, Edward. *Europe: The World of the Middle Ages*. Englewood Cliffs: Prentice-Hall, 1977.

Rosenwein, Barbara. *A Short History of the Middle Ages*. Peterborough: Broadview, 2001.

Tierney, Brian. *Western Europe in the Middle Ages 300–1475*. 6th ed. New York: Knopf, 1999.

Multiple-Volume Series

The most important work of this sort is Cambridge University Press' *New Cambridge Medieval History*, an ongoing project. Each volume contains chapters written by experts on specific topics, and the bibliographies are valuable. The older *Cambridge Medieval History* contains useful essays despite its age. There is also a handsome *Cambridge Illustrated History of the Middle Ages*.

There are also some more focused multivolume histories. A good example is R. W. and A. J. Carlyle, *A History of Medieval Political Theory in the West* (London: William Blackwood and Sons, rpt. 1962). An interesting new series is the Oxford University Press *Great Medieval Thinkers* that already contains studies of Duns Scotus, Robert Grosseteste, John Scotus Eriugena, and Bernard of Clairvaux.

As with series containing primary sources, there are several that are larger in scope than the Middle Ages but contain important medieval volumes.

The Cambridge Companions. Cambridge: Cambridge University Press. These volumes contain specially commissioned articles by leading scholars written with students and nonspecialists in mind. There are already *Cambridge Companions* to Augustine, Aquinas, Chaucer, Dante, Ockham, Medieval Romances, and Giotto in print.

General History of Europe. New York: Holt, Rinehart and Winston. Several volumes deal with the Middle Ages, and the books dealing with the end of the ancient world and with the Renaissance and Reformation are also helpful.

Handbook of Church History. Montreal: Palm Publishers. The first four volumes deal with the early Christian and medieval periods and include extensive bibliographies.

History of European Civilization Library. New York: Harcourt, Brace and Jovanovich. The volumes dealing with the Middle Ages are well illustrated.

A History of Christian Spirituality. New York: Seabury. The first two volumes are of interest to medievalists.

A Longman History of Italy. London: Longman. The first two volumes are about Italy during the Middle Ages.

The Making of European Civilization. New York: McGraw-Hill. The medieval volumes contain useful essays and lavish illustration.

Major Issues in History. New York: Wiley. Individual volumes contain some source material as well as interpretative essays.

The Oxford History of England. Oxford: Oxford University Press. The first six volumes cover England before 1485.

The Pelican History of Art. New York: Penguin.

The Pelican History of the Church. New York: Penguin. There are volumes on the early Church, the Church in the Middle Ages, and the Reformation.

Problems in European Civilization. Boston: D.C. Heath. Each volume contains several essays that provide a wide range of interpretations, and some are accompanied by relevant source materials. The coronation of Charlemagne and the pontificate of Innocent III are important medieval volumes in this series.

Encyclopedias and Other Useful Reference Materials

There is a growing number of research tools with multiple listings and entries that are valuable both for their articles and their bibliographies. The burgeoning number of encyclopedias is especially important because they collect the work of hundreds of scholars writing about their specialties, and the entries are long enough to be valuable for even advanced researchers.

Atlas of Medieval Europe. Ed. Angus Mackay. London: Routledge, 1997.

Augustine through the Ages: An Encyclopedia. Grand Rapids, MI: Eerdmans, 1999.

The Cambridge History of Medieval English Literature. Cambridge: Cambridge University Press, 1999.

Chronology of the Medieval World, 400–1491, compiled by R. L. L. Storey. New York: D. McKay, 1973.

The Dante Encyclopedia. New York: Garland, 2000.

A Dictionary of Biblical Tradition in English Literature. Grand Rapids, MI: Eerdmans, 1992

Dictionary of the Middle Ages. Ed. Joseph Strayer. 13 vols. New York, Scribner's, rpt.1989.

Encyclopedia of Early Christianity. New York: Garland, 1990.

Encyclopedia of the Early Church. 2 vols. Cambridge: Lutterworth Press, 1992.

Encyclopedia of the Middle Ages. 2 vols. Cambridge: Lutterworth Press, 2001. Edited by André Vauchez, these volumes contain 3,200 entries by 600 scholars.

Iconography of Christian Art. Ed. Gertrude Schlller. Trans. Janet Seligman. 2 vols. Greenwich, CT: New York Graphic Society, 1971. Incomplete but nevertheless valuable.

Medieval Studies: An Introduction. Ed. James Powell. 2d ed. Syracuse: Syracuse University Press, 1992. Each chapter is an orientation to a subfield of medieval studies from paleography (ancient handwriting) to canon law to music. Each chapter has a useful bibliography.

The Middle Ages: A Concise Encyclopedia. London: Thames and Hudson, 1999.

The New Catholic Encyclopedia. New York: McGraw-Hill, 1967.

The Oxford Classical Dictionary. Ed. N. G. L. Hammond and H. H. Scullard. 2d ed. Oxford: Oxford University Press, 1970.

The Oxford Dictionary of the Christian Church. Ed. F. L. Cross. Oxford: Oxford University Press, 1966.

The Times Atlas of World History. Ed. Geoffrey Barraclough. Maplewood, NJ: Hammond, 1979.

SPECIALIZED STUDIES AND BOOKS
Reprints

There are several important reprint series, designed to keep certain older books in print and to collect journal articles so that they are easily accessible. The most important of the first type is *Medieval Academy Reprints for Teaching*, published by the University of Toronto Press in association with the Medieval Academy of America. Some of these reprints are primary texts such as the *Defensor Pacis* of Marsilius of Padua, but most are secondary works such as R. W. Southern's *The Making of the Middle Ages*. Some works, such as Brian Tierney's *The Crisis of Church and State, 1050–1300*, combine primary texts with modern analysis. The most important series of reprinted articles is *Variorum Reprints* and includes the collected articles of scholars such as Giles Constable, David Herlihy, and Walter Ullmann. It is especially strong in the fields of the Crusades and the history of the Byzantine Empire.

An Online Discussion

There is a Medieval Academic Discussion Group in which a wide range of topics is discussed. This is a largely scholarly group and not a place for casual browsers or people who are only interested in making medieval costumes or recipes. It is ⟨http://www.towson. edu/~duncan/acalists.html⟩.

Periodical Literature

Much of the important scholarly work done in medieval studies appears in articles published in journals. There are journals that publish medieval work exclusively and many others that contain medieval articles from time to time. Literally hundreds and perhaps thousands of journals at least occasionally contain studies of interest to medievalists. It is important to be aware of the fact that many periodicals now have online versions, and there are some journals that exist only electronically. When searching for periodicals in libraries, it is not sufficient to browse through the current or bound periodicals because many journals, especially older volumes, are found in microtext versions.

Speculum, Traditio, Exemplaria, Journal of Medieval and Early Modern Studies, Medium Aevum, Medievalia et Humanistica, Medieval Studies, Viator, and the *Journal of Medieval History* are among the most important periodicals in English devoted entirely to the study of the Middle Ages. Journals such as the *American Historical Review, Art Bulletin, Publication of the Modern Language Association (PMLA),* and *Church History* publish important studies of medieval topics. Many journals published in non-English-speaking countries often contain articles written in English. Thus, researchers should search for materials in publications with foreign language titles.

There are virtually countless specialized journals that contain articles of value to those interested in the Middle Ages. We can illustrate this point by looking at the topic of Saint Francis of Assisi. First, articles about Francis of Assisi and his Order can be found in all of the publications listed in the previous paragraph. However, there is also much more about Francis and his Order in specialized publications. There are scholarly journals such as *Franciscan Studies* that contain the latest scholarship. There are also more popular journals, for example *The Cord*, that sometimes have articles of interest to people studying the history and spirituality of Francis and the Order. There are many Franciscan journals published in other countries, for example *Franziskanische Studien* and *Studi francescani*, that contain articles written in English. Often, articles in such journals that are published in other languages are preceded or followed by an English summary. The Franciscan journal *Greyfriars Review* regularly publishes English translations of important articles originally published in other languages. What we have said here about Franciscan studies can be applied to many other subfields of medieval studies.

Books

The following list of books is once again selective and representative rather than comprehensive. It is a place to start. There are several principles that we used in creating this bibliography that the reader needs to be aware of. Generally, we have given precedence to new works, in part because they incorporate ideas of older works and in part because they contain more up-to-date bibliographies. Sometimes an older book is listed because there is no more recent work on the subject. An example is T. S. R. Boase's biography of Pope Boniface VIII, published in 1933. Other older works that we include are often regarded as "classics" in the field. Most of books included here are what are generally called monographs, specialized studies written for those who have some previous knowledge of the field. But we have also included many books that were written for a general reader. We have ordinarily not given the subtitles of books unless they clarify the subject matter of an otherwise general or ambiguous title. An example of the latter is Margaret Miles, *Desire and Delight: A New Reading of Augustine's Confessions*. The main title does not suggest the subject matter. On the other hand, we do not give the subtitle for A. B. Cobban, *The Medieval Universities: Their Development and Organization* because the title itself is descriptive of this work, which is an overview of the universities of medieval Europe. Often we add brief annotations to clarify the subject matter, point out particular features of a book, state the level of generality or specificity of a book, or give our opinion of its value. Of course, the very fact that a book appears here suggests that we believe it to be of some value.

Abulafia, David. *Frederick II: A Medieval Emperor*. New York: Penguin, 1988.

Ackroyd, P. R., and C. F. Evans, eds. *The Cambridge History of the Bible*. Vol. 1, *From the Beginnings to Jerome*. Cambridge: Cambridge University Press, 1970. Articles by major scholars on important "founders" of the Middle Ages including Origen, Jerome, and Augustine.

Adams, Marilyn McCord. *William Ockham*. 2 vols. Notre Dame: University of Notre Dame Press, 1987.

Alexander, Jonathan J. G. *Medieval Illuminators and Their Method of Work*. New Haven: Yale University Press, 1992.

Allen, Judson Boyce. *The Friar as Critic: Literary Attitudes in the Later Middle Ages*. Nashville: Vanderbilt University Press, 1971.

Allmand, Christopher. *The Hundred Years War: England and France at War, c.1300–c.1450*. Cambridge: Cambridge University Press, 1988.

Andrews, Francis. *The Early Humiliati*. Cambridge: Cambridge University Press, 1999.

Artz, Frederick. *The Mind of the Middle Ages*. 3d ed. Chicago: University of Chicago Press, 1980.

Auerbach, Erich. *Literary Language and Its Public in Late Antiquity and the Middle Ages*. Princeton: Princeton University Press, 1965.

————. *Mimesis: The Representation of Reality in Western Literature.* Princeton: Princeton University Press, 1953. One of the most influential books of literary criticism ever written, it is also a penetrating study of the relationship between literature and culture, describing the concept of "reality" that undergirds works from Homer to the twentieth century. Six chapters deal especially with the Middle Ages.

Baldwin, John. *The Scholastic Culture of the Middle Ages 1000–1300.* Lexington, MA: D.C. Heath, 1971.

Barraclough, Geoffrey. *The Crucible of Europe: The Ninth and Tenth Centuries in European History.* Berkeley: University of California Press, 1976.

Barron, Robert. *Heaven in Stone and Glass.* New York: Crossroad, 2000.

Bartlett, Anne Clark. *Male Authors, Female Readers: Representation and Subjectivity in Middle English Devotional Literature.* Ithaca and London: Cornell University Press, 1995.

Bartlett, Robert. *The Making of Europe: Conquest, Colonization, and Cultural Change 950–1350.* Princeton: Princeton University Press, 1983.

Becker, Marvin. *Medieval Italy: Constraints and Creativity.* Bloomington: Indiana University Press, 1981.

Beckwith, Sarah. *Christ's Body: Identity, Culture, and Society in Late Medieval Writings.* London and New York: Routledge, 1993.

Bennett, Judith, et al., Eds. *Sisters and Workers in the Middle Ages.* Chicago: University of Chicago, 1989.

Bernstein, Alan. *The Formation of Hell.* Ithaca: Cornell University Press, 1993.

Bestul, Thomas H. *Texts of the Passion: Latin Devotional Literature and Medieval Society.* Philadelphia: University of Pennsylvania Press, 1996.

Black, Anthony. *Political Thought in Europe, 1250–1450.* Cambridge: Cambridge University Press, 1992.

Bloch, Marc. *Feudal Society.* 2 vols. Chicago: University of Chicago Press, 1961. Despite many important subsequent studies of the feudal era of European history, this book remains the most important study of the subject.

Bloom, Jonathan, and Sheila Blair. *Islam: A Thousand Years of Faith and Power* New York: TV Books, 2000.

Boase, T. S. R. *Boniface VIII.* London: Constable and Company, 1933.

Bolgar, R. R. *The Classical Heritage.* New York: Harper and Row, 1964.

Boswell, John. *Christianity, Social Tolerance, and Homosexuality.* Chicago: University of Chicago Press, 1980.

————. *The Kindness of Strangers.* New York: Pantheon, 1998. A fascinating study of how people in the Middle Ages dealt with abandoned and orphaned children.

Bougerol, J. Guy. *Introduction to the Works of Bonaventure.* Paterson, NJ: St. Anthony Guild Press, 1964.

Bowersock, G. W., et al., eds. *Interpreting Late Antiquity.* Cambridge: Cambridge University Press, 2001. A collection of essays by leading scholars, primarily dealing with intellectual changes.

Bowsky, William. *A Medieval Italian Commune: Siena under the Nine, 1287–1355.* Berkeley: University of California Press, 1981. This book is a model of medieval urban history.

Bradbury, Jim. *Philip Augustus: King of France 1180–1223.* London: Longman, 1998.

Brentano, Robert. *A New World in a Small Place: Church and Religion in the Diocese of Rieti, 1188–1378.* Berkeley: University of California Press, 1994.

————. *Rome before Avignon: A Social History of Thirteenth-Century Rome.* London: Longman, 1974.

————. *Two Churches: England and Italy in the Thirteenth Century.* Berkeley: University of California Press, 1968. The three volumes by Brentano are a kind of trilogy, examining from a variety of perspectives the cultural, intellectual, and social changes of the thirteenth century

Bright, Pamela, ed. and trans. *Augustine and the Bible.* Notre Dame: University of Notre Dame Press, 1999. A collection of essays by various scholars.

Brooke, Christopher. *The Monastic World, 1000–1300.* New York: Random House, 1974. Lavish illustrations and a readable text make this book a good introduction to medieval monasticism.

————. *The Structure of Medieval Society.* Garden City: Doubleday, 1971.

Brooke, Rosalind. *Early Franciscan Government.* Cambridge: Cambridge University Press, 1959.

Brooke, Rosalind, and Christopher Brooke. *Popular Religion in the Middle Ages.* London: Thames and Hudson, 1984.

Brown, George. *Bede the Venerable.* Boston: Twayne, 1987.

Brown, Peter. *Augustine of Hippo.* Berkeley: University of California Press, 1967. This masterful biography is also an excellent guide to the writings of Augustine.

————. *Authority and the Sacred: Aspects of the Christianization of the Roman World.* Cambridge: Cambridge University Press, 1995.

————. *The Body and Society: Men, Women, and Sexual Renunciation in Early Christianity.* New York: Columbia University Press, 1988.

————. *The Making of Late Antiquity.* Cambridge: Harvard University Press, 1978.

————. *Power and Persuasion in Late Antiquity: Towards a Christian Empire.* Madison: University of Wisconsin Press, 1992.

————. *The Rise of Western Christendom: Triumph and Diversity, AD 200-1000.* Oxford: Basil Blackwell, 1996.

————. *Society and the Holy in Late Antiquity.* Berkeley: University of California Press, 1982.

————. *The World of Late Antiquity A.D. 150–750.* New York: Harcourt, Brace and Jovanovich, 1971.

Brown, Raymond. *An Introduction to the New Testament.* New York: Doubleday, 1997. A very impressive survey of Christian biblical literature by a renowned scripture scholar.

Brundage, James. *Law, Sex, and Christian Society in Medieval Europe.* Chicago: University of Chicago Press, 1987.

————. *Medieval Canon Law.* London: Longman, 1995.

Burckhardt, Jacob. *The Civilization of the Renaissance in Italy.* New York: Penguin, 1990. This classic, originally published in 1860 and available in several English translations, is the most influential book ever written about the Renaissance. It is largely responsible for the still all-too-common view that the Renaissance in Italy was the beginning of individualism and was a rejection of the barbarism of the Middle Ages.

Burke, Peter. *The Renaissance Sense of the Past.* New York: St. Martin's, 1969. Burke begins with a discussion of the medieval sense of the past and discusses continuity and change during the Renaissance.

Burns, Thomas. *A History of the Ostrogoths.* Bloomington: Indiana University Press, 1984.

Burr, David. *The Spiritual Franciscans: From Protest to Persecution in the Century after Saint Francis*. University Park: Pennsylvania State University Press, 2001.

Burton-Christie, Douglas. *The Word in the Desert: Scripture and the Quest for Holiness in Early Christian Monasticism*. New York: Oxford University Press, 1993.

Bynum, Caroline. *Jesus as Mother*. Berkeley: University of California Press, 1982. A study of a spirituality of the feminine side of Christ that largely developed in the twelfth century.

————. *Holy Feast and Holy Fast: The Religious Significance of Food to Medieval Women*. Berkeley and Los Angeles: University of California Press, 1987.

————. *The Resurrection of the Body in Western Christianity, 200–1336*. New York: Columbia University Press, 1995.

Cadden, Joan. *The Meaning of Sexual Difference in the Middle Ages: Medicine, Science, and Culture*. Cambridge: Cambridge University Press, 1993.

Cahill, Thomas. *How the Irish Saved Civilization*. New York: Doubleday, 1995.

Calkins, Robert. *Illuminated Books of the Middle Ages*. Ithaca: Cornell University Press, 1983.

Canning, Joseph. *A History of Medieval Political Thought, 300–1450*. London: Routledge, 1996.

Cantor, Norman. *The Invention of the Middle Ages*. New York: William Morrow, 1991. A controversial and opinionated discussion about how the best known scholars of the twentieth century contributed to the formation of ideas concerning the Middle Ages.

Carruthers, Mary. *The Book of Memory: A Study of Memory in Medieval Culture*. Cambridge: Cambridge University Press, 1990.

Chadwick, Henry. *The Early Church*. Baltimore: Penguin, 1967. A volume of the *Pelican History of the Church*. Still a good introduction to the first centuries of Christian history.

————. *John Cassian*. 2d ed. Cambridge: Cambridge University Press, 1968.

Chenu, M.-D. *Nature, Man, and Society in the Twelfth Century*. Chicago: University of Chicago Press, 1968. Excellent essays on intellectual changes of the twelfth century.

————. *Toward an Understanding of St. Thomas*. Chicago: Henry Regnery, 1964.

Chitty, Derwas. *The Desert a City*. London: Mowbray's, 1966. A study of the earliest monks of the desert of Egypt.

Cipolla, Carlo. *The Fontana Economic History of Europe: The Middle Ages*. London: Fontana, 1972.

Clanchy, M. T. *From Memory to Written Record: England 1066–1307*. Cambridge: Harvard University Press, 1979.

Cobban, A. B. *The Medieval Universities*. London: Methuen, 1975.

Cochrane, C. W. *Christianity and Classical Culture*. Oxford: Clarendon Press, 1940.

Colish, Marcia. *Medieval Foundations of the Western Intellectual Tradition*. New Haven: Yale University Press, 1997.

Constable, Giles. *The Reformation of the Twelfth Century*. Cambridge: Cambridge University Press, 1996.

————. *Three Studies in Medieval Religious and Social Thought*. Cambridge: Cambridge University Press, 1995.

Cook, William. *Francis of Assisi: The Way of Poverty and Humility*. Dover, DE: Michael Glazier, 1989 (also Collegeville, MN: Liturgical Press).

————. *Images of St Francis of Assisi in Paintings, Stone, and Glass from the Earli-*

est Images to ca.1320 in Italy: A Catalogue. Florence: Leo S. Olschki, 1999. This catalogue is not just of use in studying Franciscan art but also for learning how art is connected to other aspects of the medieval experience.

Copland, Rita. *Rhetoric, Hermeneutics, and Translation in the Middle Ages: Academic Traditions and Vernacular Texts*. Cambridge: Cambridge University Press, 1991.

Copleston, F. C. *A History of Philosophy*. Vol. 2, *Medieval Philosophy*. Garden City: Doubleday, 1962.

Cowdrey, H. E. J. *Gregory VII, 1973–1085*. Oxford: Oxford University Press, 1998.

Crocker, Richard L. *An Introduction to Gregorian Chant*. New Haven: Yale University Press, 1996.

Crombie, A. C. *Medieval and Early Modern Science*. 2 vols. Garden City: Doubleday, 1959.

Cross, Richard. *Duns Scotus*. Oxford: Oxford University Press, 1999.

Curtius, Ernst. *European Literature and the Latin Middle Ages*. Princeton: Princeton University Press, 1953. Traces, with exceptional scholarly precision, the continuity of literary commonplaces, or "topoi," from antiquity through the Middle Ages.

Cusack, Pearce. *An Interpretation of the Second Dialogue of Gregory the Great*. Lewiston, NY: Edwin Mellen Press, 1993.

Daniel, E. Randolph. *The Franciscan Concept of Mission in the Middle Ages*. Lexington: University of Kentucky Press, 1975.

Daniélou, Jean. *The Bible and the Liturgy*. Notre Dame: University of Notre Dame Press, 1956.

Davis, Brian. *The Thought of Thomas Aquinas*. Oxford: Clarendon Press, 1993.

Dawson, Christopher. *The Making of Europe*. New York: Meridian Books, 1956.

Delahaye, Hippolyte. *The Legends of the Saints*. Notre Dame: University of Notre Dame Press, 1961. This still has value as an introduction to medieval hagiography even though the author is not always sympathetic to the genre he writes about.

De Lubac, Henri. *Medieval Exegesis: The Four Senses of Scripture*. 2 vols. Grand Rapids: Eerdmans, 1998. This French work of 1959–1964 is now in English translation. Indispensable for the study of medieval understandings of the Bible.

DeWulf, Maurice. *Philosophy and Civilization in the Middle Ages*. New York: Dover, 1953.

Dodds, E. R. *Pagan and Christian in an Age of Anxiety*. New York: Norton, rpt.1970.

Dronke, Peter. *Women Writers of the Middle Ages: A Critical Study of Texts from Perpetua (203) to Marguerite Porete (1310)*. Cambridge: Cambridge University Press, 1984.

Duby, Georges. *The Early Growth of the European Economy*. Ithaca: Cornell University Press, 1974.

———. *The Europe of the Cathedrals, 1140–1280*. Cleveland: World, 1964.

———. *France in the Middle Ages, 987–1460: From Hugh Capet to Joan of Arc*. Trans. Juliet Vale. Oxford: Basil Blackwell, 1991.

Duckett, Eleanor. *Carolingian Portraits: A Study of the Ninth Century*. Ann Arbor: University of Michigan Press, 1962.

———. *The Gateway to the Middle Ages*. 3 vols. Ann Arbor: University of Michigan Press, 1961.

Duffy, Eamon. *The Stripping of the Altars: Traditional Religion in England, c.1400–c.1580*. New Haven: Yale University Press, 1992.

Duhem, Pierre. *Medieval Cosmology: Theories of Infinity, Place, Time, Void, and the*

Plurality of Worlds. Ed. and trans. Roger Ariew. Chicago: University of Chicago Press, 1985.

Dunn, Marilyn. *The Emergence of Monasticism: From the Desert Fathers to the Early Middle Ages.* Oxford: Blackwell, 2000.

Dyer, Christopher. *Standards of Living in the Later Middle Ages: Social Change in England, c. 1200–1520.* Cambridge: Cambridge University Press, 1989.

Elliott, Dylan. *Fallen Bodies: Pollution, Sexuality, and Demonology in the Middle Ages.* Philadelphia: University of Pennsylvania Press, 1999.

Ellis Davidson, H. R. *Gods and Myths of Northern Europe.* Baltimore: Penguin, 1961.

Emmerson, Richard K. *Antichrist in the Middle Ages: A Study of Medieval Apocalypticism, Art, and Literature.* Seattle: University of Washington Press, 1981.

Emmerson, Richard K., and Ronald B. Herzman. *The Apocalyptic Imagination in Medieval Literature.* Philadelphia: University of Pennsylvania Press, 1992.

Emmerson, Richard K., and Bernard McGinn, eds. *The Apocalypse in the Middle Ages.* Ithaca: Cornell University Press, 1993.

Erdmann, Carl. *The Origin of the Idea of Crusade.* Princeton: Princeton University Press, 1977.

Evans, G. R. *The Language and Logic of the Bible: The Earlier Middle Ages.* Cambridge: Cambridge University Press, 1984.

Evans, Joan. *Monastic Life at Cluny 910–1157.* New York: Anchor Books, rpt.1968.

Ferrante, Joan. *The Political Vision of the Divine Comedy.* Princeton: Princeton University Press, 1984.

Fichtenau, Heinrich. *The Carolingian Empire.* Trans. Peter Munz. Toronto: University of Toronto Press, 1978.

———. *Living in the Tenth Century: Mentalities and Social Orders.* Trans. Patrick Geary. Chicago: University of Chicago Press, 1991.

Fleming, John. *Classical Imitation and Interpretation in Chaucer's Troilus.* Lincoln: University of Nebraska Press, 1990.

———. *An Introduction to the Franciscan Literature of the Middle Ages.* Chicago: Franciscan Herald Press (now Quincy, IL: Franciscan Press), 1977.

Fletcher, Richard. *The Barbarian Conversion from Paganism to Christianity.* New York: Henry Holt, 1997.

Folz, Robert. *The Coronation of Charlemagne: 25 December 800.* London: Routledge and Kegan Paul, 1974.

Fortini, Arnaldo. *Francis of Assisi.* Trans. Helen Moak. New York: Crossroad, 1981. This is a useful abridgement of the most detailed (2,000+ pages) biography of Saint Francis.

Fowler, David. *The Bible in Early English Literature.* Seattle: University of Washington Press, 1976.

———. *The Bible in Middle English Literature.* Seattle: University of Washington Press, 1984.

Frank, Isnard. *A Concise History of the Medieval Church.* New York: Continuum, 1996.

Freccero, John. *Dante: The Poetics of Conversion.* Ed. Rachel Jacoff. Cambridge: Harvard University Press, 1986.

Fudge, Thomas. *The Magnificent Ride: The First Reformation in Hussite Bohemia.* Aldershot: Ashgate, 1998.

Geary, Patrick. *Before France and Germany: The Creation and Transformation of the Merovingian World.* New York: Oxford University Press, 1987.

Gehl, Paul F. *A Moral Art: Grammar, Society, and Culture in Trecento Florence.* Ithaca: Cornell University Press, 1993.

Gilson, Etienne. *Heloise and Abelard.* Ann Arbor: University of Michigan Press, 1960.

———. *Reason and Revelation in the Middle Ages.* New York: Scribner's, 1966. Gilson was one of the greatest students of medieval philosophy in the twentieth century, and this short work is a valuable synthesis of his thought.

Goffart, Walter. *Barbarians and Romans A.D. 418–584: The Techniques of Accommodation.* Princeton: Princeton University Press, 1980.

———. *The Narrators of Barbarian History (A.D.550–800): Jordanes, Gregory of Tours, Bede, and Paul the Deacon.* Princeton: Princeton University Press, 1988.

Gottfried, Robert. *The Black Death.* New York: The Free Press, 1983.

Grabar, André. *Christian Iconography: A Study of Its Origins.* Princeton: Princeton University Press, 1968.

Hallam, Elizabeth. *Capetian France 987–1328.* New York: Longman, 1980.

Hardison, O. B. *Christian Rite and Christian Drama in the Middle Ages.* Baltimore: The Johns Hopkins University Press, 1965.

Haskins, Charles Homer. *The Renaissance of the Twelfth Century.* Cambridge: Harvard University Press, 1927. Haskins "invented" the idea of a medieval renaissance in this landmark book in the field of medieval studies.

Hayes, Zachary. *Bonaventure's Mystical Writings.* New York: Crossroad, 1999.

Heer, Friedrich. *The Medieval World.* New York: Mentor Books, 1961.

Heffernan, Thomas. *Sacred Biography: Saints and Their Biographers in the Middle Ages.* New York: Oxford University Press, 1988.

Henzelmann, Martin. *Gregory of Tours: History and Society in the Sixth Century.* Cambridge: Cambridge University Press, 2001.

Herlihy, David. *The Black Death and the Transformation of the West.* Cambridge: Harvard University Press, 1997.

———. *Medieval Households.* Cambridge: Harvard University Press, 1985.

———. *Opera Muliebria: Women and Work in Medieval Europe.* Philadelphia: Temple Univeristy Press, 1990.

Herrin, Judith. *The Formation of Christendom.* Princeton: Princeton University Press, 1987.

Hinnebusch, William. *The History of the Dominican Order.* 2 vols. New York: Alba House, 1966, 1973.

Hoeberichts, J. *Francis and Islam.* Quincy, IL: Franciscan Press, 1997.

Hollywood, Amy M. *The Soul as Virgin Wife: Mechtild of Magdeburg, Marguerete Porete, and Meister Eckhart.* Notre Dame: University of Notre Dame Press, 1995.

Hudson, John. *The Formation of English Common Law.* London: Longman, 1996.

Huizinga, Johan. *The Autumn of the Middle Ages.* Trans. Rodney Payton and Ulrich Mammitzsch. Chicago: University of Chicago Press, 1996. This book, originally published in 1921, appeared in an earlier translation under the title *The Waning of the Middle Ages.* Although some regard the book as outdated, it has received a new round of plaudits in this more modern and accurate translation.

Hussey, J. M. *The Orthodox Church in the Byzantine Empire.* New York: Oxford University Press, 1986.

Jacoff, Rachel, and Jeffrey T. Schnapp, eds. *The Poetry of Allusion: Virgil and Ovid in Dante's Commedia.* Stanford: Stanford University Press, 1991.

Jaeger, C. Stephen. *The Envy of Angels: Cathedral Schools and Social Ideals in Medieval Europe, 950–1200.* Philadelphia: University of Pennsylvania Press, 1994.

————. *The Origins of Courtliness: Civilizing Trends and the Formation of Courtly Ideals, 930–1210*. Philadelphia: University of Pennsylvania Press, 1985.

Jaeger, Werner. *Early Christianity and the Greek Paideia*. Oxford: Oxford University Press, 1961.

Jager, Eric. *The Book of the Heart*. Chicago: University of Chicago Press, 2000

Jantzen, Grace. *Power, Gender, and Christian Mysticism*. Cambridge: Cambridge University Press, 1995.

Jeffrey, David L. *The Early English Lyric and Franciscan Spirituality*. Lincoln: University of Nebraska Press, 1975. This study links Franciscan spirituality with one form of vernacular literature.

————. *People of the Book: Christian Identity and Literary Culture*. Grand Rapids: Eerdmans, 1996.

Jones, A. H. M. *Constantine and the Conversion of Europe*. Baltimore: Penguin, rpt.1972. A readable account by a great scholar.

Jordan, William. *The Great Famine: Northern Europe in the Early Fourteenth Century*. Princeton: Princeton University Press, 1996. This study makes clear the population loss in Europe in the fourteenth century involves many more factors than the arrival of the bubonic plague bacillus.

Justice, Stephen. *Writing and Rebellion: England in 1381*. Berkeley and Los Angeles: University of California Press, 1994.

Kantorowicz, Ernst. *The King's Two Bodies: A Study in Medieval Political Theology*. Princeton: Princeton University Press, 1957. A standard work. The subtitle suggests how the author looks at kingship from a theological perspective.

Kardong, Terrence. *Benedict's Rule: A Translation and Commentary*. Collegeville, MN: Liturgical Press, 1996. The translation included in this volume is the *RB 1980* listed in the primary sources section.

Keen, Maurice. *Chivalry*. New Haven: Yale University Press, 1984.

Kelly, J. N. D. *Jerome: His Life, Writings, and Controversies*. New York: Harper and Row, 1975.

Kieckhefer, Richard. *Unquiet Souls: Fourteenth-Century Saints and Their Religious Milieu*. Chicago: University of Chicago Press, 1984.

King, Peter. *Western Monasticism*. Kalamazoo: Cistercian Publications, 1999.

Knowles, David. *Christian Monasticism*. London: Weidenfeld and Nicholson, 1969.

————. *The English Mystical Tradition*. New York: Harper and Row, 1961.

————. *The Evolution of Medieval Thought*. New York: Random House, 1962. This work is something of a classic of modern scholarship.

Kolve, V. A. *The Play Called* Corpus Christi. Stanford: Stanford University Press, 1966. A study of the origins of drama in the Middle Ages.

Kretzmann, Norman, Anthony Kenny, and Jan Pinborg, eds. *The Cambridge History of Later Medieval Philosophy: From the Rediscovery of Aristotle to the Disintegration of Scholasticism, 1100–1600*. Cambridge: Cambridge University Press, 1982.

Kretzmann, Norman, and Eleonore Stump, eds. *The Cambridge Companion to Aquinas*. Cambridge: Cambridge University Press, 1994.

Künstler, Gustav, ed. *Romanesque Art in Europe*. Greenwich, CT: New York Graphic Society, 1968.

Kuttner, Stephan. *Harmony from Dissonance*. Latrobe, PA: St. Vincent Archabbey, 1960. This little-known gem is an introduction to canon law in the Middle Ages that draws a comparison between the development of law and music.

Lackner, Bede. *Eleventh-Century Background of Citeaux*. Kalamazoo: Cistercian Pub-
     lications, 1972. This volume begins with the ninth-century monastic reforms as-
     sociated with Benedict of Aniane and examines the revival of eremetical life in Eu-
     rope before the founding of Citeaux in 1098.
Ladner, Gerhart. *The Idea of Reform*. New York: Harper and Row, rpt.1967. A good
     example of "biography of an idea."
Laistner, M. L. W. *Thought and Letters in Western Europe A.D. 500–900*. Ithaca: Cor-
     nell University Press, 1957.
Lambert, Malcolm. *The Cathars*. Oxford: Basil Blackwell, 1998.
———. *Medieval Heresy: Popular Movements from the Gregorian Reform to the Re-
     formation*. 2d ed. Oxford: Basil Blackwell, 1992.
Lampe, G. W. H., ed. *The Cambridge Companion of the Bible*. Vol. 2, *The West from
     the Fathers to the Reformation*. Cambridge: Cambridge University Press, 1969.
     Excellent essays about the Bible both in Latin and in the vernacular in the Mid-
     dle Ages, including works by Beryl Smalley and Jean Leclercq.
Lapanski, Duane V. *Evangelical Perfection: An Historical Examination of the Concept
     in the Early Franciscan Sources*. St. Bonaventure, NY: Franciscan Institute Pub-
     lications, 1977.
Larner, John. *Italy in the Age of Dante and Petrarch, 1216–1380*. London: Longman,
     1980.
Lawrence, C. H. *The Friars: The Impact of the Early Mendicant Movement on West-
     ern Society*. London: Longman, 1994.
Leclercq, Jean. *The Love of Learning and the Desire for God*. New York: Fordham Uni-
     versity Press, 1974. A masterful study of monastic culture, beginning with the Fa-
     thers of the Church and culminating in the twelfth century. The best single book
     on the monastic experience.
———. *Monks and Love in Twelfth-Century France*. Oxford: Clarendon Press, 1979.
Leff, Gordon. *The Dissolution of the Medieval Outlook*. New York: Harper and Row, 1976.
———. *Medieval Thought: St. Augustine to Ockham*. Baltimore: Penguin, 1958.
Lekai, Louis. *The Cistercians: Ideals and Reality*. Kent, OH: Kent State University
     Press, 1977.
Lerer, Seth. *Boethius and Dialogue: Literary Method in the* Consolation of Philoso-
     phy. Princeton: Princeton University Press, 1986.
Lesnick, Daniel. *Preaching in Medieval Florence: The Social World of Franciscan and
     Dominican Spirituality*. Athens, GA: University of Georgia Press, 1989.
Lewis, C. S. *The Allegory of Love*. Oxford: Oxford University Press, 1936. Though
     Lewis is better known to young people as a writer of fantasy and to Christians as
     a powerful apologist, he was an important medieval scholar. Though many ideas
     in this book have been called into question, it is still an elegant introduction to
     medieval courtly literature.
———. *The Discarded Image*. Cambridge: Cambridge University Press, 1964. Although
     Lewis wrote this book primarily as an introduction to medieval and Renaissance
     literature, it is also a gracefully written introduction to medieval cosmology.
Leyser, Henrietta. *Hermits and the New Monasticism: A Study of Religious Commu-
     nities in Western Europe, 1000–1150*. New York: St. Martin's, 1984.
Lindberg, David. *The Beginnings of Western Science: The European Scientific Tradi-
     tion in Philosophical, Religious, and Institutional Context, 600 B.C. to A.D. 1450*.
     Chicago: University of Chicago Press, 1992.
Little, Lester. *Religious Poverty and the Profit Economy in Medieval Europe*. Ithaca:

Cornell University Press, 1978. Little examines the ways that various religious groups dealt with the development of a money economy. Although the author deals at length with the mendicant orders, he also discuses religious movements of the eleventh and twelfth centuries.

Lopez, Robert. *The Commercial Revolution of the Middle Ages, 950-1350.* Englewood Cliffs: Prentice-Hall, 1971.

Lynch, Joseph. *The Medieval Church: A Brief History.* New York: Longman, 1992.

Lyon, Bryce. *The Origins of the Middle Ages: Pirenne's Challenge to Gibbon.* New York: Norton, 1972. An examination of the historiography of the beginning of the Middle Ages.

MacMulllen, Ramsay. *Christianity and Paganism in the Fourth to Eighth Centuries.* New Haven: Yale University Press, 1997.

———. *Christianizing the Roman Empire.* New Haven: Yale University Press, 1984.

———. *Constantine.* New York: Harper and Row, 1969.

Macy, Gary. *Treasures from the Storeroom: Medieval Religion and the Eucharist.* Collegeville, MN: Liturgical Press, 1999. Contains a good article on the doctrine of transubstantiation.

Maginnis, Hayden B. J. *Painting in the Age of Giotto.* University Park: Pennsylvania State University Press, 1997.

———. *The World of the Early Sienese Painter.* University Park: Pennsylvania State University Press, 2001.

Mâle, Emile. *The Gothic Image: Religious Art in France of the Thirteenth Century.* New York: Harper and Row, 1958.

———. *Religious Art in France in the Twelfth Century: A Study of the Origins of Medieval Iconography.* Princeton: Princeton University Press, 1978. Beautifully illustrated.

Manselli, Raoul. *St. Francis of Assisi.* Chicago: Franciscan Herald Press, 1988.

Markus, Robert. *The End of Ancient Christianity.* Cambridge: Cambridge University Press, 1990.

Martines, Lauro. *Power and Imagination: City States in Renaissance Italy.* New York: Alfred Knopf, 1979. Although the subtitle suggests that this is a book about Renaissance Italian city-states, it is as much about the Middle Ages as the Renaissance because Martines "begins" the Renaissance extraordinarily early.

———. *Strong Words: Writing and Social Strain in the Italian Renaissance.* Baltimore: Johns Hopkins University Press, 2001.

Mathews, Thomas. *The Clash of Gods: A Reinterpretation of Early Christian Art.* Princeton: Princeton University Press, 1993. Mathews argues that the inventiveness and quality of Christian art played a significant role in the triumph of Christianity in the Roman Empire. Well illustrated.

Matter, E. Ann. *The Voice of My Beloved: The Song of Songs in Western Medieval Christianity.* Philadelphia: University of Pennsylvania Press, 1990.

McGinn, Bernard. *The Calabrian Abbot: Joachim of Fiore in the History of Western Thought.* New York: Macmillan, 1985.

———. *The Presence of God: A History of Western Christian Mysticism.* Vol. 1, *The Foundations of Mysticism*; Vol. 2, *The Growth of Mysticism*; Vol. 3, *The Flowering of Mysticism.* New York: Crossroad, 1991–1998.

McKittrick, Rosamond, ed. *Carolingian Culture: Emulation and Innovation.* Cambridge: Cambridge University Press, 1994. An excellent collection of essays concerning the main facets of the Carolingian Renaissance.

McNamara, Jo Ann. *Sisters in Arms: Catholic Nuns through Two Millennia*. Cambridge: Harvard University Press, 1996.

Menocal, Maria Rosa. *The Arabic Role in Medieval Literary History*. Philadelphia: University of Pennsylvania Press, 1987.

Merinbon, John. *Early Medieval Philosophy (480–1150): An Introduction*. London: Routledge and Kegan Paul, 1983.

Meyendorff, John. *Imperial Unity and Christian Divisions: The Church 450–680 A.D.* Crestwood, NY: St. Valdimir's Seminary Press, 1989.

Miles, Margaret. *Desire and Delight: A New Reading of Augustine's Confessions*. New York: Crossroad, 1992.

Mollat, Michel. *The Poor in the Middle Ages*. Trans. Arthur Goldhammer. New Haven: Yale University Press, 1990.

Moorhead, John. *Justinian*. London: Longman, 1994.

Moorman, John. *A History of the Franciscan Order from Its Origins to the Year 1517*. Oxford: Clarendon Press, 1967 (rpt. Quincy: Franciscan Press, 1998).

Morris, Colin. *The Discovery of the Individual 1050–1200*. London: SPCK, 1972 (rpt. Toronto: University of Toronto Press, 1991).

———. *The Papal Monarchy: The Western Church from 1050 to 1250*. Oxford: Oxford University Press, 1989.

Murray, Alexander, ed. *After Rome's Fall: Narrators and Sources of Early Medieval History*. Toronto: University of Toronto Press, 1998. A collection of essays dealing with problems in early medieval historiography.

———. *Reason and Society in the Middle Ages*. New York: Oxford University Press, 1986. More oriented toward social than intellectual history.

Newman, Barbara. *Sister of Wisdom: St. Hildegard's Theology of the Feminine*. Berkeley and Los Angeles: University of California Press, 1987.

———. *From Virile Woman to WomanChrist: Studies in Medieval Religion and Literature*. Philadelphia: University of Pennsylvania Press, 1995.

Nirenberg, David. *Communities of Violence: Persecution of Minorities in the Middle Ages*. Princeton: Princeton University Press, 1996.

Noble, Thomas. *The Republic of St. Peter: The Birth of the Papal State, 680–825*. Philadelphia: University of Pennsylvania Press, 1984.

Norwich, John Julius. *The Normans in Sicily*. London: Penguin, 1991.

O'Donnell, James. *Cassiodorus*. New York: Harper and Row, 1969.

Oberman, Heiko. *The Dawn of the Reformation*. Grand Rapids: Eerdmans, 1992.

———. *Forerunners of the Reformation*. New York: Holt, Rinehart and Winston, 1966.

———. *The Harvest of Medieval Theology*. Cambridge: Harvard University Press, 1963.

Orme, Nicholas. *From Childhood to Chivalry: The Education of English Kings and Aristocracy, 1066–1530*. London: Methuen, 1984.

Ozment, Steven E. *The Age of Reform (1250–1550): An Intellectual and Religious History of Late Medieval and Reformation Europe*. New Haven: Yale University Press, 1980.

Panofsky, Erwin. *Gothic Architecture and Scholasticism*. New York: World, 1957. There are newer works that study this relationship but none better.

Patch, Howard. *The Goddess Fortuna in Medieval Literature*. New York: Octagon, rpt.1967.

Pedersen, Olaf. *The First Universities: Studium Generale and the Origins of University Education in Europe*. Cambridge: Cambridge University Press, 1997.

Pelikan, Jaroslav. *The Excellent Empire: The Fall of Rome and the Triumph of the Church*. New York: Harper and Row, 1987.

———. *What Has Athens to Do with Jerusalem? Timaeus and Genesis in Counterpoint*. Ann Arbor: University of Michigan Press, 1997.

Pennington, Kenneth. *Pope and Bishops: The Papal Monarchy in the Twelfth and Thirteenth Centuries*. Philadelphia: University of Pennsylvania Press, 1984.

Peters, Edward. *Inquisition*. New York: Free Press, 1988.

Peterson, Ingrid. *Clare of Assisi: A Biographical Study*. Quincy, IL: Franciscan Press, 1993.

Peterson, Joan. *The Dialogues of Gregory the Great in Their Late Antique Cultural Background*. Toronto: Pontifical Institute of Medieval Studies, 1984.

Pieper, Joseph. *Scholasticism: Personalities and Problems of Medieval Philosophy*. New York: McGraw-Hill, 1969.

Pounds, N. J. G. *An Economic History of Medieval Europe*. 2d ed. New York: Longman, 1994.

Power, Kim. *Veiled Desire: Augustine on Women*. New York: Continuum, 1996.

Raby, F. J. E. *A History of Christian Latin Poetry from the Beginnings to the Close of the Middle Ages*. Oxford: Oxford University Press, 1927.

———. *A History of Secular Latin Poetry in the Middle Ages*. 2 vols. Oxford: Oxford University Press, 1934.

Ramsey, Boniface. *Ambrose*. London: Routledge, 1997.

Reames, Sherry. *The Legenda Aurea*. Madison: University of Wisconsin Press, 1985. A study of Jacopus de Voragine's *Golden Legend*, the Middle Ages' most important collection of saints' lives.

Reeves, Marjorie. *The Influence of Prophecy in the Later Middle Ages*. Oxford: Clarendon Press, 1969.

———. *Joachim of Fiore and the Prophetic Future*. New York: Harper and Row, 1976

Reynolds, L. D., and N. C. Wilson. *Scribes and Scholars: A Guide to the Transmission of Greek and Latin Literature*. 2d ed. Oxford: Clarendon Press, 1974.

Reynolds, Susan. *Fiefs and Vassals: The Medieval Evidence Reinterpreted*. New York: Oxford University Press, 1994.

Richards, Jeffrey. *Consul of God: The Life and Times of Gregory the Great*. London: Routledge and Kegan Paul, 1980.

———. *The Popes and the Papacy in the Early Middle Ages*. London: Routledge and Kegan Paul, 1979.

Riché, Pierre. *The Carolingians: A Family Who Forged Europe*. Trans. Michael Allen. Philadelphia: University of Pennsylvania Press, 1993.

———. *Education and Culture in the Barbarian West*. Columbia: University of South Carolina Press, 1976.

Riley-Smith, Jonathan. *The Crusades: A Short History*. New Haven: Yale University Press, 1987.

Robertson, D. W. *A Preface to Chaucer*. Princeton: Princeton University Press, 1962.

Robinson, I. S. *Henry IV of Germany, 1056–1106*. Cambridge: Cambridge University Press, 1999.

———. *The First Crusade and the Idea of Crusading*. Philadelphia: University of Pennsylvania Press, 1986.

Rorig, Fritz. *The Medieval Town*. Berkeley: University of California Press, 1971.

Rousseau, Philip. *Ascetics, Authority, and the Church in the Age of Jerome and Cassian*. New York: Oxford University Press, 1978.

Rubin, Miri. *Corpus Christi: The Eucharist in Late Medieval Culture.* Cambridge: Cambridge University Press, 1991.

Runciman, Steven. *A History of the Crusades.* 3 vols. New York: Harper and Row, 1951–1954.

Russell, Jeffrey Burton. *A History of Medieval Christianity: Prophecy and Order.* New York: Crowell, 1968.

———. *Lucifer: The Devil in the Middle Ages.* Ithaca: Cornell University Press, 1984.

———. *A History of Heaven.* Princeton: Princeton University Press, 1997,

Ryan, John. *Irish Monasticism.* Ithaca: Cornell University Press, rpt.1972.

Saenger, Paul Henry. *Space between Words: The Origins of Silent Reading.* Stanford: Stanford University Press, 1997.

Sahlin, Claire L., *Brigitta of Sweden and the Voice of Prophecy.* Rochester, NY: Boydell and Brewer, 2001.

Sauerländer, Willibald, and Max Hirmer. *Gothic Sculpture in France, 1140–1270.* New York: Harry Abrams, 1972. Lavishly illustrated.

Sayers, Jane. *Innocent III. Leader of Europe, 1198–1216.* London: Longman, 1994.

Schnapp, Jeffrey T. *The Transfiguration of History at the Center of Dante's Paradise.* Princeton: Princeton University Press, 1986.

Schneider, Michael. *A Beginner's Guide to Constructing the Universe: The Mathematical Archetypes of Nature, Art, and Science.* New York: Harper Collins, 1995. A large portion of this book deals with medieval cosmology and number symbolism.

Sears, Elizabeth. *The Ages of Man: Medieval Interpretations of the Life Cycle.* Princeton: Princeton University Press, 1986.

Seay, Albert. *Music in the Medieval World.* Englewood Cliffs: Prentice-Hall, 1965.

Setton, Kenneth, ed. *The Crusades.* 5 vols. Madison: University of Wisconsin Press, 1969ff. Each volume contains chapters written by scholars with special expertise.

Seznec, Jean. *The Survival of the Pagan Gods.* Princeton: Princeton University Press, 1954.

Shannon, William. *Anselm: The Joy of Faith.* New York: Crossroad, 1999.

Siberry, Elizabeth. *Criticism of Crusading, 1095–1274.* New York: Oxford University Press, 1985.

Smalley, Beryl. *Historians of the Middle Ages.* London: Thames and Hudson, 1974.

———. *The Study of the Bible in the Middle Ages.* Notre Dame: University of Notre Dame Press, 1964.

Sorrell, Roger. *St. Francis of Assisi and Nature.* New York: Oxford University Press, 1988.

Southern, R. W. *The Making of the Middle Ages.* New Haven: Yale University Press, 1953. Generations of students have been introduced to the Middle Ages through this brilliant work.

———. *Medieval Humanism and Other Studies.* New York: Harper and Row, 1970.

———. *St. Anselm and His Biographer.* Cambridge: Cambridge University Press, 1966.

———. *Western Society and the Church in the Middle Ages.* Baltimore: Penguin, 1970. A volume in the *Pelican History of the Church.* It lacks a strong chronological framework but contains the insights of one of the twentieth century's greatest medievalists.

Spade, Paul Vincent, ed. *The Cambridge Companion to Ockham.* Cambridge: Cambridge University Press, 1999. Like other volumes in this series, it contains essays accessible to non-experts by leading scholars.

Stewart, Columba. *Cassian the Monk*. New York: Oxford University Press, 1998.

Stock, Brian. *The Implications of Literacy: Written Language and Models of Interpretation in the Eleventh and Twelfth Centuries*. Princeton: Princeton University Press, 1983.

Straw, Carole. *Gregory the Great: Perfection in Imperfection*. Berkeley: University of California Press, 1988.

Strayer, Joseph. *Medieval Statecraft and the Perspectives of History*. Princeton: Princeton University Press, 1971.

———. *On the Medieval Origins of the Modern State*. Princeton: Princeton University Press, 1970. A brief and brilliant overview.

Strohm, Paul. *Social Chaucer*. Cambridge: Harvard University Press, 1989.

Stuard, Susan Mosher, ed. *Women in Medieval History and Historiography*. Philadelphia: University of Pennsylvania Press, 1987. Several of the essays deal with historiographical issues involving the history of medieval women.

Stump, Eleonore, and Norman Kretzmann, eds. *The Cambridge Companion to Augustine*. Cambridge: Cambridge University Press, 2001. Like other volumes in the Cambridge Companion series, this is a collection of essays by leading contemporary scholars written for nonspecialists.

Sumption, Jonathan. *Pilgrimage: An Image of Medieval Religion*. London: Faber and Faber, 1975.

Swanson, R. N. *Religion and Devotion in Europe, ca.1215–ca.1515*. Cambridge: Cambridge University Press, 1995.

Szittya, Penn R. *The Antifraternal Tradition in Medieval Literature*. Princeton: Princeton University Press, 1988.

Taylor, H. O. *The Medieval Mind*. 2 vols. 4th ed. New York: Macmillan, rpt. 1975.

Tellenbach, Gerd. *Church, State, and Society at the Time of the Investiture Contest*. New York: Harper and Row, 1970.

Tierney, Brian. *The Crisis of Church and State 1050–1300*. Englewood Cliffs: Prentice-Hall, 1964 (rpt. Toronto: University of Toronto Press, 1988).

———. *Foundations of the Conciliar Theory*. Cambridge: Cambridge University Press, 1955. Tierney focuses a great deal on the ideas of the canon lawyers of the twelfth and thirteenth centuries.

———. *The Idea of Natural Rights: Studies on Natural Rights, Natural Law, and Church Law, 1150–1625*. Atlanta: Scholars Press for Emory University, 1996.

———. *Origins of Papal Infallibility 1150–1300*. Leiden: Brill, 1972. An important study of canon law and mendicant traditions that places the origin of the idea of an infallible pope in a new context.

Tuchman, Barbara. *A Distant Mirror: The Calamitous Fourteenth Century*. New York: Knopf, 1978.

Turner, Victor, and Edith Turner. *Image and Pilgrimage in Christian Culture*. New York: Columbia University Press, 1978.

Tyerman, Christopher. *The Invention of the Crusades*. Toronto: University of Toronto Press, 1998.

Ullmann, Walter. *The Growth of Papal Government in the Middle Ages*. London: Methuen, 1955.

———. *Law and Politics in the Middle Ages*. London: The Sources of History, 1975.

———. *Medieval Political Thought* (originally published as *A History of Political Thought: The Middle Ages*). Baltimore: Penguin, 1970.

———. *A Short History of the Papacy in the Middle Ages*. London: Methuen, 1972.

Van Os, Henk. *The Art of Devotion in the Late Middle Ages in Europe 1300-1500.* London: Merrell Holberton, 1994.

Van Steenberghen, Fernand. *Aristotle in the West: The Origins of Latin Aristotelianism.* Louvain: Nauwelaerts, 1970.

Vauchez, André. *The Laity in the Middle Ages: Religious Beliefs and Devotional Practices.* Ed. Daniel Bornstein. Trans. Margery Schneider. Notre Dame: University of Notre Dame Press, 1993.

———. *Sainthood in the Later Middle Ages.* Trans. Jean Birrell. Cambridge: Cambridge University Press, 1997.

Vicaire, M.-H. *St. Dominic and His Times.* London: Darton, Longman, Todd, 1964.

Von Simson, Otto. *The Gothic Cathedral.* New York: Harper and Row, 1956. This work contains a valuable analysis of the influence of Pseudo-Dionysius on medieval thought in addition to its examination of Gothic aesthetics.

Vitto, Cindy. *The Virtuous Pagans in Middle English Literature.* Philadelphia: American Philosophical Society, 1989.

Wagner, David L. *The Seven Liberal Arts in the Middle Ages.* Bloomington: Indiana University Press, 1983.

Wakefield, Walter. *Heresy, Crusade, and Inquisition in Southern France, 1100–1250.* Berkeley: University of California Press, 1974.

Wallace, David. *Chaucerian Polity: Absolutist Lineages and Associational Forms in England and Italy.* Stanford: Stanford University Press, 1997.

Wallace-Hadrill, J. M. *The Barbarian West,* rev. ed. New York: Harper and Row, 1962. A brief but excellent overview of the Germans who settled in the Roman Empire.

———. *The Frankish Church.* Oxford: Clarendon Press, 1983.

———. *The Long-Haired Kings.* New York: Barnes and Noble, 1962.

Ward, Benedicta. *Miracles and the Medieval Mind: Theory, Record, and Event, 1000–1215.* Philadelphia: University of Pennsylvania Press, 1982.

Weisheipl, James. *Friar Thomas d'Aquino.* Garden City: Doubleday, 1974.

Wemple, Suzanne. *Women in Frankish Society: Marriage and the Cloister, 500–900.* Philadelphia: University of Pennsylvania Press, 1981.

White, Lynn. *Medieval Technology and Social Change.* New York: Oxford University Press, 1966. A pioneering work in this area.

Wickham, Chris. *Early Medieval Italy.* London: Macmillan, 1981.

Wills, Garry. *Saint Augustine.* New York: Viking, 1999.

———. *St. Augustine's Childhood.* New York: Viking, 2001. A translation of and commentary on Book I of Augustine's *Confessions* plus a translation of *The Teacher,* a dialogue Augustine composed based on a discussion he had with his son.

Witt, Ronald. *In the Footsteps of the Ancients: The Origins of Humanism from Lovato to Bruni.* Leiden: Brill, 2000. Witt argues that Humanism began in the mid-thirteenth century and that Petrarch was a third generation humanist.

Wolff, Philippe. *The Awakening of Europe.* Baltimore: Penguin, 1968.

———. *Western Languages A.D.100–1500.* New York: McGraw-Hill, 1971.

Wolfram, Herwig. *The Roman Empire and Its Germanic Peoples.* Trans. Thomas Dunlap. Berkeley: University of California Press, 1997.

Wood, Charles. *The Quest for Eternity: Medieval Manners and Morals.* Garden City: Doubleday, 1971.

Zarnecki, George. *The Monastic Achievement.* New York: McGraw-Hill, 1972.

INDEX

Note: Page numbers in *italics* refer to illustrations.